JOURNEYS OF FAITH

Stories of Pilgrimage from Medieval Ireland

JOURNEYS *of* FAITH

Stories of Pilgrimage
from Medieval Ireland

LOUISE NUGENT

columba
BOOKS

First published in 2020 by

columba BOOKS

23 Merrion Square North
Dublin 2, Ireland
www.columbabooks.com

ISBN: 978-1-78218-372-3

Set in Adobe Garamond Pro 11/15
Book design by Alexis Sierra | Columba Books
Cover design by Alba Esteban | Columba Books

Front cover pictures: Pilgrims climbing Croagh Patrick, Co. Mayo, Ireland. © Tom Szustek / Wikimedia Commons; Murrisk Abbey with Croagh Patrick in background. © Louise Nugent; St James dressed as a pilgrim at Kilconnell Friary. © Louise Nugen; Skelllig Michael. © National Monuments Service, Department of Culture, Heritage, and the Gaeltacht.

Back cover pictures: Stones left by modern pilgrims at St Patrick's holy well Ballyshannon. Co. Donegal. © Louise Nugent; Image of Reproduction of St Patrick's Bell Shrine. © MMA / Wikimedia Commons; Medieval ecclesiastical ruins at the Rock of Cashel, Co. Tipperary. © Louise Nugent.

Printed by L&C, Poland

To my parents Mary and John Joe

Contents

Acknowledgements

I am grateful to Columba Press for giving me the opportunity to write this book. There are so many who have helped throughout the process, but I would like to extend special thanks to Damian Shiels, Br Colmán Ó Clabaigh and Sharon Greene, without who's support, encouragement and advise this book would not have been finished.

Writing this book has been a humbling and overwhelming experience. I have been amazed by the generosity of specialists from so many fields Irish History, Archaeology, Hagiography and Art History, too many to mention, who have generously shared their time and knowledge, provided articles/books, images and translations of texts. I extend my heartfelt thanks to you all. Many thanks to all the readers who have cast their discerning eye over sections of this manuscript especially Damian Shiels, Pádraig Ó Riain, Dagmar Ó Riain-Raedel, Colmán Ó Clabaigh, Michael Haren, Finbarr McCormick, Francis Young, Stuart Kinsella, Fr La Flynn, Malgorzata Krasnodebska D'Aughton. Jessica Smyth, Neil Jackman and Christy Cunniffe. I am very grateful for their discussion, comments and suggestions, but any errors in the book are my own. Thanks also to the Rachel Finnegan, Áine Foley, Paul Duffy and the team at Lough Derg for their generosity and kindness providing access to Saints and Station Island.

Many thanks to all the institutions and individuals who provided images for the book: National Monuments Service, National Museum of Ireland, Hereford Cathedral, York Minster & Westminster Abbey. Also Ronan Foley, Neil Jackman, James Dempsey, Sarah Blick, Aidan O Sullivan, Maurice Hurley, Diarmuid Healy, Ryan Lash, Chris Corlett, Eleanor Parker, Finbarr McCormick, Jimmy Barry, Amanda Clarke, Finnola Finlay and Sara Nylund. A very special thanks JG O'Donaghue, whose wonderful images of the journey of Friar Simeon and reconstruction of pilgrims in prayer at an early medieval shrine they have exceeded all my expectations and help to bring this story to light. I am very grateful to Richard Clutterbuck and Johnny Ryan for creating the wonderful maps that accompany this book.

Introduction

Pilgrimage means many things in modern Ireland. For some, it is a distant practice carried out by previous generations, while for others it remains an active part of spiritual and religious life, with people still making pilgrimages to holy wells, grottos and churches all over Ireland. Predominantly local, these pilgrimages are performed by individuals throughout the year or in groups on the saint's feast day. As well as being an expression of personal devotion, a local pilgrimage reinforces the bonds of local community and acts as a cohesive force. Pilgrimage brings people together, an example being the ecumenical services held at certain holy wells. Pilgrimage can also take the form of endurance or penance: each year, large numbers of pilgrims climb Croagh Patrick on Reek Sunday or spend time fasting and in prayer on the penitential island of St Patrick's Purgatory in Lough Derg. Irish Catholics also travel to holy places outside Ireland, such as Rome and Jerusalem, and to Marian shrines associated with healing, such as Medjugorje in Bosnia and Herzegovina, Fatima in Portugal and Lourdes in France. Tourism- and spiritual-based pilgrimage are also very popular in Ireland and across the world. There has been an increase in the numbers of people walking along modern routes inspired by older medieval pilgrim routes, with Irish people travelling to Spain to walk the Camino to Santiago de Compostela or walking one of the many Irish pilgrim paths. Such activities are undertaken largely as journeys of self-discovery, spiritual growth or adventure, with fewer people participating for purely religious motives.

Pilgrimage as it is practised today, in all its varying forms, traces its roots back to earlier times, particularly the medieval world. This book explores pilgrimage in medieval Ireland and traces the tradition across a time span of a thousand years, from the 7th century to the Reformation. The time period has been broken into the early medieval period (AD 600–1200) and the later medieval period (AD 1200 to the Reformation). The following chapters will tell the stories of pilgrims who lived in Ireland and shed light on what pilgrimage meant to individuals and communities, as well as exploring why people engaged in the practice with such enthusiasm.

This book must be read with a number of caveats: Firstly, medieval pilgrimage is poorly documented in Ireland and the literary evidence that survives allows us to catch glimpses of its practice at certain points in time. Secondly, the surviving historical sources overemphasise long-distance pilgrimage, but this does not reflect trends in contemporary pilgrimage. Throughout the period discussed in the book, local pilgrimage was practised more widely and by greater numbers of people than pilgrimage to distant places.

The reader will also see that while pilgrimage was ever changing, a number of key aspects – the physical journey, devotion to the saints and a quest for cures – have remained constant and are as relevant to pilgrims today as they were in earlier centuries.

Irish Pilgrims: Who Were They?

Pilgrimage was one of the most popular forms of personal devotion in the medieval world. Although the Irish historical sources mention pilgrimage only sporadically between the 7th century and the Reformation, it is clear that it was practised by men and women of all social classes in much greater numbers than recorded.

Who were Irish pilgrims and what can we learn about their personal stories? In the following chapters, the stories of Irish pilgrims are told by means of archaeological and historical evidence. We see that pilgrimage was undertaken by men and women, the wealthy and the poor, the old and young, the sick and repentant. Over the course of 1,000 years a tapestry of individual pilgrims is revealed, including clerics, kings, lords and ladies, poets, mayors and bailiffs. The religious devotees included priests, abbots of early medieval monasteries and, after the 12th century, members of religious orders such as the mendicant Augustinians and Cistercians.

What is missing from the historical texts is the story of the majority – ordinary people who were not recorded by name. We catch only an occasional glimpse of them referenced, in passing, in historical documents, as part of groups of pilgrims at monastic sites or holy wells. While archaeological evidence for pilgrimage generally relates to the infrastructure of pilgrimage, such as roads, guesthouses or the cult of the saint, traces of the individual are occasionally found.

The Forms of Medieval Pilgrimage

Christianity arrived in Ireland during the 5th century, bringing with it devotion to the saints and ideas about Christian pilgrimage. The concept of pilgrimage would not have been unknown to the pre-Christian population and strong evidence survives for Irish people making pilgrimages to spring wells, holy mountains and other holy places from at least the Iron Age.[1] By the 7th century, Christianity had become the dominant religion in Ireland and it is around this time that we first see Christian pilgrimage mentioned in the historical records. By the 12th century it was very much an established and familiar form of popular devotion across the Christian world. The importance of pilgrimage to Irish society from an early date is clearly seen in the variant of the tradition that existed.

Three types of pilgrimage were known in early medieval Ireland. The first was a severe, ascetic pilgrimage involving a lifelong, voluntary self-exile from one's native place and, in more extreme cases, from the island of Ireland. Ascetic pilgrimage was performed primarily by devout clerics – examples include St Colmcille (Columba), St Columbanus and St Fursa. Known by the Latin term *peregrinatio,* pilgrimage remained popular among the religious of Ireland and the island of Britain until the 9th century, when changes in monastic rules and the implementation of a diocesan system on the Continent brought the practice to an end.[2]

Many of the churches established by these early Irish pilgrims grew from remote hermitages into monastic settlements and in turn became important pilgrimage sites; for example, those at Iona in Scotland, founded by St Colmcille, and Bobbio in Italy, founded by St Columbanus.

The second type of pilgrimage occupied the middle ground, between the extreme ascetic type and the universal kind practised by most of the Irish population. Recorded in annals from the 7th and 8th centuries up to the beginning of the 14th century, the pilgrim entered a monastery for a set duration of time – for days, weeks, months or even years and sometimes up to the time of death. These pilgrims were generally high-ranking individuals in the Irish Church or the nobility. For example, in

> 1118 Dervorgilla daughter of Murchad O'Mealsechlainn and wife of Tiernan O'Rourke went to Drogheda on pilgrimage.[3]

The monasteries chosen by these pilgrims, both men and women, were all of high status.[4] Extended pilgrimages are recorded at Clonmacnoise, Co. Offaly, Glendalough, Co. Wicklow, and Armagh, Co. Armagh, before the year AD 1200, and from this point the annals record similar pilgrimages at Cloyne, Co. Cork, Kilbeggan, Co. Kildare, and Ballintubber Abbey, Co. Mayo.[5]

The third kind of pilgrimage, still practised today, could be described as universal pilgrimage, which involved a journey of varying length to and from a holy places following a period of prayer. This type of pilgrimage was undertaken by the majority of medieval people and it is their stories that will be told in the following pages.

NOTES

1 Séan Duffy, 'A Site for Sore Eyes: A Hiberno-Roman Curative Cult at Golden, Co. Tipperary,' *Archaeology Ireland* 16, no. 2 (2002): 8-9; Eamonn P. Kelly, 'Antiquities from Irish Holy Wells and Their Wider Context,' *Archaeology Ireland* 16 no. 2 (2002): 24-28; Christiaan Corlett, 'The Prehistoric Ritual Landscape of Croagh Patrick, Co. Mayo', *JIA* 9 (1998):9-26; Geraldine Stout, *Newgrange and the Bend of the Boyne* (Cork: Cork University Press, 2002); Máire MacNeill, *The Festival of Lughnasa* (Dublin: Folklore of Ireland Council, 2007).

2 Thomas Charles-Edwards, 'The Social Background to Irish Peregrinatio,' *Celtica* 11 (1976): 43-59; Kathleen Hughes, 'The Changing Theory and Practice of Irish Pilgrimage,' *JEH* 11 no. 2 (1960): 143-51.

3 ALC.

4 Aghaboe (AFM 1100), Armagh (AFM 974, AFM 976, CS/AFM/CS/AU 981/987/988/989; AFM 987, AFM/AU 1003/1004, AFM 1004, AI 1029, AU/AFM/ALC/CS 1037, AU/AFM died here; AU1043, AC 1063, AU 1073, AU/AFM, 1103, AFM 1151) Ballintubber (AFM 1224), Boyle (AU/AFM/ALC/ACon 1231, AFM/ALC/ACon 1242, ALC/ACon 1307), Cend Ri Monaidh (AFM/CS 963/956), Clonard (AFM 1056, 1070 AFM, 1185 AFM/ALC, AI 1092), Clonmacnoise (AFM/CS 606/610; AFM/CS 610/615; AFM/AC 753/754; AC/CS 832; AFM/CS 834, AFM 1100; AU 1118, AFM 1204), Cloyne (AI 1208), Cong (AFM1150, AU 1168, ALC 1183/1184, MCB 1x98)], Cork (AI 1028], Derry (AU 1122, 1188 AU/AFM.ALC], Drogheda (AU 1186 (died here in ALC 1193), Glendalough (AFM 951; AU/ALC/AFM 1030; 1122 AFM) InishCathaig (AI 1024), Inish Clothrann/Inchcleraun Lough Ree (AlC 1193, ALC 1220, AFM 1231), Kilbeggan (AC 1213, AC 1218), Killaloe (AFM 1159), Lismore (AFM 1056, AI 1116 ALC 1136, AU/AI 1123/1126), Lough Cre (AFM 1138), Sruthair-Bracain (?) (ALC 1204), Sruhir/Shrule Abbey (AC 1239), Tuam (1170 AFM).

5 Clonmacnoise (AFM 1205), Cloyne, Co. Cork (AI 1208), Kilbeggan, Co. Kildare (AC 1213), Inish Clothrann/ Inchcleraun Lough Ree (ALC 1220; AFM 1231), Ballintubber Abbey, Co. Mayo (AC/AFM 1224), Boyle Abbey, Co. Roscommon (AFM/AU 1231, AFM/ALC/ACon, 1242; ALC/ACon 1307), Sruhir/Shrule Abbey (AC,1239), Sruthair-Bracain [?] (ALC 1204).

CHAPTER 1

The Landscape of the Irish Pilgrim

Medieval sources from across the Christian world suggest that each region and country had its own unique landscape of sacred places with either local, regional or, less often, national appeal. Pilgrim landscapes could extend beyond regional and national boundaries and some holy locations like Rome and the Holy Land had an international importance. Medieval Ireland was no different and pilgrims regularly made pilgrimages in the country, with fewer numbers going abroad to visit holy places.

Local sites were by far the most popular pilgrim places. Local pilgrimage involved short journeys that required little investment of time or finances and was especially popular among women who, for much of their lives, were tied to the family home by obligations such as managing the home and caring for children, the elderly and the sick.[1] Studies of medieval English miracle stories (*miracula*) connected to pilgrim places suggest that the majority of pilgrims who attended local shrines – centres of pilgrimage[2] – were women, with men featuring more prominently at more distant shrines. The English evidence suggests that some shrines were more popular with different genders. Places like the shrine of St Godric of Finchale at Norfolk, St Frideswide of Oxford and Our Lady of Walsingham were predominantly visited by women.[3] There are exceptions, and some women, from the middle and upper classes, such as the English pilgrim Margery Kempe, undertook epic journeys to foreign pilgrim places. The popularity of pilgrim places seems to have also been influenced by the type of miracles offered. People from lower levels of society were mentioned more frequently in the miracle tales at places that offered relief from blindness and crippling disease, while upper-class men tended to frequent places with non-healing miracles. This was certainly true of the visitors to St Patrick's Purgatory in Co. Donegal, who were predominantly men from the upper echelons of society.[4]

The cost of long-distance pilgrimage prevented most people from undertaking journeys outside local or regional territories. In the later medieval period, as relics from the Holy Land flooded into Europe, it became possible for the lower classes to have a connection with the Holy Land at a local church or abbey close by, without travelling thousands of kilometres. While this did not quell the desire to experience such places at first hand, it did make a connection with these exotic places possible on home soil.[5]

Early Adopters: Ireland's Early Medieval Pilgrimage Landscape

If early pilgrims were restricted in the distance they travelled, they did not want for variety of holy places to visit. Holy wells, trees and stones, the grave and relics of local saints could be easily found locally, regionally and further afield.

Many pilgrimages were to places associated with the saints, in particular to their graves and relics.[6] Irish pilgrims, in common with their counterparts throughout the medieval Christian world, had a strong relationship with local and regional saints and many pilgrimages were undertaken out of devotion to a particular saint. Growth in devotion to a saint could result in a monastery or church or place associated with that saint becoming a place of pilgrimage. Numerous early medieval monasteries were founded by saints and possessed treasured relics and, in some cases, their graves.

Some of the earliest accounts of pilgrimage in Ireland concern monasteries and churches and are found in the biographical accounts (or 'Lives') of the Irish saints. The 7th-century *Life of St Brigit* of Kildare mentions large groups of pilgrims arriving at the monastery at Kildare on the saint's feast.[7] Pilgrims are also recorded in 7th-century *Life of St Patrick*, written by Muirchú. The *Life* relates that the relics of St Ercc, a disciple of Patrick, were 'worshipped in the city of Slane'.[8] It is impossible to quantify the number of pilgrims who visited Slane but it must have been significant, and the pilgrimage well established, to warrant notice in this document. This theory is strengthened by the survival of fragments of a stone outdoor reliquary shrine, known as a gable shrine, at the site today. The stone reliquary represents an investment in the cult of relics and the presence is a clear indicator of pilgrimage.

A century later, the Latin *Life of St Molua* (c. AD 800) mentions groups of pilgrims arriving at the monastery of Clonfert Molua (now *Clonfertmulloe)* in the territory of Osraigi and Éli and Loígsi, in modern-day Co. Laois.[9] The pilgrims went there to pray at the grave of their beloved St Molua.

Further evidence of pilgrims at holy graves is found in the early 9th-century *Martyrology of Oengus*, where it is recorded that pilgrims visited the grave of St Maelruain (d. 792), the founder and abbot of the monastery of Tallaght in Co. Dublin. The saint's grave is represented as a place of healing.

> Mael Ruáin after this pious service, the great sun on Meath's south plain, at his grave with purity is healed, the sigh of every heart.[10]

The Hill of Slane the site of St Erc's early medieval monastery, Co. Meath.

Tallaght was also in possession of other important relics, such as an epistle said to have been thrown to Maelruain by St Michael the Archangel, from Heaven, which would also have been of interest to pilgrims.[11]

The desire to visit the graves of saints does not seem to have abated in later centuries. The author of the 12th-/13th-century *Life of St Ita* of Kileedy refers to multitudes gathering at the saint's tomb;[12] similar claims are made in the Latin *Life of St Máedóc* (Aidan) regarding his tomb at Ferns.[13]

The increasing numbers of pilgrims visiting graves was often accompanied by the efforts of the caretakers to make the physical remains of the saints more accessible. This involved exhuming the remains and placing them in specially constructed containers known as reliquary shrines. Literary and archaeological evidence of such events, known as 'translation' (from the Latin *translatio*), suggests that pilgrimages were already taking place at these sites and that the events marked an increase in (or an attempt to increase) pilgrim traffic.[14]

As with pilgrimage, the earliest written accounts of the translation of Irish saints are documented in the Lives. The 7th-century *Life of St Brigit* records that the bones of St Brigit and St Conlead, the first bishop of Kildare, rested in elaborate containers or reliquary shrines inside the main church on either side of the altar at Kildare.[15] Niamh *Wycherley,* in her book *The Cult of Relics in Medieval Ireland,* highlights several other early examples of translations. Tírechán's late 7th-century

St Ita of Kileedy by Harry Clarke, Honan Chapel, UCC. © Louise Nugent

Life of St Patrick, for instance, refers to the translation of the body of the priest Bruscus, who had been ordained by Patrick at Mag Réin. Following his death, Bruscus appeared three times in a dream to a holy man, bemoaning the location of his burial place and asking to be removed from the deserted church and placed somewhere more suitable. Eventually, the holy man took a shovel, dug up his bones and moved them to his own monastery, where they could be properly venerated.[16] Muirchú's *Life of St Patrick* records the translation of a female saint called Monesan, the daughter of a foreign king. Despite being pushed into marriage by her family, the girl, who was filled with the holy spirit, sought out St Patrick so that she could be baptised. After her baptism, she fell down dead and 'gave up her spirit into the hands of the angels'.[17] At that very moment, Patrick prophesied that 'after twenty year her body would be conveyed to a nearby chapel with great ceremony'. Muirchú goes on to say that this was done and that the 'relics of the virgin from across the sea are there an object of worship to the present day'.[18] The phrase 'great ceremony' suggests that this event was performed with an elaborate religious ceremony and possibly a procession from the saint's grave to the chapel, attended by the clergy and devotees of her cult.[19]

The Irish annals start to record additional translations of other Irish saints in the 8th and 9th centuries and are further evidence of devotion and pilgrimage. In 801, the relics of St Ronan at Dromiskin, Co. Louth, were placed in a shrine made of gold and silver.[20] Although translations are recorded in the early centuries of the Irish Church, the practice was not necessary for the success of a pilgrimage site and not every church that possessed a saint's grave went on to remove the saint from his or her final resting place.[21]

Physical evidence of devotion to the saint's burial place in early medieval Ireland survives, at several monastic and ecclesiastical sites, in the form of outdoor reliquary shrines made of stone. These structures were built as repositories for the relics of the saints, the most precious of these being their bones. The above literary examples of translations in early medieval Ireland contrast with the surviving archaeological evidence, which points to liturgical space in the church, especially around the altar, kept separate from the corporeal or bodily relics of the saint.[22] It was not until the 11th and 12th centuries that it became more common for corporeal remains to be moved inside Irish churches. This divergence between the two records suggests variety in how translations were conducted and the way in which the saints' corporeal relics were treated in the early Irish Church.

Archaeology suggests that initially the grave of the founding saint was simply marked by a cross or lintel stone. At the early medieval monastery of Caherlehillan, Co. Kerry, a late 5th-/early 6th-century burial place, identified as that of a holy person or saint, was marked by a simple stone-lined grave covered with a flat lintel stone. In the 8th century, the original grave was covered with a more elaborate structure called a corner shrine, whose construction was likely brought about by increased numbers of pilgrims to the site.[23]

Corner shrine at the early medieval ecclesiastical site of Caherlehillan, Co. Kerry.
© John Sheehan

At the monastery on the island of Iona, in Scotland, St Colmcille's grave was marked by a stone known as the pillow stone, until his bones were moved to a shrine in the mid-8th century.[24]

On the windswept island of Árd Oileán (High Island), off the coast of Co. Galway, eight elaborate graves identified as belonging to 'holy people' were deliberately incorporated into the east wall of the church, perhaps as a means of bring the saint(s) into the church without the bones being physically inside the building. The elaborate nature of the burials and their location suggest that the dead were seen as holy men – perhaps even saints – and venerated by the religious community. Each grave was marked by elaborate cross-inscribed head and foot stones and three of the graves were covered with slabs. The burials are not contemporary and date from the 9th to the 12th centuries. One of the graves may contain the

Graves of holy people built into the gable of church at High Island, Co. Galway. ©National Monuments Service, Department of Culture Heritage and the Gaeltacht.

remains of St Gormgal, an anchorite whose virtuous life made him famous outside the island and whose death is recorded in the annals as 1017/1018.[25]

As the cult of holy men and women developed, their graves were also marked by more elaborate structures known as outdoor reliquaries or shines. One of the earliest known examples was uncovered during excavations of an early Christian cemetery at Scotch Street, Armagh, in the late 1980s. The cemetery, identified as '*Ferta Martyrum*' or 'the burial ground of the Martyrs', is mentioned in Muirchú's 7th-century *Life of St Patrick*. The cemetery was part of the early medieval ecclesiastical foundation of Armagh.[26] The shrine was made of wood and its base incorporated a rectangular pit cut into the ground.[27] During excavation, fragments of two long bones and a skull were revealed in the east end. Wider than all the other excavated graves in the cemetery, it was too short to have contained an extended adult skeleton. The size of the grave, along with the disarticulated remains, suggests that the bones were interred some time after the body. Dating to between the 5th and the 7th centuries, this may be the earliest evidence for the translation of the bones of a holy person in Ireland. Two square posts at its western end may have acted as a grave marker and a focus for pilgrims.[28] It is very likely that similar reliquary structures, made of wood, existed elsewhere in Ireland.

Gable shrine at Temple Cronan, Co. Clare. © Louise Nugent

The remaining Irish outdoor reliquary shrines are made of stone. They come in a variety of forms and date from the 7th/8th through to the 13th centuries. In many cases, local folklore also identifies them with the burial places of the founding saints, referring to them as '*leaba*' or 'bed'.

Dating to the 7th and 8th centuries, the gable or tent reliquaries are the earliest outdoor

Shrine chapel known as St Declan's Oratory at Ardmore, Co. Waterford. © Louise Nugent

stone reliquaries found in Ireland. These triangular structures, consisting of two long stones and two smaller triangular stones, arranged like a tent, were designed to hold the disarticulated bones of the saint.[29] Examples survive at the early medieval ecclesiastical sites of Killoluaig, Killabuonia and Illaunloughan, Co. Kerry, and at Temple Cronan, Co. Clare.[30]

Box shrines are another distinctive type of outdoor shrine that date to the 8th century. These are made from flat slabs of stone built into a box shape. A box-shaped reliquary was recorded during excavations of a multi-period graveyard in Ballyhanna, Co. Donegal.[31] The contemporary corner post shrine is a variant of the box shrine. It is composed of four upright stone posts that hold flat slabs of stone arranged to form a box that is roofed with a large flat slab of stone.[32] Examples survive at the monastic sites of Kildrenagh, on the windswept island of Valencia, Co. Kerry, and on the remote Church Island, Co. Kerry.[33]

The shrine chapels are more complex outdoor reliquaries. Similar in design to full-scale mortared churches, they share many of their features, such as antae and a western doorway, but are significantly smaller, measuring less than 12 square metres. They seem to have been designed to act as repositories for relics.[34] Early examples, dating to the 8th and 9th centuries, have been identified at the ecclesiastical sites of Iona, Argyll, Scotland; Clonmacnoise, Co. Offaly, and Ardmore, Co. Waterford.[35]

In most cases, they appear to be built over a grave or incorporate a special area associated with the saint's grave. They were perhaps built as a way of developing the saint's cult, without translating the relics from the original grave.[36]

St Mologa's grave at Labbamolaga, Co. Cork.
© Finola Finlay

At St Declan's Oratory at Ardmore, the saint's grave is marked by a rectangular hole in the corner of the building, while at the shrine known as St Mologa's Bed at Labbamolaga, Co. Cork, the saint's grave is said to lie in the building, under an early medieval grave slab.

Excavations of the interior of the shrine chapel known as Temple Ciarán, at Clonmacnoise, in the 1950s, uncovered a stone box (cist) that predated the chapel. The box was too short to be a grave and may have been used to house the disarticulated bones of the saint. The chapel was used to store relics of the saint up to the 17th century and, during the visit of Bishop Doping in 1648, a relic of St Ciaran's hand was still kept there.[37]

A few double-vaulted stone-roofed churches built in the late 11th to the early 12th centuries appear to have functioned in the same way as the earlier shrine chapels.[38] Examples include St Flannan's Church at Killaloe, Co. Clare, St Mochta's House, Co. Louth, and St Columba's House, Kells, Co. Meath.[39]

These structures not only housed relics, but were sometimes designed for worship and even to be used by anchorites.[40] An un-vaulted, late 12th-century chapel known as St Molaise's House, on Devenish Island, Co. Fermanagh, may have acted as a reliquary chapel.[41]

St Mochta's House, Co. Louth.
© Finola Finlay

The Skull House in the late 19th century, Cooley, Co. Donegal. ©National Monuments Service, Department of Culture Heritage and the Gaeltacht.

A small group of buildings found in the north-west of the island, and known as mortuary houses, also functioned as outdoor reliquaries. Larger, but of a similar design to the earlier shrine chapels, they may also have housed the disarticulated human remains of saints. The smallest of the group, at Cooley, Co. Donegal, is known as the skull house.[42] Examples are found in Co. Derry at Bovevagh, Tamlaght and Banagher.[43]

All the outdoor reliquaries are physical evidence of pilgrimage and many identify places of pilgrimage that are not recorded in the historical sources. The pilgrims' interactions with the shrines took place outside the main church buildings.

The *Leachta:* Enigmatic Reminders of Early Irish Pilgrimage

Many Irish pilgrim places are associated with a monument known as a *leacht* (plural *leachta*). *Leachta* appear to have been built from the 8th to the 9th centuries, continuing up to the post-medieval period. The medieval examples had a variety of functions: as grave markers for individual saints; memorials;[44] pilgrim stations (the focal point in the landscape where pilgrims performed rituals and said prayers); and outdoor altars.[45] In modern Ireland, *leachta* are used as stations or points of prayer and are ritually circled by pilgrims reciting set prayers. It is thought that medieval pilgrims may have interacted with them in a similar way and attended liturgies (see Chapter 7). At active pilgrim sites, several of the larger *leachta* also function as altars in modern pilgrimages, as for example in Caher Island, Co. Mayo.

The shape and size of the *leachta* are as varied as their function. Some are low, rectangular, dry-stone-faced mounds, while others are small, square/rectangular constructions made of stones, boulders or slabs. Some were made of 'a neat rough-masonry block, with a flat top on which a variety of decorated stones or

Early medieval *leacht* at Caher Island Co Mayo, used as an altar during the patron day mass in 2016. © Louise Nugent t

Early Medieval *leacht* at Gallarus, Co. Kerry. © Louise Nugent

slabs may stand affixed'.[46] The majority of the surviving *leachta* are found along the west coast of Ireland, at pilgrimage sites such as Caher Island, Co. Mayo, Skellig Michael, Co. Kerry, and Inismurray, Co. Sligo.[47]

A few, such as those at Killabuonia and Illaunloughan, are found with gable shrines. At Illaunloughan, the gable shrine was built on top of one of its two *leachta*, and at Killabuonia the *leacht* is adjacent to the gable shrine.[48] Excavations at Inishmurray, Co. Sligo, suggest that the island's *leachta,* constructed in the 9th to the 10th centuries, were originally used in processional rituals, as well as acting as pilgrim stations.[49]

The 11th and 12th centuries saw a marked rise in the number of Irish saints being translated into elaborate shrines. The Irish Church was undergoing many changes at the time, including being reorganised around a diocesan structure.

Leacht at Illaunloughan Co. Kerry surmounted by a gable shrine.
© Jim@megalithcireland.com

During this period, individual churches used their associations with saints to help them compete for diocesan status and attract royal patronage. The promotion of links to the saints prompted the building of churches, the writing of the Lives of the saints, the translation of the saints' remains, and the placing of them and other relics in elaborate reliquary shrines. Some of these reliquaries were designed to contain the exhumed bodies of saints (or fragments of their bodies) and others enclosed items originally owned by the saint. Politically, Ireland was also changing, with moves towards a more centralised government, as power became concentrated and controlled by a few political dynasties.

In 1122, the bones of St Colmán of Lann, were rediscovered at Lann Ela, now Lynally, Co. Offaly, and placed in a new shrine.

> The shrine of Colmán son of Luachán was found in the burial place of Lann *Ela*, a man's cubit in earth, on Spy Wednesday 22 March.[50]

The church at Lann Ela was by this time an established place of pilgrimage, but the discovery of the saint's body during Easter week would have reinvigorated his cult and was undoubtedly timed to take advantage of the increased numbers worshippers who had come to celebrate one of the most important feasts in the Church calendar.[51]

Forty years later, in 1162, at the monastery Clonfert, Co. Galway, the

> Clergy of Brendan removed from the soil the bones of Moinnean and Cummian Fada and placed them in a shrine.[52]

This event shows a tradition of devotion and pilgrimage to SS Moinnean and Cummian, in addition to Brendan, the patron of the site.[53] A fragment consisting of a single, decorative ridge stone of a high-status Romanesque house shrine was recently discovered at Clonfert, Co. Galway. The date of the shrine makes it a strong candidate for the example recorded in the annals in 1162.[54] Unfortunately, given its fragmentary state, it is not possible to establish if it was located inside or outside the church.

Irish reliquaries kept in churches took many forms. St Manchan's shrine, a 12th-century portable reliquary,[55] was displayed at the monastery of St Manchan at Lemanaghan, Co. Offaly.

This outstanding example of early decorative metalwork was most likely manufactured at the nearby monastery of Clonmacnoise.[56] Today, the shrine is still the focus of local veneration and devotion and can be seen at the parish church of Boher, Co. Offaly.

The 12th-century portable reliquary known as St Manchan's shrine, at Boher, Co. Offaly.
© Louise Nugent

Solid stone shrine said to mark the grave of St Tigernach at Clones, Co. Monaghan.
© Louise Nugent

Similar portable reliquaries must have existed elsewhere. A contemporary stone copy of a wood and metal reliquary large enough to contain a full-length body can be seen today among the ruins of the medieval monastery of Clones, Co. Monaghan. The shrine is traditionally believed to mark the grave of St Tigernach, the founder of the monastery, and sits on top of a vaulted tomb that would have contained the saint's relics.[57]

Elaborate portable reliquary shrines are known to have existed at other locations in Ireland. At Roscommon, in 1170, the relics of St Comman, the patron and founder of the monastery, were 'removed from the earth' and put into a gold and silver shrine by Gilla Iarlaithe Ua Carmacain,[58] the head of the church at Roscommon.[59] The shrine and its relics were surely a focus for pilgrims.

The annals tell us nothing of the process involved in translations, but the removal of the body from the ground must have taken much consideration and was surely accompanied by an elaborate ceremony.

In 929, the bones of Columbanus were removed from his grave at Bobbio Abbey, in the Province of Piacenza, Italy, with great pomp and ceremony.

> … the abbot of Bobbio and four monks dressed in liturgical vestments descended into the crypt of their abbatial church. The group approached the sarcophagus (which they had opened the night before with trepidation) containing the body of their saint and patron, Columbanus. They prostrated themselves on the ground in prayer and implored the saint to allow them to remove his body from its resting place. Then, they reverentially lifted the body of the saint and placed it in a pine chest, securing it with iron bars. As the small group left the crypt and ascended the steps into the church they were greeted by a throng of people holding candles, lamps, and incense burners. The packed church resounded in song as they carried the saint towards a throne set before the altar of St Peter, where the congregation, moved to tears, cried out: 'Saint Columbanus, come to our aid! We are your people and we ask you to beseech the Lord, lest we perish.'[60]

While we must allow for regional variations, this account provides some insight into the rituals involved in translation process. The 12th-century *Life of St Flannán* of Killaloe provides a very brief description of the translation of the bones of this saint. First, permission was sought from Rome by 'the prelates of the church and the king and nobles of the entire Kingdom' to disinter Flannan's body from his burial place and have it put into a shrine of precious metal.[61] The *Life* also

The tomb of St Columbanus, Bobbio, Italy. © Diarmuid Healy

tells us that owing to 'an injunction of the saint when dying there was difficulty in getting persons to disinter and touch the body'.[62] The bones of Flannan were removed by two holy men, who presumed the saint's forgiveness. However, the saint was not so forgiving: when the coffin was taken from the earth, a strong vapour rose from it, blinding one of the men and paralysing the other.[63] The saint was placed 'with due solemnity' in a special gold and silver shrine. His staff and bell were also covered in gold.[64] Pilgrims and others devoted to the saint would have travelled to be part of the occasion and, in the immediate aftermath, devotion to the saint would have increased.

The 12th century was a time of political upheaval with the invasion and conquest of vast parts of the island by the Anglo-Normans. The arrival of the new settlers also played a role in the creation of new pilgrim sites and the rejuvenation of existing cults. The Anglo-Normans were aware of the political importance of cultivating native cults, which could be used as a means of maintaining control over newly colonised areas.[65] For example, John de Courcy, an Anglo-Norman knight responsible for the conquest of Ulster,[66] instigated the 'rediscovery' of the bodies of three principal Irish saints, Patrick, Colmcille and Brigit, at Downpatrick.[67]

The graves were discovered after the location was miraculously revealed to St Malachy in a vision. An entry in the 12th-century calendar of St Werburg, at Chester, tells that the saint's remains were discovered on 24 March, in the Octave of the feast of St Patrick.[68] The bones were then placed in a shrine in Downpatrick Cathedral. As part of his promotion of the cult, John de Courcy also restored the cathedral of the Holy Trinity at Downpatrick and rededicated it to St Patrick. He commissioned Jocelyn of Furness to write a new Life of St Patrick, and all this helped to fan the fires of devotion and increase pilgrim numbers.[69] The feast of the translation of the relics was celebrated by the Augustinian canons at Christ Church in Dublin up to the 15th century and was recorded in *The Book of Obits and Martyrology of the Cathedral Church of Holy Trinity [Christ Church]*. The saint's feast day was one of the busiest times for pilgrimage in Ireland, so the discovery of the saint's remains so close to this date would have had a special significance for pilgrims.[70]

St Flannan's Oratory at Killaloe, Co. Clare, where relics of St Flannan were once kept.
© Louise Nugent

Modern stone placed over the traditional site of St Patricks grave at Downpatrick, Co. Down.
© Louise Nugent

Early Lives of St Patrick claim that his burial place was either Saul or Downpatrick. Muirchú's *Life of Patrick* tells us that when the time came for him to leave this world, an angel ordered him to Saul, although later, due to divine intervention, he was buried at Dún Lethglaise (Downpatrick).[71] In his version of the saint's life, Tírechán states, 'nobody knows where his bones rest', until St Columcille, moved by the Holy Spirit, 'showed where Patrick's grave was and confirms this, that is in Saulpatrick, in a church near the sea'.[72] While this reference suggest that he was buried at Saul, St Patrick's Church at Saul is at an inland location, while Downpatrick is located on the tidal River Quoile. Given the proximity of both sites, and earlier links with Saul as the place of the saint's death, it can be argued that Downpatrick is inferred here as the place of his burial.

It was not unusual in the medieval world for one or more churches to claim possession of the same relics. The annals in 1293 record the bodies of Brigit,

Patrick and Colmcille being rediscovered at Saul, perhaps in an attempt to rival Downpatrick and poach some of its pilgrims.

> It revealed to Nicholas Mac Maelisa (Coarb of St. Patrick) that the relics of Patrick, Columbkille, and Bridget were at Sabhall; they were taken up by him, and great virtues and miracles were afterwards wrought by *means of* them, and, after having been honourably covered, they were deposited in a shrine.[73]

It is not clear if the church in question is Saul, Co. Down, or Saul (Sabhall) at Armagh, and it has been suggested that this event was part of a 'counter scheme of the anti-English party in the Irish church' to rival Downpatrick in their claims to the patron saints.[74]

In the medieval world, many churches fought over legitimate claims to the bodies of saints. In England, the churches of Canterbury and Glastonbury both claimed to possess the body of St Dunstan, while Dorchester and Winchester argued over who possessed the true remains of St Birinus.[75] Furthermore, in France, the monasteries of Poitiers and Tours were in dispute over who possessed the body of St Martin.[76]

There was a similar politicising of the cult of St Finnian of Clonard and St Cíanán of Duleek, in Meath, where both saints were actively promoted by the Anglo-Normans.[77] Duleek had begun as a monastery founded by St Cíanán in the 6th century and by the 12th century the Augustinian canons had built an abbey there.[78] The body of the founder, St Cíanán, is mentioned in the 9th-century *Martyrology of Oengus*, as having remained 'without corrupting, without dissolving, in the tomb to the east of the damliac [Church]'. The tomb was presumably an outdoor shrine and, as such, located in the monastic graveyard.[79] During the 14th century, the saint was moved by one of the bishops of Meath and placed in a shrine in the Augustinian church. Deeds relating to the Priory of Llanthony in Monmouthshire, Wales, known as the *Cartularies of Llanthony Secunda*, mention that St Cíanán was reburied in the chancel of the church. Llanthony was a priory of Augustinian monks; in the 1170s the De Lacy family had granted them lands to establish a grange at Duleek.[80] A renewed pilgrimage to Duleek was likely to have been a welcome side effect of the translation.

Later sources record the presence of translated saints in a number of other Irish churches, and it is very possible that these events reinvigorated existing pilgrimages or initiated new ones. The bones of St Cainnech at Aghaboe, Co. Laois, were housed in the church there until the mid-14th century. Aghaboe began as an early monastery, founded in the 6th century by St Cainnech, and by the 12th

St Mary's Abbey
Duleek, Co. Meath.
© Louise Nugent

century it was the principal church in Ossory until superseded by Kilkenny.[81] As with Duleek, the Augustinian Canons established a priory here in the 13th century. In 1346, the 'bones and relics' of the saint were destroyed when Diarmuid Mac Gillapatrick[82]

> burnt the town of Aghaboe and the cemetery and church and cruelly forsaking St Canice, abbot, patron of the neighbourhood and founder of the place, he burnt and completely destroyed, with the cruellest fire, the saint's shrine with his bones and relics.[83]

Such a violent act may have resulted in the end of the pilgrimage at this place. The memory of the translation of the bones of St Boice, the founder of the early medieval monastery at Monasterboice, Co. Louth, was recorded in the 16th century in the *Life of St Colmcille*. In the text, Colmcille, when visiting Monasterboice, rediscovered Boice's grave and had the relics enshrined.[84] Confirmation of an earlier translation of the saint's remains is found in a 1521 case at the ecclesiastical court in Armagh. The case related to a suit for slander by Dominus Patrick McEgyr against Dominus Gabriel, for having publicly stated that McEgyr stole the head of St Boice.[85] These references suggests that the body of St Boice has been translated in the past and that by the 16th century the head had been separated from the rest of the body and placed in its own reliquary. This process must have taken place before the decline of the monastery.

The fragmentation or division of a saint's body became relatively common in the later medieval period and a side effect was the widening of the pilgrim landscape, as multiple churches could house corporeal relics from the same saint. There are many examples of contemporary head, foot and arm-shaped reliquaries throughout Europe. Irish examples include the shrine of St Lachtin's Arm, from the Donoughmore Church in Co. Cork, now on display in the National Museum of Ireland, and the 14th-century hand shrine of St Patrick, in the Ulster Museum, both designed to hold fragments of bone.[86] Historical records also tell us that arm reliquaries were kept at the monasteries of Clomacnoise, Co. Offaly, and Lorrah, Co. Tipperary.[87]

Pilgrimage to Items Owned by the Saint

The bones of saints were not the only type of relics venerated in medieval Ireland. Any item associated or perceived to be associated with the saint could become a relic. These relics could include items of clothing, books, bells and even farm implements.[88] Associative relics were far more common than corporeal ones in early medieval Ireland and a significant number have survived. Non-corporeal relics had a variety of important functions in Irish society, since they were used for the swearing of oaths, the collecting of tribute[89] and the declaration of laws.[90] Relics such as books, bells and croziers were also seen as symbols of religious office.[91] Symbolically, they conferred the saints' stamp of approval on the activities of their successors and this was especially true in the case of bells and croziers, many of which were originally displayed over their graves in the 8th and 9th centuries.[92] While the majority of medieval church sites possessed relics of some sort, not all relics attracted pilgrims, as was the case of the relics of the Holy Blood at Norwich Cathedral in England.[93]

Image of Reproduction of St Patrick's Bell Shrine. (Metropolitan Museum of Art / Wikimedia Commons / CC0 1.0 Universal Public Domain Dedication).

Relics associated with healing miracles were highly prized by pilgrims, and Irish medieval sources suggest that some bells were famed for their ability to heal.

The *Life of Colmán of Lann* tells of a bell that belonged to St Mochuta, which could cure disease and plague visited on any man and beast. A second bell associated with Colmán of Lann could produce cures when filled with water.[94] The *Life of St Mac Creiche* tells that the saint left a bell to his community. When the bell was washed in water, the water developed healing properties.

> … any pestilence of sore disease shall visit your land, the water in which my bell has been washed, and the prayer of my steward shall repel it.[95]

This holy water was also said to have cured a man of boils and restored his speech and memory.[96] These accounts provide a glimpse of how some relics were used in healing rituals, a topic which will be discussed in detail in Chapter 7.

The clothing of the saints – perhaps because it had rested on their bodies – was held in high esteem across the Christian world. A medieval poem known as 'The shrine of Adomnán' lists several items of clothing in St Adomnán's relic collection: a piece of clothing of the blessed Virgin; a cloth with Christ's blood; a girdle of St Paul; and a mantle or cloak belonging to St Enda of Aran.[97] In the Irish tradition, items worn by the saints are often associated with cures and healing. Miraculous girdles belonged to SS Kevin,[98] Moninna[99] Mochuda[100] and Crónán.[101] The miracles performed by the girdles of Irish saints were varied, with some girdles, like that of St Kevin, providing physical protection. A 15th-century Irish poem invokes the protection of the belts of SS Fínán, Finnian and John.[102]

The girdle of St Mobí of Glasnevin was able to detect untruths and would never close around anyone telling a lie.[103] The girdles of some Irish saints had the power to quell sexual desire,[104] while wearing St Moninna's girdle could repel unwanted male attention by transforming a beautiful women into old woman.[105] St Colman Mac Duagh's girdle, a treasured relic of the monastery of Kilmacduagh, was worn to test an individual's chastity. The belt would refuse to tie on the unchaste but would close on any chaste person, no matter the size of their waistband.[106]

Some Irish girdles could cure ill health and emotional turmoil. One 10th-century Irish poem praises the healing qualities of St Finnian's girdle against 'disease and grief'.[107]

Holy places that possessed a girdle with healing properties could expect a stream of pilgrims. The 12th-century Irish belt reliquary shrine known as the Moylough Belt Shrine, now on display in the National Museum of Ireland, has a distinctive wear pattern. It has been suggested that this is a result of it being repeatedly opened and closed, so that it could be placed around the limbs or head of sick pilgrims.[108] Accounts from outside Ireland suggest that many clothing relics were placed on, or worn by, the pilgrim seeking healing.[109] During the late medieval period, Canterbury Cathedral regularly lent St Anselm's girdle to pregnant women, to ensure a safe birth.[110] The hat and belt of St Thomas of Lancaster, at Pontefract Abbey, were also used as remedies for headaches and to ward against the perils of childbirth; and the blood-stained belt of St Thomas à Becket, worn by the saint when he was murdered, was wrapped around the necks of pilgrim's as a cure for a stiff neck.[111] The *Life of St Cuthbert* tells that a young man whose limbs were paralysed was healed at Cuthbert's tomb, after he had worn the saint's shoes on his feet.

A hat that belonged to 19th century holy man Fr Moore and believed to have healing properties is placed on a devotee's head at Father Moore's well, Co. Kildare. © Dr Ronan Foley

Pilgrims did not have to physically touch the relic for healing to take place. The *Life of St Brigit*, the *Vita Prima Sanctae Brigita*, from the middle of the 8th century, tells of a cure for the sick:

> You'll have my girdle. For you tell me there are many sick people in your part of the country and you will heal them in the name of Jesus Christ by means of my girdle dipped in water and they will give you food and clothing.[112]

Some Irish monasteries kept very strange relics. The Odhar Chiaráin, the 'hide of St Ciaran the dun cow', was a treasured possession of Clonmacnoise. The dun cow was first mentioned in the 8th-century Martyrology of Óengus.[113] It was believed that whoever died on the hide would go straight to heaven.[114] In 900, the Annals of Innishfallen recorded that Tadgh, King of Connaught, died at Clonmacnoise "after he had renounced the world on the hide of Cairn's Dun Cow.'[115]

In the later medieval period, the Bacall Íosa, or 'Staff of Jesus', attracted large numbers of pilgrims to Christ Church Cathedral in Dublin. The crozier, said to have belonged to Christ, later became a possession of St Patrick. It was repeatedly mentioned in the annals and was believed to have performed numerous miracles.[116] Originally kept at Armagh, from the 12th century it was a prized possession of Christ Church Cathedral until it was destroyed during the Reformation.[117] During the 16th century, prior to its destruction, the Bachall Íosa was visited by the women of Dublin, to ensure a safe childbirth.[118]

Irish Saints in the Landscape

Not all relics were located in churches or monastic graveyards. In Ireland, relics also included places in the natural landscape, such as holy wells, caves, stones and even mountains. They could occur as independent pilgrim places or as part of an extended sacred landscape associated with the burial place of a saint or a church.

Holy wells are still places of pilgrimage in modern Ireland. They are, in essence, a body of water, usually a natural spring or hollow containing water, that is seen as holy because of an association with a saint. Irish wells are not all contemporary and have come into existence at different points in time. In the majority of cases it is impossible to accurately determine when they first became places of pilgrimage. Certainly, devotions at some Irish wells began as early as the Iron Age.[119] Some of the oldest wells became Christian places in the early medieval period, but others came into existence throughout the late medieval period and in later centuries following the Reformation. In folklore and hagiography holy wells were created by the saints, who either blessed an existing water source or, by a miraculous act, caused water to burst forth from rock or earth. The Lives of early Irish saints suggest that some wells were used by the saints for baptisms and healing.[120] The holy wells recorded in the Irish saints' Lives were seen as holy places at the time the texts were written, and were most probably the focus of some level of devotional activity and pilgrimage. The location of some of these wells can still be identified; for example, the holy well at Aghagower/Achaidh Forbair (field of the spring), Co. Mayo, was mentioned in the 7th-century *Life of St Patrick*.[121] Other examples include St Attracta's holy well at Cell Adroctae/Killaraghta, Co. Sligo, mentioned in Tírechán's *Collectanea,* while the *Tobar Ultáin* of Toberultan, Co. Meath, is mentioned in other texts relating to St Patrick.

Gerald of Wales (Giraldus Cambrensis), writing in the 12th century, also makes reference to the veneration of holy wells by the Irish in his *History and Topography of Ireland.*[122]

St Attracta's holy well at Killaraghta (Cell Adroctae), Co. Sligo. © Louise Nugent

St Mac Duagh's Cave at St Mac Duagh's Hermitage in the Burren, Co. Clare. © Louise Nugent

Caves are part of the pilgrim landscapes at a number of holy places in Ireland. Most holy caves are found close to monastic sites or holy wells. In folklore, they were used by the saint for temporary accommodation, which is why they are often referred to as the saint's bed. It has been suggested that links between a saint and a particular cave led to the construction of some monasteries at a particular location or, if a cave happened to exist in a monastic complex, it may have been appropriated by an anchorite, and association with the saint developed at a later date.[123]

St Kevin's Bed, a cave at the upper lake Glendalough, Co. Wicklow, was a central part of the 19th-century pilgrimage landscape at Glendalough. Folklore tells us that the saint lived there as a hermit prior to founding his monastery at the lower lake. The cave was first mentioned in the 12th-century, Latin *Life of St Lau-*

rence O'Toole. Laurence, or Lorcán, as he is known in the Irish language, retreated to the cave in prayer for 40 days and nights.[124] The cave is situated in a jagged cliff face 10 meters above the lake. A man-made cave, it was hewn out of the rock face, probably some time in the 12th century, as a response to the holy cave at Lough Derg.[125] It was also recorded in a penitential pilgrimage in the mid-16th century but the tradition of pilgrimage probably dates to its formation (see Chapter 5). The cave was also referred to in a 17th-century *Life of St Kevin*.[126] Two other caves associated with the saint are found at the small village of Hollywood, also in Co. Wicklow, and were also visited by 19th-century pilgrims.

The most famous medieval Irish cave was St Patrick's Purgatory at Lough Derg, Co. Donegal. The cave supposedly acted as a portal for pilgrims to experience Purgatory on earth and was a place of pilgrimage from at least the 12th century.[127] According to one legend, when St Patrick was carrying out his missionary work, many people were confused about the doctrine of Purgatory. The saint went to Lough Derg and prayed. He was divinely inspired to circle his staff on the ground.

St Kevin's cave, Glendalough.
Photo by Christiaan Corlett, courtesy of Culture Stock

Pilgrims praying at St Kieran's tree at Seir Kieran, Co. Offaly.
© Louise Nugent

This action opened a pit of fire and when local people saw this miniature fiery hell, they converted in great numbers. It is said the cave was created from this.[128]

Irish pilgrims also visited holy trees, as their modern counterparts still do at Seir Kieran, Co. Offaly, and Clonfert, Co. Galway. Several holy trees are recorded in the medieval Lives of the Irish saints. Most were miraculously created from the saint's staff; for example, when St Mochaomhog forgot the staff that he had placed in the ground, it turned into a holy tree.[129] A sacred hazel tree associated with St Máedóc was mentioned in his 12th-century Latin Life.[130] Another example is found in the *Life of Colum of Terryglass*, which describes a miraculous hazel tree that took root from St Colum's finger, at a place called Eadarghabhal, in Leinster.[131]

Irish pilgrims also visited stones, both natural and those worked by man. Bullaun stones are often cited as evidence of medieval pilgrimage. They are stones or boulders with one or more man-made hollows or bowls in their surface and are thought to be of early medieval date. The majority are found at early medieval ecclesiastical sites and holy wells.[132] The relationship between bullaun stones and early medieval pilgrimage is ambiguous. While some argue that they were created by the ritual turning of stones in the basin by early pilgrims, there is a much stronger case for their use as mortars for grinding ores or herbs.[133] It seems probable that they originally had a practical purpose but over time some developed an association with a saint, and it was this association that prompted later pilgrimage. It is impossible to gauge when this process began, but by at least the 18th and 19th centuries, bullaun stones were important devotional points, either in their own right or as part of a larger pilgrim landscape.

The Keelers na Beistí. A multiple bullaun stone at Kilmalkedar, Co. Kerry. © Louise Nugent

Natural stones and rock outcrops could also become a focus for pilgrimage. One such example is found in the 7th-century *Life of St Patrick.* We are told that Patrick went to Leinster and established a church at Druimm Hurchaille (Dunmurraghill near Donadea, Clane, Co. Kildare). The church was situated on the great road in the valley, beside a stone called 'Patrick's rock' (*petra Patricii*).[134] Another example is St Declan's stone, located close to the monastery of St Declan at Ardmore, first mentioned in the 12th-century *Life of St Declan,*[135] suggesting that at the time the text was written, the stone was already viewed as a landscape relic of the saint. During the 19th and 20th centuries, pilgrims crawled under this stone as part of their pilgrim ritual, in search of a cure from backache and rheumatism.

Holy stones visited by modern pilgrims: **Left:** St Declan's stone Ardmore, Co. Waterford. **Right:** St Colmcille's chair, Glencholmcille Co. Donegal. © Louise Nugent

The *Bethu Brigte* (*Irish Life of Brigit*) also mentions a miraculous stone associated with healing.[136] Having fallen from her chariot, the saint hit her head on a stone, curring her head and bloodying the stone. The Life then notes that the saint's holy blood cured two women and the stone that caused her injury 'often heals many' and any 'head with a disease of the head which is placed on it returns from it cured'. [137] The 17th-century *Register for the Diocese of Clogher* contains a collection of documents relating to the diocese, compiled by Bishop Patrick Cuilinn (1517–34). It contains a reference to a holy stone, whereby St Patrick was said to have ejected a demon from the stone at Clogher.[138] It also records another story relating to St Patrick: When making a journey to Lough Erne, he pitched his tent in the valley of Crucha and, as was his custom, spent the night sleeping on a stone, using another as his pillow. The place was from then on known as *Pobul Patric* or Patrick's Tent. What is of particular interest, and reinforces the idea of stones being relics of the saint, is that the two stones of Crucha, consecrated by the saint's touch, were placed in front of the church, where they miraculously gave 'health of body' to the sick.[139]

Stone said to mark the spot where St Colmcille was born at Gartan, Co. Donegal.
© Louise Nugent

Croagh Patrick, Co. Mayo.
© James McKee

A holy stone associated with the birthplace of St Colmcille, at Gartan, Co. Donegal, was a focus of pilgrimage from at least the 16th century. The *Life of St Colmcille*, written in the 16th century, relates how the saint's mother gave birth on a flagstone which, from that day forth, was 'working miracles and wonders'.[140] A stone pointed out as this very site is still a focus of modern pilgrimage at Gartan.[141]

Irish pilgrims also made pilgrimages to holy mountain-tops, Mount Brandon and Croagh Patrick being two of the better-known examples. Both have been identified as places of prehistoric pilgrimage associated with the ancient festival of Lughnasa,[142] and by the early medieval period they had become centres of Christian pilgrimage.

Pilgrimage to Croagh Patrick was first documented in the 12th century.[143] In 1432, Pope Eugene IV granted an indulgence of two years to all penitents who climbed to the summit, and three pilgrims from outside Ireland are recorded as having visited there in the year 1485. Johannes Garhi and Franciscus Proly, said to be priests of the city of Lyon, accompanied by their servant Johannes Burges, are

View of Mount Brandon from the Saint's Road at Currauly, Dingle, Co. Kerry. © Louise Nugent.

known to us only from a letter of the Archbishop of Armagh stating that they had fulfilled the proper penitential exercises at Lough Derg and Croagh Patrick.[144] The latter has remained an important place of pilgrimage to the present day.

Mount Brandon was associated with St Brendan by the 9th century. Tentative evidence for pilgrimage can be discerned in references to the wealth of the church on the summit in the 12th and 14th centuries.[145] The 17th-century *Life of Aodh Mac Bric* alludes to pilgrimage on the summit of Slieve League, Co. Donegal, while other likely locations include Slieve Donard, Co. Down, and Church Mountain, Co. Wicklow. Medieval pilgrimage may also have occurred at other mountain-top sites that had previously been identified as prehistoric *Lughnasa* sites.

As we have seen, pilgrims in early medieval Ireland visited a wide range of site types, such as holy wells, stones and mountain-tops, and corporeal and secondary relics at small and large monastic sites. It must be remembered that these pilgrim landscapes were never static. Those that managed to survive through the centuries often expanded and contracted at different points in history, while others fell out of use and new pilgrim sites came into existence.

An Established Tradition: The Landscape of Later Medieval Irish Pilgrimage

The 12th century was a time of significant change in Irish society. The introduction of the diocesan system and the arrival of new religious orders, followed closely by the Anglo-Norman invasion, all changed Irish society, and brought changes to the pilgrim landscape. Some pilgrim places popular in earlier centuries would have fallen in popularity and others would have stopped attracting pilgrims. Orders like the Augustinian Canons helped to keep many older pilgrimage places

The "Yellow Steeple" at St. Mary's Abbey Trim, Co Meath, where the holy statue of Our Lady of Trim once resided. © Louise Nugent

in the focus of pilgrims, rejuvenating them through the translation of relics and by promoting the cults of their saints. These new religious orders also created pilgrim places at their newly established monasteries, one of the most famous examples being the shrine of Our Lady at the Augustinian Abbey, in Trim, Co. Meath.

Archaeological evidence for pilgrimage at these new pilgrimage places is not as obvious as at some early medieval sites. This may be partially due to the fact that these pilgrimages were focused on monastic churches, which first suffered the wrath of reformers and, in later centuries, suffered from neglect, so that the interiors were destroyed, together with any evidence of what the shrines looked like. Other churches were restored, and subsequent renovations changed their interiors.

Architectural evidence of pilgrimage, either in the form of deliberate alterations to accommodate pilgrims or stone reliquary shrines, is rare. The stone reliquaries and stands for shrines that are seen so often in English churches are very rare in Ireland. It is difficult to know if they were unfashionable or merely failed to survive. Two stone reliquary shrines dating to the 15th century survive at Holycross Abbey, where they are used to display relics of the True Cross (see Chapter 7). Archaeologist Jim Higgins has identified fragments of the base or pedestal of a stone shrine, along with parts of an upper storey, at Claregalway Abbey, Co. Galway.[146] The upper level, in common with contemporary English examples, would have held a feretory or relics casket, possibly covered with a canopy.[147] Fragments of similar shrines have been identified at Abbeyknockmoy, Co. Galway[148] and part of a stone reliquary shrine was found during recent excavations of St Thomas Abbey in Dublin.

Part of the base of a stone reliquary shrine identified by Jim Higgins at Claregalway Abbey, Co. Galway. © Louise Nugent

However, without historical accounts we cannot know what type of relics they contained.[149] Numerous later medieval metal reliquaries survive in the National Museum of Ireland collections. While most of these have no direct record of being the focus of pilgrimage, some were used in post-medieval pilgrimage rituals.

Christ Church Cathedral, Dublin. © Louise Nugent

Christ Church Cathedral, Dublin, founded in 1030, went on to become one of, if not the most important pilgrimage destinations in Leinster. It had one of the largest and finest collections of relics in medieval Ireland, assembled by Dúnán, Bishop of Dublin, before 1074, and enshrined in a reliquary shrine between 1121 and 1161.[150] The collection included the miracle-working *Bachall Íosa* (Staff of Jesus), and a marble altar said to belong to St Patrick, along with relics of other Irish

Holycross Abbey, Co. Tipperary. © Louise Nugent

saints, including St Laurence O'Toole, St Brendan and St Brigit. Non-Irish relics included a portion of the True Cross, the Cross and Chain of St Peter, fragments of the Holy Sepulchre, and the vestments of St Olaf of Norway and St Herbert of Cologne. The relics of SS Oswald, Wulfstan, Edward the Confessor and Catherine of Alexandria were also included.[151]

Relics of the crucifixion were highly regarded in late medieval Europe and any church that had a piece of the True Cross, or nails that had held Christ to the cross, had the potential to attract pilgrims. The Cistercian monastery of Holycross Abbey, Co. Tipperary, founded in 1180 by Domhnall Ó Briain, King of Thomond (Limerick),[152] had between one and three relics of the True Cross and attracted large numbers of pilgrims in the 15th and 16th centuries.[153] A relic of the True Cross was kept at Tracton Abbey, a Cistercian monastery near Carrigaline, Co. Cork.[154] The abbey, founded as a daughter house of the Welsh abbey of Whitland, by Odo de Barry in 1225, drew pilgrims especially around the feast of Easter.[155]

Crosses and symbols of the crucifixion (especially rood crosses) also became a focus of pilgrimage in the late medieval world. Ballyboggan, Co. Meath, the Priory of De Laude Dei, founded in the 12th century by Jordan Comin, attracted many pilgrims, who went to see its most valued possession – a miraculous crucifix.

A few accounts of miracles from the 14th and 15th centuries alert us to additional places of pilgrimage. Miracles occurred before the Holy Cross of Raphoe, at Raphoe Cathedral, in the years 1397[156] and 1411.[157] The *Annals of the Four Masters* also record a miraculous cross that appeared at lake Baile-an-Chuilinn in 1482. This miraculous event surely inspired pilgrimage, at least in the immediate aftermath of its discovery, as much as the moving statues of the 1980s did at places like Mellary, Co. Waterford.

Statues, especially those of the Blessed Virgin, could inspire pilgrimage. A significant number of newly developed pilgrim places in late medieval Ireland were associated with Marian statues and images. Miracles are recorded in the 14th and 15th centuries at the statues of the Blessed Virgin at Trim and Navan,[158] Co. Meath. In Munster, pilgrims visited a miraculous plaque of the Blessed Virgin, known as Our Lady of Graces, kept at the Dominican Priory in Youghal.159 This tiny plaque is now on display at St Mary's church at the Dominican priory at Pope's Quay, Cork.

Medieval plaque known as Our Lady of Graces. © Louise Nugent

Medieval statue of Our Lady of Clonfert. © Louise Nugent

Our Lady of Navan and Trim, like many other statues, were burned during the Reformation. Thankfully, a few medieval statues have survived and are on display in the National Museum of Ireland, providing some insight into what these lost statues may have looked like. Two other medieval statues are the focus of modern pilgrimage. Our Lady of Clonfert, a late 13th- early 14th-century wooden statue of the Madonna and Child is a focus of a modern month-long pilgrimage in May by the parishioners of the parish of Eyrecourt, Meelick and Clonfert, in East Co. Galway. The statue came either from the medieval cathedral of Clonfert or the Abbey of St Mary de Portu Puro, to the south-east of the cathedral. A small oak statue of St Gobnait is still venerated at Ballyvourney, Co. Cork. This is now housed in the parish church and the earliest references to pilgrims praying before the image date to the late 17th century.[158] Unfortunately, there is no way of knowing if either of these statues was visited by pilgrims in earlier centuries.

Very Local Pilgrimage – St Richard of Dundalk

Late medieval records of pilgrimage occasionally allow us to identify pilgrim places of local importance. One of the most interesting is the Shrine of St Richard of

Dundalk, at Dundalk, Co. Louth. Pilgrimage was centred around the cult of St Richard FitzRalph, and began after the bones of the holy man were brought back to Dundalk by the Bishop of Meath, Stephen de Valle, 10 years after the saint's death at Avingon, in 1360. In 1377, the *Chronicon Angliae,* written by a monk of St Alban's, recorded that 'great miracles worked daily' occurred at Richard's tomb, housed in St Nicholas's Church, in the medieval town of Dundalk. Evidence of continued devotion and pilgrimage to the saint's remains is found in the *Register of the Archbishop of Armagh*, where the then archbishop directed the chaplain of the deanery of Trim to undertake a penitential pilgrimage there, in 1437.[159]

Despite a number of attempts, the saint was never officially canonised, and his cult remained local. In 1545, a Synod held at St Peter's Church in Drogheda passed a decree for the feast of St Richard, to be celebrated the day following the feast of SS John and Paul, on 27 June. Little is known about how pilgrimage fared in the ensuing centuries. The tomb seems to have been located in the chancel of St Nicholas's Church and although it was much defaced, it was still present in 1624.[160] Richards continued to be referred to as a saint as late as the year 1634, when a priest who was then engaged in a controversy with the friars reminded his opponents that FitzRalph was 'called by the inhabitants of this country S. Richard of Dundalk'.[161] The memory of the pilgrimage remained locally long after it had ceased and is clearly seen in a couplet recited in the Dundalk area during the early 1800s:

> Many a mile did I go, and many did I walk,
> But never saw I a holier man than Richard of Dundalk.[162]

A fleeting reference to a local pilgrimage to the Church of the Blessed Virgin Mary at Thurles, Co. Tipperary, can be found in the 1432 *Calendar of Ormond Deeds*, when the Earl of Ormond granted safe conduct to all pilgrims visiting Thurles on the feast of the Assumption of Our Lady.[163] Another local pilgrimage to the holy statue of St Dominic at the Dominican Priory of Cork was recorded when the local people were outraged at its destruction during the Reformation. This occurred in 1578, when Matthew Sheyne, the Protestant bishop of Cork, ordered the statue to be dragged from the abbey and carried to the high cross of the city, where it was publicly burned, much to the dismay of the people of Cork.[164]

NOTES

1 Sarah Hopper, *Mothers, Mystics and Merry-makers: Medieval Women Pilgrims* (Stroud: Sutton Publishing, 2006), 3.

2 The word shrine is used to denote a centre of pilgrimage as well as a reliquary container and both meanings will be found throughout this book.

3 Susan Morrison, *Women Pilgrims in Late Medieval England* (London: Routledge, 2002), 3.

4 Morrison, *Women Pilgrims*, 3.

5 Diana Webb, *Pilgrimage in Medieval England* (London: Hambledon, 2000), xiii; Patrick J. Geary, *Living with the Dead in the Middle Ages* (Ithaca and London: Cornell University Press, 1994), 164.

6 For discussion of the role of relics in early medieval Ireland see Niamh Wycherley, *The Cult of Relics in Early Medieval Ireland* (Turnhout: Brepols Press, 2015).

7 *Life of St Brigit*, 27.

8 Ludwig Bieler, ed., *The Patrician Texts in the Book of Armagh* (Dublin: The Dublin Institute for Advanced Studies, 2000), 89, I.17(16).

9 VSH Vol. II, 216.

10 Whitley Stokes, ed., *The Martyrology of Oengus the Culdee* (Dublin: Dublin Institute for Advanced Studies) (1984), 26 no. 225.

11 Stokes, *The Martyrology of Oengus*,13.

12 VSH Vol. II, 130 §36. Thanks to Elva Johnston for alerting me to this reference.

13 VSH Vol. II, 162-163

14 Christy Cunniffe, 'Medieval Clonfert: The Genesis, Development and Decline of a Gaelic Cathedral Town' (PhD thesis, NUI Galway, 2010), 112.

15 *Life of St Brigit*, 25 (32.1).

16 Bieler, *The Patrician Texts*, 137, 16 (8–10).

17 Bieler, *The Patrician Texts*, 99–100 I.27(26).

18 Bieler, *The Patrician Texts*, 99–100, I.27(26).

19 Wycherley, *The Cult of Relics*, 83–85.

20 AU, AFM.

21 Wycherley, *The Cult of Relics*, 73–99.

22 Tomás Ó Carragáin, 'The Architectural Setting of the Cult of Relics in Early Medieval Ireland,' *JRSAI* 133 (2003): 130.

23 John Sheehan, 'A Peacock's Tale: Excavations at Caherlehillan, Kerry,' in *The Archaeology of the Celtic Churches. The Society for Medieval Archaeology Monograph 2*, ed. Nancy Edwards (Leeds: Maney, 2009), 197–99.

24 VC, 228 (III.28).

25 Jenny White Marshall and Grellan D. Rourke, *High Island: An Irish Monastery in the Atlantic* (Dublin: Town House and Country House, 2000), 102–21.

26 Chris Lynn, 'Excavations at 46–48 Scotch Street, Armagh, 1979–80,' *UJA* 51 (1988): 69; Bieler, *The Patrician Texts*, 108–9, I.24(1–4).

27 The cut of pit measured 1.3 metres long, c. 0.7 metres wide and 0.35 metres deep.

28 Lynn, 'Excavations at 46–48 Scotch Street,' 69-84, esp. 80; Nancy Edwards, 'Celtic Saints and Early Medieval Archaeology,' in *Local Saints and Local Churches in the Early Medieval West*, ed. Alan Thacker and Richard Sharpe (Oxford: Oxford University Press, 2002), 239.

29 Jenny White Marshall and Claire Walsh, *Illaunloughan Island: An Early Medieval Monastery in County Kerry* (Bray: Wordwell Press, 2005), 55–58; Charles Thomas, *The Early Christian Archaeology of North Britain* (London: Oxford University Press, 1971), 141–43.

30 The ruins of a shrine are also found at Cill Comhla, Inishmore. The gable stone at Cill Cheannannach on Inis Méan and a shrine formerly existed at Slane. See White Marshall and Walsh, *Illaunloughan Island*, 55–56; Thomas Johnson Westropp, '"Slane in Bregia" Co. Meath,' *JRSAI* 31 (1901): 418.

31 Philip MacDonald and Naomi Carver, 'Archaeological Excavations at Ballyhanna Graveyard – Chronology,' in *The Science of a Lost Medieval Gaelic Graveyard: The Ballyhanna Research Project*, ed. Catriona J. McKenzie, Eileen M. Murphy, and Colm J. Donnelly (Dublin: Transport Infrastructure Ireland (TII), 2015), 54–56.

32 Thomas, *The Early Christian Archaeology*, 150.

33 Other examples include Kilruane near Bantry Harbour, Co. Cork, and Caherlehillan, Co. Kerry. Excavation of the later confirms an 8th-century date. See Sheehan, 'A Peacock's Tale', 197–99.

34 Ó Carragáin, 'The Architectural Setting of the Cult,' 130–34.

35 Also found at Inishmurray, Co. Sligo, Inishcleraun, Co. Longford, Labamolaga, Co. Cork, and Inishcealtra, Co. Clare.

36 Ó Carragáin, 'The Architectural Setting of the Cult,' 136.

37 John O'Donovan, 'The Registry of Clonmacnoisee; With Notes and Introductory Remarks,' *JKSEIAS* 1 no. 2 (1857): 446–47; Ó Carragáin, 'The Architectural Setting of the Cult,' 136; Peter Harbison, *Pilgrimage in Ireland. The Monuments and the People* (London: Syracuse University Press, 1991), 14.

38 Tomás Ó Carragáin, *Churches in Early Medieval Ireland: Architecture, Ritual and Memory* (London: Yale University Press, 2010), 291.

39 Ó Carragáin, *Churches in Early Medieval Ireland*, 291. St Dairbhile's house at Fallmore, Co. Mayo, and St Kevin's House at Glendalough, Co. Wicklow, had a similar function.

40 Ó Carragáin, *Churches in Early Medieval Ireland*, 291.

41 Helen Lanigan Wood, 'The Monastery of St Molaisse in Devenish from Early Chrisitain Period until the End of the Medieval Period,' in *An Archaeological Survey of County Fermanagh. Volume 1. Part 2*, ed. Claire Foley, Ronan McHugh, and Brian Scott, vol. 1 (Belfast: HMSO, 2014), 879. During the mid-19th century, antiquarians excavated the interior and found the remains of a single skeleton, although there is no way of knowing if it had a connection to the saint.

42 Measuring 1.80 x 1.50 metres, 1.4 x 0.81 metres, and 2.50 metres in height, respectively.

43 Dudley Waterman, 'An Early Christian Mortuary House at Saul, Co. Down, with Notes on Similar Monuments in Ulster,' *UJA* 23 (1960): 83–88; Herity, 'The Forms of the Tomb-Shrine of the Founder Saint in Ireland,' 193–94; Harbison, *Pilgrimage in Ireland*, 154–56. Waterman, in his article 'An Early Christian Mortuary House at Saul, Co. Down', identified a further example at Saul ,Co. Down, but recent excavations here have shown it was of post-medieval date (personal communication with Finbar MacCormack).

44 Excavations at the Clochán Leo Complex, Inishark, Co. Galway, suggest that the *leachta* on the island were constructed as monumental commemorations or cenotaphs. Ryan Lash et al., '"Differing in Status, but One in Spirit": Sacred Space and Social Diversity at Island Monasteries in Connemara, Ireland,' *Anitquity* 92 (2018): 447–48.

45 Aidan O'Sullivan, Conor McDermott, and Graham Warren, 'Stratigraphical Report on Archaeological Excavations at Templeteenaun (Ballinagee Townland), Co. Wicklow. Preliminary Report. School of Archaeology UCD.' Unpublished Excavation Report, 2008, 43; Jerry O'Sullivan and Tomás Ó Carragáin, *Inishmurray: Archaeological Survey and Excavations 1997–2000* (Cork: Collins Press, 2008), 316–51; White Marshall and Walsh, *Illaunloughan Island*, 46–57; Michael Herity, 'The Antiquity of an Turas (the Pilgrimage Round) in Ireland,' in *Lateinische Kultur Im VIII. Jahrhundert. Traube-Gedenkschrift*, ed. Albert Lehner and Walter Berschin (St Ottilien: EOS, 1989), 95–143.

46 Thomas, *The Early Christian Archaeology*, 169.

47 Examples also existed at larger ecclesiastical sites like Glendalough and Clonmacnoise. See White Marshall and Walsh, *Illaunloughan Island*, 47.

48 Ann O'Sullivan and John Sheehan, *The Iveragh Peninsula: An Archaeological Survey of South Kerry* (Cork: Cork University Press, 1996), 248.

49 O'Sullivan and Ó Carragáin, *Inishmurray*, 316–35.

50 AU.

51 Marie Therese Flanagan, *The Transformation of the Irish Church in the Twelfth and Thirteenth Centuries* (Woodbridge: Boydell & Brewer, 2013), 222.

52 AFM.

53 Cunniffe, 'Medieval Clonfert,' 111.

54 Cunniffe, 'Medieval Clonfert,' 112–24.

55 Made of yew wood, it is decorated in elaborate metal work and measures c. 498 millimetres in height and its rectangular base measures 597 x 356 millimetres. The base is mounted on small feet with large metal rings attached, allowing the shrine to be transported using poles.

56 For a detailed discussion of reliquaries, see Karen Eileen Overbey, *Sacral Geographies: Saints, Shrines and Territory in Medieval Ireland* (Brepols, 2012), Chapter 2.

57 Harbison, *Pilgrimage in Ireland.*, 155; Peter Harbison, 'The Clones Sarcophagus: A Unique Romanesque-Style Monument,'

Archaeology Ireland 13 no. 3 (1999): 13–16; William Wakeman, 'Monastic Antiquities of Clones,' *Clogher Record* 3 (1975): 32–36.

58 AFM.

59 Flanagan, *The Transformation of the Irish Church*, 222.

60 Alexander O' Hara and Faye Taylor, 'Aristocratic and Monastic Conflict in Tenth-Century Italy: The Case of Bobbio and the Miracula Sancti Columbani,' *Viator* 44 no. 3 (2013): 62.

61 Rev. Sylvester Malone, *Life of St. Flannan* (Dublin: James Duffy & Co, 1902), 51; The translation of St Flannan's remains was also recorded in a Martyrology at Regensburg, in Germany, for 26 August. Regensburg was part of a group of Benedictine monasteries known as the *Schottenklöster*, which had close links with Munster. See Flanagan, *The Transformation of the Irish Church*, 222-23.

62 Malone, *Life of St. Flannan*, 51

63 Malone, *Life of St. Flannan*, 51.

64 Malone, *Life of St. Flannan*, 52.

65 Raghnall Ó Floinn, *Irish Shrines & Reliquaries of the Middle Ages* (Dublin: Town House and Country House, 1994), 8.

66 He captured a large collection of relics belonging to Armagh during the Battle of Downpatrick in 1177. Only the Book of Armagh and St Tigernach's bell were returned; the others were kept either for ransom or to enhance the prestige of the church at Downpatrick. See Raghnall Ó Floinn, 'Insignia Columbae,' in *Studies in the Cult of Saint Columba*, ed. Cormac Bourke (Dublin: Four Courts Press, 1997), 141.

67 The promotion of St Patrick's cult was also an attempt to promote a more stable political situation in north-east Ulster.

68 Flanagan, *The Transformation of the Irish Church*, 223.

69 Ó Floinn, 'Insignia Columbae,'141.

70 Anon, 'Historical Notes on Downpatrick Cathedral,' *JRSAI* 41 (1911): 293–94; Ó Floinn, *Irish Shrines & Reliquaries*, 8

71 Bieler, *The Patrician Texts*, 120–21, II.11(9).

72 Bieler, *The Patrician Texts*, 164–65, III.5 54.

73 AMF.

74 Ó Floinn, 'Insignia Columbae,' 143.

75 Ronald C. Finucane, *Miracles and Pilgrims: Popular Beliefs in Medieval England* (London: J. M. Dent and Sons., 1977), 29.

76 Finucane, 29.

77 Kathleen Hughes, *Church and Society in Ireland A.D. 400-1200*, ed. David Dumville (London: Variorum Reprints, 1987), 345-346 V; 354-55 V.

78 Aubrey Gwynn and Richard Neville Hadcock, *Medieval Religious Houses: Ireland* (Dublin: Irish Academic Press, 1988), 75, 173.

79 Stokes, *The Martyrology of Oengus*, 245.

80 Hughes, *Church and Society*, 355 (V); Susan Leigh Fry, *Burial in Medieval Ireland 900-1500: A Review of the Written Sources* (Dublin: Four Courts Press, 1999), 164-65.

81 Andy Halpin and Conor Newman, *Ireland. An Oxford Archaeological Guide to Sites from the Earliest Times to AD 1600* (Oxford: Oxford University Press, 2006), 257.

82 A penitential pilgrimage was recorded here in 1100, when 'Macraith Ua Flaithen, successor of Ciaran, and Cronan of Tuaim-Greine, died on his pilgrimage at Achadh-bo', AFM.

83 Bernadette Williams, *The Annals of Friar John Clyn* (Dublin: Four Courts Press, 2007), 238.

84 Brian Lacey, *Colum Cille and the Columban Tradition* (Dublin: Four Courts Press, 1997), 58; Laurence P. Murray, 'Archbishop Cromer's Register (Continued),' *JLAS* 8, no. 3 (1935): 259.

85 Murray, 'Archbishop Cromer's Register (Continued),' 273 no. 140.

86 Ó Floinn, *Irish Shrines & Reliquaries*, 16.

87 Ó Floinn, *Irish Shrines & Reliquaries*, 16.

88 VSH Sal, 89; A. Lucas, 'The Social Role of Relics and Reliquaries in Ancient Ireland,' *JRSAI* 116 (1986): 10.

89 For example, in 793 (AU) 'The taking on tour of the relics of Tóla', in 794 (AU) 'The taking on tour of the relics of Trian'. In 908 (FM), Muireann, successor of Brigit, along with a large group of clergy and many relics, escorted him to Mag n-Airb, and when he arrived in Munster he made peace there. The second Irish *Life of St Kevin* also makes reference to swearing on the saint's relics. See *BNÉ*, vol. 2, 142.

90 For example, in 811, the *Annals of Ulster* tell us that abbot of Armagh used the relics of St Patrick when promoting the 'law' of Patrick in Connacht: 'Nuadu, abbot of Ard Macha, went to Connacht with Patrick's law and his casket.'

91 Edel Bhreathnach, *Ireland in the Medieval World, AD 400–1000: Landscape, Kingship*

and Religion (Dublin: Four Courts Press, 2014), 230.

92 Ó Carragáin, 'The Architectural Setting of the Cult,' 133; Cormac Bourke, 'Irish Croziers of the Eighth and Ninth Centuries,' in *Ireland and Insular Art A.D. 500–1200*, ed. Michael Ryan (Dublin: Royal Irish Academy, 1987), 166–73.

93 James Leslie Houlden, *Jesus in History, Thought, and Culture: An Encyclopedia* (Oxford: ABC–CLIO, 2003), 222.

94 Flanagan, *The Transformation of the Irish Church*, 225.

95 Charles Plummer, ed., 'The Life of Mac Creiche,' in *Miscellanea Hagiographica Hibernica*, Subsidia Hagiographica 15 (Brussels: Société des Bollandistes., 1925), 83.

96 'There was a man named Thomas O Godain in great and extraordinary suffering owing to the plague of boils; and he lost the faculty of speech and memory, and was almost unconscious; and after a washing (of the bell) had been made for him by a young clerk of Mac Creiche, and (the water) carried by the same young clerk, and drunk by the sick man from the bell, his speech and memory returned to him at once; and this miracle was noised abroad by everyone.' in Plummer, 'The Life of Mac Creiche,' 91.

97 Charles Doherty, 'The Use of Relics in Early Ireland,' in *Irland Und Europa: Die Kirche in Frühmittelalter*, ed. P Ní Chatháin and M Richter (Stuttgart: Klett-Cotta, 1984), 98–99; Ó Floinn, 'Insignia Columbae,'148–49. The full list of relics included a gospel book, a piece of clothing of Mary, a cloth with Christ's blood, a piece of the tree Paul was killed on, a piece of the tree Christ was crucified on, a girdle of St Paul, a cloak of St Martin, a tooth of St Patrick, a tooth of St Declan, the hair of the Blessed Virgin, a stone from Molua's Island, a rib from Camm's body and a mantle of Enda of Aran.

98 VSH Vol. I, 248, 253.

99 Mario Esposito, ed., 'Conchubrani Vita Sanctae Monennae,' *PRIA* 28 (1910): 210–11.

100 Heist, *VSH*, 338.

101 VSH Vol II, 29.

102 Whitley Stokes, 'The Klosterneuburg Incantation,' *Revue Celtique* 2 (1875): 113–15; Lucas, 'The Social Role of Relics and Reliquaries in Ancient Ireland,' 29.

103 Lucas, 'The Social Role of Relics,' 30.

104 Michael Duignan, 'The Moylough (Co. Sligo) and Other Irish Belt-Reliquaries,' *JGAHS* 24, no. 3/4 (1951): 89.

105 Ulster Society for Medieval Latin Studies, 'The Life of Saint Monenna by Conchubranus: Part I,' *Seanchas Ardmhacha* 9 no. 2 (1979): 261.

106 Duignan, 'The Moylough (Co. Sligo),' 93.

107 Hughes, *Church and Society in Ireland A.D. 400–1200*, 363.

108 Michael J. O'Kelly, 'The Belt-Shrine from Moylough, Sligo,' *JRSAI* 95 no.1/2 (1965): 183.

109 James Bugslag, 'Performative Thaumaturgy: The State of Research on Curative and Spiritual Interaction at Medieval Pilgrimage Shrines,' in *The Sacred and the Secular in Medieval Healing Sites, Objects, and Texts*, ed. Barbara S. Bowers and Linda Migl Keyser (London: Routledge, 2016), 242.

110 Hopper, *Mothers, Mystics and Merrymakers*, 107.

111 Bugslag, 'Performative Thaumaturgy,' 242.

112 V Prima, 25 no. 44.

113 Stokes, *The Martyrology of Oengus*, 203.

114 Whitley Stokes, *Lives of Saints from the Book of Lismore* (Oxford: Clarendon Press, 1890), 268.

115 The Register of Clogher (1308) recorded a miraculous sheepskin kept in a shrine called the Membrane. St Tigernach had ensured that it would a produce constant supply of wool. A sheep or badger skin of St Moline of Killevy and a badger skin cowl of St Molaise at Devenish were also kept as relics. See Kenneth Nicholls, 'The Register of Clogher,' *Clogher Record* 7, no. 3 (1971): 396–99; Cormac Bourke, 'Medieval Ecclesiastical Metalwork from the Diocese of Clogher,' in *History of the Diocese of Clogher*, ed. Henry A. Jefferies (Dublin: Four Courts Press, 2005), 28, fn. 14.

116 784 AFM; 789 AU;1027 CS; 1030 AFM; 1073 AI; 1080 AFM; 1093 AI; 1101 AFM; 1152 AFM; 1157 AFM; 1165 MIA; 1166 AFM; 1537 AFM.

117 Lucas, 'The Social Role of Relics,' 9; Cormac Bourke, *Patrick: The Archaeology of a Saint* (Belfast: HMSO, 1993), 18–20, 49.

118 Lucas, 'The Social Role of Relics,' 32.

119 Eamonn P. Kelly, 'Antiquities from Irish Holy

Wells and Their Wider Context,' *Archaeology Ireland* 16 no. 2, no. 2 (2002): 24--8.

120 VSH, Vol. I, cxliviii–clii; Bieler, *The Patrician Texts*, 79, 81, 83, 89.

121 Bieler, *The Patrician Texts*, 151.

122 Giraldus Cambrensis, *The Topography of Ireland*, Medieval Latin Series (Cambridge Ontatio: In parentheses Publications, 2000), 36–37.

123 Marion Dowd, *The Archaeology of Caves in Ireland* (Oxford: Oxbow Books, 2015), 176.

124 Charles Plummer, 'Vie et Miracles de S. Laurent Archevêque de Dublin,' *Analecta Bollandiana* 33 (1919): 141–42.

125 Conleth Manning, 'Rock Shelters and Caves Associated with Irish Saints,' in *Above and beyond: Essays in Honour of Leo Swan*, ed. Tom Condit and Christiaan Corlett (Bray: Wordwell Press, 2005), 117.

126 BNÉ Vol. II, 121.

127 Michael Haren and Yolande de Pontfarcy, *The Medieval Pilgrimage to St Patrick's Purgatory: Lough Derg and the European Tradition* (Clogher Historical Society, 1988); Dowd, *The Archaeology of Caves*, 217–21.

128 Alice Curtayne, *Lough Derg: St Patricks Purgatory* (Omagh: Graham & Sons, 1976), 7.

129 Pádraig Ó Riain, *Four Tipperary Saints. The Lives of Colum of Terryglass, Crónán of Roscrea, Mochaomhóg of Leigh and Ruadhán of Lorrha* (Dublin: Four Courts Press, 2014), 53.

130 Elizabeth FitzPatrick, *Royal Inauguration in Gaelic Ireland C. 1100–1600: A Cultural Landscape Study* (Woodbridge: Boydell Press, 2004), 58.

131 Ó Riain, *Four Tipperary Saints*, 12. For additional references to sacred trees, see A.T Lucas, 'The Sacred Trees of Ireland,' *JCHAS* 68 (1963): 16–54.

132 Judith Cuppage, *Archaeological Survey of the Dingle Peninsula* (Ballyferriter: Oidhreacht Chorca Dhuibhne, 1986), 358.

133 Brian Dolan, 'Bedrocks and Bullauns: More than One Use for a Mortar?,' *Archaeology Ireland* 23, no. 1 (2009): 16-19; Liam Price, 'Rock-Basins or 'Bullauns', at Glendalough and Elsewhere,' *JRSAI* 89 (1959): 161-88; Kathleen Hughes and Ann Hamlin, *The Modern Traveller to the Early Irish Church* (London: SPCK, 1977), 99–100.

134 Bieler, *The Patrician Texts*, 162-162, no. 51(2); Stones were also connected in inauguration rituals. See Charles Doherty, 'Kingship in Early Ireland,' in *The Kingship and Landscape of Tara*, ed. Edel Bhreathnach (Dublin: Four Courts Press for The Discovery Programme, 2005), 3–31.

135 Rev. Patrick Power, *Life of St. Declan of Ardmore and Life of St. Mochuda of Lismore* (London: Irish Texts Society, 1914), 27, 166, fn. 52.

136 Wycherley, *The Cult of Relics*, 44.

137 *Bethu Brigte*, 27 no. 29.

138 Nicholls, 'The Register of Clogher,' 401.

139 Nicholls, 'The Register of Clogher,' 401.

140 Manus O'Donnell, *The Life of Colum Cille*, ed. Brian Lacey (Dublin: Four Courts Press, 1998), 32. A similar birth legend is associated with St Colman Mac Duagh at his birth site at Kiltartan. This stone is used in the modern pilgrim stations at the site.

141 After the saint's birth, his mother 'delivered a round stone with the colour of blood, An Cloch Ruadh', which she left at Gartan to work miracles. O'Donnell, *The Life of Colum Cille*, 32–33.

142 Máire MacNeill, *The Festival of Lughnasa* (Comhairle Bhéaloideas Éireann, 1982).

143 1113 AU, AFM, ALC.

144 Haren and de Pontfarcy, *The Medieval Pilgrimage to St Patrick's Purgatory*, 96.

145 Louise Nugent, 'Exploring the Evidence for Early Medieval Pilgrimage at Kilcolman,' *JKAHS* 13, no. 2 (2013): 40–42; MacNeill, *The Festival of Lughnasa*, 103.

146 Jim Higgins, *Claregalway: Its Architecture, Archaeology and Its History* (forthcoming Galway: Crows Rock Press, 2019), 19–23;There are no records of relics at Claregalway Abbey. In 1291, an indulgence was granted to penitents who visited the church and again, in 1433, Pope Eugene IV granted an indulgence of four years and four quarantines to the faithful who visited Claregalway Franciscan friary to contribute to the renovation of the church and the completion of the tower.

147 Personal communication with Jim Higgins.

148 Higgins, *Claregalway Its Architecture*, 19–23.

149 Paul Duffy and Tadhg O'Keeffe, 'A Stone Shrine for a Relic of St Thomas Becket in Dublin?,' *Archaeology Ireland* 31, no. 4 (2017): 18–23.

150 Raghnall Ó Floinn, 'The Foundation Relics of Christ Church Cathedral and the Origins of the Diocese Dublin,' in *Medieval Dublin VII. Proceedings of the Friends of Medieval Dublin Symposium 2005*, ed. Séan Duffy (Dublin: Four Courts Press, 2006), 89–102; Ó Floinn, 'Insignia Columbae,' 148–49.

151 Ó Floinn, 'The Foundation Relics of Christ Church Cathedral.' Raghnall Ó Floinn, 'Beginnings: Early Medieval Ireland, AD 500–850,' in *Treasures of The National Museum of Ireland*, ed. Raghnall Ó Floinn and Patrick Wallace (Dublin: Gill & Macmillan, 2002), 202.

152 Roger Stalley, *The Cistercian Monasteries of Ireland: An Account of the History, Art and Architecture of the White Monks in Ireland from 1142–1540* (London: Yale University Press, 1987), 245.

153 Colmcille Ó Conbhuidhe, *The Cistercian Abbeys of Tipperary*, ed. Finbarr Donovan (Dublin: Four Courts Press, 1999), 166; Halpin and Newman, *Ireland. An Oxford Archaeological Guide*, 388.

154 Richard Mant, *History of the Church of Ireland, from the Reformation to the Revolution*, vol. 2 (London: John W. Parker, 1840), 84; Gwynn and Hadcock, *Medieval Religious Houses*, 14344.

155 Denis Sullivan, 'The Cistercian Abbey of Tracton, County Cork,' *JCHAS*, xliv (1939): 1–15; Gwynn and Hadcock, *Medieval Religious Houses*, 143–44; Stalley, *The Cistercian Monasteries of Ireland*, 249–50.

156 AFM.

157 AFM, AC, AU.

158 Nugent and Scriven, *Wells, Graves and Statues*, 35; John Richardson, *The Great Folly, Superstition, and Idolatry, of Pilgrimages in Ireland* (Dublin: J. Hyde, 1727), 71.

159 Aubrey Gwynn, *The Medieval Province of Armagh, 1470–1545* (W. Tempest, Dundalgan Press, 1946), 269–70.

160 Katherine Walsh, *Richard FitzRalph in Oxford, Avignon, and Armagh* (Oxford: Clarendon Press, 1981), 465; Robert Chambers, *The Book of Days: A Miscellany of Popular Antiquities in Connection with the Calendar, Including Anecdote, Biography, & History, Curiosities of Literature and Oddities of Human Life and Character*, vol. 2 (Edinburg: W. & R. Chambers, 1872), 186; James Ware, *The Whole Works of James Ware Concerning Ireland Revised and Improved*, vol. I (Dublin: Jones, 1739), 83.

161 Aubrey Gwynn, 'Richard Fitzralph, Archbishop of Armagh,' *An Irish Quarterly Review* 22 (87) (1933): 391.

162 John Prince, *Danmonii Orientales Illustres: Or, The Worthies of Devon* (London: Printed for Rees & Curtis, Plymouth, 1810), 367; Michael Dunne, 'Richard FitzRalph of Dundalk (c. 1300–1360) and the New World,' *Archivium Hibernicum* 58 (2004): 244. The poem was recorded in the margin of a page from the manuscript of the Martyrologium Dungallense in the National Library of Brussels. 7 Brussels, Bibl. Nat., MS 506.

163 COD Vol.3, 84.

164 Nugent and Scriven, *Wells, Graves and Statues*, 29.

CHAPTER 2

Irish Pilgrims Abroad

Irish pilgrims also made pilgrimages outside Ireland, some of the most prestigious of places being the Holy Land, Rome and Santiago de Compostela. The practicalities of travel outside the country, together with the effort, time and cost meant that foreign pilgrim destinations were not open to everyone. Most ordinary people did not have the money to go abroad, and even if they did, commitments to their family, lords or chieftains made absence for long periods difficult, if not impossible.

In early medieval Ireland, pilgrimage abroad for the lay populace was limited, but as time progressed, the opportunities to travel to more distant places both in and outside Ireland increased. The journeys of kings, lords and ladies, the middle classes, merchants, mayors and clergy are all recorded, from the 12th century onwards, in the Irish historical sources.

Ultimate Devotion – Irish Pilgrimage to Jerusalem

For all Christians, Jerusalem was the ultimate pilgrim destination. Its distance from Ireland meant that undertaking a pilgrimage to this city was an act of extraordinary devotion. Pilgrims were drawn to the Holy Land as they could literally walk in the footsteps of Christ and mentally relive all the important moments surrounding his life and death. No other place on earth could offer equal spiritual reward. The distance and cost of the journey meant that only a small minority of Irish people could ever hope to visit this prestigious destination. The earliest reference to Irish pilgrimage dates to the 11th century, but Irish pilgrims probably made the journey in earlier centuries. We

View of Jerusalem from southeast, showing city walls, the Dome of the Rock, and al-Aqsa mosque. (Library of Congress / Public Domain / Wikimedia Commons)

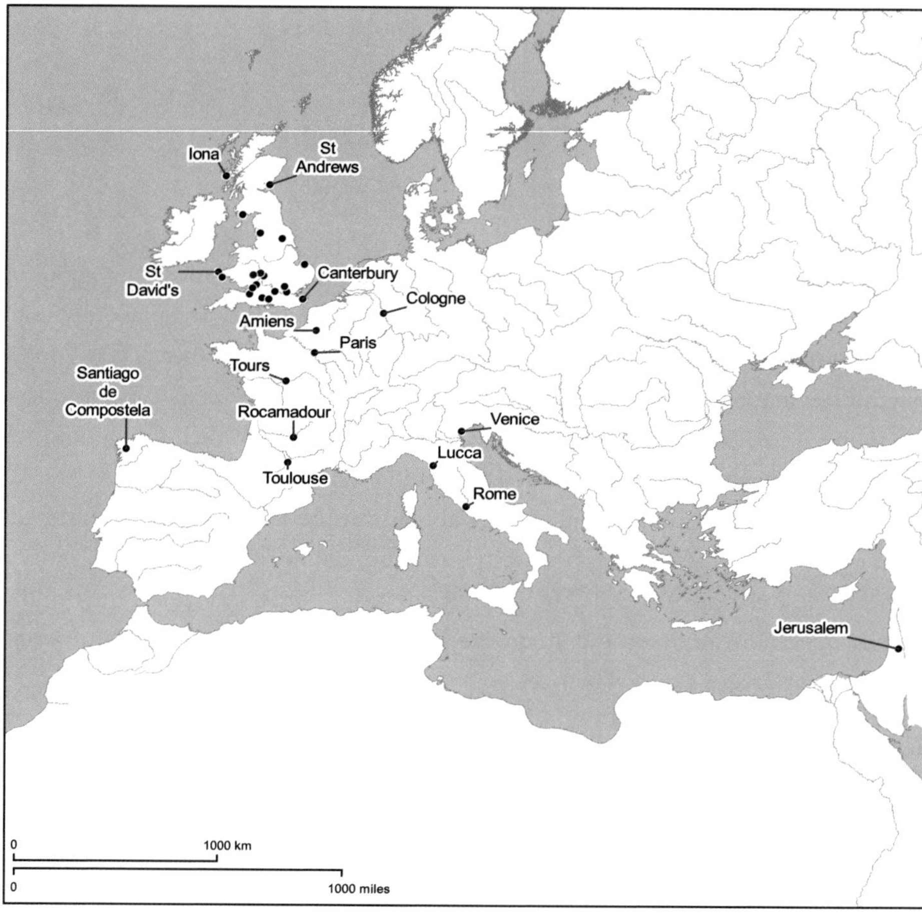

Map of foreign pilgrim destinations, visited by Irish pilgrims. Created by Richard Clutterbuck

know that pilgrims from Northern Europe had been travelling to the Holy Land from as early as the 4th century AD. The annals record four Irish pilgrimages to Jerusalem between the years 1080 to 1231, surely only a fraction of the true figure for those who travelled. Irish pilgrims must have made this journey throughout the medieval period, with numbers peaking during periods of stability and falling during periods of unrest, such as the Crusades. The pilgrims recorded in the annals are all high-status individuals, such as the king of the Decies (an ancient territory that extended over Co. Waterford into parts of South Tipperary) in 1080,[1] Hugh, son of Conor Moinmoy O'Conor, King of Connaught (1224),[2] or Ualgarc O'Rourke, the Lord of Breifne, who controlled lands in modern-day Cavan, Leitrim and parts of Sligo.[3]

From the 13th century, the historical sources record the pilgrimages of men and women from Gaelic and Anglo-Irish areas of Ireland, such as Richard and Helen de Trum (Trim, Co. Meath), who prepared for their pilgrimage to the Holy Land in the year 1230.

Occurrences of the surname Palmer may also alert us to other Irish pilgrims. During the 12th and 13th centuries, those who had been on pilgrimage to the Holy Land were often nicknamed 'Palmer'. The term comes from the Latin word, *palma* (palm tree), as pilgrims brought back palm leaves as proof of pilgrimage.[4] *The Guild Merchant Rolls of Dublin* (1190–1265) include the names of over 150 men with the surname Palmer. Some of these men were associated with English towns but many were associated with Ireland, such as Duvendalus Palmerius de Limeric (Limerick), Petrus Palmerus de Trum (Trim) and Walterus filius Palmeri de Trum.[5] The names of some, like Walterus filius Palmeri and Galgethal Palmer filius Reinaldi de Korke (Cork), imply that they were the sons of a palmer, suggesting that it was their fathers who had undertaken the pilgrimage.[6] Another pilgrim, Thomas le Palmer, a citizen of Waterford, is mentioned in the *Calendar of Documents Relating to Ireland*.[7]

Rome: The Holy City

Rome was second only to Jerusalem in popularity and prestige. The administrative centre of the Christian Church, home to its leader, the pope, it was also the burial place of the apostles Peter and Paul and had the relics of more saints than any other shrine in Christendom. Rome attracted a constant stream of pilgrims from the 3rd century AD ,and in the later medieval period there was an additional incentive for pilgrims to visit the Holy City, with the issuing of indulgences and the declaring of five Jubilee Years between 1300 and 1449.[8] Several Irish pilgrims are explicitly mentioned as having made a pilgrimage to Rome in the early and late medieval periods.[9] The earliest recorded Irish pilgrimage occurred in 926, when the abbot of Bangor, Celedabhaill, son of Scannal, 'went to Rome on pilgrimage'.[10] Irish pilgrimage would certainly have begun much earlier. Irish clerics were travelling to Rome on official Church business from the 6th century, so it is likely that many combined this with a personal pilgrimage. Again, the pilgrims recorded in the annals are all high-status individuals and include members of the clergy.[11] Donnchad, son of Brian Bóruma, travelled to Rome and died there, after being deposed as King of Munster in 1064.[12] Archaeologically, Roman pilgrimage is represented by a single pilgrim badge, a souvenir believed to have been obtained by an Irish pilgrim to the Holy City in the 13th century and several *Agnus Dei* medals from the later medieval period.[13] All are on display in the National Museum of Ireland. Porphyry, an exotic green or red stone, used in the buildings of imperial Rome, has turned up in a number of early medieval Irish contexts and may represent further evidence of Irish pilgrims at Rome. Porphyry has been found at the ecclesiastical sites of Armagh, Downpatrick, Movilla, Co. Down, Reefert Church, Glendalough, Co. Wicklow, Derrynaflan, Co. Tipperary, and Kilteel, Co. Kildare. Examples have also been found in Hiberno-Norse levels in Dublin and Waterford.[14] A piece of green porphyry was found in the burial soil of a grave at an early medieval church site at Skeam, Co. Cork.[15]

In Search of St James

Pilgrimage to Santiago began in the 9th century, following the miraculous discovery of the body of St James. By the 12th century, it had become one of most important European pilgrim shrines, second only to Rome and was a very popular pilgrimage destination in late medieval Ireland.[16] The annals, along with state documents, record the pilgrimages of high-status men and women to this place, especially during the 15th and early 16th centuries.[17] Aside from historical sources, evidence for pilgrimages to Santiago also survive in the archaeological record. Burials identified as relating to Jacobean pilgrims have been excavated on this island, all containing scallop shells, the traditional pilgrim souvenirs of Santiago. They have been recovered in Ireland in areas of both Anglo-Norman and Gaelic control, dating to as early as the 13th century.

Cathedral of St James, Santiago de Compostela, Spain.
© Maria Golpe CaminoWays.com

Continental Destinations: Irish Pilgrimage to France and Germany

Peregrini – Irish monks who, up to the 9th century, went on pilgrimages of voluntary exile to the Continent – often developed settlements that became important monasteries, and which retained links with Ireland. These places would have also been focal points for the Irish travelling on the Continent. For example, during the 14th century, Irish friar Simon Fitz Simon (Symonis Semeonis) included the monastery of Bobbio, founded by Ireland's most famous *peregrinus*, St Columbanus, on his itinerary to Jerusalem.[18]

While there is plenty evidence for Irish ascetic pilgrimage during the 7th to the 9th centuries, references to universal pilgrimage abroad are rare for this date. It was common for those going on long-distance pilgrimages to visit other holy places and churches located on, or close to, the route of their intended pilgrim destination. Therefore, some Irish pilgrims must have visited other pilgrim destinations along established pilgrim routes to Rome or Santiago. Pilgrims heading to Rome may have visited shrines in Germany and France en route. The German shrines of Wilsnack, Cologne and Aachen may have tempted Irish pilgrims to make short detours. English and Scottish pilgrims were recorded in Wilsnack in the 14th and 15th Centuries,[19] so it is likely that Irish pilgrims may also have visited this site.

In France, the shrines of St Leonard of Noblat and Our Lady of Rocamadour were accessible to pilgrims who were following French pilgrim routes to Santiago de Compostela. Irish evidence for pilgrimages to Rocamadour in France comes in the form of a 14th-century pilgrim badge uncovered in the 1800s at Lough Atrain, Co. Cavan. The focus of pilgrimage here was the tomb of St Zaccheus and a miraculous statue known as Our Lady of Rocamadour. By the later medieval period, the statue was the more popular attraction. Dedications to St Leonard in Ireland are found at holy wells in Dunnamaggin, Co. Kilkenny, and the abbey of St Leonard at Dundalk, a house of Crutched Friars.[20] Such connections may perhaps have inspired the occasional pilgrimage.

The shrine of St Martin at his monastery at Tours in France may also have appealed to Irish religious and lay pilgrims from the early centuries of the Irish Church. This idea is supported by an 11th-century Irish poem, 'De Mirabilibus Hiberniae', which details the miraculous signs and wonders of Ireland. One of the miracles relates to an Irish woman who regularly gave alms to the poor on the feast of St Martin on 11 November. One year, when her son was on pilgrimage at Tours, he saw a vision of his beloved mother handing out alms to the poor. Not only could he see the event taking place, but he was able take the lid off the

Medieval chest tomb at Kilconnell Friary, Co. Galway. St James, the central figure, is dressed as a pilgrim.
© Louise Nugent

vessel in the vision and bring it back to Ireland and present it to his mother.[21] St Martin had a strong cult following in Ireland from an early date and folk traditions relating to his feast day have endured to the present day. Another French destination of interest to Irish pilgrims was Amiens Cathedral, as evidenced by a tiny pilgrim badge depicting the head of St John the Baptist, found in excavations in Waterford. Amiens was in possession of a relic of the head of St John the Baptist brought back after the Fourth Crusade in 1206. The badge, dating to the 13th century, date is proof of at least one Irish pilgrimage to that place.[22]

The iconography on two late medieval chest tombs (see Chapter 9) points to individual pilgrimages to other pilgrim destinations. A 15th-century stone tomb at Strade Abbey in Co. Mayo tentatively suggests that the deceased had been on pilgrimage to relics of the Three Magi at Cologne, Canterbury and Rome.[23] A similar tomb at Kilconnell Friary, Co. Galway, indicates pilgrimages to Santiago de Compostela, the shrine of St Louis of Toulouse and the Abbey of Saint-Denis, in Paris.[24]

Irish Pilgrim Destinations in Britain

Irish pilgrims also went on pilgrimage to holy places on the island of Britain. The continuing development of trade networks, coupled with the early medieval transnational monastic foundations of Irish saints, ensured that close links between Ireland and the island of Britain were maintained throughout the early medieval period.

The earliest accounts of Irish pilgrimages to Britain relate to the monastery of Iona – a small island in the Inner Hebrides, off the western coast of Scotland. Iona was founded in 543 by St Colmcille, and it is here that the saint was buried. Colmcille's monastery went on to become the centre of a great monastic federation that stretched across Scotland and the north of Ireland. His cult remains

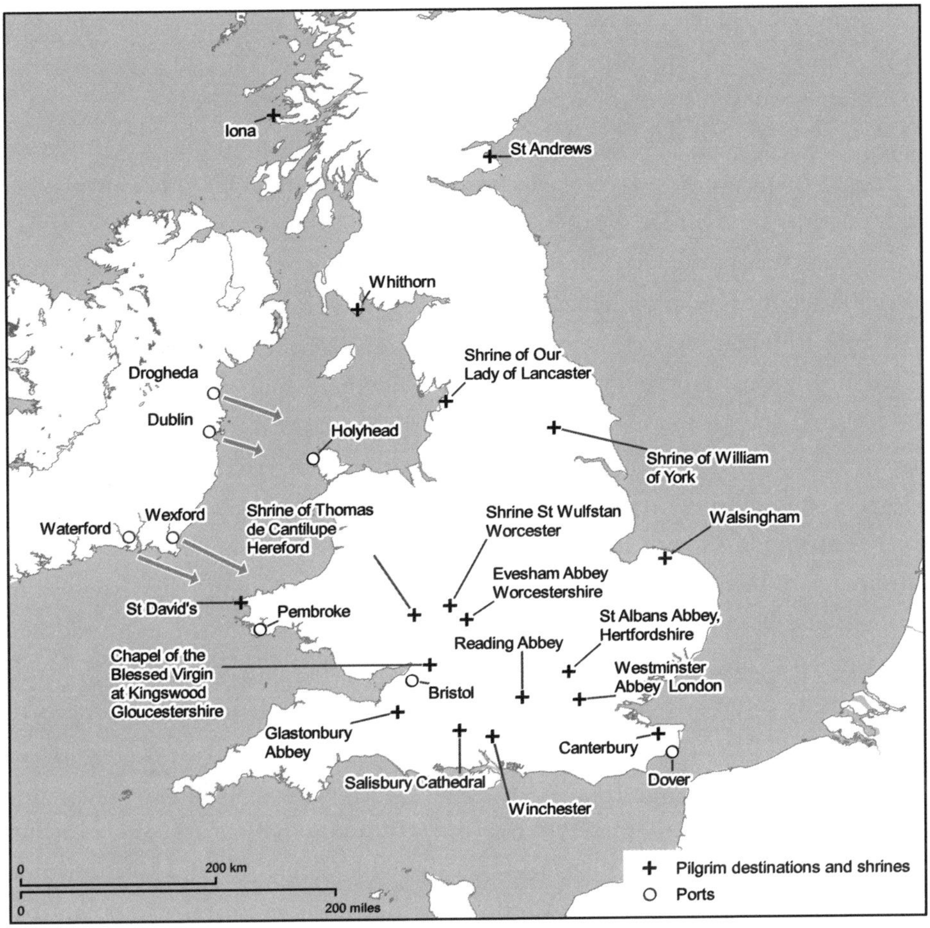

Pilgrim destinations visited by Irish medieval pilgrims on the Island of Britain. Created by Richard Clutterbuck

one of the most popular in modern Ireland and he is regarded, along with SS Patrick and Brigit, as one of three patron saints of Ireland. The 7th-century Latin *Life of Columba* by Adomnán records the arrival to the island of Irish penitential pilgrims.[25] The Irish annals mention six pilgrimages to Iona between the years 765 and 1188, all entries relating to high-status penitential pilgrims who entered the monastery and stayed until death. For example, Artdhal, King of Connaught, went on pilgrimage to Iona in 777/782[26] and his death is recorded there a few years later, in 786/790.[27] Amhlaeibh, son of Sitric, King of Dublin, died at Iona in 974/979.[28] In the year 1026, the King of Cenél Conaill, when making a pilgrimage to Rome, planned his journey to include visits to the Irish shine of Clonfert and St Colmcille's grave, as well as relics at Iona.[29]

Irish pilgrims, especially those in the north of Ireland, were surely attracted to other Scottish shrines. Scotland as a political entity came into being in the 9th century and before this, much of what is now lowland Scotland was part of the Kingdom of Northumbria. Monks from Iona, including St Aidan, established a monastery at Lindisfarne and were involved in spreading Christianity to this region.

Evidence of another early pilgrimage was to the Scottish Shrine of St Andrews, when an Irish prince, Aodh son of Maelmithig, died there in 965.[30] Although no other Irish pilgrims are recorded there, later historical sources suggest that St Andrews had an international appeal. For example, the *Chronica Gentis Scotorum* of John of Fordun (c.1380), refers to 'people of all nations' hastening to visit the relics,[31] so it is possible that some Irish pilgrims were among the international clientele.

Irish pilgrims, especially those from the northern half of the country, may have visited the great shrine of Whithorn, the burial place of St Ninnian. The presence of a 10th-/11th-century chapel dedicated to the Irish St Finnian of Moville, who studied at Whithorn before returning to Ireland, illustrates the shrine's strong links with Ireland and may tentatively represent evidence of Irish pilgrimage to this site.[32] More definitive evidence of Irish pilgrimage is found in Scottish legislation to protect pilgrims travelling to Whithorn, passed between the years 1427 and 1516. The legislation indicates that a proportion of pilgrims to the shrine came from Ireland, the Isle of Man and England.[33] For example, in 1427, King James I of Scotland granted a general safe conduct to all pilgrims to Whithorn from these regions. On 14 December 1506, Regent Albany also granted safe conduct to all persons from the same regions and, 10 years later, a further safe conduct was issued to pilgrims from these locations.[34] In the 16th century, King James V of Scotland wrote to the pope informing him of the international dimension of the pilgrimage at Whithorn, which, according to him, included people from England and Ireland.[35]

The majority of historic references to Irish pilgrims in England and Wales date to the late medieval period but, given the history of the two Islands, pilgrimage was undoubtedly taking place much earlier. The main route for Irish travellers to the Continent was via land routes in Wales and southern England, via London and on to the port of Dover (see Chapter 6). Popular Welsh and English pilgrim churches surely tempted at least occasional Irish travellers to make a short detour and break their journey. Following the Anglo-Norman conquest of Ireland, in the 12th century, the royal court in London was frequently visited by aristocrats and clergy from the Gaelic- and Anglo-Norman-controlled areas of Ireland; and some may have combined official business with pilgrimage in the city or at places nearby.

The shrine of St David's in Pembrokeshire in Wales would surely have attracted Irish pilgrims. St David and his monastery are mentioned in several Lives of

St David's Cathedral, Wales.
© Louise Nugent

Irish saints. St Finbarr of Cork visited there on his return from Rome, while SS Aidan of Ferns and Finnian of Clonard, along with Scothin and Senanus, patrons of Ossory, are all said to have studied at the monastic school in St David's. The great explorer St Brendan also supposedly spent time there.[36] This argument is strengthened by the fact that St David's shrine is geographically close to ports used by medieval Irish travellers. A late medieval tale from the miracles collection at St David's mentions the theft of an image of the saint from his shrine by a group of Irish pilgrims returning from Rome.[37] St David's cult also crossed the Irish Sea to south-east Ireland, where holy wells dedicated to him survive at Olygate, Co. Wexford, and Woodhouse, Co. Waterford.

One land route used by Irish pilgrims crossing southern England passed by the important pilgrim shrines of Glastonbury, Salisbury, Winchester and Canterbury.[38] Glastonbury had strong connections with Ireland from the early medieval period and actively promoted the cults of several Irish saints.[39] It also claimed to be in possession of the corporeal remains of SS Patrick and Benignus. Both saints are depicted alongside St Dunstan on a 14th-century seal of the abbey. Glastonbury also claimed association with St Brigit of Kildare, who was supposed to have visited there, leaving behind much-revered relics. William of Malmesbury, in *The Antiquity of Glastonbury*, written between 1129 and 1139, noted:

> The fame of Patrick brings to Glastonbury many Irish pilgrims, who, according to their unsavoury national custom, throng to kiss the remains of their favourite saint.[40]

Passing evidence of a tradition of Irish pilgrimage may also be found in the 10th-century *Life of St Dunstan*, where a boy in the monastery of St Dunstan recalled reading the books that 'Irish pilgrims' had taken to Glastonbury.[41] Evidence for pilgrimage in the 13th century relates to the archbishop of Dublin, Henry de Loundres, along with several other Irish bishops who granted indulgences to Irish pilgrims travelling to Glastonbury.[42]

Given its proximity to the main Irish land route to Dover, Irish pilgrims may also have visited the shrine of St Osmund at Salisbury Cathedral. This idea is strengthened by the fact that four archbishops of Dublin granted indulgences to anyone who travelled to Salisbury between 1280 and 1299.[43] In 1299, Bishop Nicholas of Leighlin issued an indulgence for all those praying before the tomb of Bishop William de la Corner in Salisbury Cathedral.[44] Irish bishops also actively promoted indulgences to Reading Abbey, issued for the feast and the octave of St James. The abbey had a precious relic of St James's arm.[45]

The great international shrine of Canterbury was also located on the land route used by Irish travellers to Dover. Pilgrimage at Canterbury had initially centred around St Augustine, the first archbishop of Canterbury. Augustine had been chosen by Pope Gregory the Great in 595 to lead a mission to Christianise King Æthelbert and his kingdom of Kent. From the late 12th century, Augustine was overshadowed by the cult of St Thomas à Becket. Pilgrimage in honour of St Thomas began following his murder before the high altar of the cathedral in 1170. In the centuries that followed, St Thomas's shrine developed into an international destination, attracting pilgrims from all over Europe. The earliest recorded Irish pilgrimage to Canterbury is that of St Laurence O'Toole, who visited there in 1172.[46] The *Life of St Thomas* à *Becket* mentions an Irish boy call Colonius, who was healed of a tumour at the saint's shrine.[47] It also makes a note of Daniel, a Dubliner, sent by his father on business to France, 'where he entered a monastery upon detecting signs of leprosy on his own face. Thereafter, he came to Thomas's shrine, where he was cured.'[48] Archaeological evidence of Irish pilgrimage to Canterbury during the 13th century also survives: two pilgrim *ampullae* (tiny lead flasks) recovered from excavations in medieval Dublin and a badge of similar date recovered during recent excavations at North Main Street, Cork.[49] A century later, the site was still popular among the Irish. The pilgrimage of an

Canterbury Cathedral, Canterbury, England.

Irish friar was recorded in 1425 and in 1485 an Irishman applied for a licence to undertake a pilgrimage to Canterbury.[50] Further evidence of Irish pilgrimages to Canterbury relates to the 15th-century earl of Ormond. In 1446, James Butler, 5th earl of Ormond, was accused of treason and summoned to London, where he spent some time in the Tower of London. He was later allowed to move to Smithfield due to a respiratory condition, but by royal orders he was prohibited from going beyond 40 miles of London, and was required to hold himself in readiness to respond to a summons before the king and his council.[51] The only exception to his 40-mile rule was permission to make a pilgrimage to Canterbury. This permission may have been prompted by royal recognition of the Butler family's special veneration of St Thomas à Becket, but it is not known whether the earl accepted the solace offered.

Most Irish pilgrims travelling to Dover and Canterbury passed through London and some may have taken the opportunity to rest for a day or two and visit some of the city's holy places. Irishmen on official business to the king's court may also have found time to visit and pray at some of these places. In the 12th century, at least one Irishman was recorded as making a pilgrimage to St Edward the Confessor at Westminster Abbey.[52] Several Irish bishops, including the Bishop of Armagh, helped to support the efforts of Westminster

Shrine of St Edward the Confessor.

Abbey to promote the relics of the Holy Blood, by offering indulgences to those who went to Westminster from c. 1248–1250.[53]

There is tentative evidence for Irish pilgrimage to the chapel of the Blessed Virgin at Kingswood, Gloucestershire. An indulgence of a year and 40 days was issued to penitents who visited the chapel. Miracles had taken place here previously and it was said the 'blind and lame' came from 'England, Wales, Ireland and Scotland' in search of healing.[54] Thomas of Marlborough, in his 13th-century *History of the Abbey of Evesham*, records that

> In those days many pilgrims used to come to Evesham from Aquitaine, Ireland, and many other lands … [55]

In 1233, the Bishop of Armagh, Jocelin O'Tormey, granted 15 days' indulgence to Irish people who travelled to St Alban's Abbey in Hertfordshire. The indulgence predated a period of rebuilding at the abbey. In 1250, an earthquake shook the abbey, damaging the eastern end of the church, and it was rebuilt in the following years.[56] By the 13th century, St Alban's Cathedral possessed shrines of SS Alban and Amphibalus.

Additional English shrines are mentioned in an Anglo-Norman's petition to go on pilgrimage in 1481–1482. The pilgrimage was to include a visit to the shrines of St William of York, Our Lady of Lancaster and the Our Lady of Walsingham.[57] An Irish pilgrimage to the shrine of St Wulfstan at Worcester Cathedral, in the 13th century, is represented by a single pilgrim *ampulla* found in excavations in Dublin. Evidence of other Irish pilgrimages to the shrine are found in the *Vita Wulfstani*, a Latin Life of the saint, which recalls a healing miracle bestowed on an Irishman named Pippard, whose tongue had been cut out by Hugh de Lacy, the Earl of Ulster.[58] The *Annals of Worcester* record that Pippard built a church in Ireland in honour of St Wulfstan and gave it to the church of Worcester, together with 30 carucates of land. A single carucate was the amount of land that could be tilled by a team of eight oxen in a ploughing season.[59] Worcester was relatively easy to access from the port of Bristol (located at the edge of the Diocese of Worcester). Bristol had very close trading links with Ireland and throughout the later medieval period there would have been a constant stream of ships travelling back and forth carrying items such as hides, wine and pottery from Bristol to Irish ports.[60] The cult of Wulfstan was also found in Ireland, having first arrived through the long-established trade links of Bristol and Dublin and through settlers from Bristol.[61] Interestingly, John Comyn, archbishop of Dublin, was on the panel of clerics appointed by Pope Innocent III to verify the authenticity of miracles attributed to Wulfstan prior to his canonisation.[62] Given his testament to Wulfstan's sanctity, perhaps he also had a role in promoting the saint's cult in Dublin. In 1205, a priory of the Order of St Victor, dedicated to the saint, was founded in Celbridge, Co. Kildare, by Adam de Hereford. Although not Irish by birth, he had been cured of dropsy by the intercessions of St Wulfstan at Worcester.[63] A 13th-century *ampulla* was also found in excavations of medieval Dublin.[64]

Finally, a passing reference to Irish sailors visiting the shrine of St Thomas de Cantilupe of Hereford in the 14th century highlights another Irish pilgrimage (see Chapter 7).[65]

The pilgrim destinations outlined here and in Chapter 1 represent only a fraction of those available to Irish pilgrims. The pilgrim landscape was forever changing, and Irish pilgrims were not limited in their choices of pilgrim destination, either at home or abroad.

NOTES

1 1080 AI.

2 'Hugh, the son of Moinmoy *O'Conor*, died on his return from Jerusalem and the River Jordan,' in AFM.

3 1231 (AFM). See also 1231 *ALC* & *ACon.*

4 By the 14th century, 'Palmer' had become a surname and is unlikely to indicate a connection with pilgrimage. See Patrick Hanks and Flavia Hodges, *A Dictionary of Surnames* (Oxford: Oxford University Press, 1988).

5 Philomena Connolly and Geoffrey Haward Martin, eds, *The Dublin Guild Merchant Roll, c. 1190–1265* (Dublin: Dublin Corporation, 1992) list the following people with 'palmer' in their names: Edwardus Palmer de Clunard (Clonard), p. 15; Willelmus Palmerus de Kilmainan (Kilmainham), p. 21; Galfridus Palmerous de Keneles (Kells Co. Meath date 1230–1), p. 62; Willemus Palmerus de Adhi (Athy, Co. Kildare, 1231–2), p. 63; Robertus Palmerous de Dundalk (1232–3), p. 65; Willimus Palmerus de Drocheda (Drogheda 1233–34), p. 66; Johannes Palmerus de Tristledermot (Castledermot Co. Kildare, 1235–6), p. 69; Padinus de Villa Palmeri (Palmerstown, 1236–7), p. 70; Thorfinus Palmerus de Weseford (Wexford, 1237–8), p. 72; Willelmus Palmerud de Rathoueth (Ratoath Co. Meath, 1239–40), p. 76; David Palmerus de Cnacfergus (Carrickfergus, Co. Antrim, 1243–4), p. 80; Rogerus Palmerus de Harthscul (Ardscull, Co. Wicklow, 1244–5), p. 81; Reymundus de Kilkenni (Kilkenny, 1251–2), p.92; Adam Palmerus de Balimakdun (Ballymun, Co. Dublin,1254–), p. 94; Rogerus Palmerus de Atrio Dei (Ardee, Co. Louth, 1255–6), p. 95.

6 Connolly and Martin, *The Dublin Guild Merchant Roll*, 48; Michael Potterton, *Medieval Trim: History and Archaeology* (Dublin: Four Courts Press, 2005), 310.

7 CDI (1171–1251), Vol. 1, 4; 92; 328; CDI (1252–84), Vol. 2, 140; 266; CDI (1285–96, Vol. 3, 60; 83; 155; 384. CDI (1293–1301), Vol. 4, 57, 159–60, 179.

8 Gary Dickson, 'The Crowd at the Feet of Pope Boniface VIII: Pilgrimage, Crusade and the First Roman Jubilee (1300),' *JMH*, 279–307, 25 (1999); Sumption, *Pilgrimage*, 231, 234, 245, 248–253.

9 Irish pilgrims to Rome in the annals include AFM 926 (died AFM 927), AFM 927, AFM 1024, AI 1026, ALC 1028, AI 1036, AI 1042, AU/AFM/ALC 1051, AU/ALC/CS 1064, AFM/ALC 1134, AFM 1218, AI 1218, AFM 1251, AU 1296, AU/AFM 1450, AU/AFM 1450, AU 1451, AFM 1480, AU 1491, AFM/ALC/ACon 1512.

10 AFM.

11 AFM 926, AFM297, AFM 1024, AI 1036, AFM/ALC 1134, AFM 1216, AFM 1251, AU 1450, AFM 1450).

12 AI 1026, ALC1028, AI 1042, AU/AFM/ALC 1051, AU/ALC/CS 1064, AFM 1216, AU1296, AU 1450, AFM/ALC/A Con 1512).

13 Brian Spencer, 'Pilgrim Souvenirs,' in *Miscellanea 1. Medieval Dublin Excavations 1962-81 (Series B) Vol.2 Fascicules 1–5*, ed. Patrick Wallace (Dublin: Royal Irish Academy, 1988), 43–47.

14 Chris Lynn, 'Some Fragments of Exotic Porphyry Found In Ireland,' *JIA* 2 (1984): 19-32.

15 Claire Cotter, '1990:021 Skeam West Early Church Site,' 1990, Excavations.ie (website) Accessed June 15 2015 http://www.excavations.ie/Pages/Details.php?Year=&County=Cork&id=3310.

16 For an in-depth discussion of the Irish pilgrimage to Santiago, see Bernadette Cunningham, *Medieval Irish Pilgrims to Santiago de Compostela* (Dublin: Four Courts Press, 2018).

17 Irish pilgrims in the annals include AU/AFM/ALC 1429, A Con 1445, AFM/ALC 1472, AU 1480, AFM 1507, AFM 1510. Pilgrimages were also undertaken by the mayors of Waterford (1473), and Drogheda (1473). See Roger Stalley, 'Sailing to Santiago: Medieval Pilgrimage to Santiago de Compostela and Its Artistic Influences in Ireland,' in *Settlement and Society in Medieval Ireland. Studies Presented to F.X. Martin, o.s.a.*, ed. John Bradley (Kilkenny: Boethius Press, 1988), 397–420.

18 Mario Esposito, ed., *Itinerarium Symonis Semeonis Ab Hybernia Ad Terram Sanctum*

(Dublin: Dublin Institute for Advanced Studies, 1960), 35.

19 Diana Webb, *Pilgrimage in Medieval England* (London: Hambledon, 2000), 97.

20 John Hennig, "St. Leonard in Ireland.", *JLAS* 10, no.4 (1994): 297–301.

21 Flanagan, *The Transformation of the Irish Church*, 229.

22 Brian Spencer, 'Pilgrim Signs,' in *Late Viking Age and Medieval Waterford: Excavations 1986–1992*, ed. Maurice F. Hurley et al. (Waterford: Waterford Corporation, 1997), 529–30.

23 Colmán Ó Clabaigh, *The Friars in Ireland 1224-1540* (Dublin: Four Courts Press, 2012), 194-95; Roger Stalley, 'The End of the Middle Ages: Gothic Survival in Sixteenth-Century Connacht,' *JRSAI* 133 (2003): 18.

24 Stalley, 'The End of the Middle Ages,' 17.

25 Richard Sharpe, ed., *Adomnán's Life of Columba*. (Harmondsworth: Penguin, 1995), 122 I.13; 188 II.39.

26 AFM/AU.

27 AFM/AU.

28 AU/AFM. Also, Cethernach, Bishop of Teach-Collain (Stackallan, Co. Meath) died at Iona in 1047 (AFM.

29 AI.

30 Tom Turpie, *Kind Neighbours: Scottish Saints and Society in the Later Middle Ages* (Leiden: Brill, 2015), 16.

31 Turpie, *Kind Neighbours*, 16.

32 C. A. R. Radford and G Donaldson, *Whithorn and the Ecclesiastical Monuments of Wigtownshire. Historic Scotland Guide* (Edinburgh: HMSO, 2002), 23.

33 Tom Turpie, 'Scottish and British? The Scottish Authorities, Richard III and the Cult of St Ninian in Late Medieval Scotland and Northern England,' in *Medieval and Early Modern Representations of Authority in Scotland and the British Isles*, ed. Kate Buchanan and Lucinda H.S. Dean (London: Routledge, 2016), 128; Turpie, *Kind Neighbours*, 109; David Ditchburn, "Saints at the Door Don't Make Miracles'? The Contrasting Fortunes of Scottish Pilgrimage, c. 1450–1550,' in *Sixteenth-Century Scotland: Essays in Honour of Michael Lynch*, ed. Julian Goodare and Alasdair A. MacDonald (Leiden: Brill, 2008), 92.

34 Robert Chambers, *The Book of Days: A Miscellany of Popular Antiquities in Connection with the Calendar, Including Anecdote, Biography, & History, Curiosities of Literature and Oddities of Human Life and Character*, vol. 2 (Edinburg: W. & R. Chambers, 1872), 412, fn. j.

35 *Letters and Papers, Foreign and Domestic, Henry VIII, Volume 4, 1524–1530, 379–80, no. 852; Mairi Cowan, Death, Life, and Religious Change in Scottish Towns c. 1350–1560 (Oxford: Oxford University Press, 2012), 64.*

36 David W. James, *St. David's and Dewisland: A Social History* (Cardiff: University of Wales Press, 1981), 10-11.

37 Michael J. Curley, 'The Miracles of Saint David: A New Text and Its Context,' *Traditio* 62 (2007): 143, 203 [11].

38 Ven. Archdeacon John L. Robinson, 'St. Brigid and Glastonbury,' *JRSAI* 83 (1953): 97.

39 During the 7th century, a band of Irish pilgrims were murdered by bandits outside Glastonbury. Their remains were later exhumed by King Ine of Wessex c. 700 and reburied at Glastonbury, where they became a focus for veneration. Another unlucky group of Irish pilgrims returning from Rome via this same route was murdered by bandits near Glastonbury in 851. See James F. Kenney, *The Sources for the Early History of Ireland: Ecclesiastical. An Introduction and Guide* (Dublin: Four Courts Press, 1993), 446; Robinson, 'St. Brigid and Glastonbury,' 97.

40 William Wells Newell, 'William of Malmesbury on the Antiquity of Glastonbury', *PMLAA*, 1903, 489.

41 Douglas Dales, *Dunstan: Saint and Statesman* (Cambridge: James Clarke & Co, 2013), 11.

42 Richard Mant, History of the Church of Ireland, 91; Robinson, 'St. Brigid and Glastonbury,' 97; Samantha A. Meigs, *The Reformations in Ireland: Tradition and Confessionalism, 1400–1690* (London: Macmillan Press, 1997), 9192.

43 Barra Boydell, 'Music in the Medieval Cathedral Priory,' in *Christ Church Cathedral Dublin: A History*, ed. Kenneth Milne (Dublin: Four Courts Press, 2010), 12.

44 Royal Historical Society, 'Some Pardoner's Tales: The Earliest English Indulgences,' *TRHS*, Sixth, XII (16 January 2003): 56, fn. 132.

45 Cunningham, *Medieval Irish Pilgrims*, 96-97.
46 David Farmer, ed., *The Oxford Dictionary of Saints, Fifth Edition Revised* (Oxford: Oxford University Press, 2011), 265.
47 Michael Staunton, ed., *The Lives of Thomas Becket* (Manchester: Manchester University Press, 2001), 209–10.
48 Colmán Ó Clabaigh and Michael Stanton, 'Thomas Becket and Ireland,' in *Listen, O Isles, unto Me Studies in Medieval Word and Image in Honour of Jennifer O'Reilly*, ed. Elizabeth Mullins and Diarmuid Scully (Cork: Cork University Press, 2011), 92.
49 Spencer, 'Pilgrim Souvenirs,' 35–39; personal communication with Maurice Hurley.
50 Stat. Ire. Ric. III–Henry VIII, 53; Ó Clabaigh, The Friars, 198.
51 Thomas Moore, *The History of Ireland*, Vol. 3 (London: Longman Press, 1851), 177; E Harris, *Proceedings and Ordinances of the Privy Council of England*, Vol. VI (The Commission of Public Records, 1837), x, xx, ix.
52 Marsha Dutton, ed., *Aelred of Rievaulx: The Historical Works*, trans. Jane Freeland, Cistercian Fathers Series: Number Fifty-Six (Minnesota: Liturgical Press, 2005), 162–65; Henry Richards Luard, ed., *Lives of Edward the Confessor* (London: Longman, Brown, Green, Longmans, and Roberts, 1858), 232–35.
53 Nicholas Vincent, *The Holy Blood: King Henry III and the Westminster Blood Relic* (Cambridge: Cambridge University Press, 2001), 206.
54 Diana Webb, *Pilgrims and Pilgrimage in the Medieval West* (London: I.B Tauris, 1999), 206 no. 25 for the year 1364.
55 Jane Sayer and Leslie Watkiss, *Thomas of Marlborough: History of the Abbey of Evesham* (Oxford: Clarendon Press, 2003), 169, Book III Part I.
56 Mant, *History of the Church of Ireland*, 2: 99.
57 Stat. Ire. Ric. III–Henry VIII, 335.
58 Reginald Darlington, ed., *The Vita Wulfstani of William of Malmesbury* (London: Royal Historical Society, 1928), 141.
59 Darlington, *The Vita Wulfstani*, 141; Roger Roswell, 'Medieval Painted and Stained Glass at Worcester Cathedral Priory, Part II: The Priory Cloisters,' *Vidimus Journal*, 58 (2010).
60 Clare Downham, *Medieval Ireland* (Cambridge: Cambridge University Press, 2018), 200.
61 Spencer, 'Pilgrim Souvenirs,' 39.
62 Darlington, *The Vita Wulfstani*, 141–43.
63 Darlington, *The Vita Wulfstani*, lii; Arthur Spears, *The Cult of Saint Catherine of Alexandria in Ireland. Arthur Spears* (Rathmullen: Rathmullan District Local Historical Society, 2006), 58.
64 Spencer, 'Pilgrim Souvenirs,' 39–43.
65 Tim O'Neill, *Merchants and Mariners in Medieval Ireland* (Dublin: Irish Academic, 1987), 46.

CHAPTER 3

Medieval Motives – The Impetus behind Pilgrimage

Pilgrimage has never been an official part of Church doctrine, so why did so many Irish people leave their homes, friends and family to go on pilgrimage? The answer to this question varied from person to person and changed over time. Across the centuries pilgrimage could be inspired by a combination of factors that included belief, faith, hope, the search for forgiveness or a cure, the need to do penance, following family traditions and acquiring an indulgence, as well inquisitiveness and wanderlust. Which of these factors became the overriding motivator depended on the individual and the place and time that the pilgrimage was undertaken.[1]

Faith

A belief in God was the oldest and most enduring motivate for pilgrimage. In the early centuries of the Church, faith was the primary motivational factor for pilgrimage.[2] Faith also underpins other motivations, such as the search for miracles, healing and indulgences. Pilgrimage provided ordinary people with a physical way of expressing their faith and engaging with their beliefs at a time when the majority were illiterate and so could not read the Bible. The physical act of being in the presence of holiness, the places where Christ had lived and died, or the shrines or relics of a saint where miracles had been performed made the experiences of Christ seem more real, as the pilgrim could more readily, in the words of one scholar, 'recreate in their imagination the scenes of Christ's ministry and passion. '[3]

This sentiment is clearly reflected in the writing of Paulinus of Nola (c. 352–431), in his discussion of early pilgrimage to the Holy Land:

> No other sentiment draws men to Jerusalem than the desire to see and touch the places where Christ was physically present ... Theirs is truly spiritual desire to see the places where Christ suffered, rose from the dead, and ascended into heaven ... all these things recall God's former presence on the earth and demonstrate the ancient basis of our modern beliefs.[4]

Devotion

Faith in God was very much linked to devotion to the saints. From the earliest days of Christianity, people believed that the saints, because of their human past and their privileged place in heaven, had the ability to intercede with God through their prayers.[5] Prayers to the saints could be said at any location, but many believed that their prayers would have greater meaning and be more effective when uttered beside the tomb or grave of the saint or in the presence of his or her relics. People turned to the saints for help with problems, both large and small. Pilgrimages were made to ensure a good harvest, to pray for a husband, for help in conceiving a much longed-for child and for the safe delivery of babies. Medieval pilgrimages were even made to help find lost keys, much in the same way modern Catholics will visit statues of St Anthony in local churches to pray for help in finding lost items. Pilgrimages were also made to give thanks to the saints for favours granted, be it by new mothers for delivery of a healthy child, or for cures for sickness, etc.[6]

Miraculous Healing

Some pilgrims were motivated by the desire to experience a miracle. From the 3rd century, Christians believed that saints who had performed miracles in their lifetime could continue to do so after death.[7] Belief in miracles is central to Christianity: 'just as the miracles in the New Testament are proof of Christ's authority, so the power of the individual saints was judged by the ability of their relics to work miracles'.[8]

Faith in God and devotion to the saints underpinned belief in miracles. Most people accepted miracles as part of their lived experiences and pilgrims flocked to the shrines of saints and holy places in the hope of witnessing or experiencing a miracle. Belief that saints could perform miracles through their relics was incredibly strong. Examples of this can be seen at medieval French shrines, where desperate mothers brought their stillborn babies in the hope the saint might bring them back to life to be baptised, and so save them from limbo.[9]

The search for healing miracles was one of the most common reasons for medieval pilgrimage. In modern Ireland, holy wells are associated with healing for different sicknesses and pilgrims still visit in the hope that their waters will provide a cure or relief for their illness. In the medieval period, people in much the same way hoped to gain a respite from pain and illness, not just at holy wells but also by offering prayers and visiting the graves and other relics of the saints. Death and pain were part and parcel of everyday life for the rich and the poor alike. The prospect of recovery from a serious illness was relatively low.[10] Pilgrims also went on pilgrimage on behalf of loved ones, often too ill or old to travel. The Church actively promoted the idea that physical disease was brought on by sin. Many illnesses and disabilities were thought to be a result of God's displeasure and, as such, a punishment for a sinful life.[11] Diseases such as leprosy,[12] gonorrhoea and complaints such as infertility and mental illness were all believed to have a spiritual root.[13] People believed that the saints, through their prayers or miracles, could help to cure or ease their suffering; and that doing penance at the shrine of a saint effaced not only the illness but the sin that had caused it.

There are numerous examples from across medieval Europe of sick and disabled pilgrims making their way to shrines and relics in search of healing, an Irish example being the cripple Gilla Míchíl, who made six pilgrimages to Rome. He was eventually cured by St Edward the Confessor at Westminster Abbey, after which he promptly made a seventh pilgrimage to Rome in thanksgiving for his cure.[14] Leprosy was one of the most dreaded diseases in the medieval world and many lepers left Ireland to bathe in the waters of the Jordan in the hope of recovery. An example from the late 15th century is Sir John Bellew, who tragically died en route.[15]

Most diseased and crippled pilgrims left the shrine without being healed. Pilgrims knew that healing was not guaranteed but they hoped that they might be lucky. Several *ampullae* from the shrine of St Thomas à Becket at Canterbury bear the inscription 'Thomas is the best doctor of the worthy sick'. [16] This slogan reiterates this reality. The Canterbury flasks were filled with what was known as St Thomas's water. Following the murder of Thomas à Becket by four knights of King Henry II on 29 December 1170, his blood was collected from his wounds by the monks of the cathedral. Holy water mixed with this blood became a miraculous cure for all kinds of diseases and it was even credited with bringing the dead back to life. *Ampullae* containing 'Thomas's water' were a must have for pilgrims who visited Canterbury and were sold as souvenirs.[17] The aforementioned inscription shows Canterbury's efforts to promote itself as a centre of healing and the use of the word 'worthy' implies that the success of healing was dependent on the pilgrim's moral character, as only the 'worthy' or the faithful would receive help from the saint. If a miracle was not produced, the fault was placed squarely on the pilgrim and not the saint.[18]

Cures were a feature of both local and international pilgrim sites. Many of the larger European pilgrim shrines recorded posthumous miracles of the saint in collections often referred to as *Miracula*. Surviving *Miracula* illustrate a wide range of miraculous cures, from healing cancer, restoring sight and the ability to walk,

Stained image of sick pilgrim receiving water from an ampulla at the shrine of Thomas à Becket at Canterbury Cathedral.
© Sarah Blick

to the casting out of demons. Unfortunately, there are no collections of miracles from any medieval Irish pilgrim sites. The earliest catalogue of Irish miracles is found in the 17th-century *Triumphalia Chronologica Monasterii Sancta Crucis Hibernia*, kept at Holycross, Co. Tipperary. However, there are scattered references to miracles performed at other Irish pilgrim churches. One of the earliest accounts of an Irish miracle is found in a letter written in 632 by Cummian of Armagh. The letter recalls how a holy book and relics that Cummian brought from Rome to Armagh had performed healing miracles:

> We saw with our own eyes a totally blind girl opening her eyes at these relics, and a paralytic walking, and many demons cast out.[19]

The Latin Life of St Flannan of Killaloe, written in the 12th century, recounts how, following the saint's death, large crowds gathered at his tomb and, through his intercession, miracles took place, including the healing of the lame and blind.[20]

The annals recorded miraculous events in Ireland that would not be out of place in the miracle collections of English or Continental shrines. In 1033, the shrine of SS Peter and Paul at Armagh emitted blood.[21] The shrine probably contained some of the relics mentioned by Cummian in the 7th century and it was recorded as bleeding again in 1178.[22] Bleeding relics were by no means unique to Ireland. Bleeding hosts were a common phenomenon on the Continent in the later medieval period and could attract large numbers of pilgrims.[23] The 'blood' that oozed from these relics was believed to be capable of healing and, in some cases, could even become a relic in its own right. The keepers of the shrine at Armagh may have collected the holy excretions by dipping pieces of cloth in the blood, or by diluting it with water, thereby creating secondary relics. In the years 1397 and 1411, the Holy Cross of Raphoe poured blood and miraculous cures were attributed to the excretion.[24] There are no surviving descriptions of the Raphoe cross but it is likely that its design incorporated a figure of Christ – in 1411 blood was said to have poured from the wounds of Christ.

> The Holy Crucifix of Raphoe poured out blood from its wounds. Many distempers and diseases were healed by that blood.[25]

This cross, along with the holy statue of the Blessed Virgin of Trim, is credited with restoring the sight of Hugh Mac Mahon, in 1397.[26]

Christ Church Cathedral in Dublin had several miraculous relics in its collection, including a speaking crucifix.[27] This cross and the Bachall Íosa[28] were the most important relics in the cathedral's collection.[29] The Bachall Íosa's miraculous powers were first recorded in 789.[30] Gerald of Wales, writing in the 12th century, mentions that the cathedral's cross 'earned everywhere respect and veneration '.[31] Popular devotion to these two relics is also illustrated by their frequent mention in medieval wills.[32] One bequest left to the ' … Cross of Holy Trinity a silk girdle well ornamented and two rings with jewels'.[33] The wealthy often left bequests of gold or jewels and clothing to statues of the saint and it was assumed that these would have been used to embellish statues and relics.[34] An example of this is Englishwoman Margaret Stapleton who, in 1466, left her gold ring to hang around the neck of the image of Christ at Newbridge.[35] During Strongbow's attack on Dublin in the late 12th century, a group of citizens tried to take the cross to safety. However, despite an adequate supply of manpower, it could not be moved.[36] Further miracles were recounted by Roger Hoveden in the 12th century. He describes the cross as being 'engraved ('*incisa*') with a life-size image of Christ '.[37] The fact that the cross is referred to as a 'speaking cross' implies that it had spoken at least once, if not on several occasions.

The Irish annals record another speaking relic – the crozier of Columb Mac Luighdheach, which 'openly conversed with its cleric ' in the year 1178.[38] The religious were not beyond altering their reliquaries or statues to create the illusions of miracles. During the destruction of the Holy Rood at Boxley Abbey in Kent, wires were found in the Christ figure that facilitated the moving of the eyes and lips, thus giving the effect of simulating speech.[39]

Miraculous statues, especially those connected with the Blessed Virgin, were very popular in late medieval Europe and people came from great distances to pray before them. Ireland was no different and miracles are attributed to several statues of the Blessed Virgin. In the year 1381, the *Annals of the Four Masters* state that the 'image of the Blessed Virgin Mary' at Kilmore spoke, an event which surely resulted in pilgrimage. A few decades later, in 1412, at Trim, the 'Image of [the Blessed Virgin] Mary of Ath-Trim wrought many miracles.'[40]

Further miracles performed by the statue of Our Lady of Trim were recorded in 1444, when it restored sight to a blind man, speech to a dumb man and the use of his feet to a cripple. It also stretched out the hand of a person to whose side it had been fastened and bizarrely caused a pregnant woman to deliver cats (*et foeminam gravidatam feles eniti fecit)*.[41]

The birth of cats or other animals is a common motif in miracles tales in late medieval Europe.[42] A short distance away, at the Augustinian Abbey of Navan, another miraculous statue of the Blessed Virgin was also working miracles. The Navan statue was said to have restored to health Dr Stackbolle, a dignitary of the Abbey of Navan, whose eyes had been put out and tongue cut out by order of Thomas Bathe:

> Dr. Stackbolle was carried back to the abbey, and cast before the image of the Blessed Virgin, and 'by her grace, mediation, and miraculous power, he was restored to his sight and speech'.[43]

Miracle collections from outside Ireland also record healing taking place away from the shrine, after which the healed person undertook a pilgrimage of thanksgiving. In 844, the *Annals of Clonmacnoise* reveal that St Ciaran appeared to the King of Munster on his sickbed. The King had angered the saint, who proceeded to push his *bachall* (staff) into the man's stomach, killing him:

> As king felym (soone after his return into Munster) was takeing his rest in his bed, St Queran[Ciaran] appeared to him with his habit and bachall, or pastorall stafe, & there gave him a push of his Bachall in his belly wherof he tooke his disease and ocation of Death.[44]

This tale may have strengthened belief in the miraculous powers of the saint and inspired pilgrimage to Clonmacnoise.

There are numerous accounts of medieval European pilgrims going on pilgrimage on behalf of old or sick friends and family members. Although there are no accounts of this practice surviving from medieval Ireland, there is no reason to believe things were any different there.

Such a pilgrimage is recorded in later times, in the late 17th-century prayer book of James Shee, a native of Derryhinch/Derrynahinch, in South Kilkenny. In 1694, he performed a pilgrimage to Lady's Island in Wexford in the hope of gaining a cure for his sick daughter.[45] His story survives only as a brief entry in his personal prayer book. Shee was in the habit of recording important life events such as his marriage to Mary Trapps (1660–1706) on 25 May 1684, along with the births of his children and deaths of two of his sons.[46] Some time in 1693/94, he wrote:

> My daughter Ellen being very ill, I promised to make a pilgrimage to Our Lady's Island, in honour of Our blessed Lady. This performed.[47]

Having already lost two children, James and his wife must have been very frightened for Ellen. We do not know what sickness the child had but the mortality rate for children was high in 17th-century Ireland. James and his wife are likely to have been able to afford medical care, but as there had been few medical advances since medieval times, medical intervention had limited success. The death of children from what are today preventable and curable illnesses was a harsh reality for parents, both rich and poor. James's daughter Ellen was 6 or 7 years old when she fell ill and was too young and sick to undertake a pilgrimage on her own, so it was logical that her father would go on pilgrimage on her behalf. Lady's Island is located in the south-eastern corner of Wexford in the barony of Forth and Bargy, some 80 kilometres from Derryhinch.[48] It was well known as a place of healing in the 17th century. An account of the island written in the 1680s states that:

> Impotent and infirme pilgrims and a Multitude of persons of all Qualities from all provinces and parts of Ireland, daily frequented, and with fervent devotion visited, who, praying and making some oblacions, or extending charitable Benevolence to Indigents there residing, have there miraculously cured of grievous Maladyes, and helped to the perfect use of naturally defective Limmes, or accidentally enfeebles or impaired Sences.[49]

Having completed his pilgrimage, James would have returned home. Ellen recovered from her illness and lived to adulthood; she is recorded as having married William Mulhall.[50] James and Ellen's story has parallels in both medieval and modern times and shows how a father was prepared to do all that he could to save his child.

Indulgence

From the 12th century, the quest for an indulgence was a popular reason for going on pilgrimage. An indulgence is a partial remission of the punishments due in Purgatory for sins committed on earth. It works on the theory that all the good works of the saints, the martyrs and the suffering of Christ had built up a bank of merits against which penance due in Purgatory could be offset.[51] Indulgences were first given out to encourage participation in the Crusades, but over time the net was widened, and they were given to individuals for performing penance and undertaking acts of merit, such as the building of churches, hospitals, schools, roads and bridges. Indulgences were also given out for performing acts of devotion, such as going on pilgrimage.[52]

Initially, indulgences were attached to high-status churches but from the 14th century, they were awarded by popes and bishops to pilgrim churches, ranging in importance from the very local to those with international appeal.[53] In Church teachings, Purgatory existed in real time, so indulgences were granted in real time and varied in length from days, weeks, months and years.[54] Once an indulgence was granted, it was available for a specified length of time, and could only be gained on certain days in this timespan. The humbler the destination, the smaller the indulgence and, as a rule, the length of the indulgence issued to local and regional shrines was often no more than a few days or weeks. Indulgences proved popular with pilgrims who took the opportunity to gain spiritual benefit without having to make a long, hazardous and expensive journey overseas. On rare occasions, a church offered a plenary indulgence – the complete remission of punishments in the afterlife. Plenary indulgences were largely attached to the most important destinations, such as Rome and Jerusalem. In rarer circumstances, they were issued to national and regional shrines.[55]

The indulgences could be obtained by any pilgrim who visited a church or holy place on the days that the indulgence was available, thus reducing the time that they or a loved one would have to spend in Purgatory, provided that they had made confession and received absolution and donation of alms to the Church.[56] Indulgences were available at many Irish churches during the later medieval period and were usually on offer to raise funds for church repairs. In 1432, Pope Innocent VIII issued an indulgence of two years to pilgrims to Croagh Patrick to raise funds to repair the chapel on the summit.

> Relaxation of two years and two quarantines of enjoined penance to penitents who visit and give alms for the repair or fabric of below-mentioned chapel on the Sunday before the feast of St. Peter's Chains,[57] on which day St. Patrick is specially venerated in the chapel of St. Patrick on the hill which is called Croagh Patrick (capella S.P. in Monte qui Tumulus S.P. nuncupatur sita).[58]

A plenary indulgence was issued by Pope Paul V to all pilgrims to Croagh Patrick in the year 1610, and in 1661 the procurator of the ecclesiastical province of Tuam directed that '…the plenary indulgence anciently granted to the pilgrims to the holy places of Aran and Croagh Patrick should be continued and renewed'.[59]

In 1423, the pope granted an indulgence of 10 years to the shrine of Our Lady of Trim, 'in which by the merits of the Virgin, the Lord works many miracles'.[60] Decades later, in 1453, John Bole, the abbot of St Mary's Abbey in Navan, persuaded Pope Nicholas V to grant a rare plenary indulgence to all pilgrims undertaking pilgrimages to the statue of Our Lady of Navan. The indulgence was available at Pentecost or on the three days that followed. Pilgrims were required to visit the shrine and give alms for the much-needed repair and conservation of the abbey and its buildings.[61] Two year later, the event was recorded in the *Annals of Ulster*. The inclusion of this indulgence in the annals provides evidence that religious pilgrimage often crossed Irish cultural divides and that the indulgence and pilgrimage to Navan appealed to both Gaelic Irish and Anglo-Norman pilgrims. Similarly, the monastery and pilgrim site of Derry was granted an indulgence in 1469 by Pope Paul II,[62] and in 1463, Matthew O'Hoey, the Bishop of Ardagh, confirmed that he had examined papal bulls of Popes Alexander IV, Innocent III, Honorius II, Celestine V, Gregory X, Adrian VI, Boniface VIII, Clement IV and John XXII, which granted an indulgence of a year and 40 days, and relaxation of a seventh of their penance, to those who contributed to the reparation of the fabric of the Church of Holy Trinity [Christ Church] and Holy Cross, Dublin, and were contrite and confessed.[63]

Some Irish pilgrims travelled outside Ireland to gain indulgences. Rome offered a plenary in the jubilee years of 1300, 1350, 1390, 1423, 1450, 1475 and 1500. A jubilee year, also called a holy year, is a special year of remission of sins and universal pardon. The tradition dates back to 1300, when Pope Boniface VIII called Christians to Rome to participate in a holy year. Jubilee years at Rome then began a 25- or 50-year cycle. The *Annals of Ulster*, *Loch Cé* and *Connacht* all record the jubilee year of 1300, noting:

> … a countless multitude from all the countries in Christendom were wont to go on pilgrimage to Rome at this invitation; and they would obtain forgiveness of all sins there through this grace.[64]

Plenary indulgences were also offered to pilgrims who visited the Holy Land and partial indulgence to those who could not make the journey personally.[65] Pilgrims to Santiago de Compostela could obtain a plenary indulgence during years when the feast of St James fell on a Sunday, an event which averaged once every seven years. For example, any pilgrim who set out for Santiago in the years 1445 or 1462 were able to gain this privilege.[66] The *Annals of Connacht* state that in 1445, 'many of the nobles of Ireland went to the shrine of St James', including Gaelic noblewoman Margaret O'Carroll, whose husband held lands in Co. Offaly. The second pilgrimage of James Rice, Mayor of Waterford, coincided with the jubilee year of 1483.[67] Even during an ordinary year, the pilgrim to Santiago could amass a substantial amount of indulgences. In 1456, Englishman William Wey noted that pilgrims who made the trip were given a remission of one-third of their sins. If they died on the road, they were granted a total remission. Any pilgrim taking part in any of the religious processions in the city of Compostela could gain 40 days' indulgence; and if the procession happened to be led by a bishop, it was worth an additional 200 days. If the procession was on 24 July – the eve of the feast of St James – it went up again to 600 days. Hearing Mass offered by an archbishop, dean or cardinal was worth another 200 days.[68]

Indulgences also feature in a number of late Irish saints' Lives. Several Lives refer to known pilgrim sites such as Glendalough and Derry offering indulgences equal to those gained by pilgrims going to Rome. There are no official records confirming these indulgences, so these claims are likely to have been manufactured as a way to boost pilgrim traffic, which may have been in decline following the Reformation.

The 16th-century Irish *Life of St Colmcille* tells that when the saint went on pilgrimage to Rome, the pope issued him with the following gift:

> … that is that, whichever of his own foundations Colum Cille would appoint as a pilgrimage destination for everyone, there should be the same indulgence there as for a pilgrimage to Rome.[69]

The place chosen by the saint was the monastery at Derry. The first Irish *Life of St Kevin* boldly states that one pilgrimage to the relics and bed of St Kevin at Glendalough was all that was required to gain an indulgence equal to a visit to Rome.[70]

The second and third Irish *Lives of Kevin* are less generous, informing potential pilgrims that they would have to go on seven pilgrimages to Glendalough to gain an indulgence equal to Rome.[71] The majority of Irish pilgrim churches offered indulgences that were for short periods of time, ranging from days or weeks to a couple of years. By visiting Rome, pilgrims could accrue much more substantial indulgences, especially during a jubilee year, which offered a plenary indulgence. A journey to Rome was a long and costly undertaking, which excluded many poorer people from undertaking such pilgrimages. The fact that such a substantial indulgence, even an unofficial one, could carry the same value as that of Rome, and could be gained at home in Ireland, was very appealing, and the promotion of such an indulgence would surely have attracted large numbers.

Penance

Pilgrimage was first introduced as a penance for 'offences against the moral and spiritual code' of the Church by Irish clerics in the 6th century.[72] However, it was not until the 11th and 12th centuries that the expiation of sin and guilt became one of the overriding motives for going on pilgrimage.[73] The increase in penitential pilgrimage was no doubt influenced by the developing doctrine and the promotion of concepts of sin and Purgatory in the Church. In 1415, Edmund, Earl of March and Ulster, was required to go on pilgrimage to Rome and Santiago as penance for his sins.[74] Throughout Europe, the Church did not hesitate to impose rigorous pilgrimages for serious sins, even on those of high social standing. A famous example was King Henry II of England, who went on a penitential pilgrimage to Canterbury to atone for his involvement in the murder of St Thomas à Becket.[75] During the mid-13th century, the inquisition of Languedoc had a working list of major and minor shrines in France where they could send repentant heretics. In late medieval Europe, pilgrimage could be imposed not only by a confessor but also by secular courts of law.[76] Flemish courts imposed pilgrimage as an alternative to a prison sentence for certain crimes. The courts of the cities such as Antwerp and Ghent offered those convicted of lesser crimes the choice of paying a fine or going on pilgrimage to a place of the court's choosing. Each Flemish court had its own unique list of shrines of varying status, so the pilgrimage could be chosen to suit the crime. The shrine of St James in Santiago de Compostela appears on 25 court lists, while the shrines of Canterbury, Rocamadour, Tours and Cologne are mentioned on nine court lists.[77] The Irish shrine of St Patrick's Purgatory in Lough Derg was noted on the judicial list for the court of Antwerp as a place to send repentant criminals.[78]

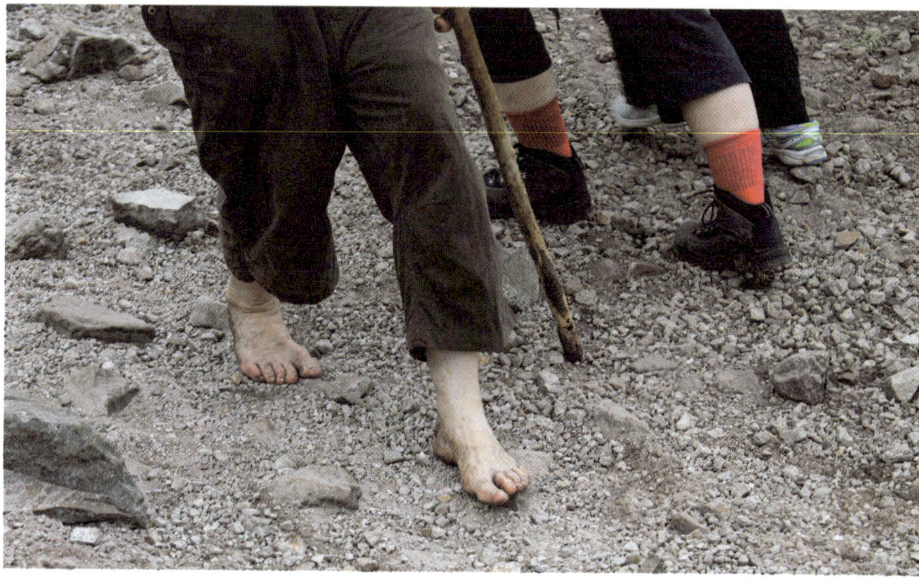

Modern pilgrim walking barefoot at Croagh Patrick. © Louise Nugent

There is no evidence for secular courts in Ireland imposing pilgrimage on criminals, but ecclesiastical courts certainly did so. The court of Armagh imposed pilgrimage as punishment for a wide variety of crimes. The most curious incident relates to an uncompleted pilgrimage imposed on John, chaplain of the deanery of Trim in 1437. John was ' … accused at Athboy of incontinence and confessed his sin'. As a punishment, he was ordered to pay 6s 8d (6 shillings and 8 pence) towards the repair of a window of the Friars Minor at Drogheda and to go on pilgrimage to the relic of the Holy Cross at Christ Church in Dublin and the shrine of St Richard at Dundalk. The court stipulated that he was to complete the pilgrimage in his bare feet. He refused to perform this penance and was promptly excommunicated.[79]

There are several interesting things about this case. Firstly, the pilgrim was required to be barefoot. At the time it was not uncommon for penitential pilgrims to walk barefoot and the practice was carried out across Europe to heighten discomfort and increase the penitential value of the pilgrimage. Secondly, it shows how pilgrimage, even if imposed, was still at its core a voluntary undertaking.

Pilgrimage was also part of the penance of Cathal O'Reilly,[80] Lord of East Breifne, the medieval territory corresponding to modern-day Co. Cavan. In September 1529, he was absolved by the Archbishop of Armagh 'from all censures, excommunications, etc., incurred by his invasion of Julianstown.' As well as taking an oath to 'make restitution to the injured tenants', he was required to undertake penance. This included the paying of two cows towards the support of the

Cathedral of Armagh and making a pilgrimage to St Patrick's Purgatory or to the statue of Our Lady of Trim.[81]

Some years earlier, in August 1460, Archbishop of Armagh John Bole imposed strict penance on Bernard McGincenan, a resident of the Armagh diocese, for forging a letter delivered to the archbishop, in the name of Henry O'Neill. Bernard was excommunicated and declared a maker of false letters. As penance, he was ordered for 12 Sundays and feasts:

> to go bare-headed and barefooted, clad only in a shirt or smock, bearing a wax candle of one pound weight in his hand, and be whipped in the manner of a penitent.[82]

He was also to walk in the solemn procession at Armagh Cathedral when required to do so by the archbishop or his officials and, afterwards, to offer the wax candle before the image of St Patrick. Within two years of this ruling, he was also to go on pilgrimage to Rome.[83]

The ecclesiastical court of Armagh also imposed pilgrimage as a punishment for the most serious of sins, murder. In the 1540s, Heneas Mac Nichaill completed a penitential pilgrimage imposed upon him by Dean Edmund MacCawell as punishment for the crime of strangling his son.[84] Mac Nichaill was to visit 19 pilgrim sites around Ireland. The itinerary was designed to take more than a year to complete and equated in length and physical demands to a pilgrimage to an international shrine such as Rome or the Holy Land.[85] The length of the list and the variety of the pilgrimage destinations suggest that Armagh had a working list of pilgrim places similar to those of the secular Flemish courts.

The *Annals of Ulster* record the pilgrimage of another Irish murderer, Henry Dillon, in 1491:

> Henry, son of Hubert, son of James Dillon, slew his own father, namely, Hubert, with thrust of knife and he himself set out for Rome after that.[86]

Henry's pilgrimage may have also been imposed upon him by a religious court. There are many European accounts of penitential pilgrims – especially those who had committed the sin of murder – wearing chains or even the murder weapon upon their person during their pilgrimage, as visible evidence of their crime.[87] Some early medieval pilgrims who had killed a family member completed pilgrimage wearing metal bands on their arms, some of which were forged from the murder weapon.

The penance was given for a specified period of time and deemed to be completed when the bands had rusted off or when they miraculously burst open through the intervention of the saints.[88] Examples include a nobleman from Lorraine, who arrived at the Cathedral of Norwich in the 1150s wearing chain mail fastened with his own sword. Another murderer arrived in 1164 at Durham Cathedral to repent at the shrine of St Cuthbert, wearing the sword he had used to kill his victim as a girdle.[89] It was common for penitents to wear sackcloth or hair shirts and to perform part or all of their pilgrimage barefoot. One cannot but wonder if Irish pilgrims Mac Nichaill and Dillion wore similar clothing, during their pilgrimages.

Crisis

People often decided to go on pilgrimage in times of crisis or danger. Storms at sea, natural disasters such as flooding, drought, famine and disease could all result in spontaneous pilgrimage. When confronted with imminent danger, some people took a vow of pilgrimage as part of a bargain with God or a patron saint for a favourable outcome.[90] There are many accounts of medieval sailors and merchants caught in severe storms, making vows to undertake pilgrimages if delivered from the power of wind and waves.[91] Medieval miracle tales record saints like Nicholas, James and Thomas à Becket saving sailors threatened with shipwreck by calming a savage storm. SS Nicholas and James were particularly popular with sailors and dedications to them are often found attached to churches in port towns; for example, St James's Church in Dingle, Co. Kerry, or St Nicholas's Collegiate Church in Galway. In 1285, St David was said to have saved a group of Irish men and women caught in a storm in the Irish Sea.[92]

Sailors and other travellers would make vows of pilgrimage when confronted by an imminent danger of a storm. Gerald Donum, a yeoman of Edward II, made such a vow to visit Rocamadour in France when his life was endangered at sea. He also pledged to maintain his beard until he reached the shrine, at which point he would shave and leave the hair as a symbol of his salvation at the hands of the Virgin.[93] In the year 1307, during the canonisation of St Thomas de Cantilupe of Hereford, a group of Irish sailors presented themselves at the shrine of the saint with a very expensive votive offering of a silver ship. The sailors had been travelling from Ireland to Gascony with a ship full of hides and cloth, when they were caught in a storm. Fearing for their lives, the men vowed to make pilgrimage in honour of the saint, if they survived their ordeal.[94]

Another Irish example happened in 1488, when Sir Richard Edgecomb was in Ireland on official royal business. His boat was caught in a storm and he was

Sailors delivered from a storm through the prayers of St Cuthbert.

forced to shelter at Lambay. The sailors on the ship made vows of pilgrimage if delivered from safety:

> aftirnoon that Day the Wind began to come large; but it Blew so much, and the Coasts were so Jeopardous of Sands and Rocks, that that Night the Mariners durst not Jeoparde to take the Sea, but lay still at Anchor about the seyd Isle, and there he and his company vowed gret Pilgrimages that God wuld cease the Tempest, and send a fair and large wind.[95]

Spontaneous pilgrimages often took place in times of plague. In the 4th century, Gregory of Tours tells that the people of Rheims, in an effort to avoid the ravages of the bubonic plague, gathered around the tomb of St Remigius in a night vigil.[96] In Italy, St Sebastian was seen as an intercessor in times of plague and was invoked by the people of Rome during the Justinian plagues of the 7th century.[97] Outbreaks of ergotism in the 12th century resulted in well-documented mass pilgrimages in Britain and France.[98] Ergotism is caused by a fungus growing on rye, the symptoms of which include hallucinations, a severe type of gangrene, a painful burning sensation and blisters. The disease was rife in the medieval period and was called St Anthony's Fire. The relics of St Anthony at the abbey of Saint-Antoine in Dauphiné in south-eastern France, were believed to be particularly beneficial for curing the disease, although the recovery of pilgrims at the shrine was probably due to the change in diet and ingestion of uncontaminated food.[99]

In 1348, the Irish friar John Clyn recorded a pilgrimage to the shrine of St Moling Luachra at Tigh Moling – now known as St Mullin's, in Co. Carlow – in response to the Black Death:

> This year, and chiefly in the months of September and October, great numbers of bishops and prelates, ecclesiastical and religious, peers and others, and in general people of both sexes, flocked together by troops to the pilgrimage and wading of the water at Tigh Moling so that many thousands might be seen there together for many days; some came out of devotion, but the greater part for fear of the pestilence which raged at that time with great violence.[100]

This is a poignant description of desperate pilgrims hoping to save themselves from the Black Death by invoking the protection of St Moling, as the disease went on to ravage the Pale and devastated urban centres such as Dublin and Drogheda.[101]

In Irish folklore, the saints are occasionally shown as the protectors against disease and plague. For example, St Gobnait (Abigail in English) spared the people of Ballyvourney, Co. Cork, by praying at the eastern boundary of the parish and preventing the plague that ravaged the country from entering the parish.[102] A plaque above her holy well in Kilshannig in North Cork states 'St Abigail Expelling The Plague A.D. 1872'. Folk memory of Irish saints healing plague is also recorded at the medieval church of Tomfinlough, Co. Clare, and a so-called plague stone, which has since disappeared, was identified there by Westropp in the 1900s.[103]

Pilgrimage by Proxy

For a variety of reasons, some vows of pilgrimage could not be fulfilled. Most vows of pilgrimage were impulsive and a change in circumstances such as ill health, old age and even a lack of interest could all result in it being unfulfilled. The Church allowed a type of 'out-clause', whereby the vow could be dispensed in exchange for a donation of money, or if someone could be found to undertake the pilgrimage on the person's behalf.[104] The belief that penance could be carried out on behalf of the dead and that an indulgence could also be obtained after death underpinned the idea of pilgrimage by proxy, where one individual could make a pilgrimage on behalf of another person, alive or dead.[105] The proxy pilgrim could be a relative or a stranger paid to complete a pilgrimage. If no willing party could be found, the vow could be offset with generous donation of money.[106] In the 12th century, Blanche of Castile made a vow to go on pilgrimage to Santiago de Compostela but was subsequently dissuaded from undertaking the journey. To discharge her vow, she donated a large sum of money to the church of St Jacques in Paris.[107] In 1320, the Archbishop of Dublin absolved Edmund Butler, along with his wife and son James, of a vow to go on pilgrimage to the Holy Land because of the rising conflict between the Gaelic and the Anglo-Irish.[108] The vow was absolved on condition that the costs of the journey were paid to the Holy Land Subsidy. Another Irish example was Elizabeth de Burgh, wife of John de Burgh, Earl of Ulster. In 1343, Elizabeth, who was 40 years of age, found she could not fulfil an earlier rather ambitious vow to undertake pilgrimage to both Santiago de Compostela and the Holy Land. We do not know why she felt she could not fulfil the vow but perhaps she had become too frail to travel. Her petition to the pope was granted, on the condition she should undertake alternative works of piety.[109]

> Elizabeth de Burgo lady de Clara, kinswoman of the queen. That she may choose a confessor, who shall transmute the vow she made in her husband's lifetime to visit the Holy Land and Santiago di Compostela, which, being forty, she cannot hope to fulfil, to some other works of piety, and to absolve her.[110]

In 1343, Matilda de Lancastria, Countess of Ulster, petitioned for absolution from her vow of pilgrimage to Santiago de Compostela.[111] This was:

> Granted, on condition of her sending thither her oblation, and within a year founding in England a chapel, value 8 marks, in honour of St James, or making a subsidy for the Christians against the Turks, to the amount of the expenses of her journey, or giving 200 florins to the papal nuncio in England for the expedition against the Turks. Villeneuve by Avignon, 2 Kal. Sept.[112]

Galway woman Margaret Athy, wife of Stephen Lynch Fitz-Dominick, Mayor of Galway City (1508–1509), made a pilgrimage Santiago around 1508. She had also intended 'to visit the Holy Land but was prevented from doing so by illness.'[113] We do not know if her vow was discharged through financial means or if she had persuaded a family member go on her behalf. There are many surviving examples from English and French wills of requests of pilgrimage by proxy to be carried out by a family member, on behalf of the deceased. By the 14th century, such requests were commonplace in English wills.[114] For example, in 1529, Scotsman George Preston proposed to undertake a pilgrimage on behalf of the late Sir Simeon Preston.[115] At one point in the later medieval period, it was fashionable for those who performed pilgrimage by proxy to carry the heart of the deceased with them on the pilgrimage.

Following objections by various popes, the practice of pilgrimage by proxy finally ceased and individuals returned to making their own pilgrimages.[116] There are no surviving Irish accounts of this practice from medieval times but, given its popularity, it surely took place in Ireland too.

Adventure

Before his pilgrimage to Rome in 926 Celedabhaill, the abbot of Bangor, was moved to compose a poem. His poem describes his attitude to pilgrimage and how for him it was a chance to escape the world and its earthly temptations, allowing him time to consider how he might become closer to Christ through inner contemplation.[117]

Not everyone thought of pilgrimage in this way and some saw it as a chance to temporarily escape the banality of everyday life. The medieval world offered the majority of people few opportunities to travel outside their local community and pilgrimage proved to be a means of escape from the daily routine, while at the same time enhancing the social status of the participant through religious merit. This was especially true for long-distance pilgrimage. For some, pilgrimage was a means to satisfy their curiosity and to see the wider world. Despite the Church trying to discourage such motivations, there are numerous texts spanning a period from the 4th to the 15th centuries attesting to this phenomenon. [118] That this was also a concern for the Irish Church can be seen in a 9th-century Irish poem:

> Who to Rome goes,
> Much labour, little profit knows
> For God, on earth though long you've sought him
> You'll miss at Rome unless you've brought him.[119]

Curiosity as a factor for pilgrimage appears to have been more common in the later medieval period, when travelling became easier and cheaper.[120] Of course, not every pilgrimage was motivated purely by adventure and it was possible to have both strong faith and a desire to explore the world and escape everyday life. The two need not have been mutually exclusive.

From an early date, pragmatic men combined pilgrimage with political and commercial business.[121] Offers of indulgences or news of a recent miracle must have been of interest to the devout and to those concerned for their mortal souls; and these possibly inspired spontaneous pilgrimages among merchants and other travellers. Irish clergy who regularly travelled to Rome, or those travelling to the royal court in London, passed many pilgrimage churches, relics and holy places and some may have stopped, thus delaying the core journey by a few extra hours or days. An Irish example of this can be seen in 1425, with an Irish friar, Nicholas, who was carrying correspondence between the Carmelite prior provincial in England and his Irish counterpart. He took the opportunity to go on pilgrimage to Canterbury.[122] Almost a century later, in 1511, Hugh Dubh O'Donnell, Lord of Tyrconnel – a territory equivalent to modern-day Donegal – spent four months in the court of Henry VIII on his return from a pilgrimage to Rome and was subsequently knighted at a banquet in Westminster. He was far from the only Irish Lord to combine political business with pilgrimage.[123] In early 1396, Tadhg Carroll embarked on a pilgrimage to Rome and on his way home stopped at the Court of Richard II of England.[124] Pilgrimage could also be used as a way of avoiding or delaying official business. When Sir Richard Edgecomb arrived at Lambay in 1488 with letters of pardon for the Earl of Kildare, for his part in the crowning of Simnel Lambert, he found that earl was missing. He was told he had gone on a pilgrimage and would not return for four or five days.[125]

Pilgrimage could also be used as a cover for espionage or for concealing politically motivated journeys. In 1593, Sir Richard Bingham wrote to Lord Burghley of 'Scots about to pass by boat into Mayo to offer at Knockpatrick'.[126] The Scots were Redshanks mercenary soldiers hired by Irish lords. It is possible that they used the excuse of pilgrimage to conceal their true intentions for being in Ireland.

Tradition

Tradition also played a part in Irish pilgrimages. Many modern pilgrims who visit a holy well on the saint's feast day will tell how they come each year because they have always done so, as had their parents and grandparents before them. For many, a pilgrimage has as much to do with tradition and connecting to past generations as it does to devotion to the saint. This must surely also have been the case for medieval pilgrims, especially to local pilgrim places like holy wells and relics of patron saints. Equally for the upper classes in late medieval Ireland, some pilgrimages may have been undertaken to uphold familial and social honour and seen as a duty to be undertaken for or with others. This view can be demonstrated in medieval Scotland.[127] Evidence of multigenerational pilgrimage can also be seen in medieval Wales, Germany and Sweden.[128]

NOTES

1 Peter Harbison, *Pilgrimage in Ireland. The Monuments and the People* (London: Syracuse University Press, 1991), 23.
2 Sarah Hopper, *To Be a Pilgrim: The Medieval Pilgrimage Experience* (Stroud: Sutton Publishing Ltd., 2002), 5.
3 Sumption, *Pilgrimage*, 89.
4 Sumption, *Pilgrimage*, 89.
5 Joseph Lynch and Philip Adamo, *The Medieval Church: A Brief History by Joseph Lynch*, 2nd ed. (London: Routledge Press, 2014), 48-49.
6 Ditchburn, 'Saints at the Door Don't Make Miracles', 74.
7 Harbison, *Pilgrimage in Ireland*, 24.
8 Richard Barber, *Pilgrimages* (Woodbridge: Boydell Press, 1991), 58.
9 John Davies, *Pilgrimage Yesterday and Today. Why? Where? How?* (London: SCM Press Ltd., 1988), 6.
10 Sumption, *Pilgrimage*, 73–77; Barber, *Pilgrimages*, 63.
11 Sumption, *Pilgrimage*, 80.
12 The word leprosy was often used to describe a variety of skin diseases in medieval sources. See Ciara Crawford, 'Disease and Illness in Medieval Ireland' (PhD thesis, NUI Maynooth, 2011), 64–65.
13 Sumption, *Pilgrimage*, 81; Crawford, 'Disease and Illness,' 64–65.
14 Dutton, *Aelred of Rievaulx*, 162–65; Luard, ed., *Lives of Edward the Confessor*, 232–35; Donnchadh Ó Corráin, *The Irish Church, Its Reform and the English Invasion* (Dublin: Four Courts Press, 2017), 33.
15 Gillian Kenny, *Anglo-Irish and Gaelic Women in Ireland c. 1170–1540* (Dublin: Four Courts Press, 2007), 100.
16 Brian Spencer, *Pilgrim Souvenirs and Secular Badges: Medieval Finds from Excavations in London* (London: HMSO, 1998), 39.
17 Spencer, *Pilgrim Souvenirs*, 38–39.
18 Spencer, *Pilgrim Souvenirs*, 39; Hopper, *To Be a Pilgrim*, 129.
19 Maura Walsh and Dáibhí Ó Cróinín, trans., *Cummian, Letter de Controversia Paschali* (Toronto: Pontifical Institute of Medieval Studies, 1988), 93-94.
20 Rev. Sylvestor Malone, trans., *Life of St. Flannan.*(Dublin: James Duffy & Co, 1902), 51.
21 AFM; AU.
22 AFM,
23 Godefridus J. C. Snoek, *Medieval Piety from Relics to the Eucharist: A Process of Mutual Interaction* (New York: Brill, 1995), 312–19; Caroline Walker *Bynum, Wonderful Blood: Theology and Practice in Late Medieval Northern Germany and Beyond* (Philadelphia: University of Pennsylvania Press, 2007); Nicholas Vincent, *The Holy Blood: King Henry III and the Westminster Blood Relic* (Cambridge: Cambridge University Press, 2001).
24 AFM; AU; AC.
25 AFM.
26 AFM.
27 James Lydon, 'The Text and Its Context, ' in *The Account Roll of the Priory of the Holy Trinity, Dublin, 1337–1346*, ed. James Mills (Dublin: Four Courts Press, 1996), xvi; James F. Lydon, 'Christ Church in the Later Medieval Irish World, 1300–1500,' in *Christ Church Cathedral Dublin: A History*, ed. Kenneth Milne (Dublin: Four Courts Press, 2000), 93.
28 Sarah Christine Erskine, 'St. Patrick's Bachall Ísu: Its Origins, Traditions, and Rise to Prominence as Armagh's Premier Relic, ' *JASIMS* 6 (2013): 41–67.
29 Raymond Refaussé, 'Introduction,' in *Christ Church Cathedral Dublin: A History*, ed. Kenneth Milne (Dublin: Four Courts Press, 2000), 15.
30 AU; Cormac Bourke, *Patrick: The Archaeology of a Saint* (Belfast: HMSO, 1993), 18.
31 Stuart Kinsella, 'From Hiberno-Norse to Anglo-Norman, c.1030–1300,' in *Christ Church Cathedral Dublin: A History*, ed. Kenneth Milne (Dublin: Four Courts Press, 2000), 46.
32 Lydon, 'Christ Church in the Later Medieval Irish World, 1300–1500,' 93.
33 M. J. McEnery and Raymond Refaussé, eds., *Christ Church Deeds* (Dublin: Four Courts Press, 2001), 132–33 no. 513.
34 Rosemay Horrox, *The Black Death* (Manchester: Manchester University Press, 1994), 219.
35 Horrox, *The Black Death*, 219.
36 Roger Stalley, 'The Architecture of the Cathedral and Priory Buildings,1250–1530,' in *Christ Church Cathedral Dublin: A History*, ed.

Kenneth Milne (Dublin: Four Courts Press, 2000), 107.

37 Stalley, 'The Architecture of the Cathedral and Priory Buildings,' 107–8; Gerald of Wales tells of an archer who had attacked the house of the archbishop and offered a penny to the miraculous cross. As the archer turned his back to leave, the penny miraculously hit him in the back.

38 AFM.

39 Ronald C. Finucane, *Miracles and Pilgrims: Popular Beliefs in Medieval England* (London: J. M. Dent and Sons, 1977), 208; Leanne Groeneveld, 'A Theatrical Miracle: The Boxley Rood of Grace as Puppet,' *Early Theatre* 10.2 (2007): 11–50; Eamon Duffy, *The Stripping of the Altars: Traditional Religion in England, c.1400–c.1580* (London: Yale University Press, 2005), 403.

40 AU.

41 AFM; *Annals of Ireland.*

42 Dianne Hall, *Women and the Church in Medieval Ireland, C.1140–1540* (Dublin: Four Courts Press, 2003), 29, fn. 58; Potterton, *Medieval Trim*, 307, fn. 17.

43 Rev. Anthony Cogan, *Ecclesiastical History of the Diocese of Meath: Ancient and* Modern (Dublin: John Fowler, Joseph Dollard, 1862), 225-26; James Hardiman, ed., *A Statute of the Fortieth Year of King Edward III: Enacted in a Parliament Held in Kilkenny, A. D. 1367, Before Lionel Duke of Clarence*, vol. 2 (Dublin: Irish Archaeological Society, 1843), 25.

44 AC 844.

45 Raymond Gillespie, *Devoted People: Belief and Religion in Early Modern Ireland* (Manchester University Press, 1997), 91; Louise Nugent, 'A 17th Century Kilkenny Pilgrim,' *Old Kilkenny Review* 67 (2015): 48–54.

46 John F. Ainsworth and Edward MacLysaght, 'Survey of Documents in Private Keeping, Second Series, ' *Analecta Hibernica* no. 20 (1958): 250-51.

47 Ainsworth and MacLysaght, 'Survey of Documents,' 250.

48 Nugent, 'A 17th-Century Kilkenny Pilgrim,' 50.

49 Herbert F. Hore, 'Particulars Relative to Wexford and the Barony of Forth: By Colonel Solomon Richards, 1682,' *JKSEIAS* IV no.1 (1862): 61. In the early 1607, Pope Paul V issued a plenary indulgence to all who visited here on the Feast of the Nativity of Our Lady (8 September) and on that of the Assumption (15 August).

50 Nugent, 'A 17th-Century Kilkenny Pilgrim,' 53.

51 R.N. Swanson, *Religion and Devotion in Europe, c. 1215–c. 1515* (Cambridge: Cambridge University Press, 1995), 217.

52 Swanson, *Religion and Devotion*, 222-24.

53 Diana Webb, *Pilgrims and Pilgrimage in the Medieval West* (London: I.B Tauris, 1999), 199.

54 Diana Webb, *Pilgrimage in Medieval England.* (London: Hambledon, 2000), xv; Swanson, *Religion and Devotion in Europe*, 220–21.

55 Webb, *Pilgrimage in Medieval England*, xv.

56 Webb, xv; Sumption, *Pilgrimage*, 144-45.

57 1 August (Lammas Day).

58 CPL Vol. VIII, year 1432; Máire MacNeill, *The Festival of Lughnasa* (Dublin: Folklore of Ireland Council, 2007), 76-77.

59 MacNeill, *The Festival of Lughnasa*, 78–79.

60 'A relaxation, during ten years, of enjoined penance to penitents who visited and gave alms for the repair of the church of the Augustinian monastery of St Mary, Trym, in which by the merits of the Virgin the Lord works many miracles'. CPL (1417–31), 254–5.

61 Anthony Lynch, 'The Administration of John Bole, Archbishop of Armagh, 1457–71,' *Seanchas Ardmhacha* 14 no. 2 (1991): 42–43; Cogan, *Ecclesiastical History of the Diocese of Meath*, vol.1, 224.

62 Michael A. Costello, *De Annatis Hiberniae: A Calendar of the First Fruits' Fees Levied on Papal Appointments to Benefices in Ireland. A.D. 1400 to 1535* (Maynooth: Saint Patrick's College for the Catholic Record Society of Ireland, 1912), 222.

63 Hugh J. Lawlor, 'A Calendar of the Liber Niger and Liber Albus of Christ Church, Dublin, ' *PRIA* 27 (1908): 22–23, no. 43.

64 AFM; see also 1296 AU.

65 Ditchburn, "Saints at the Door Don't Make Miracles', 75.

66 Ditchburn, "Saints at the Door Don't Make Miracles', 75; Indulgences were issued in 1451, 1456, 1462, 1473, 1479, 1484, 1490, 1501, 1518, 1529, 1535, 1540, 1546 and 1557.

67 Stat. Ire. Ric. III–Henry VIII, 39; Eamonn McEneaney, 'Politics and the Art of Devotion in Late Fifteenth-Century Waterford, ' in *Arts and Devotion In Late Medieval Ireland*, ed. Rachel Moss, Colmán Ó Clabaigh, and Salvador Ryan (Dublin: Four Courts, 2006), 37.

68 Francis Davey, ed., *The Itineraries of William Wey* (Oxford: Bodleian Library, 2010), 216–17.

69 Manus O'Donnell, *The Life of Colum Cille*, ed. Brian Lacey (Dublin: Four Courts Press, 1998), 114.

70 BNÉ Vol. II, 121.

71 BNÉ Vol. II, 139,155–156.

72 Ludwig Bieler, *The Irish Penitentials* (Dublin: Dublin Institute for Advanced Studies, 1963); Sumption, *Pilgrimage*, 98–99.

73 Sumption, *Pilgrimage*, 102–3.

74 CPL, Vol 6, 455—65

75 Diana J. Hall, *English Medieval Pilgrimage* (London: Routledge & Kegan Paul, 1965), 151; Hopper, *To Be a Pilgrim*, 126.

76 Sumption, *Pilgrimage*, 104–9.

77 Webb, *Pilgrims and Pilgrimage in the Medieval West*, 226.

78 Webb, *Pilgrims and Pilgrimage in the Medieval West*, 225–26.

79 Aubrey Gwynn, *The Medieval Province of Armagh, 1470–1545* (W. Tempest, Dundalgan Press, 1946), 270–71.

80 His name in Latin is Karulus O Rayly.

81 Laurence P. Murray, 'Archbishop Cromer's Register (Continued),' *JLAS* 9 no.1 (1937): 38 no. 99; Potterton, *Medieval Trim*, 308.

82 Anthony Lynch, 'A Calendar of the Reassembled Register of John Bole, Archbishop of Armagh, 1457–71,' *Seanchas Ardmhacha* 15, no. 1 (1992): 152.

83 Lynch, 'A Calendar,' 152.

84 Gwynn, in *The Medieval Province of Armagh 1470–1545,* 268–9, lists the date of completion as 1543, while the Register of Primate George Dowdall gives the date as April 1541. See Laurence, Murray, 'A Calendar of the Register of Primate George Dowdall, Commonly Called the "Liber Niger" or "Black Book" (Continued),' *JCLAS*, vol. 6, no. 3, 1927, 152.

85 Gwynn, *The Medieval Province,* 268–69.

86 AU.

87 Sumption, *Pilgrimage*, 109–10.

88 Michael Lapidge, *The Cult of St Swithun* (Oxford: Oxford University Press, 2003), 306, fn. 221.

89 Lapidge, 306, fn. 221.

90 Wendy Childs, 'The Perils, or Otherwise, of Maritime Pilgrimage to Santiago de Compostela in the Fifteenth Century,' in *Pilgrimage Explored*, ed. Jennie Stopford (York: York Medieval Press, 1999), 126.

91 Childs, 'The Perils, or Otherwise, 126.

92 Kathryn Hurlock, *Medieval Welsh Pilgrimage, c.1100-1500* (London: Palgrave Macmillan, 2018), 65.

93 Hopper, *To Be a Pilgrim*, 95.

94 O'Neill, *Merchants and Mariners*, 46.

95 Richard Edgecomb, *The Voyage of Sir Richard Edgecomb into Ireland, in the Year 1488.* (Dublin: privately published, 1747–1750), 70.

96 Snoek, *Medieval Piety from Relics to the Eucharist*, 254.

97 Duane Osheim, 'Plague Saints,' in *Encyclopaedia of Medieval Pilgrimage*, ed. Larissa J. Taylor, John Friedman, and Rita Tekippe (Leiden: Brill, 2010), 573.

98 Sumption, *Pilgrimage*, 75; M Peraica et al., 'Toxic Effects of Mycotoxins in Humans', *Bulletin of the World Health Organization* 77 (1999): 754.

99 Martin Weidenbörner, *Encyclopedia of Food Mycotoxins* (New York: Springer, 2001), 89–90.

100 Bernadette Williams, *The Annals of Friar John Clyn* (Dublin: Four Courts Press, 2007), 246.

101 Horrox, *The Black Death*, 82.

102 D.M.A. Ó hÉaluighthe, 'Saint Gobnet of Ballyvourney,' *JCHAS* 57 (1952): 59.

103 Folklore also survives relating to the ability of St Luchtighern of Tomfinlough, Co. Clare, to heal plague sores. See Thomas Johnson Westropp, *Folklore of Clare. A Folklore Survey of County Clare and County Clare Folk-Tales and Myths* (Ennis: CLASP Press, 2003), 92–93; John O'Donovan and Eugene Curry, *The Antiquities of County Clare* (Ennis: CLASP Press, 2003), 200–203 .

104 Margaret Wade Labarge, *Medieval Travellers: The Rich and the Restless* (London: Hamish, 1982), 70–71.

105 Sumption, *Pilgrimage*, 295–96.

106 Sumption, *Pilgrimage*, 299; Wade Labarge, *Medieval Travellers*, 70.

107 Wade Labarge, *Medieval Travellers*, 70–71.
108 Cunningham, *Medieval Irish Pilgrims*, 30.
109 Cunningham, *Medieval Irish Pilgrims*, 30–31.
110 CPL (1342-1419), 18-39.
111 Cunningham, *Medieval Irish Pilgrims*, 167.
112 CPL (1342-1419), 54-75.
113 Jim Higgins, *St. James' Church & Cemetery, Gleninagh Heights, Galway* (Galway: Rock Crow's Press, 1996), 78.
114 Wade Labarge, *Medieval Travellers*, 70; Sumption, *Pilgrimage*, 297-98; Webb, *Pilgrimage in Medieval England*, 196-201.
115 Ditchburn, "Saints at the Door Don't Make Miracles', 78.
116 Ditchburn, "Saints at the Door Don't Make Miracles', 78.
117 AFM 923.
118 In Christian 'dogma and culture, curiosity, that is curiosity about the world, is a sin related to the original sin and the transgression, hence identified with humanity's Fall'. See Billie Melman, 'The Middle East/Arabia: 'The Cradle of Islam', in *The Cambridge Companion to Travel Writing. Cambridge Companions to Literature.*, ed. Peter Hulme and Tim Youngs (Cambridge: Cambridge University Press, 2002), 108.
119 David Dumville, *A Palaeographer's Review: The Insular System of Scripts in the Early Middle Ages*, vol. 2. Suita, Institute of Oriental and Occidental Studies (Osaka: Kansai University, 1999), vol. II, 194.
120 Spencer, *Pilgrim Souvenirs*, 1.
121 Ditchburn, "Saints at the Door Don't Make Miracles', 79.
122 Ó Clabaigh, *The Friars*, 198.
123 Sean J. Connolly, *Contested Island: Ireland 1460–1630* (Oxford: Oxford University Press, 2007), 293.
124 Emmett O' Byrne, " A Divided Loyalty': The MacMurroughs, the Irish of Leinster and the Crown of England 1340–1420, ' ed. Thomas McGrath and William Nolan, *Carlow: History & Society. Interdisciplinary Essays of the History of an Irish County* (Dublin: Geography Press, 2008), 293.
125 Edgecomb, *The Voyage of Sir Richard Edgecomb*, 63.
126 CSPI , 128.
127 Ditchburn, 'Saints at the Door Don't Make Miracles', 77.
128 Diana Webb, *Medieval European Pilgrimage, c.700–c.1500* (Basingstoke: Palgrave, 2002), 79; Hurlock, *Medieval Welsh Pilgrimage*, 114–24.

CHAPTER 4

Pilgrim Preparations – Getting Ready for the Journey

Having decided to undertake a pilgrimage, it was essential for the pilgrim to make practical and spiritual preparations for the journey ahead. The level of preparation varied according to the distance of the pilgrimage. A journey to a local shrine or holy well required little in the way of preparation, as it would take only a few hours or days, at most. Pilgrims to local shrines may not even have had to leave their own parish, and their absence would have had little impact on family life. However, it was a very different scenario for pilgrims embarking on a long-distance pilgrimage either in or outside Ireland. Such journeys could take weeks, months and, in some cases, years to complete. A case in point is Fermanagh Lord Thomas Óg Maguire, who left on his pilgrimage to Rome a month after Lammas day (the first day of August) in 1450 and did not return until the beginning of the following year.[1] Aodh O'Donnell, Lord of Tyrconnel and north Connaught, set out on his pilgrimage to Rome in 1510, returning a year and a half later, in 1512.[2] The long duration of many foreign pilgrimages necessitated practical preparations.

Long-distance Pilgrims

Long-distance pilgrimage not only impacted the individual pilgrim, but also the personal and financial lives of his or her family. Travel to a distant shrine was a big commitment and success was dependent on factors outside the control of the pilgrim, such as shipwreck, attack by robbers, political unrest and sickness. As many pilgrims died on their journey to or from the shrine, it was essential for them to put their affairs in order before setting forth.

For the pilgrimage to be successful, it was essential for the pilgrim to be in the right spiritual frame of mind. Spiritual preparation was essential for any pilgrim planning to obtain a much-coveted indulgence or to seek absolution for sin. The Italian priest, Canon Pietro Casola, in his book *Pilgrimage to Jerusalem in the Year 1494*, wrote that, before departing on pilgrimage to the Holy Land, the pilgrim should:

> ...prepare himself to pardon the injuries done to him; to restore everything belonging to others; and live according to the law, because without this first and necessary disposition every hope and fatigue is in vain.[3]

Arguments with neighbours and friends were settled and debts repaid. Families had frank discussions about finances – who would take over business or property in the interim and what would happen if the pilgrim did not return. Property owners would make a will. The English pilgrim Margery Kempe (c.1373–1438), asked the priest to announce from the pulpit that anyone she owed money to should make themselves known, so that she could make amends before departing on pilgrimage to the Holy Land.[4]

Irishman Sir John Bellew, of Bellewstown, Co. Meath, settled his estate on his wife before he set off for the Holy Land.[5] An inquisition held when Thomas de Chaddesworth was Dean of St Patrick's Cathedral in Dublin (1284–1310) confirmed that Dublin man Adam de Ley bequeathed his house to the chapter of the cathedral. His will stipulated that his wife had the right to continue to live in the house, paying rent of half a pound of wax yearly. The document was made before Adam made a pilgrimage to Santiago.[6] David Lombard of Blarney Castle, Co. Cork, also made a will in 1479, on the eve of his departure on pilgrimage to Santiago, for the jubilee year.[7] In the later medieval period, the property of pilgrims was meant to be protected in their absence. In the year 1453, to help put pilgrims' minds at ease, Pope Nicholas V issued a papal sanction against those 'interfering with the pilgrims' on pilgrimage and, more importantly, 'against those who attacked their lands and property while they were absent on pilgrimage'.[8] This did not stop unscrupulous individuals from taking advantage, by trying to steal property and monies or lay claim to their land. Immediate family were not above such unscrupulous acts; for example, the wife of one Scottish pilgrim from Edinburgh broke into a locked box having duplicated her husband's keys while he was on pilgrimage to Whithorn.[9]

Permission to go on Pilgrimage

A married person could not go on pilgrimage without permission from his or her spouse. Margery Kempe was obliged to ask permission from her husband before undertaking her pilgrimage to Jerusalem.[10] If a man went on pilgrimage without his wife's consent, she could sue for his return in a church court.[11] Gaelic lord and pilgrim Thomas Óg Maguire, on the return leg journey of one of his pilgrimages to Santiago, was

> placed in grievous danger of death and vowed to Almighty God that in the event that he should be delivered from this danger he would no longer be of the world but would remain in some hospital as a poor man living on alms.[12]

His wife Juliana Campbell and his children were greatly opposed to this decision. In May 1439, having failed to secure his wife's support, Thomas petitioned for dispensation from his oath. The request was granted by the rector of Aghalurcher, Co. Fermanagh.[13] As with spouses, priests, monks and nuns would have had to ask permission from their bishop, abbot or abbess.[14]

In addition, people in roles of responsibility were expected to ask for permission from those they owed commitments to, such as their king, lord or chieftain, before heading away on pilgrimage. In later centuries, as well as permission from a spouse, pilgrims – especially those holding office – needed permission from the crown. During the late medieval period, a licence from government was required by wealthy pilgrims, in order to travel abroad, though bishops could also issue licences to lay pilgrims and members of the religious. Licences and letters of protection acted as a primitive type of passport. The contents of a license issued by Henry III to English pilgrim Roger la Zouch reads as follows:

> Henry to all who may inspect the present letters, greetings. Know that we have given licence to our beloved and faithful Roger la Zouch for going as a pilgrim to Saint James. Oxford, 1220.[15]

We are aware of the pilgrimages of several Irish men holding civic office or positions in the Church because of their requests for permission to travel. In the year 1405, Richard Peter, the rector of Trim, received permission from the king to travel to Rome on pilgrimage.[16] Prior to his departure on pilgrimage to Santiago de Compostela in 1483, Mayor Rice of the city of Waterford petitioned parliament for permission to leave his post. The *Statue Rolls* of the Irish Parliament record Rice's request to take up the 'pilgrim staff' and the subsequent granting of permission to embark on his pilgrimage. Permission was granted under the proviso that the mayor appointed replacements for himself and two bailiffs who travelled with him, for the duration of their absence.[17]

Mayor James Lynch FitzStephen of Galway City, who held office from 1493–94, was also obliged to ask permission from the city council before embarking on his pilgrimage to Santiago.[18] In 1472–73, John Fowling, Mayor of Drogheda, petitioned and was granted permission by parliament to go on pilgrimage to Santiago and the shrine of St Trynyan.[19] St Trynyan may be St Mothrianog, also known as Triananus or Trenanus of Ruscach, whose shrine was in the Cooley area of Co. Louth.[20]

In the year 1481–82, petition for a licence of pilgrimage was requested by William, Bishop of Meath and Chancellor of Ireland, to go on pilgrimage to several holy places in England. He stated he was ' … of late in his great infirmity' and had 'vowed certain pilgrimage'. It seems that William, aware of his impending death, hoped to perform pilgrimage, perhaps as penance to atone for past sins or to obtain indulgences in a bid to lessen the time he would spend in Purgatory. He requested to visit the shrines of St William of York, Our Lady of Lancaster, Walsingham and various other places in England. Permission was granted but the journey had to be completed in a year

> … and granted to the said bishop by authority of the said parliament that it shall be lawful for himself to absent himself out of this land of Ireland from the day of his departure next ensuing and fully completed and that during the said year[21]

The abbot of St Thomas the Martyr in Dublin also petitioned parliament to go on pilgrimage to the shrine of St Thomas à Becket at Canterbury, in 1485.[22]

Several Irish friars and monks also applied for permission to go on pilgrimage. In 1431, Friar William Macgoreolitaidh and his companion were granted permission by the Augustinian prior general to visit 'devout places in Ireland and abroad'.[23] Decades later, the Irish Augustinian lay brother Friar Donatus (1479) was given permission to go to Rome but was ordered, under pain of excommunication, to return immediately to Ireland. John Bole, Archbishop of Armagh (1457–71), granted licence to travel in 1470 to Brother Patrick O'Segill (or O'Fegill), priest and canon of the Augustinian monastery of SS Peter and Paul, Armagh, to make pilgrimage, and to be absent from the monastery for seven years.[24] In 1491, Friar Thomas Lawless, a Dominican from Waterford, was granted permission to visit Rome by the master general Friar Joachim Turriani. Another Dominican friar, David of Athenry, was granted leave to visit the shrine of James in Compostela by the master general Friar Garcia of Loaisa, 1520.[25]

Funding the Pilgrimage

Long-distance pilgrimage was expensive and Irish pilgrims faced the added cost of making a sea voyage if they wished to travel anywhere outside Ireland. It was necessary to put in place finances to fund the pilgrimage. Costs included passage by ship, expenses such as food, clothing and accommodation, and a donation or offering to the pilgrim shrine. The cost of the return journey also needed to be factored in. In mid-15th-century Scotland, it was estimated that a pilgrimage to Rome cost about £200 Scots, the equivalent of a year's income for a prosperous knight.[26] The Holy Land was the most expensive of all pilgrimages. For Irish pilgrims, the journey involved a sea voyage to Wales or England, a land journey to Dover, a second voyage to the Continent, a lengthy land journey to an Italian port and another sea voyage to north Africa, followed by a further overland journey to Jerusalem. In the 15th century, pilgrims to the Holy Land could expect passage on a ship from Venice to Jaffa to cost as much as 30 Venetian ducats – a fare that, by the 16th century, had increased to 40 Venetian ducats. A ducat was a gold coin worth something in the region of an English crown, 4s 8d. [27]

A sea voyage to Santiago was much more reasonable. When Irish ships were not available, Irish pilgrims travelled to England or Wales and sailed from there. In the reign of Richard I (1157–1199), the journey from England to Santiago de Compostela, including food, cost 13s 4d. By 1470 the sea journey there from England cost £1 2s 6d.[28] The average wage of an English labourer between the years 1412 to 1532 was 4d a day, so they needed to work for 60 days to earn £1.[29] Passage from Ireland to Galicia in 1470s was slightly cheaper, at 7s 6d, which amounted to several weeks' wages for a working man.[30] These prices indicate that the pilgrimage was within the price range of the middle classes.

The costs of a pilgrimage were covered by personal funds and many people probably saved up over several years. Proxy pilgrims could expect funds to be provided through the bequest of the deceased relative for whom they were to carry out a pilgrimage. In England, many pilgrims received funds from guilds and fraternities. It is possible that Irish guilds may also have helped their members in a similar way.[31]

The Irish sources suggest that money for pilgrimage was also donated in the form of alms. On 24 May 1413, a letter was sent by Archbishop Fleming of Armagh to clergy and parishioners in his diocese, requesting that financial aid be given to Christian Oferagaid, known in Irish as Giolla-Chríost Ó Feradhaigh, who was about to make pilgrimage to the Holy Land. To sweeten the deal, the potential donors were offered

> an indulgence of forty days to all who assist him with their goods, both the archbishop's 'parochianai' and others whose diocesans ratify the indulgence.[32]

On 28 March 1470, the Prior of St Patrick's Purgatory, in the Diocese of Clogher, offered an indulgence to 'all who provide resources' for Thomas O'Callachan, for his forthcoming pilgrimage to Rome and 'other holy places'. O'Callachan, a priest of the Diocese of Armagh, who had recently 'visited St Patrick's Purgatory, fasted, prayed and entered the cave of the Purgatory and remained within for a natural day'.[33] Finally, in the year 1490, the Archbishop of Armagh wrote to his clergy to encourage them to persuade their parishioners to give alms to a man called James Hall, of the Diocese of Meath, who intended to make pilgrimage to the Holy Land and the Sepulchre of Christ.[34]

During the pilgrimage journey, if money ran low, pilgrims had little option but to turn to begging. Some pilgrims did finance their pilgrimage by begging but this was not always a reliable way of getting money and there are many stories of pilgrims ending up destitute and stranded, unable to complete their pilgrimage or to get back home, due to lack of funds.

Spiritual Preparation

Spiritual preparation was as important as financial preparation. For any pilgrimage to be successful, the participant was expected to make a sincere and full confession and to seek the blessing of the local priest, bishop or abbot before setting forth.[35] Several European texts dating to the 8th century preserve blessings that were to be uttered over the pilgrim before departure. Over time, the blessing became more elaborate and developed into a special ceremony.[36] By the 11th century, 'the blessing ceremony' centred on the benediction or blessing of the staff and scrip (leather satchel) – items carried by most pilgrims.[37] The complete text for a blessing ceremony survives in the late 11th-century manuscript *The Worcester Pontifical*.[38] The ceremony involved presenting the pilgrim with a staff from the altar. The 11th-century *Life of St Anselm* alludes to a similar end to the ceremony, with the saint receiving his 'staff and scrip' before setting off to Rome.[39] Another text records that a group of English pilgrims had their staves and scrips consecrated in church prior to departure for pilgrimage to St Andrews in 1284.[40] Blessings were also part of the pilgrim tradition in Iceland. *The Diary of Nikolas of Munkathvera*, written in the late 1150s, tells of Icelandic pilgrims receiving a scrip, staff and a blessing before departing on pilgrimage to Rome.[41]

A blessing ceremony was also part of the preparations of Irish pilgrims. In the 12th century, Bishop Goilla (Gillebertus) of Limerick (1070–1145) wrote that in the absence of a bishop, the parish priest was to bless those who were about to make a pilgrimage.[42] The Bishop of Limerick's writing implies that during this period the blessing ceremony was a routine duty of the bishop and in his absence it fell to the parish priests. The blessing ceremony was probably part of the duties of bishops across Ireland at the time. Further evidence for Irish blessing ceremonies can be found in the 12th-century satirical tale *Aisling Meic Conglinne/The Vision of Mac Conglinne.* This source presents a parody of a pilgrim blessing for the monk Mac Conglinne, before he departs for his pilgrimage to Cork, from his monastery at Roscommon. First he wraps himself in a white cloak and picks up a 'knotty staff'; then he walks clockwise around the graveyard; and finally, he sets off, after his tutor has circled a gospel book around him.[43]

Privileges and 'Passports'

Long-distance pilgrimage bestowed certain entitlements and benefits upon pilgrims.[44] In the early medieval period, pilgrims travelling on the Continent had the right to free hospitality,[45] safe passage, exemption from the payments of tolls, and the suspension of services owed to feudal lords for the duration of pilgrimage.[46] These privileges continued and increased in the later medieval period, when the pilgrims' entitlements were extended to include the protection of property for the duration of their absence and their right to make a will.[47] To avail of entitlements and to discourage dishonest individuals from taking advantage, it was necessary for pilgrims to be identifiable to those they encountered along the way. As early as AD 341, the Council of Antioch ordered that no pilgrim should set forth without letters of recommendation. This policy was encouraged in the 8th and 9th Centuries by the Carolingians and many examples of letters of identification have survived from the records of the Merovingian and Carolingian kingdoms.[48] Irish pilgrims would have turned to their bishops and even the pope for letters, stating their intentions as pilgrims. In 1366, a letter written from the Archbishop of Armagh to the Prior of the Purgatory of St Patrick and the clergy of the Diocese of Clogher asked for the provision of hospitality to pilgrims John Bonham and Guidus Cissy, who wished to visit St Patrick's Purgatory on pilgrimage.[49] A papal letter of safe conduct, dated 9 May 1431, was given to James Butler, 4th Earl of Ormond, for himself and a retinue of up to 25 people to travel to Rome.[50] He seems not to have undertaken the pilgrimage, despite obtaining a two-year licence for absence.[51]

Once permission was granted and letters of safe passage obtained, the next concern for the pilgrim was packing. Clothing was an essential consideration. The earliest pilgrims dressed like other travellers but by the 8th century, the appearance of pilgrims had become more distinguishable. In 797, Charlemagne complained of merchants concealing themselves as pilgrims, to avoid paying tolls.[52] The dress of pilgrims evolved still further and by the 13th century, a dress code or uniform had developed that clearly identified the wearer in his/her role as a pilgrim.[53] It is unlikely that pilgrims to local shrines needed such distinctive clothing. The oldest and most distinctive parts of the pilgrim uniform were the staff and scrip, both of which appear in contemporary depictions of pilgrims. The staff is often shown with a single or double knob at the top and a metal toe or double-pronged iron spike at the other end.[54] The fictional Irish pilgrim Mac Conglinne carried an 'even-poised knotty staff, in which were five hands from one end to the other'.[55] The staff was a practical and useful accessory, as it acted as an aid when crossing difficult terrain and, if necessary, could be used as a defensive weapon, against robbers and wild animals.[56]

The scrip was a leather purse or satchel used to hold the pilgrim's food and money. It was worn tied around the waist or over the shoulder.[57] Both the scrip and the staff continued to be readily identified as the traditional symbols of pilgrimage, or *Signia peregrinationis*, and were actively promoted in the imagery of the Church. For example, images of St James the Greater often depict the saint as a pilgrim, with a staff and scrip.[58] From the 11th century, a long coarse tunic called a sclavein began to be worn by some pilgrims on the Continent. The 'uniform' was developed further in the 13th century, when it became fashionable to wear a broad-brimmed hat turned up at the front.[59] The hat was secured to the person with a long sash/scarf that was twisted around the body as far as the waist. Several late medieval paintings, woodcuts and stone carvings show pilgrims in their distinctive clothing, including the wide-brimmed hat, an Irish example being the 15th-century tomb at Kilconnell Friary, Co. Galway. These items of clothing were very much part of the iconography of St James by the 14th century. How far Irish pilgrims followed this uniform is difficult to know. They probably used the staff and a scrip, which were practical items used by all travellers. They would also have taken a good pair of shoes suitable for walking and a heavy cloak to protect themselves from the weather. The sclavein and the broad-brimmed hat are depicted on some late medieval carvings of St James in Ireland but it is not clear if they were part of Irish pilgrim dress.

Over time, the Church began to sanctify the clothing of pilgrims through the 'blessing ceremony', and to invest in it a rich and elaborate symbolism.[60] The 12th-century sermon *Veneranda Dies* (1125) assigned symbolism to the pilgrim garb, whereby the scrip was symbolic of almsgiving, while the staff signified the Blessed Trinity and the individual wearer's fight against evil.[61]

St James dressed as a pilgrim at Kilconnell Friary.
© Louise Nugent

On a more practical level, as the social status of pilgrimage increased, so too did the entitlements available to the pilgrims.[62] It was beneficial for the pilgrim to be easily distinguishable from other travellers, particularly for those travelling abroad to foreign lands and the pilgrim uniform clearly marked the pilgrim and his/her mission, in much the same way as the robes of a priest marked him out. Those who encountered pilgrims were aware of their intentions and also of their entitlement to benefit from free food, lodgings, safe passage and exemption from tolls and taxes, as per the diktat of the Church.[63] Of course, what was supposed to happen did not always work out and pilgrims, in some cases, may have had to pay all these expenses themselves.

In 2015, reenactor Steven Payne recreated a medieval pilgrimage, following the exact route of the Italian pilgrim Coluccio de Carrara, who travelled 320 kilometres by foot from Southampton to Canterbury in 1365. His journey and preparations are documented on his Facebook page, Pilgrim's Progress.[64] Steven dressed in the attire of a medieval traveller and his clothing was inspired by the dress of contemporary bog bodies in Sweden.

His outfit consisted of a heavy waterproof woollen cloak and on his feet he wore thick, leather soles. In a leather satchel, he carried soap made from wood ash and olive oil, as well as a block of alum for deodorant. He also took flint and steel for starting fires and some food that included dried apples, honey oatcakes, some cinnamon and nuts, and non-alcoholic ginger wine. Payne's pilgrimage was recorded in great detail each day on his Facebook page. It began on 16 December and, as had many medieval pilgrims before him, he arrived at Canterbury for the feast of St Thomas, 29 December.

NOTES

1 AU.
2 1510 AU/1512; *ACon.*
3 Mary Margaret Newett, ed., *Canon Pietro Casola's Pilgrimage to Jerusalem in the Year 1494* (Manchester: Manchester University Press, 1907), 10.
4 Hopper, *To Be a Pilgrim*, 78.
5 Kenny, Anglo-Irish and Gaelic Women, 100.
6 William Monck Mason, *The History and Antiquities of the Collegiate and Cathedral Church of St. Patrick Near Dublin, from Its Foundation in 1190, to the Year 1819* (Dublin: Printed William Monk Mason by W. Folds, 1820), 82.
7 Cunningham, *Medieval Irish Pilgrims*, 25.
8 Anthony Lynch, 'The Administration of John Bole, Archbishop of Armagh, 1457-71,' *Seanchas Ardmhacha* 14 no. 2 (1991): 43.
9 Ditchburn, 'Saints at the Door Don't Make Miracles', 81.
10 A. Bale, *The Book of Margery Kempe*, Oxford World Classics (Oxford: Oxford University Press., 2015), xxvii. 111.
11 Kenny, *Anglo-Irish and Gaelic Women*, 100.
12 Michael Haren, 'The Religious Outlook of a Gaelic Lord: A New Light on Thomas Óg Maguire,' *IHS*,25 no. 98 (1986): 196
13 Haren, 'The Religious Outlook,' 196; Kenny, *Anglo-Irish and Gaelic Women*, 101.
14 Hopper, *To Be a Pilgrim*, 78.
15 Finucane, *Miracles and Pilgrims*, 41.
16 Potterton, *Medieval Trim*, 310.
17 Stat. Ire. Ric. III–Henry VIII, 39; Eamonn McEneaney, 'Politics and the Art of Devotion,' 37.
18 Jim Higgins, *St. James' Church & Cemetery, Gleninagh Heights, Galway* (Galway: Rock Crow's Press, 1996), 77.
19 Stat. Ire., 12-22 Edw. IV, Vol. IV, 53–55.
20 Pádraig Ó Riain, *A Dictionary of Irish Saints* (Dublin: Four Courts Press, 2011), 501.
21 Stat. Ire. Ric. III–Henry VIII, 335.
22 Stat. Ire. Ric. III–Henry VIII, 53.
23 Ó Clabaigh, *The Friars*, 198.
24 Lynch, 'The Administration of John Bole, Archbishop of Armagh, 1457–71,' 159.
25 Ó Clabaigh, *The Friars*, 198.
26 Ditchburn, 'Saints at the Door Don't Make Miracles', 81.
27 Ditchburn, 'Saints at the Door Don't Make Miracles', 81.
28 Ditchburn, 'Saints at the Door Don't Make Miracles', 81.
29 John Lee, *Cambridge and Its Economics. Studies in Regional and Local History*, Vol.3 (Hatfield: University of Hertfordshire Press, 2005), 196.
30 Stalley, 'Sailing to Santiago,' 405. For a discussion of the cost of travelling from Scotland, see Ditchburn, 'Saints at the Door Don't Make Miracles', 81.
31 Susan Morrison, *Women Pilgrims in Late Medieval England* (London: Routledge, 2002), 69.
32 Henry Jackson Lawlor, 'A Calendar of the Register of Archbishop Fleming,' *PRIA* 30 (1912): 158. no. 229.
33 Anthony Lynch, 'A Calendar of the Reassembled Register of John Bole, Archbishop of Armagh, 1457–71', *Seanchas Ardmhacha:* 15, no. 1 (1992): 148.
34 Lawlor, 'A Calendar of the Register,' no. 145.
35 Sumption, *Pilgrimage*, 168–71.
36 Debra Birch, *Pilgrimage to Rome in the Middle Ages: Continuity and Change* (Woodbridge: The Boydell Press, 1998), 76–77; James Brundage, 'Cruce Sigari: The Rite for Taking the Cross in England', *Traditio* 22 (1966): 289–310; Sumption, *Pilgrimage*, 172–73.
37 Sumption, *Pilgrimage*, 171; Davies, *Pilgrimage Yesterday?*, 45–46.
38 Birch, *Pilgrimage to Rome*, 77; Brundage, 'Cruce Sigari,' 298.
39 William Richard Southern (ed) *The Life of St Anselm, Archbishop of Canterbury* (Oxford: Clarendon Press, 1962), 97; Birch, Pilgrimage to Rome, 76.
40 Webb, *Pilgrimage in Medieval England*, 186.
41 Francis P Magoun, 'The Pilgrim-Diary of Nikulas of Munkathvera: The Road to Rome,' *Journal Mediaeval Studies* 6 (1944): 349; Birch, *Pilgrimage to Rome*, 76.
42 John Fleming, *Gille of Limerick (c. 1070–1145): Architect of a Medieval Church* (Dublin: Four Courts Press, 2001), 156-57.
43 Kuno Meyer, *Aislinge Meic Conglinne: The Vision of MacConglinne, a Middle-Irish Wonder Tale* (London: D. Nutt, 1892), 8.

44 For detailed discussion of entitlements see Birch, *Pilgrimage to Rome*, 72–88.

45 Legislation was issued to make it compulsory to provide accommodation for rich and oor pilgrims in the Carolingian kingdoms. See Birch, *Pilgrimage to Rome*, 79.

46 From the 7th century to the end of the medieval period, laws and decrees were issued continuously by the Church (especially from the 10th century onwards) and secular rulers to protect the safe passage of pilgrims. The Lateran Council held in 1123 decreed that anyone who was convicted of robbing a pilgrim was to be excommunicated. See Birch, *Pilgrimage to Rome*, 80–85; Edwin Mullins, *The Pilgrimage to Santiago* (Devon: Readers Union Ltd, 1975), 71.

47 Birch, *Pilgrimage to Rome*, 74-86; Sumption, *Pilgrimage*, 168–71.

48 Birch, *Pilgrimage to Rome*, 72–77.

49 Lawlor, 'A Calendar of the Register,' 274, no. 193.

50 CPL (1427-47), 278.

51 E.A.E Matthew, 'The Governing of the Lancastrian Lordship of Ireland in the Time of James Butler, Fourth Earl of Ormond c. 1420–1452'. Unpublished PhD Thesis University of Durham. (PhD thesis, 1995), 252.

52 Webb, *Medieval European Pilgrimage, c.700–c. 1500*, 12.

53 Sumption, *Pilgrimage*, 171–75.

54 Sumption, *Pilgrimage*, 171.

55 Meyer, *Aislinge Meic Conglinne*, 8.

56 Sumption, *Pilgrimage*, 173.

57 Sumption, *Pilgrimage*, 171–72; Birch, *Pilgrimage to Rome*, 76; Hopper, *To Be a Pilgrim*, 73–74; Anon, *Santiago de Compostela; 100 Ans de Pelèrinage Européen, Europalia 85* (Gent: Ausstellungskat, 1985), Catalogue nos. 309, 311, 323, 334–335.

58 For a discussion of the iconography of St James, see Mark Hall, 'Crossing the Pilgrimage Landscape: Some Thoughts on a Holy Rood Reliquary from the River Tay at Carpow, Perth and Kinross, Scotland,' in *Beyond Pilgrim Souvenirs and Secular Badges. Essays in Honour of Brian Spencer*, ed. Sarah Blick (Oxford: Oxbow Books, 2007), 75–91.

59 Sumption, *Pilgrimage*, 171–172.

60 Sumption, *Pilgrimage*, 173; Webb, *Pilgrims and Pilgrimage in the Medieval West*, 21–22; Davies, *Pilgrimage Yesterday?*, 43.

61 Sumption, *Pilgrimage* , 173; Birch, *Pilgrimage to Rome*, 76.

62 Birch, *Pilgrimage to Rome,* 72.

63 Birch, *Pilgrimage to Rome,* 72.

64 'Pilgrims Progress - Posts | Facebook.' https://en-gb.facebook.com/14thcenturypilgrimsprogress/posts/?ref=page_internalhttps://en-gb.facebook.com/14thcenturypilgrimsprogress/posts/?ref=page_internal. Accessed 18 May 2018. 'Pilgrim completes 'medieval' journey from Southampton to Canterbury...'. 30 December 2015'.

CHAPTER 5

Pilgrim Journeys in Ireland

Once preparations had been made, the pilgrims began their journey. Travel to a local holy well, church or monastery was a relatively easy task: the pilgrims were familiar with the surrounding landscape and knew the best route to take. In all likelihood they or a family member had made the journey before. As a general rule, whether travelling in Ireland or abroad, pilgrims made use of established routes and roads. Untangling the exact routes used at this time is difficult. Throughout the medieval period, historical and literary sources make frequent references to the journeys of Irish saints, the clergy, kings and armies, yet the exact route of these journeys tends to be described in vague terms, making them difficult to pinpoint in the modern landscape. However, although they are vague these sources do suggest an existing infrastructure

Longer journeys were more challenging and, where possible, the would-be pilgrim sought out others who had completed the pilgrimage, finding out as much as possible about their experiences and the route they had taken. If available, travel guides and itineraries, like the 12th-century *Liber Sancti Jacobi,* a five-book compilation containing a pilgrim's travel guide, were consulted. It is difficult to know how widely available such texts were in medieval Ireland, if at all. The will of Drogheda merchant John Brent, written in the 1440s, lists a book describing the stations of the holy places in Rome, among his possessions. This volume, written in English, would have been of great interest to any pilgrim hoping to travel to Rome.[1]

Journeying Through Medieval Ireland

Throughout the medieval period, most ordinary people did not travel far from their home place. In rural Ireland up to the 20th century, it was commonplace for people to travel no further than the nearest big town, unless forced to emigrate. The social limitations on travel meant that most pilgrimages were made to local and regional destinations; but, given the resourcefulness of the human spirit, there were undoubtedly exceptions.

The 7th-century Irish law tracts, a code for how society should function, strongly suggests that few ordinary people travelled beyond the bounds of their *túath* (territorial unit of land), except in extraordinary circumstances such as military service, travelling to an *óenach* (assembly) or on the feast days of major saints.[2] The law provided varying degrees of protection to the upper classes, when travelling beyond the territory of their *túath*. For the lower classes such as farmers, there was little or no legal protection beyond the borders of the *túath*, with individuals losing all legal right to protection and becoming, in effect, non-entities or outlaws in the eyes of the law.[3] There seem to have been some exceptions for travel involving the celebration of feast days and other Church festivals, as the Irish saints' Lives often show pilgrims travelling on such occasions (see Chapters 1 and 7).

Opportunities for ordinary people to travel seem to have expanded in the 10th and 11th centuries, as Ireland moved towards a more centralised political system. It was also during this period that many of the larger monasteries increased in power and wealth, and their patron saints developed wider devotional appeal. In the 12th century, the Anglo-Normans gained control of substantial parts of the country, introducing a new social system and agricultural practices based on feudalism. It is unlikely that the lower classes of Anglo-Norman-controlled areas of Ireland, such as east Leinster and Munster, would have travelled any further than their counterparts in areas of Gaelic control, i.e. beyond their local parish or dioceses. Long-distance travel and pilgrimage continued to be predominantly performed by the elite, clergy, aristocracy, and the middle and merchant classes.[4]

Transport

Walking was the cheapest and easiest means of travel. Well into the 19th century, walking was the most popular way to get from A to B. The poor had little choice but to walk. Pilgrims on foot could expect to cover an average distance of 15 to 25 kilometres a day; or if they had the means to hire a horse, they could expect to cover 30 to 40 kilometres per day.[5] Walking also had the advantage of allowing the traveller to move through rough terrain that was unsuited to other modes of transport.[6] For the pilgrim, the physical exertion of walking increased the penitential merit of the journey, so that even those who could afford to travel in more style would often opt to walk all or part of their journey.[7] Some pilgrims even walked part or all the journey barefoot. The abbot of Bury St Edmunds travelled to Rome in 1160 in the company of a group of Scotsmen who walked barefoot, their shoes thrown over their shoulders.[8]

Wealthy pilgrims had the option of travelling by horse or mule. In medieval sources from outside Ireland, sick and infirm pilgrims were often described as travelling on mules. Anyone who chose to travel this way had to pay for the cost of purchase, feed and shoes, as well as the repair and maintenance of equipment.

The 14th-century *Account Roll of the Priory of the Holy Trinity* tells us that a day's journey of three men on horseback from Drogheda to Balscaddan and back to Drogheda, cost in 'bread, wine, ale and fish, bought 13d.; in bread, hay, and oats bought for horses cost 11d.; in shoeing the horses on same day, 2½d'.[9]

Medieval Irish Roads

The journeys of all Irish pilgrims, whether on foot or by horse, were affected by the condition of the roads. The early Irish law tracts suggests that a network of roads of varying sizes and functions existed by the 7th century. These roads consisted of the highway (*slige*), road (*rout*), by-road (*lámraite*), curved road (*tógraite*), and cow-track (*bóthar*).[10] Cormac's Glossary (c. 900) lists seven grades of road: the road (*sét, rout/rót*), road leading to residence of a king (*rámat*), highway (*slige*), by road (*lámrotae*), way to mountain land in private ownership *(túagrotae*), and cow track or drove road (*bóthar*).[11]

Most Irish roads were little more than thin strips of land, considered to be rights of way.[12] Some Irish roads had a formal construction with paving surfaces, defined on either side by banks and ditches. One law tract tells us that the '*slige*' or highway, the largest of the early medieval roads, was wide enough for two chariots to pass each other.[13] To date, chariots have not been recovered from Irish excavations. The use of wheeled traffic suggests that roads were maintained and possibly paved or metalled. Surviving sections of the Slighe Dála road in the townlands of Knocknadala, Turoe, Lackafinna and Loughrea in Co. Galway, measured 7 metres in width (excluding the banks).[14] Another surviving section of the same road close to the church site of Clonfert-Molua had the appearance of a sunken hollow way and was 4 metres wide.[15] The *bóthar* was the smallest of the roads, wide enough to fit two cows, one sideways and the other lengthways.[16] The historical sources suggest that some of these early roads had such an imposing effect on the landscape that, along with other prominent features such as rivers and bogs, they were used as boundary markers.[17] The Slige Dála, Slige Mór and Slige Assail all acted as territorial boundary markers.[18]

Archaeological evidence confirms variety in the form and construction of Irish roads. The Irish countryside is scattered with stretches of abandoned medieval and post-medieval roads. Many are sunken or hollow ways, where the road surface is below the height of the surrounding fields, a result of the continuous traffic of cattle and carts compressing the ground surface over generations.[19] Medieval examples are found at deserted villages, such as Tullamoylin, in North Tipperary.[20] Some medieval roads were defined by banks and surviving stretches of the Slighe Dála, which traditionally ran from Knockdala to Roscrea, are defined by banks in the townlands of Turoe, Lackafinna and Loughrea.[21] A stretch of the road in the townland of Boherygeela was defined by low parallel banks and ditches.[22]

There are also examples of medieval roads with cobbled surfaces. A fine cobbled road, 4 metres wide and flanked by drainage ditches 0.8 metres deep, was excavated at Phoenixtown, Co. Meath, in 2007. The upper surface of the road, which had fallen out of use around the 13th and 14th centuries, showed evidence of wheel ruts from wagons and carts.[23] St Kevin's road, the great pilgrim road that linked the plains of Kildare to Glendalough, was composed of two to three fluid routes that merged into a man-made road close to the Wicklow Gap. The constructed section of road was very likely built at the height of Glendalough's power in the 10th to 12th centuries. By the 17th century, the surface of the road was completely covered in peat but it remained a favoured route for travellers until the mid-19th century, providing a dry island in the surrounding mountainous land. Unfortunately, a 1,000-metre section of the peat-covered road in the townland of Brockagh was exposed and severely damaged in the early 2000s. A series of rescue excavations carried out by University College Dublin's School of Archaeology in 2005–06 revealed that the road had a complex construction. Layers of gravel and small stones had been placed upon the peat, acting as the foundation and core of the road. The upper surface was covered in compacted gravel that changed to large patches of small cobbles, to areas of paving composed of flat slabs of granite. The road was flanked on either side by a ditch.[24] The building of St Kevin's road required a considerable labour force. The land had to be prepared, ditches dug, foundation deposits laid, and granite boulders split to create the sections of paving and cobbles laid in other sections. When first built, the road must have looked striking in the surrounding landscape, and on sunny days its granite surface would have glistened and sparked, an impressive sight for those who walked along it.[25]

Many places in the modern landscape that we might consider as isolated or hard to reach, such as bogs, were not viewed that way in earlier times. Irish bogs, fens and callows had been traversed by roads and trackways from prehistoric times.[26] Bog trackways range from simple tracks made of brushwood or woven wattle to more substantial structures of timber planks lain over brushwood. Bog roads known as *toghers* were composed primarily of stone or gravel and flagstones, and could sustain the weight of a cart in some places.[27] Wetland trackways and roads date from the Mesolithic period to the 19th century and were constructed in piecemeal fashion to connect islands of dry land in the bogs. Many of these roads had a short life-span, although there were some roads that were repaired and used over long periods of time.[28] Two bog roads that formed part of a wider

Surface of St Kevin's Road at Brockagh, Co. Wicklow, revealed during the 2005 excavations undertaken by the School of Archaeology, UCD. ©Louise Nugent

road network around the pilgrim shrines of Clonmacnoise and Lemanaghan have been excavated in the Bloomhill and Lemanaghan Bogs, Co. Offaly. The Bloomhill road was constructed sometime between AD 566 and 770 and was in use until the mid-13th century. It was traced for a distance of 950 metres from close to the monastery of Clonmacnoise to a dry land island in the townland of Cloncraff/Bloomhill and on into the townland of Ballynahownwood in Co. Westmeath. The road was around 3.40 metres wide[29] and was rebuilt and repaired many times in the course of its life. It was built with layers of clay, gravel, timber and brushwood, and was covered with a substantial flagstone surface. In a later phase, the flagstones were covered by a birchwood track.[30] Even when the road was covered in peat in later centuries, it remained visible in the landscape and was used by people travelling through the bog up until the 19th century.[31]

A similar multiphase road was excavated at Derrynagun bog in 1996. The road brought people across the bog to the nearby ecclesiastical settlement at Lemanaghan,[32] built on a dry land island in the bog.[33] Excavation of the road revealed five phases of rebuilding with a lifespan of over 600 years. The road was first built in the 650s[34] and initially had the appearance of a longitudinal plank walkway made of split oak, 1 metre wide. Towards the end of its life, in the later 12th century, it was rebuilt and resurfaced with horizontal split planks defined by double row of posts at the edges of the road, sitting on top of layers of brushwood. It was 4.2m metres wide.[35] The first phase of construction, the plank walkway, is broadly contemporary with the establishment of the monastery by St Manchan at Lemanaghan in 645. As the monastery developed and expanded, the road became part of a network of routeways that crossed the large expanses of bog in the midlands and linked with important places like Clonmacnoise.[36] Both the Lemanaghan and the Bloomhill roads required a considerable amount of physical labour during the construction period and significant investment was also required to maintain them. Bog roads like the Bloomhill road linked into other dry land routes, which would have required little or no construction.[37]

Waterways

The importance of Irish waterways to travel in medieval Ireland is often underestimated. In medieval times, Irish rivers were deeper and wider, having fewer obstructions to their channels.[38] They acted as corridors for the transport of goods and people. Waterways such as the Shannon, Liffey, Lee, Blackwater, Nore, Suir, Barrow, Erne and Boyne were navigable for much of their courses, providing alternative routes for travellers. Rivers such as the Shannon, Barrow and Suir provided vital links to the coast. Rivers and lakes linked in to wider networks of roads and coastal routes. It is not surprising that many important medieval ecclesiastical and secular settlements were located close to, or beside navigable waterways.

Travellers who chose to travel along land routes would encounter waterways – lakes, rivers and streams – along the routes. They would have to cross streams and rivers at suitable fording points or take a boat across a lake.[39] Small rivers and streams could be crossed on foot, where the riverbed was firm and the water level shallow.[40] To make the crossing easier, the level of the riverbed at some fords was built up with stones and planks.[41] Hurdles – woven wicker mats – were also laid down and spiked into the mud of the river bed. One of the crossing points on the River Liffey at Dublin was known as Áth Cliath, the 'ford of the hurdles'. The townland name of Annakisha or Áth na Cise, 'ford of the wickerwork causeway', near Mallow, Co. Cork, preserves evidence of a similar crossing.[42] Fording points on rivers were also crossed by stepping stones, and in larger rivers, there were causeway-type structures built of stones, punctuated by gaps, enabling the water to flow through, as at Skeagh on the River Shannon.[43] Larger, deeper rivers had to be crossed by canoe, raft or ferry/barges or by bridge.

Ferries were used to bring people and goods across unbridged rivers that were too wide or deep to be crossed on foot. Log boats have been recovered at or near bridges in places where, in earlier times, a ferry service was needed.[44] Eleven canoes of medieval date were discovered on the bed of the River Shannon during the excavation of a medieval timber bridge close to the monastery of Clonmacnoise.[45] The late 12th-/early 13th-century Latin *Life of St Moling* mentions the saint ferrying travellers across the Barrow to his monastery at St Mullens.[46]

Bridges were rare in the early medieval Ireland. They did not become common until the 11th century, when bridges at places such as Athlone, Athleague, Ath Caille (Athlunkard) and Killaloe were constructed.[47] Medieval bridges were made from either wood or stone, or a combination of both. The Clonmacnoise bridge is the earliest known timber bridge built in Ireland. Spanning a 160-metre-wide section of the River Shannon, it was built to accommodate the crossing of the Slighe Mór[48] over the Shannon.[49]

THE PERILOUS ROAD: CHALLENGES FOR THE TRAVELLER

Weather

The weather was an obstacle over which the pilgrim had little control but something that could greatly affect the time scale of a journey. Heavy rain turned unsurfaced roads to mud and made fords impassable. Many pilgrimages were timed for the summer months to avoid the heavy rains of winter. Apart from rain, winter brought the risk of snow, which could make roads impassable.

Pilgrims and Crime

Travellers in and outside Ireland were vulnerable to unscrupulous people. Attacks by robbers could involve serious assault and even death.[50] Long-distance pilgrims who needed to carry substantial sums of money to meet their expenses were attractive targets. European sources abound with stories of pilgrims who suffered at the hands of innkeepers, robbers and kidnappers. Women – especially those travelling alone – were particularly vulnerable to assault and robbery.[51] On the Continent the abduction of rich pilgrims and their subsequent ransom was a common event during the medieval period.[52] The *Annals of Ulster* for 913 record the abduction and ransom of a pilgrim in Ireland:

> Máel Brigte son of Tornán went to Mumu (Munster) to ransom a Welsh pilgrim.[53]

Máel Brigte was the abbot of Armagh (883–927) and, as such, was one of the most important clerics in Ireland. The fact that such a high-ranking cleric travelled all the way to Munster is very significant and suggests that the Welsh pilgrim was of high standing or that the holding of pilgrims for ransom was a very unusual event in Ireland.[54]

Where possible, pilgrims stayed on busy roads and avoided isolated tracks. Roads passing through areas of forest were particularly dangerous, as robbers could easily lie in wait, camouflaged by the dense trees and scrub. That these threats were very real is demonstrated by a letter written to Bishop Franco of Liège (854–901) by an Irish pilgrim returning from Rome, in which he requested the return of property stolen from him by people from the bishop's diocese.[55] A rare entry in the annals for the year 1224 records the robbery of an unnamed man, most likely a pilgrim, along a road leading to Croagh Patrick. The entry states this was one of the only crimes to take place in Connacht during the peaceful reign of Aodh Ó Conchobhair. The perpetrator of the crime was severely punished by having his hands and feet cut off:

> … one act of plunder on the road to Cruach, and his hands and feet were cut off the person who committed it.[56]

In 1242, the annals recorded that the Lord of Tireragh, who controlled an area of land in the north east portion of Co. Mayo, was murdered on his way to Boyle Abbey.

> Brian son of Donough O'Dowda, Lord of Tireragh, Tirawley, and Erris, was killed as he was going on a pilgrimage to the Abbey of Boyle.[57]

It is not clear if this attack was carried out by criminals or rival political factions, but the incident shows how vulnerable people were when travelling outside their own territory. The first *Life of Máedóc of Ferns* provides another rare description of pilgrims being attacked

> As he drew near to the Irish coast, he saw robbers on one side of a road, robbing and killing pilgrims and feeble folk … He then rang his bell, and the chief of the brigands heard it. 'Tis the sound of the bell of a devout and godly man,' said he, 'and he rings his bell to bid us cease this work.' They let the pilgrims be after this.[58]

Political Unrest

At certain times, travelling into and through enemy or rival territory could be very dangerous. In the year 1351, Hugh O'Rourke was taken prisoner by Philipin McWilliam Burke, when travelling through McWilliam territory.[59] This territory lay close to Aghagower Church, a prominent site on the Irish pilgrim road known as the Tóchar Phádraig, which tentatively suggests that O'Rourke may have been travelling along the Tóchar on pilgrimage to Croagh Patrick. Another incident happened in 1501, when Edmond Burke was taken captive by Mac Williams of Clanrickard, on his return from Santiago.

> Edmond, the son of Rickard Burke, was taken by Mac William of Clanrickard, on his return from the pilgrimage of St James in Spain.[60]

He was later released, once a ' great ransom' had been paid. Relations between Anglo-Norman and Gaelic communities were often strained and pilgrims from Gaelic-controlled areas of Ireland, or vice versa, could at certain times in history be travelling through hostile territory. During the 15th century, pilgrim shrines located in the Anglo-Norman-controlled areas, fearing the loss of valuable revenue from Gaelic pilgrims, enlisted state protection to ensure the safety of pilgrims travelling from Gaelic lordships. Thanks to pressure from the shrines, the crown responded by issuing warrants of protection to all pilgrims travelling to these shrines. In 1400, the abbot of St Mary's Abbey, Trim, penned a desperate letter to Henry IV, complaining that Gaelic pilgrims who up to this point had been free to make pilgrimage to the miraculous statue at his abbey, were now reluctant to do so due to the imprisonment of a number of Gaelic pilgrims by crown forces. The abbot was clearly concerned about the impact these events would have on the numbers of pilgrims and the revenue they generated. He stressed that obligations made by pilgrims constituted the primary income for the abbey. The king confirmed ' an ancient privilege of immunity of such pilgrims from the suits of the king, of the lords of Meath, or any other persons whatsoever'.[61] Further royal protection was granted to the shrine at Trim in 1402, 1415, 1450 and 1472/1473.[62]

St Mary's Abbey, Trim, Co. Meath.
© Louise Nugent

A royal warrant to protect all pilgrims travelling to Christ Church Cathedral for a duration of three years was issued on 26 October 1462.[63] The pilgrims could stay in the city for eight days. A similar protection was enacted in 1491, and later confirmed by the provincial council of the Archdiocese of Dublin in 1495, threatening all perpetrators with excommunication.[64] The efforts by Christ Church to protect Irish pilgrims and the potential wealth that they brought is all the more intriguing, given attempts by the Dublin municipal assembly to drive all Irish men and women from the city during the same period.[65]

The chapel of St Catherine at Fieldstown, Co. Dublin,[66] also benefited from royal protection. At this time, a steady stream of pilgrims came 'by sea and by land' to pray for salvation and ' to obtain their petitions and prayers'. Nicholas Dovedale, Prebendary of Clonmethan, petitioned parliament, in 1474, for the protection of Gaelic pilgrims who came to pray to the Virgin and St Katherine the Martyr. He described how the once-thriving pilgrimage had declined, as 'persons have been at divers times vexed and molested'.[67] It is clear that the pilgrims provided a much-needed source of income for the chapel. Nicholas also expressed his concern for the pilgrims who had made vows of pilgrimage but were unable to fulfil them due to the dangers of travel. Parliament granted protection to the pilgrims and their property and anyone caught 'molesting, vexing or grieving' them was liable to 'forfeit 20 pounds half to the king' and half to the complainant.[68]

Accommodation

Shelter was a vital consideration for long-distance pilgrims. Irish travellers could also expect to find lodgings in one of the hostels (secular and religious) and religious guesthouses scattered around the countryside. The more affluent may have stayed at the homes of their peers. In isolated areas of Ireland, travellers would wrap themselves up in their cloak and sleep under the stars.[69] After the 12th century, shelter could also be found on the floor of the parish church.[70]

Hostels run by lay people were in existence in Ireland throughout the medieval period. They were located in prominent positions at road junctions, crossroads and fording points of rivers. The principle of free hospitality was seen as the cornerstone of Christian charity and was actively promoted by the Church from an early date.[71] The Church had a moral duty to provide accommodation and shelter for travellers and pilgrims for at least a limited period of time.[72] Religious-run hostels that were governed by independent communities of monks were found beside some monasteries. The majority of larger monasteries in early and late medieval Ireland had a guesthouse or hospital attached, where pilgrims could find shelter. There are numerous references to guesthouses at monastic sites in the early saints' Lives, suggesting that duty of care for guests was taken seriously.[73] Many early medieval Irish monasteries were located close to, or beside busy routes, maximising accessibility for travellers. Clonmacnoise and its guesthouse were built at the junction of two important medieval routeways, the River Shannon and Slighe Mór.[74]

The guesthouse attached to the monastery of Roscrea was located at the junction of three important routes: the Slighe Dála, the River Moneen and an unnamed north-south road.[75]

In late medieval Ireland, urban centres had more choice of types of accommodation, but religious houses were still the main providers.[76] For example, a pilgrim to Dublin could stay at the hostel of St James or at the guesthouses attached to St Thomas's and St Mary's Abbeys. Both regularly housed large numbers during the holding of parliament and occasions when the city was at its most crowded.[77]

Catering for large numbers of people was expensive and needed careful organisation. The monastic guesthouses were run by the guestmaster/*airchinnech*, whose responsibility it was to order supplies and monitor the comings and goings of people.[78] The Latin *Life of St Molua* (c. 800) tells that the monks of Clonfertmollua wished to build the saint a house, but Molua refused this offer, insisting they should instead build a guesthouse and hand over a large portion of their estates for its use.[79]

Hospitality was not limitless: as a general rule, travellers could expect to stay a maximum of three days and three nights at the '...residence of nobleman, humble home or ordinary household, guesthouse or monastery...'[80] In late medieval Ireland, visitors to Holycross Abbey was allowed to stay for two days and two nights in the guesthouse and, following dinner on the third day, they were expected to leave.[81] The standard of accommodation and the treatment of pilgrims and other travellers varied from place to place. Poor-quality accommodation is highlighted in the 12th-century satirical tale *Aislinge Meic Conglinne*. When Meic Conglinne arrives at the monastery of Cork, he encounters ungracious hosts and deplorable accommodation, with his bedding '...rolled and bundled in the bed and walls full of lice and fleas'.[82] Hostels and guesthouses seem to have provided guests with food, fire, bedding and bathing facilities.[83] Adomnán's *Life of St Columba* describes the guesthouse at Iona as being built of wattle.[84] During the early medieval period, Irish monastic buildings were constructed largely of timber (with exceptions on the west coast, where they were predominantly of stone), and even when stone buildings came into vogue in the 10th century, they were usually restricted to churches. The domestic buildings associated with the monastery continued to be built in perishable materials, such as timber or post and wattle, so they are no longer traceable without excavation. The fact that the guesthouses and infirmaries of continental orders in Ireland rarely survived may indicate that many of these structures were also built of timber. At Holycross Abbey, a 15th-century infirmary survives, and the size of the building indicates that it may also have been used to facilitate pilgrims to the shrine.

The late medieval guesthouse at Holycross Abbey.
© Louise Nugent

Possible early medieval guesthouse at the ecclesiastical site of Templeteenaun, Co. Wicklow, located outside the entrance to the ecclesiastical enclosure.
© Louise Nugent

Archaeological remains of two possible early medieval guesthouses have been identified at the pilgrim centres of High Island, Co. Galway, and Templeteenaun, Co. Wicklow. Both structures are located outside the entrance of the main monastic enclosure.[85] At High Island, the guesthouse is only 5.5 x 3.8 metres. Built of stone, the outline of the walls suggest it was sub-rectangular/trapezoidal in shape.[86] A structure of similar shape and size, and probable function, exists at Church Island.[87] A rectangular pit designed to collect water in its southern wall may have provided water for the washing of the guests.[88] At Templeteenaun, a small structure constructed of sod walls, possibly a guesthouse,[89] is located outside the entrance to the monastery.[90]

In later medieval Ireland, pilgrims could stay at hospitals and inns, usually located near or in urban centres. While hospitals initially catered for the sick as well as pilgrims, over time the emphasis shifted to the sick. Even in earlier centuries, the distinction between a guesthouse to care for travellers visiting the monastery and a hospital to care for the sick was often blurred, and in early medieval Ireland, the same building could fulfil both functions.[91]. Unfortunately, Irish hospitals and inns have attracted little historical or archaeological attention, so we know very little about them. Hospitals seem to be located at places that were easily accessible to travellers: on the edge of towns or outside their walls, alongside main roads or at bridging points of rivers and at ports.

Irish Pilgrim Journeys in Medieval Literature

Lough Derg: The Pilgrim Route to St Patrick's Purgatory

St Patrick's Purgatory, in Lough Derg, Co. Donegal, is the only Irish pilgrimage site with a significant literature relating to the pilgrimage. There are 29 literary accounts written by foreign pilgrims who travelled to St Patrick's Purgatory at Lough Derg between the years 1185 and 1517. Irish people also made a pilgrimage to this site, but unfortunately there are no detailed accounts of their experiences or the routes taken to the island. The European pilgrims came from a wide geographical area, including modern-day France, Hungary, Germany, Catalonia, Italy, Switzerland, the Netherlands and England. They were all young men from the upper echelons of society, who were attracted to St Patrick's Purgatory by the penitential nature of the pilgrimage.[92] The style of the surviving foreign accounts are more literary works, than historical accounts, with a focus on the experience at the cave and the horrors of Purgatory. However, when considered as a group, they provide some insight into the routes travelled by the pilgrims to Lough Derg.

The pilgrimages of all foreigners follow roughly the same pattern. On arrival in Ireland they first sought out the Archbishop of Armagh, in whose archdiocese St Patrick's Purgatory was located. They then travelled to Lough Derg. In some cases, they sought the Bishop of Clogher prior to arriving at the lake. Having arrived at Lough Derg, they entered the Augustinian Priory on Saints Island, where they asked the prior's permission to complete pilgrimage to St Patrick's Purgatory, located on Station Island. The community of Augustinian Canons on Saints Island were guardians of St Patrick's Purgatory, so permission from the prior was essential. Once permission had been granted, the men performed appropriate rituals and entered the cave. They then returned to the east coast of Ireland and arranged passage on a ship to take them home.

The journey of the pilgrims from the point at which they set foot on Irish soil until their arrival at Lough Derg is largely ignored. However, a handful of the accounts contain details that allow us to construct a general route to the island.

Route taken by the pilgrim Laurence Rathold of Pászthó to and from St Patrick's Purgatory. Created by Richard Clutterbuck

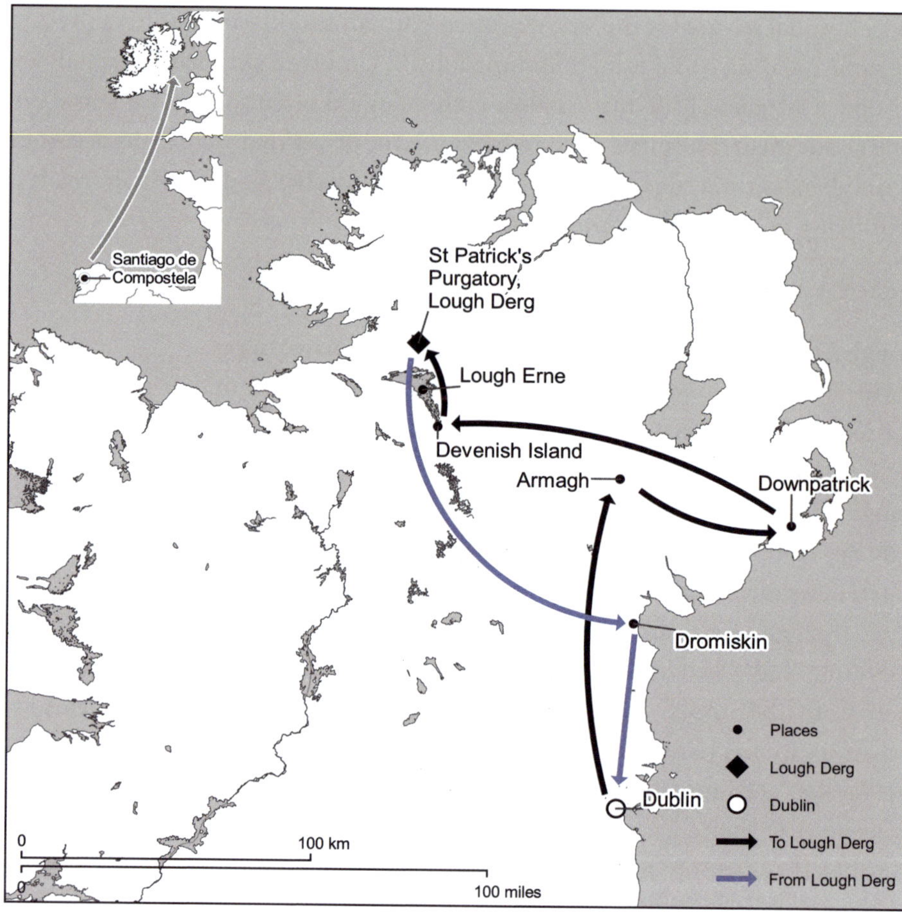

All foreign pilgrims landed on the east coast of Ireland – either at the port of Dublin or Drogheda. In 1411, Laurence Rathold of Pászthó, a Hungarian knight, arrived in Dublin in late summer, having just completed a pilgrimage to Santiago de Compostela.[93] He had probably sailed directly from La Coruña to Dublin, perhaps on one of the many Irish ships that sailed regularly between the two places. Laurence was a high-ranking retainer of Sigismund, King of Hungary and Holy Roman Emperor. As befitting his station, he was accompanied by his herald and a retinue of servants.[94] The hostel of St James, near the quayside, would have made a convenient place to rest after the journey but it may not have been grand enough for his tastes. His account does not say where he stayed when in Dublin, but we know that in 1398 the Catalan pilgrim and aristocrat Ramon de Perellós was entertained by the Earl of March.

Laurence Rathold began his Irish pilgrimage with a visit to Christ Church Cathedral, where he visited the relic known as the Bachall Íosa. He then presented his letter of safe conduct to the mayor and his bailiffs, the official representatives of the citizens of Dublin.[95] Laurence then left Dublin with his followers and set out to find the Archbishop of Armagh, Nicholas Fleming. He hoped to present Fleming with a letter from King Sigismund requesting, on his behalf, safe conduct and admittance to the Purgatory cave.[96] His party was joined by Italian banker Antonio Mannini, who had been resident in Ireland for three years. A letter written by Mannini to a friend at a later date suggests that Rathold's party did not leave Dublin until late September, a month after he first arrived.[97]

Having tracked down the Archbishop, he presented him with his letter of safe conduct, which was promptly entered in the register at Armagh.[98] It began with Sigismund listing his credentials and titles, before announcing that:

> ... Laurence Ratholdi of Pastoch, master of the seneschals (dapiferorum) and supreme dispenser, of noble descent, brought up from childhood in his royal court, proposes to visit the shrine (limina) of St James in Compostela and the Purgatory of St Patrick in Ireland, and to wander through various regions in search of military adventure. Desire for him and his company a favourable reception and free passage without payment of tribute or other extraction.[99]

Archbishop Fleming granted permission for Rathold to complete the pilgrimage and presented him with another letter of safe conduct.[100] From Armagh, the group made a detour to Downpatrick, where they spent several days in prayer and fasting before the relics of SS Brigit, Patrick and Colmcille. Downpatrick was a customary stop for many of the foreign pilgrims en route to Lough Derg.[101] From Downpatrick, Rathold and his party headed west to Lough Derg. No details are given for this part of the journey, but he probably travelled through modern-day Co. Fermanagh via Lough Erne. The group may have stopped along the way at other holy places such as Devenish Abbey – the burial place of St Molaise and an important pilgrimage destination. Having completed the pilgrimage, the group travelled back to the east coast. Laurence again sought out Archbishop Fleming, who was at the time staying at his manor at Dromiskin, in Louth. He presented him with a letter confirming completion of the pilgrimage. The group seems to have spent Christmas with the Archbishop – hospitality unlikely to be extended to those of a lesser station. The pilgrimage had taken three and a half months to complete. Rathold spent a further four to six weeks in Dublin waiting to secure passage on a ship to take him to England.[102]

The account of the pilgrimage of Catalan pilgrim Ramon de Perellós is also of interest, as it provides details of his journey from Paris through England and Wales, as well as through Ireland. He had arrived in Ireland in 1398, having set out from Avignon via the French court in Paris, carrying with him a letter of safe conduct from Pope Benedict.[103]

In Paris, the king provided him with additional letters of recommendation to be presented to the King of England. We are told little about his journey to Ireland but some of the places he mentions provide a general overview of the route taken. From Paris, he travelled 'by daily stages' to Calais, where he took a ship to England, presumably landing in Dover and making his way to London, 'passing by St Thomas of Canterbury'. In London, he sought out the King and, 'on account of the letters of the King of France which [he] brought [he] was very well received'.[104] He spent 10 days at court.[105] The King provided him with a guide for the next stage in his journey and they set out, arriving at Chester

> after several days' journey in a district called Cheshire, which is on the border of Wales; I arrived at the city of Chester, and there I hired a ship to pass into Ireland; and in this I went along the coast of Wales; I reached a place called Holyhead.[106]

From Chester they traveled to Holyhead, where he set sail 'and crossed the deep' towards Ireland, stopping at the Isle of Man before finally arriving in Dublin.[107]

His status afforded him consideration and care while in Ireland that would not have been shown to pilgrims of lesser social standing. In Dublin, he was entertained by the Earl of March, a cousin to King Richard of England. The earl even gave Perellós the use of horses and two squires, one named John Talbot, who spoke Irish and acted as an interpreter. He also covered the costs accrued.[108]

As was customary, the group set out to meet with the Archbishop of Armagh, who was at the time in Drogheda. He presented 'the letters of the king and queen of England and of the Earl of March,' and with reluctance the archbishop granted permission to continue to Lough Derg, but not before warning of the dangers of the Purgatory cave and also of the Irish whose territories the party had to travel through. Having made a confession to the Archbishop, he set forth to find Lord Niall Mór O'Neill of Tyrone, whose territories he needed to travel through. O'Neill was at Armagh and the pilgrim received hospitality there and even spent Christmas with him.

> … the king who received me well in their fashion and sent me a gift of food, that is to say beef because they neither eat bread nor drink wine, because they have none; but they drink water and the great lords drink milk for their nobility and some drink meat broth.[109]

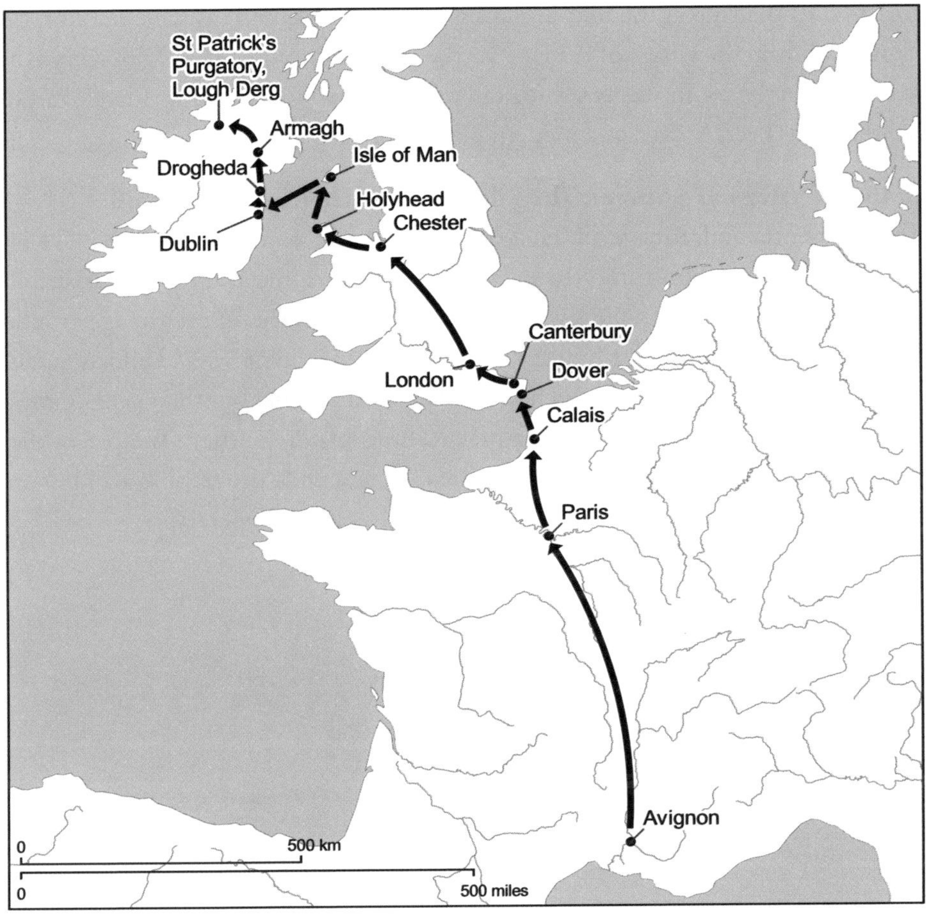

Route taken by Catalan pilgrim Ramon de Perellós to and from St Patrick's Purgatory.
Created by Richard Clutterbuck

After Christmas, Ramon departed on horseback 'and followed the road for several days', on to a place called La Pross[es]iho, probably Termon Magrath, Co. Donegal. From here, we are told he travelled on foot to the Purgatory, most likely following the route of an old road known as the Saints Road.[110]

The Belgian pilgrim Ghillebert de Lannoy arrived in the port town of Drogheda in 1430, via Scotland. Having gained an audience with the Archbishop of Armagh, who was at the time resident at Termonfeckin, Co. Louth, he travelled along a route that took him through the towns of Kells and Cavan, before passing the 'little churches and abbeys' of Lough Erne.[111] All the pilgrims, whether Irish or European, would have approached the final stage of their pilgrimage along the old road. Physical traces of this stage of the journey survived until recent times as a track known locally as the Saints Road. The Saints Road was first mentioned in historical sources in the 19th century, but it was at that time an old structure. Until the afforestation of this area around the lake in the mid-20th century, the road could easily be traced for 8 kilometres from the village of Pettiago via the Portneillinmore hill to Portcreevy Bay, to a point on the south-western shore of Lough Derg, opposite Saints Island. Part of the route has been revived as a modern pilgrim path.[112]

In the Footsteps of a Sinner: The Pilgrimage of Heneas MacNichaill

The penitential pilgrimage of Heneas MacNichaill, completed in 1543/1544, presents another opportunity to partially reconstruct the route of an Irish pilgrimage.[113] MacNichaill's pilgrimage took him to 19 places of pilgrimage around Ireland as a punishment for murdering his son (see Chapter 3).[114] Unfortunately, we do not know the order in which these places were visited but their geographical locations give some insight into the practicalities of the journey. The places that make up MacNichaill's pilgrimage are spread over a wide geographic area but are clustered in the north-east and north-west and in south Tipperary.

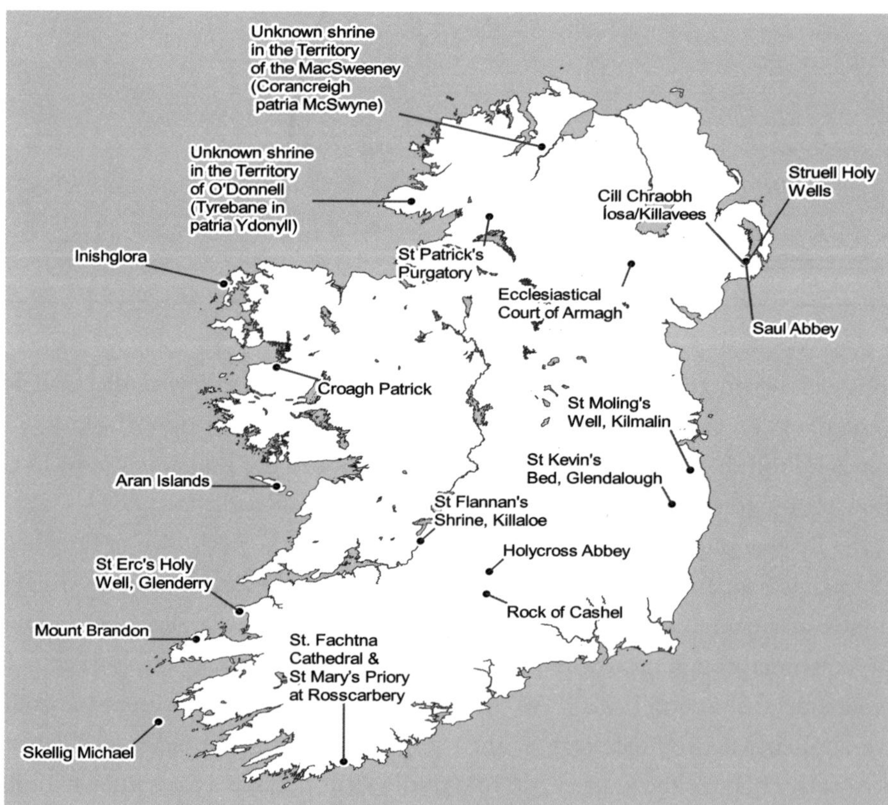

Pilgrim sites visited by Heneas MacNichaill during his penitential pilgrimage. Created by Richard Clutterbuck created by Richard Clutterbuck.

Pilgrim destinations relating to the pilgrimage of Heneas MacNichaill, as listed in Armagh Ecclesiastical Court Records

1	Struhmolyn in Reghterlaegen in Patria Kewan (or Rewan?)	St Moling's well, in the townland of Kilmalin, Powerscourt Demesne, Co. Wicklow
2	Lectum Cayn in Glendalough	St Kevin's Cave, Glendalough, Co. Wicklow
3	Rosse Hyllery O Garbre in patria McCarbre Rewa, principale hic ut dicit	Rosscarbery, Co. Cork
4	Skellig Meghyll in patria McCathiremore	Skellig Michael, Co. Kerry
5	Arayn Nenaw	Aran Island, Co. Galway
6	Cruake Brenan in patria militis Kerray	Cnoc Bréanainn/Mount Brandon, Co. Kerry.
7	Sanctorum Flanani	St Flannan's Shrine in Killaloe, Co. Clare
8	McEdeaga in Momonia	St Erc's Holy well, Glenderry, Ballyheigue, Co. Kerry
9	Collum Sti. Patricii in Conacia in patria Ymaille	Croagh Patrick, Co. Mayo
10	Purgatorium Sti Patricii apud Loughdirge in patria Ydonyll	St Patrick's Purgatory, Lough Derg, Co. Donegal
11	Enysskworym StGworain Anmerrys Downyll in Conacia	Inishglora, Co. Mayo
12	Corancreigh in patria McSwyne	Unknown pilgrim site in Donegal, in the territory of the MacSwine
13	Tyrebane in patria Ydonyll	Unknown pilgrim site in Donegal, in the land of the O'Donnell
14	Sanctum Crucem apud Woghterlawan in patria Comitis Ormond	Holycross Abbey, Co. Tipperary
15	Carrek Caissill	The Rock of Cashel
16	Dwyne	Downpatrick
17	Sawyll	Saul, Co. Down
18	Craen Yssa (or Crave Yssa)	Cill Chraobh Íosa ' Church of the branch/ tree of Jesus' , at Killavees, Co. Down
19	Strwyll	Struell Holy Wells, Co. Down

View of medieval ecclesiastical ruins at the Rock of Cashel, Co. Tipperary.
© Louise Nugent

Two of the pilgrim destinations are in modern-day Co. Wicklow – St Moling's Well, now in the Powerscourt Demesne[115] and the cave, known as St Kevin's Bed, at the great monastery of Glendalough. Two of the places are in Co. Tipperary – Holycross Abbey and the nearby Rock of Cashel. A cluster of four destinations is found in Co. Down – Downpatrick Cathedral, Saul Abbey, the church of Killavees and the holy wells of Struell. Three more are found in modern-day Co. Donegal, but only St Patrick's Purgatory, now Station Island in Lough Derg, can be identified with certainty. Of the two unidentified destinations, Tyrebane may have been located in Tír Baoighill, now the Barony of Banagh in south-west Donegal, an area of many important pilgrim destinations such as Inishkeel and Glencolmcille. The other was somewhere in territory of the Mac Sweeneys. The list also included St Flannan's Shrine at Killaloe, Co. Clare, home to the relics of St Flannan.

The other destinations are all located in coastal areas along the west coast of Ireland and include the islands of Skellig Michael, Co. Kerry, the Aran Islands, Co. Galway, and Inishglora, Co. Mayo, as well as the mountain-top pilgrimages of Croagh Patrick, Co. Mayo, and Mount Brandon, Co. Kerry.

Rosscarbery, in West Cork, known in medieval times as *Ros Ailithir,* the home of St Fachtna's Cathedral and St Mary's Benedictine Priory, was close the coast, as was the holy well of McEdeaga in Munster. The well probably St Erc's holy well, is found at Glenderry, in Ballyheigue, Co. Kerry, and overlooks the Kerry coastline.[116] Although the places assigned to Mac Nichaill cover a wide geographical footprint, there is a marked absence in the list of sites in the midlands of Ireland.

St Fachtna's Cathedral Roscarbery, Co. Cork.
© Louise Nugent

It is clear that MacNichaill had to travel by land and water. If the pilgrimage was organised in a practical manner, we can assume any clusters of sites were visited together. Given the serious nature of his crime – murder – he may very well have walked on foot, even barefoot, for large parts, or all, of the land journey.

St Flannan's shrine at Killaloe could be approached by land routes but it was also located on the River Shannon and the edge of Lough Derg, Co. Clare, waterways that were part of a regional travel network. The pilgrim had to travel by boat to get to the island pilgrim sites. The coastal sites of Croagh Patrick and Mount Brandon could be easily accessed by both land and sea and Rosscarbery overlooks an estuary providing easy access to the sea.

MacNichaill must have made use of existing shipping routes along the west coast, as well as local fishing boats to travel from location to location. Due to their manoeuvrability in choppy waters, medieval leather-covered curraghs would have been the most suitable vessels for travelling to island pilgrim sites, some of which were difficult

Skellig Michael, Co. Kerry. © National Monuments Service, Department of Culture, Heritage, and the Gaeltacht.

to land on.[117] Access to the islands would have been weather dependent: in normal weather conditions, travellers had little difficulty landing on the islands of Aran or Skellig Michael. This was not the case with the island of Inishglora, a very low-lying island, swept by large seas, which made landing difficult, even in good weather.[118] Local knowledge would have been essential for safe landing.

In keeping with the nature of his pilgrimage, a significant number of the places on the list are penitential, such as St Kevin's Bed, St Patrick's Purgatory, Croagh Patrick, Mount Brandon and the island sites. St Patrick's Purgatory allowed the pilgrims to confront their sins and the punishments due in the afterlife for these crimes, through a mental pilgrimage to Purgatory. At the holy wells of Struell, pilgrims engaged in penitential bathing to cleanse their sins. Island pilgrim sites were set apart from the mainland in more ways than one and had layers of meaning and symbolism for the medieval mind. Some islands were seen as deserted places, the equivalent of desert, which is why many eremitic monastic sites were located on them. They were also seen as staging posts between this world and the next – ' intermediate stations on the way to the supreme glory in Paradise' .[119] The physical act of getting on a boat and leaving the mainland gave the pilgrim a feeling of stepping out of the normal world.

MacNichaill's pilgrimage also included pilgrimage destinations based around relics. The relic of the True Cross at Holycross Abbey attracted pilgrims from all over Munster. The True Cross was the most potent symbol of the Christian faith and of the sacrifice of Christ. Gazing upon this relic may have brought some hope of redemption for MacNichaill.

A second relic of the True Cross may have been kept at the church of the Killavees, Co. Down. Killavees was known in historical records as Craobh Íosa, the ' branch/tree of Jesus' , although it is possible that the name may also relate to a holy tree that no longer survives.[120] Killaloe possessed the relics and bones of its patron St Flannan, the patron saint of the Diocese of Killaloe, who might be persuaded through prayer to act as an intercessor. Cashel, the seat of the Archbishop of Cashel and Emly, must have had its own extensive collection of relics, although apart from MacNichaill's account, there is no record of any other medieval pilgrimages to this place or to its relics.

Relic of the True Cross at Holycross Abbey, Co. Tipperary.

Downpatrick claimed to have the corporeal relics of SS Patrick, Brigit and Colmcille during this period and was a secondary pilgrimage stop for many pilgrims heading to Lough Derg.

It is possible that MacNichaill came here and visited the sites of Struell, Saul and Killavees before continuing on to St Patrick's Purgatory at Lough Derg and the other Donegal sites. As MacNichaill's penance was prescribed by the dean of the Augustinian foundation at Armagh, it is not surprising that a large proportion of the places on the list relate to St Patrick or are associated with the Augustinian canons. St Patrick's Purgatory, Croagh Patrick, Downpatrick, Saul and Struell were all places where St Patrick was said to have spent time either in prayer or fasting. From the 12th century, the Rock of Cashel was known as St Patrick's Rock, and was said to be the spot where the saint baptised the first Christian ruler of Ireland. Inishglora and Mount Brandon are connected with St Brendan. He was also connected to the place called McEdeaga, now known as St Ercc's holy well at Glenderry, Co. Kerry. The well and a nearby medieval church are dedicated to St Erc, who baptised St Brendan.[121]

The Augustinian canons are associated with a large portion of the 16 sites that we can identify with certainty. They had foundations at Glendalough and Saul. The island sanctuaries of Skellig Michael, Co. Kerry, and Inishglora, near Erris, Co. Mayo, were also in the care of the canons.[122] Both originated as early medieval eremitic foundations, whose communities had transferred to the mainland by the 12th century, when they became Augustinian foundations. Skellig Michael was dedicated to St Michael the Archangel and was controlled by the Augustinian

Modern cathedral at Downpatrick, built on site of medieval cathedral and pilgrim site. © Louise Nugent

priory at Ballinskelligs, Co. Kerry. Inishglora was administered by the canons of Cross Abbey, Co. Mayo.[123] In both cases the communities fulfilled a role similar to that of their confrères at Aughris Priory and Inishmurray, acting as caretakers and controlling pilgrims' access to the sites. The islands of Aran had several ecclesiastical sites associated with different saints, particularly St Enda.

By the 12th century, the communities of Skellig Michael and Inishglora, which began as eremitic foundations, had moved to the mainland at Ballinskelligs and Cross Abbey and became Augustinian foundations. Even after the move to the mainland both communities controlled the access of pilgrims to the two islands. The church of Killavees[124] was under the control of the Priory of St Thomas the Martyr, otherwise called the Priory of Toberglorie (the Spring of Glory), a Augustinian priory of regular canons. This monastery was located around 3 kilometres north of Grangicam, on the south-east side of Downpatrick town.[125] While many of the sites had Augustinian links, not all of them did. Downpatrick Cathedral was a Benedictine establishment. There was also a Benedictine priory at Rosscarbery and Holycross Abbey was a Cistercian foundation.

MacNichaill must have spent at least a few days at each pilgrim site. He may have undertaken some rituals barefoot and fasting. At each shrine he would have asked for letters of proof of completion of pilgrimage, to be presented at Armagh at the end of his arduous journey. One wonders how he was received and treated by other pilgrims and the keepers of the shrines he visited. Did his crime weigh heavy on his mind as he made his journey around Ireland? Perhaps he found relief in the hardships of his penance and was genuinely trying to atone for his crime. Unfortunately, we know nothing else about this man as, having completed his pilgrimage, he disappeared from historical sources.

Uncovering Our Pilgrim Past: The Archaeology of Irish Pilgrim Routes

We know from the historical sources and archaeological excavations that an infrastructure for travel existed in early and late medieval Ireland. Many important pilgrim destinations at early monasteries like Clonmacnoise and Glendalough, or in medieval towns like Trim and Dublin, were connected to networks of roads and navigable waterways. We are fortunate that the physical remains of several medieval routes and roads connected with pilgrimages survive in the modern Irish landscape. The better-known examples include St Kevin's road, leading to Glendalough, Co. Wicklow, the Tóchar Phádraig, to Croagh Patrick and the Saint's Road, to Mount Brandon. Some have been incorporated into, or inspired, modern walking routes such as the Pilgrim Paths initiative.[126] Prior to the 1700s, Irish roads are seldom mentioned in historical sources or marked on early maps, unless connected with events such as cattle raids, war parties or in land grants or boundary descriptions.[127] Before the 18th century, roads were depicted only in a sporadic manner, and when they do feature on 16th- and 17th-century maps, those noted are predominantly connected to military activity.[128] Knowledge of Irish pilgrim roads has survived only because stretches of their routes were recorded on maps and in local histories in the 19th century or survived in folklore memory. When combined, 19th-century sources and surviving physical remains and folklore allow us to recreate the general route of these roads, but the more local details for much of the routes are now lost.

Tóchar Phádraig – Pilgrim Route to Croagh Patrick

Croagh Patrick, overlooking Clew Bay, is one of modern Ireland's most iconic pilgrim destinations, with tens of thousands of pilgrims climbing to the summit each year on the last Sunday in July. The mountain has been a focus of pilgrimage from prehistoric times, with Christian pilgrimage taking place from at least the 10th century.

There are several routes to the summit of this holy mountain, folklore suggests two are associated with medieval pilgrimage. The first, the northern approach, is a path created by generations of feet, called the Casán Phádraig (Patrick's Path). It is used still by most modern pilgrims and tourists who climb to the summit. The second route, the eastern approach, travels along a more complex route known as the Tóchar Phádraig (Patrick's Causeway).

Casán Phádraig – the Northern Approach

The Casán stretches for 3.55 kilometres from the ruins of Murrisk Friary, at the edge of Clew Bay, to the mountain summit. Murrisk, an Augustinian friary, was founded in the year 1456 by Hugh O'Malley and played a key role in the pilgrimage from this time. In medieval times, maritime pilgrims from outside the local area could arrive in Clew Bay by boat and many took the Casán to the mountain summit. From the mid-5th century, the Casán may have been the preferred route of maritime pilgrims and those coming from the west and north. Murrisk Friary was known as Mons S. Patrittii, Chruach Padruig or the Monastery of St Patrick at Croagh Patrick. From the time of its foundation, it was an integral part of the pilgrimage to the summit. Indeed, the choice of its location may have been influenced by the existing Casán. The friary would have been a place of prayer for pilgrims prior to their ascent and decent. They would have come to pray before relics of St Patrick, kept in the friary church. Long after the friary's suppression, it was common for 19th-century pilgrims to pray at Murrisk before making their ascent. The friary's relics included the Black Bell of St Patrick, used in the pilgrimage rituals on the summit until the 1800s. Unfortunately, we cannot know if the bell was used in early pilgrim rituals.[129]

Modern statue of St Patrick at base of Croagh Patrick, Co Mayo. © Louise Nugent

The experiences of medieval and modern pilgrims on the Casán are relatively similar. While the clothing of the pilgrims has changed over the centuries, the physical experience of the climb has remained relatively unaltered. The Casán climbs steadily from the base of the mountain until it reaches the mountain's distinctive cone-shaped top.

The ground underfoot changes and becomes more challenging as the gradient increases sharply and the path deteriorates into moving scree. A 19th-century penitential cairn, the Leacht Mionnáin,[130] marks the base of the cone and the beginning of the more challenging ascent. The final stage is particularly gruelling, as the stony scree moves constantly underfoot – conditions that each year give rise to sprained limbs and broken bones. The unpredictable weather conditions can occasionally put climbers at risk of heat stroke or hypothermia, depending on the time

Murrisk Friary with Croagh Patrick in background. © Louise Nugent

Modern pilgrims walking the Casán Phádraig at Croagh Patrick. © Louise Nugent

of year. Despite its perils, Mayo Mountain Rescue notes that only a few pilgrims have died trying to reach the summit. In recent years, the mountain has been put at risk with severe damage from erosion caused by the ever-increasing numbers of pilgrims and tourists, and the sports enthusiasts who run up the mountain.

On the Trail of St Patrick – Walking the Tóchar Phádraig

Pilgrims travelling to Croagh Patrick from the east followed the Tóchar Phádraig.[131] Today the road can be traced for around 35 kilometres from Ballintubber Abbey up the side of Croagh Patrick to the point at which it merges with the Casán Phádraig, close to Leacht Mionnáin. Folklore suggests that the road may have extended further east to the great pilgrim site of Balla, also in Co. Mayo.

Much of what we know about Tóchar comes from folklore and the first edition Ordnance Survey 6-inch map of Mayo created in 1839, that records significant sections of the route, many of which are no longer identifiable on the ground.

The route of the Tóchar Phádraig, as it is known today, travels through areas of marsh and bog, modern pastures and pockets of trees. We can assume that the medieval pilgrim travelled through a less enclosed landscape with larger pockets of trees.

It is difficult accurately to determine the true age of the Tóchar, due to lack of excavation and historical sources, but parts of it may have been established before the Christian pilgrimage came into its own. Monuments in proximity to the route of the road are of early and late medieval date, with some dating back further to prehistory. The presence of prehistoric monuments known as standing stones suggest that parts

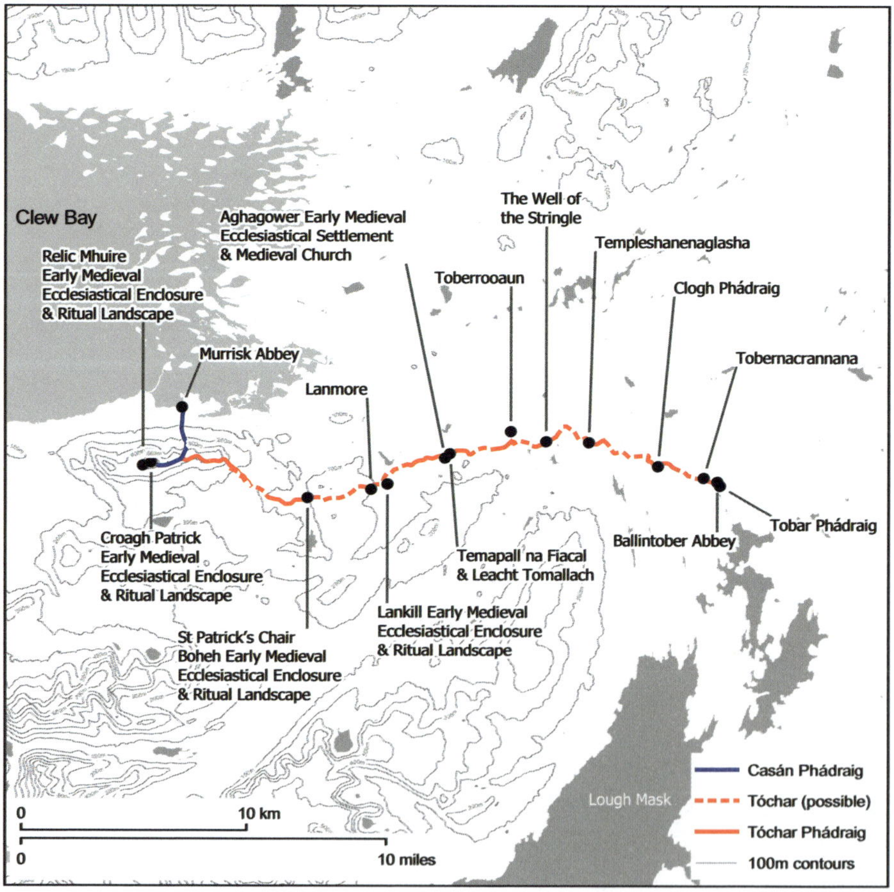

Map of the route of the Casán Phádraig and the Tóchar Phádraig. Created by Richard Clutterbuck

of the Tóchar's route at Lankill and Boheh date to the Bronze Age,[132] while the road's proximity to early medieval monuments like holy wells, ring forts and ecclesiastical sites suggest that it was in use in early medieval times. The continued investment in religious monuments on nodal points on its routes, such as the Augustinian Abbey at Ballintubber and the church at Aghagower suggest a continued use of the road in later centuries. The Tóchar appears to have fallen out of use in the late 18th to 19th centuries, as new and better roads were built in the area.

From what we know of other medieval roads, paving and more complex construction were probably confined to small sections of the route such as marshy wet

View of the merging of the Casán Phádraig and Tóchar Phádraig from the summit of Croagh Patrick.
© Louise Nugent

Ballintubber Abbey, Co. Mayo, the traditional starting point of the Tóchar Phádraig.
© Louise Nugent

View of Tóchar Phadraig as it leaves Ballintubber Abbey. © Louise Nugent

areas[133] and approaches to important settlements. The rest of the road probably had a more informal construction. Today the route of the Tóchar Phádraig can be traced running across fields, alongside field and townland boundaries, under sections of grassy lanes and in modern tarmacked roads. Paved sections can still be seen in upland and boggy areas.

When the road arrives at the base of Croagh Patrick, it becomes a mountain track that zigzags to the summit before merging with the Casán Phádraig at the penitential cairn Leacht Mionnáin. For the medieval pilgrim, the most challenging parts of this route were the boggy areas and river crossing. Throughout its course, the Tóchar crosses four rivers: the Claureen, the Aille, the Camoge and the Ownee. During the summer months, the Clareen is shallow and can be crossed by foot, but care would have been needed in the winter and in times of flood, when its water were faster and deeper. Today the Tóchar is carried over the Claureen by a series of stepping stones of unknown date. [134] The exact crossing point used by medieval pilgrims at the Aille, Camoge or Ownee Rivers is uncertain. The waters of the Aille are fast-flowing and the area is prone to flooding, so crossing without a bridging point would have been very challenging.

The medieval pilgrims who walked the Tóchar were a mix of people who lived alongside or close to the road and those who had travelled from other parts of Ireland, along with the occasional foreigner. The needs of local people were few: those who lived near its furthest point could, as 19th-century pilgrims did, walk from Ballintubber to the summit of Croagh Patrick in a day, making their pilgrimage and returning home the following day.

Pilgrims from outside the hinterland of Croagh Patrick needed shelter and food and the bulk of the work of caring for pilgrims was carried out by the Church. However, some may have found shelter at one of the many ringforts and habitation sites found along the route of the road.

The road as we know it today begins at Ballintubber Abbey. The abbey was run by Augustinians and was founded in 1216, on the site of an earlier monastery, by

A. Tóchar Phádraig as a grassy trackway in Boheh townland. © Louise Nugent

B. Tóchar Phádraig as a paved path in the townland of Boheh. © Louise Nugent

C. A paved section of the Tóchar in Pollawaddy. © Louise Nugent

Tóchar it approaches the summit of Croagh Patrick. © Louise Nugent

Tóchar Phádraig as it crosses the Claureen River.
© Louise Nugent

Cathal Crovderg O'Connor, the King of Connacht. From an early date, land at and around the abbey had a connection with St Patrick, who was said to have blessed a well and founded a church here during his mission. A small building that has undergone much restoration and rebuilding in the grounds of the abbey was pointed out by antiquarians as being the original church founded by the saint. The blessed well that gave its name to the townland is likely one of two holy wells associated with the saint in the vicinity of the abbey: one is found in the grounds of the abbey and the other is 150 metres to the south-east of the abbey church. The latter is known today as Tobermore, but was marked on the first edition of the Ordnance Survey map as Tobar Patrick. The importance of the well to pilgrims is suggested by how the abbey is known –*Monasterium Sanctae Trinitatis de villa fontis Patricii* – the Monastery of the Holy Trinity of the town of St Patrick's Well.

Any early medieval pilgrims who travelled along the Tóchar would surely have visited the holy well and early monastery. The well continued to be important to later medieval pilgrims who came to pray and find shelter at the Augustinian abbey. Pilgrims would have offered prayers at the abbey church and attended liturgical celebrations and listened to stirring sermons about penance and St Patrick. The abbey church originally had a cruciform plan with a low tower over the crossing, defining the junction between the open un-aisled nave and the chancel and choir. They may also have spent time in the chapels in the east transept.

As modern pilgrims leave the abbey grounds, they pass what appear to be the ruins of a structure. Known as Dancora, or Dabhach an Chóra – the bath of the righteous – it has been suggested that it was a bathing area for pilgrims. However, it has the appearance of the foundations of a building rather than a type of well or bath.

A short distance from the abbey, pilgrims passed by a holy well in Skehanagh, a townland known as Tobar na Cannuána or the Well of the Canons. It is a small spring enclosed by a stone wall and is said to have a cure for eye disease. Unfortunately, we don't know if the well had a significance for medieval pilgrims, but it was visited by pilgrims into the mid-20th century.

Leaving the abbey, the pilgrims headed west. Over the course of their journey, they would have passed several religious sites, churches, wells and stones that were associated with the pilgrimage, at least for a short period of time.

Shortly after crossing the Claureen River, the pilgrims passed a holy stone at Derrynacanna. Modern pilgrims will find the stone beside the field boundary marked by a small plaque. Originally, the stone, known as Clog Phádraig or St Patrick's Chair, was found on the north side of a paved section of the Tóchar Phádraig. It was moved to its current located after the road was destroyed during land reclamation.

Structure known as Dancora or Dabhach an Chóra – the bath of the righteous – at Ballintubber Abbey. © Louise Nugent.

It is possible that the stone's association with the road may date to medieval times but we cannot be sure. It certainly had a great significance for more modern pilgrims in the 19th and early 20th centuries.

The next religious site encountered by pilgrims is the ruin of a small church at Templeshaunaglasha/Teampal Seán na Glasha in the townland of Bellaburke.

Little is known about the history of the church and it seems to have no direct association with St Patrick, but it appears to date to the later medieval period. It is possible that it may have provided shelter for the weary traveller.

Continuing on an eastward course, as the pilgrims approached the mid-point of their journey, they moved through a landscape layered with the folklore and

Structure known as Dancora or Dabhach an Chóra – the bath of the righteous at Ballintubber Abbey. © Louise Nugent.

Tobar na Cannúana – the well of the Canons – Co. Mayo. © Louise Nugent.

connections to their beloved saint. In the townland of Toberoàun, the road passes close to a holy well dedicated to Rodan, a disciple of Patrick. Further west in the townland of Gorteen, the road passes a small slab-and-concrete structure called the Leacht Tomaltach. According to folklore, it marked the grave of Tomaltach who, following an altercation with St Patrick, fell from his horse and died. Less than 400 metres to the south-west, the Tóchar took pilgrims past a church known as Teampall na BhFiacal. Today, all that remains are the footings of a small rectangular building. The church was said to be part of a convent built for Mathana,

View of the former location of the Clogh Phádraig and Tóchar Phádraig in Derrynacranna. During land improvements the road was destroyed and the stone moved to its current location beside a nearby field wall.
© Louise Nugent

The Clogh Phádraig in a secondary location at Derrynacranna, Co. Mayo.
© Louise Nugent.

Templeshaunagliasha/Temple Seán na Glasha, Co. Mayo.
© Louise Nugent.

Aghagower round tower and medieval church.
© Louise Nugent

the daughter of Senach, the abbot of nearby Aghagower monastery and a contemporary of St Patrick. The name Teampall na BhFiacal, or church of the tooth, suggests that a relic of a tooth – perhaps even one thought to have belonged to St Patrick – was once venerated there. If so, it would have attracted pilgrims to stop and pray here.

The monastery of Aghagower, only a short distance to the south-east, was a mid-point on the Tóchar. Today it sits at the centre of a small village of the same name. Aghagower, or field of the spring, was said to have been founded by St Patrick in the 5th century, during the saint's missionary work in Mayo. He gave the monastery to St Senach before continuing westwards, evangelising the locals. Aghagower went on to become a wealthy and important monastery and was a pilgrim site. It controlled the pilgrimage at Croagh Patrick well into late medieval period and continued to be a place of pilgrimage until the 19th century, when pilgrims stopped here en route to the holy mountain.[135] Aghagower provided medieval pilgrims with a place to rest and recharge, as well as acting as an additional place of pilgrimage, having several landscape relics in its grounds.

Leaba Phádraig – St Patrick's Bed – Aghagower monastery. © Louise Nugent

The modern visitor will find the ruins of a round tower, a late medieval church, a penitential cairn known as the Leaba Phádraig (St Patrick's Bed), where the saint is reputed to have slept, and two large holy wells. The wells – Tobar na nDeochaun (The well of the deacons) and the Dabhach Phádraig (St Patrick's Bath) – are surrounded by stone enclosures, with steps leading to the interiors. Both are now dry. The monastery's close links to Croagh Patrick in later centuries are clearly seen in an indulgence granted in 1440 to pilgrims to Croagh Patrick. Part of the alms raised through the offerings of penitents were to be used for the upkeep of the church at Aghagower.[136]

As pilgrims – medieval and modern – left Aghagower, they continued on a westward course.

In the townland of Lankill, the road may have passed by the small, early medieval ecclesiastical enclosure with a large cross-inscribed pillar stone dedicated to St Brendan. Beside the enclosure is a holy well dedicated to St Brendan and a bullaun stone, both of which were visited locally up to the 20th century. It is possible that the church and enclosure may have provided some facilities to early medieval pilgrims but at present there is no way of knowing how long it was active. It was later used as a burial ground for unbaptised children.

Further dedications to Patrick are attached to several boulders and prehistoric stones, scattered along the Tóchar's route. Some of these stone may have functioned

Holy wells at Aghagower.
Top left and right: Tobar na nDeochaun.
Bottom Left and right: Dabahach Phádraig.
© Louise Nugent

St Patrick's Chair and site of prehistoric rock art at Boheh.
© Louise Nugent

The Tóchar Phádraig as it crosses heathland in Boheh. © Louise Nugent

as route markers, while others may have been places of devotion, where pilgrims might have stopped to pray; for example, 'Cloch Phádraig', a large boulder, in the townland of Derrynacanna. A similar boulder, now destroyed, called St Patrick's Chair, was located beside the road in the townland of Ballyhean. Several standing stones are situated close to or along the western end of the route. One of these stones in the townland of Lanmore is known as Clogh Phádraic and can be seen clearly from the Tóchar. Close to the eastern side of the Tóchar, as it heads through the townland of Boheh, is Patrick's Chair, a natural outcrop decorated with prehistoric rock art; and to the south another standing stone.[137]

It has been argued that the pillar stones at Lankill, Lanmore and Knappaghmanagh, together with the Boheh rock art, were prehistoric route markers for prehistoric pilgrims travelling to Croagh Patrick.[138] The dedication of these prehistoric stone to St Patrick in Christian times made them part of the Christian landscape.

Close to St Patrick's Chair in Boheh are the ruins of a small early medieval ecclesiastical enclosure. As at Lankill, it was also used as a children's burial ground. We know little of the history of the site and all that remain today are the footprints of a small structure, possibly a church, several early medieval cross slabs and a *leacht*. A holy well dedicated to St Patrick, now dry, is to be found beside the enclosure. It is difficult to know what role, if any, this church played in the medieval

View of Croagh Patrick from the Tóchar Phádraig at Boheh.
© Louise Nugent

View of Croagh Patrick in Boleybrian close to the route of the Tóchar.
© Louise Nugent

pilgrimage or for how long it was an active site, but it may have been able to offer pilgrims food and shelter at some point during the early medieval period.

For modern and medieval pilgrims, for much of the route the holy mountain Croagh Patrick is the dominant mark on the horizon and, as the pilgrims moved through this landscape, their final destination was never far from their minds.

NOTES

1 Brendan Smith, *Crisis and Survival in Late Medieval Ireland: The English of Louth and Their Neighbours, 1330–1450* (Oxford: Oxford University Press, 2013), 136.

2 Thomas Charles-Edwards, *Early Christian Ireland* (Cambridge: Cambridge University Press, 2000), 14.

3 Liam de Paor, 'The Early Historic Period: Monks and Traders,' in *Travel and Transport in Ireland*, ed. Kevin Nowlan (Dublin: Gill & Macmillan, 1973), 19; Maria Kelly, *A History of the Black Death in Ireland* (Gloucestershire: Tempus, 2001), 1–5.

4 Terry Barry, 'Transport and Communication in Medieval and Tudor Ireland,' in *Travel and Transport in Ireland*, ed. Kevin Nowlan (Dublin: Gill & Macmillan, 1973), 32–46.

5 de Paor, 'The Early Historic Period: Monks and Traders,' 20 (personal communication with Dr Rena Maguire).

6 de Paor, ' The Early Historic Period,' 20.

7 Davies, *Pilgrimage Yesterday*, 49.

8 Peter Yeoman, *Pilgrimage in Medieval Scotland* (London: Batsford, 1999), 110.

9 James Mills, ed., *The Account Roll of the Priory of the Holy Trinity, Dublin, 1337–1346* (Dublin: Four Courts Press, 1996), 93-94.

10 Fergus Kelly, *Early Irish Farming* (Dublin: The Institute for Advanced Studies, 1997), 391.

11 Kelly, *Early Irish Farming*, 391.

12 Linda Doran, 'Medieval Communication Routes Through Longford and Roscommon and Their Associated Settlements,' *PRIA* 104 no. 3 (2004): 69.

13 Kelly, *Early Irish Farming*, 391.

14 Kieran Jordan and Tom O'Connor, 'Archaeological Sites of Interest Surrounding the Turoe Stone,' *JGAHS* 55 (n.d.): 112–13.

15 Elizabeth FitzPatrick, 'On the Trail of the Ancient Highway: Rediscovering Dála's Road,' in *Lost and Found: Discovering Ireland's Past*, ed. Joe Fenwick (Dublin: Wordwell, 2003), 169.

16 Kelly, *Early Irish Farming*, 391.

17 Pádraig Ó Riain, 'Boundary Association in Early Irish Society,' *Studia Celtica* 7 (1972): 12–29.

18 Ó Riain, Boundary Association,' 23.

19 Jean Farrelly and Camin O' Brien, *Archaeological Inventory of County Tipperary/ Compiled by; Dúchas, The Heritage Service.* Vol. 1, North Tipperary, vol. 1 (Dublin: Stationary Office, 2002), 160.

20 Farrelly and O'Brien, Vol 1:160; Terry Barry, *The Archaeology of Medieval Ireland* (London: Routledge, 1987), 78–79.

21 Jordan and O'Connor, ' Archaeological Sites of Interest Surrounding the Turoe Stone,' 112–13. A short section of the road close to the site of Clonfert-Molua appears as a sunken hollow way about 1 metre below the modern field surface. See FitzPatrick, 'On the Trail,' 169.

22 Margaret Gowan, '1986: 41. Boherygeela (BGE). 'Ancient? Road/Trackway', Data Base of Excavation Reports, 1986.' http://www.excavations.ie/Pages/Details.php?-Year=&County=Limerick&id=3677. Accessed 18 April 2016.

23 Ed Lyne, 'Lives through Time,' *Archaeology Ireland* 22 (2008): 18–19. Other roads had paved or cobbled surfaces. Excavations at the medieval mass paths at Boherygeela revealed that the road was paved with a rough metalled surface. Other roads were paved or had cobbled surfaces. Excavations at the medieval Mass paths at Boherygeela revealed that the road was paved with a rough metalled surface. See Gowan, '1986:41. Boherygeela (BGE).'

24 Louise Nugent, 'St Kevin's Road: Relics of a Pilgrim Landscape in the Wicklow Mountains,' In *Archaeology, People, and Landscapes: Essays in Honor of Jenna Higgins*, ed. Thomas. Finan (Institute of European Archaeology Press: St. Louis, 2012), 186

25 Nugent, 'St Kevin's Road,' 186; Conor McDermott et al. 2006. Preliminary Site Investigation at St Kevin's Road Brockagh townland, Co. Wicklow. Unpublished Report.

26 Anna Brindley and Jan Lanting, 'Radiocarbon Dates for Irish Trackways,' *JIA* 9 (1998): 62. These types of routeways have a very high survival rate compared to other roads and tracks, as they are preserved under layers of peat and bog.

27 Brindley and Lanting, 'Radiocarbon Dates,' 45.

28 Brindley and Lanting, 'Radiocarbon Dates,' 59.

29 Thaddeus C. Breen et al., 'Excavation of a Roadway at Bloomhill Bog, County Offaly,' *PRIA* 88 (1988): 323.

30 Breen et al., 'Excavation of a Roadway,' 321, 323-327; Conor McDermott, 'A Paved Way In Bloomhill Bog in Counties Westmeath and Offaly,' in *Blackwater Survey and Excavations: Artefact Deterioration in Peat Lands, Lough More, Co. Mayo. Trans.*, ed. A Moloney, vol. 4 (Dublin: Crannóg Publications, 1995), 59–66.

31 Breen et al., 'Excavation of a Roadway,' 332; Elizabeth FitzPatrick and Camin O'Brien, *The Medieval Churches of County Offaly* (Dublin: Government of Ireland, 1998), 7.

32 A small causeway/road paved with large flat slabs connects the main ecclesiastical settlement with small oratory known as St Mella's cell.

33 Ellen O'Carroll, '1996:327. Lemanaghan Togher,' Database of Irish Excavation Reports, 1996. http://www.excavations.ie/Pages/Details.php?Year=&County=Offaly&id=215. Accessed 2 April 2015.

34 The earliest phase of construction produced a radiocarbon dates of AD 653 ± 9. This is a complex road and for a detailed discussion of its construction, see O' Carroll, '1996: 327. Lemanaghan Togher.'

35 O'Carroll, '1996: 327. Lemanaghan Togher.'

36 O'Carroll, '1996: 327. Lemanaghan Togher.'

37 McDermott, 'A Paved Way,' 65.

38 Peter O' Keeffe and Tom Simington, *Irish Stone Bridges. History and Heritage* (Dublin: Irish Academic Press, 1991), 24.

39 O'Keeffe and Simington, *Irish Stone Bridges*, 23–25.

40 Kelly, *Early Irish Farming*, 393.

41 Kelly, *Early Irish Farming* 393.

42 O'Keeffe and Simington, *Irish Stone Bridges*, 24.

43 John Bradley, 'Bridges,' in *Medieval Ireland: An Encyclopaedia*, ed. Séan Duffy (London: Routledge Press, 2005), 47; O'Keeffe and Simington, *Irish Stone Bridges*, 24–25.

44 Malcolm Fry, *Coití: Logboats from Northern Ireland* (Antrim: Greystone Press on behalf of the Environment and Heritage Service, Dept. of the Environment, 2000), 3–4.

45 Aidan O'Sullivan and Donal Boland, 'The Clonmacnoise Bridge: An Early Medieval River Crossing in County Offaly,' *Archaeology Ireland. Heritage Guide No. 11*, (Bray: Wordwell, 2000).

46 Patrick O' Leary, *St. Mullins Illustrated: A Local History and the Life of St. Moling* (Graig-na-Managh: s.n., 1913), 23.

47 Kelly, *Early Irish Farming*, 393; Bradley, 'Bridges,' 48; Doran, 'Medieval Communication Routes,' 68.

48 An eastwest running routeway, which followed the line of the Esker Riada from Dublin to Clarenbridge in Co. Galway.

49 O'Sullivan and Boland, 'The Clonmacnoisee Bridge'; Nugent, 'Pilgrimage in Medieval Ireland, AD 600–1600' (PhD thesis, University College Dublin, 2009), Vol. I, 187–88.

50 Sumption, *Pilgrimage*, 175–84.

51 Sumption, *Pilgrimage*, 179–84; Sarah Hopper, *Mothers, Mystics and Merrymakers*, 141–54.

52 Sumption, *Pilgrimage*, 180–84.

53 AU.

54 Colmán Etchingham, *Church Organisation in Ireland, A.D. 650 to 1000* (Maynooth: Laigin Publications, 1999), 205; Louise Nugent, 'Pilgrimage in Medieval Ireland,' Vol. 1, 150.

55 Kenney, *The Sources for the Early History of Ireland*, 601.

56 ALC.

57 AFM. Also recorded in the same year, 1242, in ALC.

58 BNÉ Vol. II, 205. For additional hagiographic references, see BNÉ Vol. II, 37, 41.

59 ALC.

60 ALC.

61 Potterton, *Medieval Trim*, 306.

62 Potterton, 306–7.

63 M. J. McEnery and Raymond Refaussé, eds., *Christ Church Deeds* (Dublin: Four Courts Press, 2001), 90, no. 297.

64 Lydon, 'Christ Church in the Later Medieval Irish World, 1300–1500,' 86, fn. 69.

65 Lydon, 'Christ Church,' 86.

66 Its mother church was the church of Clonmethan, in the barony of Balrothery.

67 Stat. Ire. 14 Edw VI, 217–221

68 Stat. Ire. 14 Edw VI, 221.

69 Ohler, The Medieval Traveller, 30; James Harpur, *Sacred Tracks: 2000 Years of Christian Pilgrimage* (London: Frances Lincoln Ltd, 2002), 81.

70 Catherine O'Sullivan, *Hospitality in Medieval Ireland 900–1500* (Dublin: Four Courts Press, 2004), 120.

71 Sumption, *Pilgrimage*, 198.

72 Aidan MacDonald, 'Adomnán's Monastery of Iona,' in *Studies in The Cult of Saint Columba*, ed. Cormac Bourke (Dublin: Four Courts Press, 1997), 39; O'Sullivan, *Hospitality in Medieval Ireland 900–1500*, 164–65.

73 O'Sullivan, *Hospitality*, 142.

74 O'Brien and Sweetman, *Archaeological Inventory of County Offaly*, 94; Also mentioned in 1031, AFM.

75 O'Sullivan, *Hospitality*, 145; Michael Hallinan, *Tipperary County: People and Places: An Anthology of the Evolution of County Tipperary, Some Historic Events and the History of the Principal Towns in the County* (Dublin: Kincora Press, 1993), 121.

76 For an in-depth discussion, see Cunningham, *Medieval Irish Pilgrims*, 101–5.

77 James Lydon, 'The Text and Its Context,' in *The Account Roll of the Priory of the Holy Trinity, Dublin, 1337–1346*, ed. James Mills (Dublin: Four Courts Press, 1996), xviii.

78 Annette Kehnel, *Clonmacnoise-the Church and Lands of St. Ciarán. Change and Continuity in an Irish Monastic Foundation* (6th to 16th Century) (Münster: LIT Verlag, 1995), 41.

79 From the latin '*Et uolentes fratres sancti Moluae domum ei in claro loco construere, in primis ait eis: Christus abbas noster est; ipse iam in hospite recipitur. Domum igitur hospitum hic facite, et meliores de agris vestries in vssum eius tradite.*' VSH Vol. II, (xxviii), 217. Paraphrase provided by Charles Doherty.

80 O'Sullivan, *Hospitality*, 212–13; MacDonald, 'Adomnán's Monastery of Iona', 39.

81 Geraldine Carville, *The Heritage of Holy Cross* (Belfast: Blackstaff Press, 1973), 49.

82 Meyer, *Aislinge Meic Conglinne*, 5; O'Sullivan, *Hospitality*, 220.

83 O'Sullivan, 143.

84 VC II.3, 155.

85 O'Sullivan, et al., ' Stratigraphical Report,' 6, 17–20; White Marshall and Rourke, *High Island*, 50.

86 White Marshall and Rourke, *High Island*, 50.

87 Michael J. O'Kelly, 'Church Island Near Valencia, Co. Kerry,' *PRIA* 59 (1957): 3–74,124–25.

88 O' Kelly, 'Church Island,' 74–75.

89 The hut has a sub-rectangular plan and measures internally 5.60 metres east–west x 3.40 metres north–south. See Aidan O'Sullivan et al. 'Archaeological Excavations at Templeteenaun, Co. Wicklow: A Medieval Chapel on St Kevin's Pilgrim's Road to Glendalough'. *PRIA forthcoming;* According to White Marshall & Rourke (2000, 51), 'Archaeological evidence of guesthouses can only be inferred from their position relative to the other monastic structures; in material remains they are identical to those of other dwellings'.

90 O'Sullivan et al., 'Stratigraphical Report,' 17–20.

91 Adomnán records several pilgrims dying in the guesthouse of Iona. See MacDonald, 'Adomnán's Monastery of Iona,' 39.

92 Michael Haren and Yolande de Pontfarcy, *The Medieval Pilgrimage to St Patrick's Purgatory: Lough Derg and the European Tradition* (Clogher Historical Society, 1988).

93 The account of his pilgrimage was written by Irishman James Yonge, a notary in Dublin. See Theresa O'Byrne, 'Centre or Periphery? The Role of Dublin in James Yonge's Memorial (1412),' in *Dublin: Renaissance City of Literature*, ed. Kathleen Miller and Crawford Gribben (Oxford: Oxford University Press, 2017), 16–37.

94 O'Byrne, 'Centre or Periphery?' 21; Haren and de Pontfarcy, *The Medieval Pilgrimage*, 159.

95 Haren and de Pontfarcy, *The Medieval Pilgrimage*; O'Byrne, 'Centre or Periphery?' 22.

96 O'Byrne, 'Centre or Periphery?' 22; Haren and de Pontfarcy, *The Medieval Pilgrimage*, 160.

97 O'Byrne, 'Centre or Periphery?' 23–24.

98 Lawlor, 'A Calendar of the Register,' 122–23.

99 Lawlor, 'A Calendar of the Register,' 144.

100 Haren and de Pontfarcy, *The Medieval Pilgrimage*, 160.

101 Haren and de Pontfarcy, *The Medieval Pilgrimage*, 159–60; O'Byrne, 'Centre or Periphery?' 24.

102 O'Byrne, 'Centre or Periphery?' 9–30.

103 Alan Mac an Bhaird, ed., *The Journey of Viscount Ramon De Perellós to Saint Patrick's Purgatory* (Cork: CELT, 2012), 5. https://celt.ucc.ie/published/T100079A.html . Accessed 6 October 2017.

104 Mac an Bhaird, *The Journey*, 6.
105 John Mahaffy, '*Two Early Tours in Ireland*,' *Hermathena*, 18(40) (1914): 40, 5.
106 Mahaffy, '*Two Early Tours,*' 5
107 Mahaffy, '*Two Early Tours,*' 5; Mac an Bhaird, *The Journey*, 6.
108 Mac an Bhaird, *The Journey*, 6.
109 Mac an Bhaird, *The Journey*, 7.
110 Haren and de Pontfarcy, *The Medieval Pilgrimage*, 111–12.
111 Haren and de Pontfarcy, *The Medieval Pilgrimage*, 93.
112 Brian Lacey, *Archaeological Survey of County Donegal: A Description of the Field Antiquities of the County from the Mesolithic Period to the 17th Century A.D.* (Lifford: Donegal County Council, 1983), 280–83; Daniel O'Connor, *St. Patrick's Purgatory, Lough Derg: Its History, Traditions, Legends, Antiquities, Topography* (Dublin: J. Duffy, 1895), 62–63.
113 Gwynn, *The Medieval Province of Armagh 1470–1545,* 268–9. The Register of Primate George Dowdal gives the date as April 1541. See, Murray, 'A Calendar of the Register,' 152.
114 The list of sites visited by MacNichaill is published in Murray, 'A Calendar of the Register,' 152. I am very grateful to Pádraig Ó Riain, Thomas Cannon and Brian Lacey for help in identifying locations on the list.
115 St Moling's Holy Well is located in the townland of Kilmalin, barony of Rathdown, Co. Wicklow. This lies in Íochtar Laighean and in St Kevin country.
116 Ó Riain, *A Dictionary of Irish Saints*, 284-285.
117 White Marshall and Rourke, *High Island*, 23.
118 Personal communication with Michael Gibbons.
119 Tomás Ó Carragáin, 'The View from the Shore: Perceiving Island Monasteries in Early Medieval Ireland,' *Hortus Artium Medievalium* 19 (2013): 220.
120 www.placenamesni.org, n.d., Accessed July 18, 2018.
121 Ó Riain, *A Dictionary of Irish Saints*, 284–85.
122 For a discussion of pilgrimage to Inishglora, see Michael and Myles Gibbons, 'Inishglora – "The Western Threshold Between Land and Wave"', in *Recent Explorations and Discoveries in Irish Heritage*, ed. Jim Higgins (Galway: Rock Crow's Press, 2017), 24–40.
123 Ann O'Sullivan and John Sheehan, *The Iveragh Peninsula: An Archaeological Survey of South Kerry* (Cork: Cork University Press, 1996), 346; Aubrey Gwynn and Richard Neville Hadcock, *Medieval Religious Houses: Ireland: With an Appendix to Early Sites* (Dublin: Irish Academic Press, 1988), 168, 192.
124 http://www.placenamesni.org/resultdetails.php?entry=17513. Accessed 18 July 2018.
125 http://www.placenamesni.org/resultdetails.php?entry=17506. Accessed 18 July 2018.
126 See www.irishpilgrimpaths.ie. Accessed 21 January 2018.
127 Doran, 'Medieval Communication Routes,' 57.
128 Elizabeth FitzPatrick, 'Roads and Routes,' in *Medieval Ireland: An Encyclopaedia*, ed. Séan Duffy (Abingdon: Routledge, 2005), 414.
129 Harry Hughes, *Croagh Patrick (Cruach Phádraig – The Reek): An Ancient Mountain Pilgrimage* (Westport: Harry Hughes, 1991), 56; http://monastic.ie/history/murrisk-augustinian-friary/. Accessed 2 February 2019.
130 Also known as *Leacht Benan*.
131 The following discussion is based on Louise Nugent, 'Pilgrimage in Medieval Ireland,' Vol. 2 60–68; 98—4.
132 See Christiaan Corlett, 'Prehistoric Pilgrimage to Croagh Patrick,' *Cathair Na Mart* 16 (1996): 54–61; Corlett, 'The Prehistoric Ritual Landscape,' 9–26.
133 A section of the road in Derrynacranna destroyed by land improvements in the 1980s was described as paved.
134 Not recorded on the early Ordnance Survey maps of the area.
135 Bieler, *The Patrician Texts*, 151–153 37(1–4).
136 CPL (1427–1447), Vol. VIII, 440.
137 Nugent,' Pilgrimage in Medieval Ireland,' 111-116, Vol. II.
138 Christiaan Corlett, 'The Prehistoric Ritual Landscape,' 12—4, 19–22.

CHAPTER 6

The Irish Abroad: Irish Pilgrims Travelling outside Ireland

Irish pilgrims who travelled abroad required the same services as those visiting Ireland.[1] Accessing shelter, food, ferries, boats or ships could be more challenging in territories where people spoke different languages. Even in Ireland, this could pose a problem for Gaelic-speaking pilgrims travelling through Anglo-Irish areas or vice versa. This was one of several factors that caused pilgrims to favour established roads and routeways. These routes also included rivers and a journey could combine an overland and water route along a navigable river or lake.

Many of the infrastructural needs of medieval Europe were fulfilled by pre-existing and ancient routes such as Roman roads.[2] On the Continent, Roman roads were the backbone of the medieval road network. At the height of the Roman Empire, roads radiated out from Rome for over 4,800 kilometres, connecting the capital to the furthest regions of the empire. Many European states did not have an equivalent road network until the 18th century. Roman roads had been designed for the easy and rapid movement of armies and, although they were highly efficient for moving troops, they were less ideal for use by wagons and draught animals, as the surface became very slippery when wet, causing animals to stumble and unshod hooves to wear down very quickly. Roman roads were also quite narrow, 4–5 metres wide, causing problems if two wagons or carts were to meet.[3] Compounding the problem, many Roman roads had fallen into disrepair by the early medieval period and the surfaces of many had been quarried for their paving.[4] Ironically, the removal of the road surface made the roads easier to use and less difficult to repair.[5]

New roads and pathways were also constructed to meet the needs of the local communities and facilitate trade.[6] Some had no formal construction, and were little more than dirt tracks with fluid, elastic and changeable routes.[7] The old Roman roads continued to be a core part of English or continental pilgrim journeys.[8]

Accommodation

As in Ireland, the Church provided the bulk of accommodation for pilgrims in early medieval Europe. The Council of Tours (c. 813) decreed that bishops were responsible for providing accommodation and food for pilgrims.[9] Monasteries shouldered the brunt of this responsibility and from the 9th century were expected to set aside part of their revenue to cater for guests.[10] The Church's continuing obligation to provide hospitality was further emphasised in the 11th, 12th and 13th centuries.[11] Irish pilgrims travelling on through France and Germany could expect to find special welcome at the monasteries that had Irish connections.

On busy routes, large monasteries often had to build substantial guesthouses to accommodate large numbers of pilgrims. During the 8th century, a large guesthouse was built at the monastery of St Gall in Switzerland. St Gall was an Irish saint and one of 12 disciples of St Columbanus, and the medieval monastery had developed out of the saint's hermitage.[12] Free accommodation and food for pilgrims and travellers were provided for a limited period of time at some medieval monasteries. The social status of the traveller often determined the standard of care they received. The hierarchical treatment of guests can readily be seen in the ground plans of St Gall Abbey, where separate accommodations were provided for the poor, visiting monks and high-status visitors.[13] Also, the quality and standard of the hospitality varied according to the finances of the monastery.[14] A surviving example of the level of hospitality one might receive in England can be seen in the Statutes of the Archbishop of Winchelsea, which assured the right of hospitality for pilgrims who stayed at the guest hall of Christ Church priory at Canterbury. Pilgrims could expect to be fed daily with meat and bread, and if they died while staying there, they had the right to burial in the grounds of the cathedral.[15] Although technically a free service, monasteries did their best to encourage guests to make donations by ensuring that their own in-house relics were on display. In the later medieval period, some monasteries could even offer indulgences of varying lengths to their pilgrim guests.[16]

During the 8th century, *hospita,* or hospices/hostels, provided additional accommodation for pilgrims.[17] Many of the hospices were connected to monasteries with strong Irish connections. Examples include those at Péronne, Honau and St Omer in France. Monasteries founded by Irish saints continued to have strong connections with Ireland and were probably sought out by Irish pilgrims. In the early medieval period, pilgrims travelling to Rome from Ireland could stay at a network of hostels with Irish links.[18] In Rome, there was even a small hospice dedicated to the Trinity, used by Irish pilgrims.[19] In 850, Bishop Donatus of Fiesole, an Irishman, established a small hospice attached to the Church of St Brigit in the city of Piacenza in Northern Italy. This was on one of the main routes to Rome used by Irish pilgrims, the Via Emilia.[20] In 883, Carolingian

Emperor Charles III built an Irish monastery in Viktorsberg in Rhaetia, and two years later he gave additional monies for the upkeep of a hospice there.[21] During the 9th and 10th centuries, the Irish-run hospices went into a marked decline and a century later they had almost entirely disappeared. From this point on, Irish pilgrims would have relied on monastic guesthouses for accommodation. An increase in the numbers of pilgrims in the 11th century saw a surge in new hospices being built across Europe.[22]

At the height of the pilgrimage movement, all the major routes in Europe were equipped with hostels about a day's walk apart.[23] The majority of routes to Santiago had hospitals and hostels every 25km, all within a day's walk of each other,[24] while roads leading to the shrine of the Volto Santo in Lucca, in Northern Italy were equipped with hostels every three to four kilometres.[25] Generally, hospices provided basic accommodation. Travellers would have slept on straw placed on the floor and were expected to provide their own meals; only the wealthier establishments were able to offer beds and food.[26]

On 25 October 1492, on his journey back to Ireland from Rome, Irishman Thaddeus McCarthy died at a pilgrim's hostel at Ivrea, Northern Italy. Ivrea was an important location on the Via Francigena to Rome, and the *Life of St Malachy* mentions that the saint passed by there on his way to the Holy City in 1139.[27] McCarthy would have been buried as an unknown pilgrim had it not been for the fact that the Bishop Nicholas Garigliatti had a dream of Thaddeus's death and his ascension to heaven. After waking, the bishop came to collect the body. Many miracles occurred following Thaddeus's death and he soon came to be regarded locally as a saint. Bishop Garigliatti had him buried under the altar of the cathedral church at Ivera, alongside the body of St Eusebius.[28] In modern times, relics of the saint made their way to Ireland and are now on display at St Colman's Cathedral, Cobh, and at St Mary and St Anne's Cathedral in Cork.

Pilgrims could also stay at hospitals. Though modern hospitals are primarily associated with the care of the sick, in medieval times four types of hospitals existed: '… those which sheltered the poor; those which cared for the sick poor; leper houses, and hospices for travellers'.[29] Before the 9th century, the words guesthouse (*xenodochium*) and hospital (*hospitium*), tended to imply the same thing and there was no clear difference between the functions of the two. By the 12th century, guesthouses provided board and lodging, and hospitals as charitable institutions cared for the sick and needy. However, the functions of the hospital as provider of care for the sick and of shelter for travellers could still overlap; for example, hospitals dedicated to the sick occasionally provided temporary accommodation

Image of Volto Sancto from the "Von dem heiligen Kreuz in der Stadt Lucca, das man Sunte Hulpe oder Gottes Hilfe nennt". Woodcut from the Lübeck Passional 1492. (unknown artist / public domain / Wikimedia Commons)

for healthy travellers who usually stayed only one night.[30] Some hospitals catered specifically for pilgrims. In the Holy Land, military and knightly orders such as the Knights Templar and the Knights Hospitaller played an important role in the foundation and running of hospitals for pilgrims (sick and healthy), while foundations run by the order of Altopascio had a strong presence along pilgrim routes to Santiago de Compostela.[31] The Hospital of St Nicholas at Harbledown, a mile from the great shrine of Canterbury, and the hospital of St Bartholomew's at Smithfield, were founded to care for sick pilgrims.[32] St Thomas's Hospital at Eastbridge in Canterbury fulfilled a similar function, caring primarily for sick pilgrims; the undercroft where the pilgrims once stayed still survives. The statutes of the Hospital of St Thomas the Martyr for the year 1342 make provision that a healthy traveller/pilgrim could stay here for no more than one night, as priority was to be given to poor and sick pilgrims. In 1440, the hospital of St John at Hildesheim offered a similar policy of providing accommodation for one night only to healthy pilgrims.[33]

Eleventh-century Irish pilgrims often travelled to the Holy Land by a route that passed through Vienna and along the Danube. By the late 11th and 12th centuries,

Southern Germany witnessed the establishment of a group of Benedictine monasteries, dependent on the mother-house of St James at Regensburg. Commonly known as *Schottenklöster,* they had strong connections with Munster. There is little doubt that some Irish pilgrims travelling to Rome or the Holy Land diverted to, and found shelter and accommodation in, these monasteries.

In the late medieval period, inns provided additional accommodation in urban centres and along very busy routes. They ranged in standard from small, dingy hovels to relatively grand establishments. They all offered board, lodging and stabling, but some also supplied medicines and a laundry service.[34] Inns were relatively inexpensive; for example, a traveller in 14th-century England could expect to pay a penny for a bed for a night. However, food was expensive and the price of a bed was often less than the price of a dinner.[35] Guests staying at inns usually shared both the room and the bed; it was normal to have at least two to a bed and it was not uncommon to have three to five sharing a bed.[36] Surviving examples of medieval inns include the remains of the courtyard and gateway of the Old Georges Inn at Salisbury and the medieval inns at Gloucester and Glastonbury.[37]

The Economy of the Pilgrim Route

Those providing accommodation to pilgrims also offered them financial services. This is well illustrated by the following account of an Irish pilgrim in Lucca, Italy. On 13 July 1250, Rogerius de Irlanda was on his deathbed in a small inn in Lucca. Lucca was located on the Via Francigena, one of the main Italian pilgrim routes to Rome. The town was also a place of pilgrimage in its own right, possessing a holy cross known as the Volto Santo.[38] The inn that Rogerius lodged at was run by an Englishman named Gilbertus, to whom Rogerius entrusted the execution of his will. It is very likely that because of its management, the inn was regularly frequented by English and Irish pilgrims.[39] The will, which still survives, listed a series of bequests. They included 4d. for the roof of Lucca Cathedral, 4d for the altar of St Martino and 4d for oil for the Volto Santo.[40]

Reputable places of hospitality also provided safekeeping for the pilgrims' valuables, as shown by another account relating to an Irish pilgrim in Lucca. Maurice FitzGilbert[41] had arrived in Lucca in late July/early August 1402, on his way to Rome. He stayed at the Hospital of the Misericordia, an establishment that maintained 27 beds for male pilgrims and 23 beds for female pilgrims. It also had a 23-bed infirmary.[42] As with many other Italian hospitals, the Misericordia offered a service akin to a safety deposit box in a bank and would hold valuables in safekeeping, while the pilgrims continued to Rome. The valuables could then be collected on their return, thus ensuring that their finances were in place for the return leg of their journey. Maurice wished to leave 2 gold nobles, worth a total of 13s 4d. The arrangement stipulated that if he did not return, the money was to be paid out to an authorised claimant, once he had performed a secret signal: closing his right eye and touching the treasurer's right hand with the index finger of his right hand. Maurice returned safely and collected his money on 15 August 1402, presumably travelling safely back to Ireland afterwards.[43]

Treacherous Travels: Extreme Weather and Disease

Irish pilgrims abroad encountered more extreme weather conditions than they were used to at home. At higher altitudes, they faced many of the same difficulties of modern hill walkers, such as heavy fog causing poor visibility and disorientation. At the same time, the travellers were at risk of hypothermia and frostbite when they encountered heavy rain or snow in areas without shelter. Most Irish pilgrims travelling to Rome had to cross the Alps. The safest time to travel in this region was in summer, before heavy snows set in. Those who waited until winter put themselves at risk of avalanches and even frostbite.[44] An example of the dangers of a winter crossing is seen in the tragic journeys of Ælfsige, Archbishop of Canterbury, who froze to death crossing the Alps in 959, or John de Liro, who suffered the same fate when travelling from Liege to Rome in 1215.[45] Over the centuries, hundreds if not thousands of pilgrims perished there and there were surely some unfortunate Irish pilgrims among them. Pilgrims to Santiago de Compostela faced similar challenges when crossing the Pyrenees in the winter months.

While travel in winter held the most obvious dangers, travel during summer months could also be difficult. In warmer climates, pilgrims needed to take care to avoid over-exposure to the sun. Heatstroke and bad sunburn could cause great discomfort and even delay journeys. This may be why the wide-brimmed hat became a popular part of pilgrim dress in the late medieval world. Heat was certainly a major risk factor for pilgrims travelling to destinations such as the Holy Land, where they could potentially face other dangers such as sandstorms.

The ideal time to travel to Rome was from late summer to late autumn, as the traveller avoided the intense heat of summer and the dangerous winter conditions of the Alps.[46] Warm weather provided optimum conditions for the spread of disease. Anyone arriving in Rome at the height of summer not only had to deal with the intense heat but also the risk of malaria. At the time, Rome was surrounded by swampy land and outbreaks of malaria in the historical texts show a marked increase in the summer. A particularly bad outbreak of the disease occurred in 1188, killing many pilgrims.[47] In Rome, plague epidemics occurred during the jubilee year of 1400 and again in 1435, 1448–50, 1457, 1468, 1476, 1478, 1480–81,1485, and 1493–94.[48] We know that Irish pilgrims were affected; for example, in 1450 the annals record the death of the Irish pilgrim Muirchertach Ua Flannagan, who held lands in Tuath-Ratha, barony of Magherboy, Co. Fermanagh, and who succumbed to plague while in Rome.[49] Muirchertach had gone to Rome during a jubilee year and his family may have gained some comfort from his death, knowing that he obtained the plenary indulgence through his pilgrimage.

Robbers

Irish pilgrims also had to contend with issues of personal safety when travelling abroad. The danger was perhaps heightened as they were travelling through unknown terrain. Robbery, assault and kidnappings of pilgrims were frequently recorded in Europe during the early and late medieval period.[50] Pilgrims were particularly vulnerable when travelling through wooded areas, as thieves would often hide and ambush them as they passed by. In 1168, the unfortunate Earl of Salisbury was murdered by thieves when travelling home from his pilgrimage to Santiago de Compostela.[51] The ever-present dangers attached to the pilgrim's journey were acknowledged by the author of the medieval *Life of St Fursey.* In the text, Fursey (Fursa), an Irish saint who left Ireland as a *peregrinus*, reached Rome, having travelled through the hindrances of Burgundy, the dangers of Italy, the assaults of the Passerella, the tricks of Pavia, the treachery of Sutri and the deceits of Carbonella.[52]

From the 12th century onwards, pilgrims tended to travel in small groups for reasons of safety. These groups were often formed as a matter of convenience rather than from a desire to travel together. That such groups were common is evident from their depiction in later medieval literature, such as Chaucer's *Canterbury Tales*. Literary themes often imitated real-life situations; for example, the real-life pilgrim Margery Kempe, when undertaking her many pilgrimages, also travelled with groups of other pilgrims. There is also evidence from England to suggest that pilgrims travelled in family groups, on pilgrimage to long-distance or local shrines.[53] The historical sources suggest that many upper-class Irish pilgrims travelling to foreign pilgrimage destinations also travelled in groups. These groups were made up of family members and the typical retinue of an aristocratic household. Examples of this are commonplace: in 1051, Laidhcenn Ua Leocain, Lord of the Gaileanga, went on pilgrimage to Rome accompanied by his wife;[54] King Sitric of Dublin went to Rome in 1028 and was accompanied by his retinue, referred to as 'many others' (multialii);[55] and James Butler, in 1431, planned to travel to Rome accompanied by a retinue of 25 of his followers and servants.[56]

The year 1445, a year of indulgence at the Shrine of St James, inspired a great many Irish nobles to go on pilgrimage, each travelling with a retinue of their followers[57]. Among them was Irish noblewoman Margaret O'Carroll, the wife of Calbhach Ó Conchobhair Failghe (Calvach O'Connor Faly), the Lord of Eile, a territory that corresponds to Co. Offaly.[58]

The *Annals of Lecale* record the names of other nobles like Tomaltach Mac Diarmoda, King of Maghluirg, Mageochagan (Mageoghegan), the ruler of the Cenel Fiachach.[59]Garret, son of Thomas of the Geraldines of Kildare, and O'Drisceoil Óg of Baltimore also travelled in this year. Evilin, daughter of Edmond FitzThomas O'Feargail, was another who made pilgrimage in this year. As the wife of Pierce Dalton, who ruled a territory corresponding to the barony of Rathconrath, Co. Westmeath, she would have travelled in a style befitting her station. She, like the others ,would have travelled with her own retinue of servants and supporters.[60]

The Cork chieftain Fineen O'Driscoll, lord of Baltimore, died in 1472,[61] having completed his pilgrimage to Santiago de Compostela in the company of his son, Teige. These men were surely accompanied by supporters. Other Irish examples of pilgrims travelling with a retinue or companions include James Rice, the Mayor of Waterford, who was accompanied on his second pilgrimage to Santiago, in 1483, by his two bailiffs, Patrick Mulgane and Philip Bryane.[62] Finally, Gaelic Lord Barry Roe made a pilgrimage to Santiago de Compostela in 1507, attended by 'many chiefs of his people'.[63]

Pilgrims would also have encountered decent and kind people, who gave them alms and food. Margery Kempe, when travelling on her pilgrimage to Rome, on her return from the Holy Land, was rejected by her compatriots, who found her company tiresome. Finding herself alone in Venice, she placed her trust in God and was provided with an unlikely guide, described by her as a broken-backed Irishman named Richard. The pair travelled together to Assisi, where they joined a party of pilgrims that included wealthy noblewoman Margaret Florentyne, continuing with them to Rome. Margery seems to have given away both her own and Richard's money to the poor, leaving them both destitute by the time they arrived in Rome. She obtained help from another benefactor and completed her pilgrimage and returned home. We are not told what happened to Richard, but he too seems to have landed on his feet, as Margery met him again at a later date when she was travelling to Santiago de Compostela. Her fortunes had changed by this time and she was able to repay her debt to Richard.[64]

Political Turmoil

Throughout the medieval period, political conflicts outside Ireland had a disruptive effect on pilgrimage. During times of war, there was an increase in criminal acts such as piracy and robbery that targeted travellers.[65] Major conflagrations like the Hundred Years War (1337–1453) and the various Crusades all had a major affect on pilgrimage, causing many people to think twice before travelling through areas of conflict. The dangers that could be met on the road can be clear seen in the 11th-century *Life of St Colmán*. Colmán was completing his pilgrimage from Ireland to the Holy Land around 1012, when he was murdered at Stockerau, near Vienna, after being mistaken for a Hungarian spy.[66] Stockerau was on a land route to the Holy Land that passed through Hungary and Greece.

By Sea to Santiago

Anyone who hoped to make pilgrimage outside Ireland had to travel by sea. From the 12th century pilgrims to Spain made use of existing trade routes when travelling between the two countries. Irish pilgrims in the 14th century travelled to Santiago almost exclusively by ship from ports such as Drogheda, Dublin, Wexford, New Ross, Waterford, Youghal, Cork, Kinsale, Dingle, Limerick and Galway. They boarded ships that sailed directly to the Spanish port of La Coruña, and from there went on foot to the shrine of St James.[67]

If luck was on their side, passage could be secured on a ship in a day or two of arrival at the port, otherwise there was a wait that could extend to weeks. If patience ran out, there was the option of travelling to an English port such as Bristol and setting sail to Spain from there.[68] In some cases, the wait for a ship could be longer than the sea voyage itself. In 1456 the English pilgrim William Wey spent five days sailing from Plymouth to Coruña, having waited almost six weeks for a ship. Margery Kempe spent six weeks waiting for a ship at Bristol. Her voyage took only seven days and her return journey only five days.[69]

Initially, the boats used by pilgrims were trading vessels that carried pilgrims as an additional stream of income. Sources from Britain suggest that by the 14th/15th centuries, the popularity of pilgrimage had led vessels to carry pilgrims exclusively. It is estimated that a typical ship from this era could hold an average of 60 to 80 pilgrims, although larger numbers were also recorded.[70]

All pilgrims who embarked on sea voyage did so with trepidation. Bad weather was the biggest threat to a successful voyage and every storm had the potential to cause a shipwreck. Even short voyages, such as crossing the Irish Sea to the island of Britain, was not without its dangers. In 1268, for example, Maurice FitzGerald drowned when his ship got into difficulty crossing from Ireland to England.[71] Tragedy struck again in 1313, shortly after Walter Thornbury, Lord Chancellor of Ireland, was elected by the canons of Christ Church Cathedral as Archbishop of the See of Dublin. Thornbury had just begun his journey to see Pope John XXII in Avignon, when his ship perished in a great storm in Dublin Bay.[72] There are many vivid descriptions of the terror and feelings of helplessness experienced by passengers and sailors caught in storms. The sense of fear and dread was heightened by the sounds of shrieking winds, creaking wood, cracking masts and inpouring of water, as ships were tossed about on the waves.[73] It is no wonder that in these situations people turned to the saints for help and bargained for their lives by making vows of pilgrimage. Felix Fabri, writing in the 15th century, describes his experience of a storm while sailing from Venice to Alexandria.

> When day broke, as the storm still continued, we remained quiet, and bore our lot with patience, we were without food or drink, for there was no fire in the galley, and the kitchen on deck was full of water; beside which we *were* all sea-sick, and loathed all food and drink, because our stomachs were upset. Indeed, if anyone had eaten while that storm lasted he would not have kept it down, but would have vomited it up again. There is nothing better than to keep one's stomach empty during storms. Moreover, all our bread was spoilt and uneatable with salt water, and therefore we were compelled to fast.[74]

Even if a vessel survived the storms, any damage could extend the time frame of the journey. The *Mary Leybourne* had broken its mast on its last voyage from Portugal to Ireland in 1476/1477. Repairs to the vessel delayed its next voyage from Kinsale to La Coruña.[75]

The return voyage had the same dangers, and small comfort could be taken by pilgrims who had effaced some of their sins, now that their pilgrimage was completed.

The journey to and from the shrine could be stressful on the body and exacerbate underlying medical conditions. The Gaelic Lord Ó Drisceoil Óg died at sea on his return voyage from the shrine of St James in 1445.[76] In 1450, Andrew Ua Droma, 'a polished, conscientious man', who travelled to Rome for the jubilee year, died at the age of 55 having returned to Ireland.[77] A similar fate was met by the poet Donnell O'Higgin, after his return from pilgrimage to Santiago de Compostela in 1501:

> Donnell O'Higgin, Chief Preceptor to the schools of Ireland in poetry, died, after his return from the pilgrimage of St James.[78]

In 1507, the Irish chief Barry Roe went on pilgrimage to the shrine of his namesake at Santiago, accompanied by his retinue of Irish chiefs. After performing their pilgrimage, the party boarded a ship to return home but, tragically, they were all lost at sea and never heard of again.[79]

Pirates could pose another danger and were known to attack ships, kidnap and ransom or enslave those on board; and in the worst-case scenario, they could kill the passengers. A Lübeck chronicle dating to 1453 records pirates capturing 300 pilgrims on their return journey from the Holy Land.[80] In 1473, *La Mary London*, carrying 400 Irish pilgrims on their return journey from Santiago, was captured by pirates. The ship had sailed out from New Ross. It seems that the pilgrims were ransomed, as they were later released in the port of Youghal, Co. Cork, although the ship had originally been destined to dock in Waterford.[81]

Even when not in life-threatening situations, pilgrims found that conditions on board ship were unpleasant. Apart from sea sickness, they were confined in cramped and unhygienic spaces. For longer sea voyages, shortages of food and water were common. To make a profit, some ship owners would cram into their boats as many pilgrims as they could fit, and the cramped quarters often gave rise to arguments among travellers. Adding to the tensions were disturbed sleep, the snoring of other passengers, the cries and moans of the sick, as well as the rats, fleas and lice that inhabited the ship.

It must have been such a relief for pilgrims to set foot again on solid ground, especially if they had experienced bad weather conditions. Ports like La Coruña were bustling places. William Wey, who sailed from Plymouth to La Coruña 'noted 84 ships moored in harbour' that came from England, Wales, Normandy, Brittany and Ireland, suggesting that up to 5,000 pilgrims had arrived in the space of a few days. At La Coruña, Irish pilgrims disembarked into a crowded and exotic port and, as they walked the small narrow streets, they were hit by strange smells and the sound of numerous languages being spoken. Most pilgrims would have needed some time to recover from the voyage before beginning the next leg of their pilgrimage to Santiago. William Wey rested in La Coruña for three days.[82] Fighting disorientation and adjusting to solid ground, pilgrims were easy prey for pickpockets. One of the pilgrims aboard Wey's ship had his purse cut from his belt; apparently, thanks to a miracle by St James, it was later returned.[83]

From La Coruña, the pilgrims headed on foot to Santiago. It must have been a relief for them to stretch their legs after the cramped conditions on board ship. Anticipation and excitement would have increased as the pilgrims drew nearer to Santiago.

A favourite resting place for pilgrims was Mount Joy, and it was here pilgrims got their first glimpse of the city. For some, this was an emotional experience, as the hardship of their journey were now behind them. Many pilgrims sat on the hill and removed their shoes, walking barefoot into the city.

Unfortunately, though we know that Santiago was a popular destination for the Irish, no Irish pilgrim left a record of his or her experiences at Santiago, or at least none have survived. By looking at contemporary accounts of pilgrims from other countries, we can piece together what their experiences might have been.

One of the first things all pilgrims did was secure a bed in one of the many hostels or inns in the city. Washing was a priority. As well as being a practical matter, it symbolised purification. If pilgrims arrived on the feast of St James, they spent the first night of their pilgrimage at a vigil in St James's Cathedral.[84] Pilgrims entered the building through the doorway known as the Portico de la Gloria, which had no doors until the 16th century.[85] Medieval accounts suggest that pilgrims divided into regional groups and spent the night singing hymns, chanting prayers and playing music.[86] The next day they offered their prayers before the high altar. Mass took place at the high altar around midday and the priest would announce the indulgence granted for that day. After Mass, the offerings brought by pilgrims were presented before the high altar and in many smaller chapels in the cathedral. The poor were given gifts to present at the ceremony but people with means were expected to have brought an offering with them or purchased a gift for the saint in the city.[87] After the gift-giving ceremony, pilgrims visited the other chapels and altars in the cathedral. They also descended into the crypt to pray at the tomb of St James.[88] The 12th-century *Codex Calixtinus* makes reference to the saint's tomb being accessible only at certain times.[89]

> The tomb was lit by the otherworldly gleam of carbuncles, honoured without cease by heavenly fragrance, bathed in the glow of celestial candles and watched over by attendant angels.[90]

By the 15th century, pilgrims also climbed the stairs behind the high altar to touch and kiss a statue of St James. German pilgrim Arnold Von Harff, writing in 1497, recorded his experience at the shrine:

Reliquary of Saint James at Cathedral of Santiago de Compostela (cropped) ©MAbW / Wikimedia Commons / CC BY-SA 4.0

> On the high altar is a great wooden shrine made in honour of St James. On it is a crown, and the pilgrims ascend behind the altar and place the crown on their heads, wherefore the inhabitants make fun of us Germans.[91]

The staff of St James, encased in silver, was another relic at which pilgrims paid their respects. This was attached to a crossing pier[92] and it was customary for them to touch the staff as part of their prayers.[93]

It was also customary for pilgrims to make a confession to a priest, before going on to obtain a certificate known as the *Compostelana* at the Capillia del Rey de Francia. The certificate stated that the pilgrim had completed the pilgrimage and gained the indulgence. It also stipulated that the pilgrim could stay in the city for three days and nights, which was plenty of time in which to explore the cathedral and the surrounding city.[94]

All Roads Lead to Rome

Irish pilgrims travelling to Rome and the Holy Land shared a similar route for much of their journey. Northern Europeans tended to travel to Italy when making their way to the Holy Land, some continuing to Rome before sailing from one of the many southern Italian ports. All Irish pilgrims travelling to Rome or other continental shrines made their way to Britain, taking a route through Wales and England. Many headed to London and on to Dover via Canterbury, where they caught another boat to the Continent. From there, they travelled through the Low Countries and the Rhineland, before heading up-river to Switzerland, over the Alps and on to Rome.[95] Most northern-European pilgrims travelling to Rome followed the Via Francigena, also popular with tradesmen, merchants and churchmen. One of the earliest descriptions of the route is found in the late 10th-century diary of Archbishop Sigeric of Canterbury.[96] The Francigena crossed the Alps by way of passes at Mont Cenis and Mont Joux (further north), as well as at the Great and Little St Bernard's Passes, before diverging into four separate routes that crossed four different topographical areas of Italy, all leading to Rome. The most eastern route passed through Lucca and Siena and, as we have seen above, was used by Irish pilgrims.[97] There are no surviving accounts of Irish pilgrims' activities in Rome. Rome possessed many relics, but none were as adored as the bodies of the apostles Peter and Paul. The shrine of St Peter was the highlight of all pilgrimages. Up until the 13th century, pilgrims had direct access to the shrine.[98] In 1300, a special route was devised around the city for those seeking to gain the plenary indulgence. By visiting all the points on the route, including the basilicas of SS Peter and Paul, the pilgrim obtained the longed-for plenary indulgence. The pilgrim landscape was ever changing and expanding in Rome, and by the 14th century, pilgrims could visit more than a thousand churches, many of which were mentioned in late medieval guidebooks. The guidebooks also listed different relics of martyrs and saints, telling pilgrims in which churches they could be found.[99]

In the Footsteps of Christ – Travel to the Holy Land

Over the centuries, many different routes were taken by pilgrims from Northern Europe to the Holy Land. Most involved travel by sea, journeys over land, along river routes or a combination of all three. In the early centuries, pilgrims travelled to Italy and sailed on from its southern ports. Depending on the political situation, it was also possible for pilgrims to travel by land through the Balkans and Asia Minor.[100] By the 14th century, most northern Europeans travelled to the Italian ports of Venice and Bari, sailing to Egypt and travelling overland to Jerusalem.[101]

A single comprehensive account of an Irish pilgrimage to the Holy Land can be found in a Latin text called *Itinerarium Symonis Semeonis Ab Hybernia Ad Terram Sanctam,* a personal account of pilgrimage made by the Irish Franciscan friar Simon Fitz Simons to the Holy Land in 1323. Simon was a high-ranking member of the Irish Franciscans and came from a prominent Anglo-Irish family.[102] He was accompanied on his pilgrimage by another Franciscan, Hugh the Illuminator. There were many routes leading to any one pilgrim destination, local or interna-

Speculative reconstruction of a blessing ceremony Friar Simon and Hugh may have participated in before departing on their pilgrimage to Jerusalem. By JG O'Donoghue

tional. The decision about how pilgrims should get to where they wanted to go was often dictated by where they needed to avoid; for example, areas of flooding, famine or war. People also picked routes in order to stop at additional pilgrim sites. Simon's route was heavily influenced by his connections to the Franciscan order, and he stopped at many holy places associated with the Franciscans.[103] The pilgrimage gave Simon and Hugh the opportunity to immerse themselves in the places of the Bible and to follow in the footsteps of their founder, St Francis, who had made a pilgrimage to Jerusalem in 1219.[104]

Before setting forth, both men would have acquired letters of introduction from their superiors, stating that they were pilgrims and asking for safe passage and hospitality. They probably also attended a blessing ceremony, which would have been an emotional experience. All present were keenly aware they might not meet again. The Dominican Felix Fabri, who travelled to the Holy Land in the 15th century, describes receiving his own blessing while lying prostrate before the altar in front of his community. He describes a very emotional departure:

> I received a blessing from the altar, amid the exceeding bitter weeping of the Prior of the convent and all the brethren. When I had received my blessing, my sobs and tears made me unable to bid my brethren farewell in words, but my tears, my sorrowful face and my sobs spoke for me. I therefore embraced and kissed each of the brethren and begged to be remembered in their prayers.[105]

Simon tells us nothing about the Irish part of the journey or where he sailed from. We know that he sailed out of Ireland on 16 March, crossing the 'very stormy and dangerous' Irish Sea, landing at Holyhead in Wales.

The pair travelled on to Chester, arriving by 24 March and spending Easter there.[106] Chester was an important pilgrim destination and the pair probably made time to pray at the relics of St Werburgh. After Easter, they travelled to Lichfield, another important pilgrim destination. Simon wrote of Lichfield: 'There is the most beautiful church in honour of St Chad, with most lofty stone towers and splendidly adorned with pictures, sculptures and other ecclesiastical ornaments.'[107] Leaving Lichfield, they headed east to London, where they attended Mass in the Lady Chapel of St Paul's Cathedral.[108] As they entered the city, they passed by the Chapel of St Thomas on London Bridge. From London, they continued to the shrine of St Thomas à Becket at Canterbury, via Rochester. The route from London to Canterbury was frequently used by Irish pilgrims. There was a strong devotion to St Thomas in medieval Ireland[109] and the saint's relics were the goal of many Irish pilgrims. London became a nodal point for pilgrimages to Canterbury. As well as being the birthplace of St Thomas, it also had a number of pilgrim sites, which the friars and other Irish pilgrims may also have visited (see Chapter 2). Many pilgrims en route to, or returning from, Canterbury made sure to visit St Thomas's Chapel on the ninth pier of London bridge.[110] The chapel was a likely stop for Simon, as he mentions it directly in his writings:

> Traffic continuously reached London by the famous river Thames over Which is the well-known bridge full of inhabitants and wealth, in the middle of which is the church of St Thomas, archbishop and martyr.[111]

The pair may even have attended one of the daily Masses held on the bridge.[112] At Canterbury, a Benedictine foundation, Simon describes St Thomas's shrine as

> all of gold and adorned with innumerable precious stones and pearls, glittering like a gate of Jerusalem and even covered with an imperial diadem.[113]

It is clear that the opulence of the shrine and its reliquary greatly impressed the pair, as it did other pilgrims.

From this point on many of the places where Simon and Hugh stopped along their chosen route had relics from the Holy Land. In the years immediate to the sacking of Constantinople, in April 1204, during the Fourth Crusade, relics from

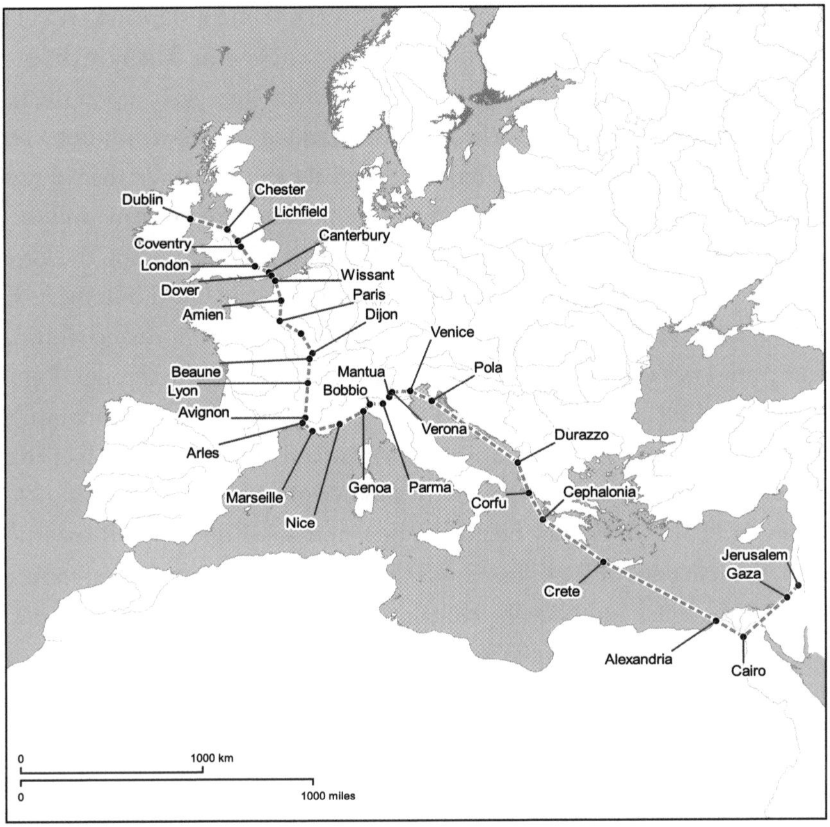

Map detailing the route taken by Friar Simeon to Jerusalem.
Created by Richard Clutterbuck

the east had flooded into Europe. In a sense, the presence of these relics brought part of the experience of the Holy Land to northern Europe. They allowed pilgrims to experience and connect with the Holy Land without travelling there and were of comfort for those unable to, due to sickness and old age, or when conflict in the Holy Land made it a dangerous destination. Seeing these relics from the Holy Land must have instilled in Simon the strength to continue his journey, reminding him of his ultimate goal: Jerusalem.[114]

Throughout their journey through Wales, England and across continental Europe, the friars relied on the hospitality of fellow religious, finding lodgings and food at monasteries along their route. Both men had taken a vow of poverty on entering the order, so they would have had no funds of their own. They may have received a donation to pay for their sea voyages from a benefactor, but most of the expenses were met through the charity of those they encountered along the way. There are frequent references to the Benedictines, who were associated with many of the places they stopped at along journey.

Leaving Canterbury, they continued on to Dover, found a ship and set sail across the English Channel, landing at the port of Wissant in France. The French leg of the journey took them to great cathedral at Amiens, where they gazed upon the head of St John the Baptist (obtained as a result of the sacking of Constantinople) and the miraculous image of the Blessed Virgin.[115] From there, they made their way to the bustling city of Paris, spending time at the great monastery of St Denis and the Saint Chapelle.[116] The latter had a fine collection of biblical relics, including the Crown of Thorns, part of the True Cross, two of the nails that crucified Our Lord, the lance that pierced his side and milk and hair of the Blessed Virgin.[117] In normal circumstances, pilgrims from Paris travelling to the Holy Land followed a route through Lombardy to Northern Italy. This route was closed to Simon and Hugh, due to political unrest caused by a war between the territories of Milan and Naples, so they had to plot a new course that made a detour through the Dijon region.[118] The new route took them to the city of Lyon, where they boarded a boat and sailed down the River Rhône to Avignon, the residence of Pope John XXII. From Avignon, they travelled to Arles and overland to Marseilles and Nice, before taking a ship to Genoa, in Italy. From Genoa they travelled over land via Bobbio to the port of Venice.[119] The leg of the journey from Genoa to Bobbio was extremely challenging and we are told the pair moved through '… mountains, valleys, thick forests and districts peopled with robbers'.[120]

Bobbio provided a place to rest and sleep, as well as for another spiritual experience. The monastery was the burial place of the great Irish Saint Columbanus, a *peregrinus* who had left Ireland in the 7th century and founded several monasteries in modern-day France, before ending his days at Bobbio. His achievements would have been well known to Simon and Hugh.

Mountains surrounding Bobbio.
© Diarmuid Healy

View of Bobbio with the monastery of St Columbanus in background.
© Diarmuid Healy

As well as holding the bones of the Irish saint, Bobbio was in possession of a significant number of relics from the Holy Land, such as of the Jars of Cana. The interaction of Simon and Hugh with items from the Holy Land reminded them of the miraculous works of Christ and deepened their resolve to reach their ultimate goal of Jerusalem.[121]

From Bobbio, the friars travelled towards the eastern coast of Italy, arriving at Venice on 28 June. They had been travelling for more than three months. Securing passage on a ship to the Holy Land took several weeks.[122] The pair may have used this time to rest and recuperate from the journey, as well as to plan the route ahead. They surely took the opportunity to visit the city's many relics, such as the body of St Mark the Evangelist, Theodore the martyr and the holy virgins Lucia and Marina.[123]

The body of St Mark was taken to Venice by two Venetian merchants in 828 and was by far the city's most popular relic.[124] In the ensuing centuries, the churches of Venice acquired one of the most extensive collections of relics in Europe. Much of the collection was developed during the era of the Crusades, when 'merchants, monks and pilgrims presented the churches of Venice with an exceptional quantity of relics which was especially enriched by the sack of Constantinople.'[125]

Reconstruction of Friars Simon and Hugh boarding a ship to Jerusalem in Venice. By JG O'Donoghue

The Venetians had the monopoly on travel to the Holy Land in later centuries and many surviving travel itineraries recommended taking Venetian boats rather than those from other ports, which were seen as less safe. By the 14th century, Venice offered the equivalent of a package holiday for pilgrims to the Holy Land, with licensed ship owners providing transport, food and accommodation.[126] There was even a tourist office to help pilgrims secure lodgings and negotiate with ship owners.[127]

From Venice, pilgrims could either sail directly to Jaffa or take a route passing through Alexandria in Egypt. Simon and Hugh chose the latter, a longer and more arduous journey, with frequent stops at ports along the way. In good weather it took on average five weeks to sail from Venice to Alexandria.[128] Simon and Hugh departed Venice on Thursday 18 August. Simon does not tell us what conditions were like on board the ship or the costs of the voyage but contemporary accounts suggests that the passage from Venice to Alexandria cost 17 gold ducats, the equivalent of £8 in contemporary English money.[129] Their ship sailed along the Adriatic coast, stopping at places such as Pola, Zara and Crete, which are described in the friars' writings. Finally, on 14 October, the ship docked in Alexandria, whereupon it was immediately boarded by the harbour master and examined by customs officials,[130] who checked through their belonging, which included books brought from Ireland and images of Christ and the Blessed Virgin. The customs officers ridiculed the friars and their religious belongings, but they did not confiscate anything.[131] The friars and their fellow pilgrims were taken under armed guard to the gates of the city, where they remained until all the relevant travel permits had been arranged. They arrived in Cairo on 23 October.[132] At this stage in the journey, Hugh became ill with dysentery. After a sickness that lasted five weeks, he died and was buried at the Church of St Martin.[133] Hugh's death was a blow to Simon. Not only had he lost a friend, but also his one link with home. Simon's disappointment and heartbreak following Hugh's death were obvious:

> How bitter and sharp was the storm of grief ... This poisoned arrow has pierced my bowels without pity and wounded me sorely with a sharp point of grief and pain.[134]

Following a brief period of mourning, Simon decided to continue and made his way to the Sultan's palace, where he obtained papers that allowed him to travel freely throughout Egypt and the Holy Land. In contrast with lay pilgrims, the authorities allowed all Franciscans to travel free from taxes because of their vow of poverty. Simon was able to join a small group of pilgrims who were also travelling to Jerusalem. The group hired two camels and a guide. The camels carried the four pilgrims, along with supplies such as tents, food, water and fodder.[135] This part of Simon's account provides details of some of discomfort of the journey. He notes that he

> slept deprived of all comforts of a house, amidst the sand and the dung of the animals, with the stars only as a covering. Wishing for twigs to lie upon and to place under our head as a cushion instead of heaps of dung and sand, they would without doubt have been worth a French bed.[136]

The landscape that Simon travelled through was very different from that of Ireland, yet it was strangely familiar, as the places he passed through were well known to him from his readings of the Old and New testaments of the Bible.[137] The party crossed the desert to the town of Gaza, an important customs station, where road tax had to be paid by travellers.[138] The desert ended about 3 kilometres from Gaza and Simon mentions that the town was surrounded by gardens and orchards.[139] From there, he began the final leg of his journey. As he neared Jerusalem, which

Reconstruction of Friar Simon seeing Jerusalem for the first time.
By JG O'Donoghue

sits 807 metres above sea level, he would have noticed the road begin to rise. Many pilgrims chose to walk barefoot into the city.

The first glimpse of Jerusalem could be very emotional. In 1414, Margery Kempe was so moved by the sight of the city that she had a vision of the heavenly Jerusalem.[140] Some pilgrims fell to their knees and prayed, while others were moved to tears. Geoffrey of Beaulieu, when describing Louis IX's pilgrimage from Acre to Nazareth, noted as he approached Nazareth:

> When he saw from afar the holy place, getting down from his horse, he worshipped it devoutly on bended knees and went forward in this way until he humbly entered the sacred city.[141]

Giovanni Adorno gave an account of his visit to the holy places in Jerusalem:

> For they would not be human beings, but rather devils, were they not moved to tears upon seeing the places where the Lord and Creator of heaven and earth and all things that exist.[142]

Simon walked through the gates of the walled city of Jerusalem on 10 December, after travelling for almost nine months.

The magnificent Jerusalem described in medieval literature was a far cry from the city that pilgrims of this period encountered. The constant fighting of the Crusades had taken its toll on the city and one wonders how Simon felt as he walked around Jerusalem. Some pilgrims were disappointed and saddened by the physical state of the city, which was in stark contrast to the elaborate relics of the Holy Land in their jewel-covered containers found across Europe.[143]

After resting, Simeon arranged a visit to the Holy Sepulchre.

> This church is large and beautiful, its nave being spherical and closely resemble a pigeon house, except that it is built upon columns and all round it an ambulatory. In its centre there is a small chapel of marble in which is the Sepulchre of Our Lord, which is nine palms in length. It is entirely covered over with a slab of white marble in such a manner that it can nowhere be touched nor seen except through three small holes which are on its southern side.[144]

Simon makes note of the 18 steps leading to the summit, where there is a round hole in which the cross of Christ was fixed. It is here that his account breaks off and ends. Because his descriptions are focused on the architecture of the city, we get little sense of how Simon felt or what rituals he engaged in as a pilgrim.

Felix Fabri, writing in 1483, gives us some sense of how emotional an experience pilgrimage at Jerusalem could be for pilgrims. He describes scenes of mass outpourings of emotion at the door of the Holy Sepulchre church, where pilgrims wailed and sobbed as they entered the holy shrine.[145] Pilgrims tried to re-enact the final footsteps of Christ and,during the 12th century, it was common for pilgrims to have themselves flagellated at the pillar in the Church of Mount Sion. We know that from 1231, the route taken by Christ from Pilate's prison to Calvary was marked out on the streets of the city.[146] In the decades following Simon's pilgrimage, the Franciscan friars established a presence in Jerusalem. The order welcomed and helped pilgrims and became 'guardians' and guides of the Holy Places for the Latin Church.[147] By the 14th century, pilgrims usually spent an average of 10 to 14 days in Jerusalem. Simon spent 7 weeks there, and may also have visited other holy places, such as Bethlehem and the River Jordan. As his account of the pilgrimage breaks off abruptly, we are not told how he gets home. He left Jerusalem on 24 January and it is implied that his return route took him through Cairo, Milan, Rome and Germany.[148] From this point, he disappears from the pages of history.

NOTES

1 Norbert Ohler, *The Medieval Traveller*, trans. Caroline Hillier (Woodbridge: Boydell Press, 1989), 22.
2 Paul Hindle, *Roads and Tracks for the Historian* (London: Philmore, 2001), 35.
3 Ohler, *The Medieval Traveller*, 22, 26.
4 R.S. Lopez, 'The Evolution of Land Transport in the Middle Ages,' *Past and Present* IX (1956): 19–20.
5 Lopez, 'The Evolution,' 19–20.
6 Lopez, 'The Evolution,' 23.
7 Hindle, *Roads and Tracks*, 195.
8 Lopez, 'The Evolution,' 26; Ohler, *The Medieval Traveller*, 25.
9 Birch, *Pilgrimage to Rome in the Middle Ages*, 79–80.
10 Sumption, *Pilgrimage*, 198—03.
11 Birch, *Pilgrimage to Rome*, 80.
12 Sumption, *Pilgrimage*, 198–99.
13 Sumption, *Pilgrimage*, 198–99.
14 Hopper, *To Be a Pilgrim*, 111.
15 Hopper, *To Be a Pilgrim*, 110–11.
16 Hopper, *To Be a Pilgrim*, 111.
17 Sumption, *Pilgrimage*, 198.
18 Harbison, *Pilgrimage in Ireland*, 31.
19 Harbison, *Pilgrimage in Ireland*, 31.
20 Diana Webb, *Pilgrims and Pilgrimage in Medieval Europe*, 18.
21 Harbison, *Pilgrimage in Ireland*, 31.
22 Sumption, *Pilgrimage*, 199.
23 Hopper, *To Be a Pilgrim*, 88.
24 Margaret Wade Labarge, *Medieval Travellers: The Rich and the Restless* (London: Hamish Hamilton, 1982), 84; Jennie Stopford, 'Some Approaches to the Archaeology of Christian Pilgrimage,' *World Archaeology* 26, no. 1 (1994): 66.
25 Colin Morris, *The Papal Monarchy: The Western Church from 1050 to 1250* (Oxford History of the Christian Church) (Oxford: Oxford University Press, 1991), 313.
26 Sumption, *Pilgrimage*, 201–2.
27 Rev. Anthony Hurley, 'Blessed Thaddeus McCarthy, Bishop of Cork and Cloyne, 1490-2.', *JCHAS*, 2, 2 no. 24, no. 24 (1896): 506–7; Rev P Hurley, 'Blessed Thaddeus McCarthy, Bishop of Cork and Cloyne, 1490–1492 (Contd.),' *JCHAS* 3 no. 27, no. 27 (1897): 94.
28 Hurley, 'Blessed Thaddeus,', 96.
29 Roger Price and Michael Ponsford, *St Bartholomew's Hospital, Bristol: The Excavation of a Medieval Hospital 1976–1978. CBA Research Report 110* (York: Council for British Archaeology, 1998), 214.
30 Hopper, *To Be a Pilgrim*, 113; Price and Ponsford, *St Bartholomew's Hospital, Bristol*, 204.
31 Hopper, *To Be a Pilgrim*, 114; Edwin Mullins, *The Pilgrimage to Santiago* (Devon: Readers Union Ltd, 1975), 72.
32 Hopper, *To Be a Pilgrim*, 214; Price and Ponsford, *St Bartholomew's Hospital, Bristol.*
33 Hopper, To Be a Pilgrim, 115; Diana Webb, Pilgrims and Pilgrimage in the Medieval West, 91.
34 Harpur, *Sacred Tracks*, 82.
35 Sumption, *Pilgrimage*, 203.
36 Harpur, *Sacred Tracks*, 82.
37 Hopper, *To Be a Pilgrim*, 117.
38 Rogerius appears to have been on the return leg of his pilgrimage from the Holy Land via Rome. This coincided with the Louis IX's Crusades and he had probably gone to Jerusalem. Given his infirmity, he was unlikely to have been a crusader, but he may have taken advantage of the greater availability of shipping and the security of travelling with a large group of well-armed men. See Christine Meek, 'Beyond the Frontier: Irishmen and Irish Goods in Lucca in the Later Middle Ages,' in *Colony and Frontier in Medieval Ireland*, ed. Terry Barry, Robin Frame, and Katherine Simms (London: Hambledon Press, 1995), 228–29.
39 Meek, 'Beyond the Frontier,' 230.
40 Meek, 'Beyond the Frontier,' 229–230.
41 In Latin, Mauritius Ghiliberti de Ybernia.
42 Meek, 'Beyond the Frontier,' 231.
43 Meek, 'Beyond the Frontier,' 231.
44 Harpur, *Sacred Tracks*, 78–79.
45 Birch, *Pilgrimage to Rome*, 56.
46 Birch, *Pilgrimage to Rome*, 56–8.
47 Birch, *Pilgrimage to Rome*, 57.
48 Joseph Patrick Byrne, *Encyclopedia of the Black Death* (Oxford: ABC–CLIO, 2012), 315.
49 'Ua Flannaga[i]n (namely Muircertach) of Tuath-Ratha went to Rome this year and died of the plague.' AU.

50 Birch, *Pilgrimage to Rome*, 68–70.
51 Birch, *Pilgrimage to Rome,* 69.
52 Birch, *Pilgrimage to Rome,* 68.
53 Webb, *Medieval European Pilgrimage, c.700–c.1500*, 78–79.
54 AU.
55 Stuart Kinsella, 'From Hiberno-Norse to Anglo-Norman, c.1030–1300,' in *Christ Church Cathedral Dublin: A History*, ed. Kenneth Milne (Dublin: Four Courts Press, 2000), 28.
56 E.A.E Matthew, 'The Governing of the Lancastrian Lordship of Ireland in the Time of James Butler, Fourth Earl of Ormond c. 1420–1452.' Unpublished PhD Thesis, University of Durham. (PhD thesis, 1995), 252; K Ralph, 'Medieval Antiquarianism: The Butlers and Artistic Patronage in Fifteenth-Century Ireland,' *Eolas* 7 (2014): 4.
57 Cunningham, *Medieval Irish Pilgrims*, 143.
58 ACon.
59 A branch of the Southern Uí Néill.
60 Cunningham, *Medieval Irish Pilgrims*, 143.
61 AFM.
62 Stat. Ire. Ric. III–Henry VIII, 39.
63 AFM,
64 Diana Watt, 'Margery Kempe's Overseas Pilgrimages,' in *A Place to Believe In: Locating Medieval Landscapes*, ed. Clare Lees and Gillian Overing (University Park, PA: Penn State University Press., 2006), 179; Jennifer Ward, *Women in Medieval Europe 1200–1500* (London: Routledge Press, 2016), 232.
65 Karina Holton, 'From Carters: Aspects of Fairs and Markets in Medieval Leinster,' in *Irish Fairs and Markets. Studies in Local History*, ed. Denis Cronin, Joe Gilligan, and Karina Holton (Dublin: Four Courts Press, 2001), 27.
66 Flanagan, *The Transformation of the Irish Church*, 227.
67 Stalley, 'Sailing to Santiago,' 398.
68 Stalley, 'Sailing to Santiago,' 399.
69 Childs, 'The Perils, or Otherwise,' 129.
70 Stalley, 'Sailing to Santiago,' 399.
71 AI; Goddard H Orpen, 'The Fitz Geralds, Barons of Offaly,' *JRSAI* 4, no. 2 (1914): 100.
72 James Lydon, 'Alexander Bicknor: Archbishop and Peculator,' *History Ireland* 1 (2) (1993): 15.
73 Olivia Remie Constable, 'Storms at Sea on a Voyage between Rhodes and Venice, November 1470,' in *Medieval Chrisitianity in Practice*, ed. Miri Rubin (Princeton and Oxford: Princeton University Press, 2009), 83.
74 A. Steward, trans., *Flelix Fabri (Circa 1480–1483 A.D). The Library of the Palestine Pilgrims' Text Society*, vol. 1 (London: London Committee of the Palestine Exploration Fund, 1896), 41.
75 Stalley, 'Sailing to Santiago,' 403; Cal. Pat. Rolls 147–85, 78.
76 Cunningham, *Medieval Irish Pilgrims*, 143.
77 AFM.
78 AFM.
79 AFM.
80 Ohler, *The Medieval Traveller*, 48–49; Harpur, *Sacred Tracks*, 79.
81 Cal. Pat. Rolls 1476–85, 78; Stalley, 'Sailing to Santiago,' 397.
82 Francis Davey, ed., *The Itineraries of William Wey* (Oxford: Bodleian Library, 2010), 211–12.
83 Davey, *The Itineraries,* 213.
84 Sumption, *Pilgrimage*, 212–13.
85 Bugslag, 'Performative Thaumaturgy,' 230.
86 Sumption, *Pilgrimage*, 213.
87 David M. Gitlitz and Linda Kay Davidson, *The Pilgrimage Road to Santiago: The Complete Cultural Handbook* (New York: St. Martin's Press, 2000), 344.
88 Harpur, *Sacred Tracks*, 104.
89 Bugslag, 'Performative Thaumaturgy,' 220, fn. 4.
90 Harpur, *Sacred Tracks*, 104.
91 Gitlitz and Davidson, *The Pilgrimage Road to Santiago*, 344.
92 A square or composite pillar performing a similar function to a column. Found at the junction of the nave, chancel and transepts of a cruciform church.
93 Bugslag, 'Performative Thaumaturgy,' 220, fn. 4.
94 Gitlitz and Davidson, *The Pilgrimage Road to Santiago*, 344; Hopper, *To Be a Pilgrim*, 50.
95 Kenney, *The Sources for the Early History of Ireland*, 601; Ven. Archdeacon John L. Robinson, 'St. Brigid and Glastonbury,' *JRSAI* 83 (1953): 97.
96 Hopper, *To Be a Pilgrim*, 97; Birch, *Pilgrimage to Rome*, 41; Stopford, 'Some Approaches to the Archaeology,' 63.

97 Hopper, *To Be a Pilgrim*, 97–98. See also Webb, *Medieval European Pilgrimage, c.700–c.1500*, 128–35.
98 Sumption, *Pilgrimage*, 222.
99 J. F. Romano, 'Rome,' in *Encyclopedia of Medieval Pilgrimage*, ed. L. Taylor (Boston: Brill, 2010), 644.
100 Jacoby, 'Evolving Routes,' 77.
101 Harpur, *Sacred Tracks*, 79; Webb, *Medieval European Pilgrimage*, 143.
102 Ó Clabaigh, *The Friars*, 195. The text mentions the chapter in Clonmel, but it is not clear if he was a member of the monastery there.
103 M. Krasnodebska-D'Aughton, 'Relics and Riches: Familiarising the Unknown in a Fourteenth-Century Pilgrimage Account from Ireland,' in *The Art, Literature and Material Culture of the Medieval World. Transition, Transformation and Taxonom*, ed. J Boulton, J Hawkes and M Herman (Dublin: Four Courts Press, 2015), 113–14.
104 Michael Robson, *St. Francis of Assisi: The Legend and the Life* (London: Continuum, 1999), 188.
105 Steward, *Flelix Fabri*, vol. 1, 57.
106 Esposito, *Itinerarium Symonis Semeonis*, 25.
107 Esposito, *Itinerarium Symonis Semeonis*, 25.
108 Esposito, *Itinerarium Symonis Semeonis*, 27.
109 Colmán Ó Clabaigh and Michael Stanton, 'Thomas Becket and Ireland,' in *Listen ,O Isles, unto Me Studies in Medieval Word and Image in Honour of Jennifer O'Reilly*, ed. Elizabeth Mullins and Diarmuid Scully (Cork: Cork University Press, 2011), 87–101.
110 Bruce Watson, Trevor Bringham and Tony Dyson, *London Bridge: 2000 Years of a River Crossing. MoLAS Monograph 8* (London: Museum of London Archaeological Service, 2001), 111.
111 Esposito, *Itinerarium Symonis Semeonis*, 27.
112 Watson et al., *London Bridge*, 111.
113 Esposito, *Itinerarium Symonis Semeonis*, 27. Canterbury was the burial place of John Pecham, the great Franciscan theologian and archbishop of Canterbury. See Ó Clabaigh, *The Friars*, 196.
114 For an in-depth discussion of the topic, see Krasnodebska-D'Aughton, 'Relics and Riches.'
115 Esposito, *Itinerarium Symonis Semeonis*, 29.
116 Esposito, *Itinerarium Symonis Semeonis*, 29.
117 Esposito, *Itinerarium Symonis Semeonis*, 29.
118 Esposito, *Itinerarium Symonis Semeonis*, 31.
119 Esposito, *Itinerarium Symonis Semeonis*, 31–33.
120 Esposito, *Itinerarium Symonis Semeonis*, 35.
121 Esposito, *Itinerarium Symonis Semeonis*, 35.
122 From the early 13th century, Venice 'began to stand out as a port of embarkation to the Holy Land. Thanks to its maritime predominance in the Eastern Mediterranean, following her involvement in the Fourth Crusade (1204).'' Paola Modesti, 'Venice,' in *Encyclopedia of Medieval Pilgrimage* (Boston: Brill, 2010), 788.
123 Esposito, *Itinerarium Symonis Semeonis*, 35.
124 Modesti, 'Venice,' 784, 788.
125 Modesti, 'Venice,' 788.
126 Harpur, *Sacred Tracks*, 115.
127 Nicole Chareyron, *Pilgrims to Jerusalem in the Middle Ages* (New York: Columbia University Press, 2005), 41.
128 Esposito, *Itinerarium Symonis Semeonis*, 37–43.
129 Esposito, *Itinerarium Symonis Semeonis*, 9.
130 Esposito, *Itinerarium Symonis Semeonis*, 37–45.
131 Esposito, *Itinerarium Symonis Semeonis*, 47.
132 Esposito, *Itinerarium Symonis Semeonis*, 65.
133 Many pilgrims died on their way to the Holy Lands, such as Irish pilgrim Ualgary O'Rourke, Lord of Breifney, who died on his way to the River [Jordan] in 1231 (AFM).
134 Esposito, *Itinerarium Symonis Semeonis*.95.
135 Esposito, *Itinerarium Symonis Semeonis*, 97—9.
136 Esposito, *Itinerarium Symonis Semeonis*, 103.
137 Krasnodebska-D'Aughton, 'Relics and Riches,' 116.
138 Esposito, *Itinerarium Symonis Semeonis*, 105.
139 Esposito, *Itinerarium Symonis Semeonis*, 18.
140 Anthony Bale, *The Book of Margery Kempe*, Oxford World Classics (Oxford: Oxford University Press, 2015), 79.
141 Denys Pringle, *Pilgrimage to Jerusalem and the Holy Land 1187-1291* (London: Routledge Press, 2016), 186.
142 Jan Van Herwaarden, *Between Saint James and Erasmus: Studies in Late-Medieval Religious Life: Devotions and Pilgrimages in the Netherlands* (Brill, 2003), 52.
143 Esposito, *Itinerarium Symonis Semeonis,*107; Krasnodebska-D'Aughton, 'Relics and Riches,' 119.
144 Esposito, *Itinerarium Symonis Semeonis*, 107. This was a church that, according to tradition,

dated back to at least to the 4th Century and contained the two holiest sites in Christendom: the site where Christ was crucified and the empty tomb of Jesus, where he is said to have been buried and resurrected. Within the church proper are the last four Stations representing the final episodes of the Passion of Christ.

145 Harpur, *Sacred Tracks*, 118–19.

146 Sumption, *Pilgrimage*, 146.

147 For accounts of other contemporary descriptions of pilgrimage, see Mary Margaret Newett, ed., *Canon Pietro Casola's Pilgrimage to Jerusalem in the Year 1494* (Manchester: Manchester University Press, 1907), 259–60.

148 Esposito, *Itinerarium Symonis Semeonis*, 6; Ó Clabaigh, *The Friars*, 198.

CHAPTER 7

Pilgrim Performance: Rituals at the Pilgrim Shrine – Right Place, Right Time

People made pilgrimages throughout the year, but certain times of the year were more popular than others. The saint's feast day was very much favoured, as medieval people believed the saint's presence was at its most potent on this day, with a greater chance of prayers being answered and miracles performed. It was also a more eventful time: larger numbers of pilgrims, combined with more elaborate religious ceremonies, created a more energetic atmosphere. Outside Ireland, some pilgrim churches rarely exhibited their relics and viewings were confined to set times of the year, including the saint's feast day. Close contact with relics – either physical or visual – outside these times was often a luxury afforded only to the rich.[1]

The 7th-century *Life of St Brigit* is the earliest account of an Irish pilgrimage. We are told that pilgrims arrived at the monastery of Kildare 'to join in the solemn celebration of the feast of the saint Brigit', on 1 February.[2] Kildare was not alone in having a tradition of commemoration of the saints. The 7th-century *Life of St Colmcille* refers to special Masses held at Iona on the feast day of the saints Columcille and Bathéna.[3] As Iona was the head of a federation of monastic churches that stretched across Scotland and Ireland, it is likely that all churches in the Columban sphere of influence celebrated these feast days in a similar manner. An 8th-century *Additamenta* attached to Tírechán's *Life of St Patrick* notes that on St Patrick's feast day all monasteries and churches under the control and influence of Armagh were to celebrate 'his proper Mass' and chant hymns dedicated to St Patrick.[4] Further evidence for the popularity of the pilgrimage focused on the feast days of saints is found in the 8th/9th-century annals. Viking raids at monasteries frequently coincided with important Church festivals such as Christmas and feast days of the saints.[5] For example, in 869, the Vikings attacked Armagh on 17 March, the feast of St Patrick, and in 933 on the feast of St Martin.[6] Similarly, Kildare was raided on 1 February 929.[7] These raids appear to have been planned to take advantage of the presence of lay people and pilgrims.[8]

Following trends in the wider Christian world, pilgrimage on the feast days of saints continued to be popular in later centuries in Ireland. For example, the

Medieval cathedral of Kildare built on the site of the early medieval monastery founded by St Brigit. © Louise Nugent

Annals of Ulster recorded the death of a group of pilgrims at Croagh Patrick on the eve of St Patrick's feast day in 1113. The 12th-century text *Aislinge Meic Conglinne* also makes passing reference to pilgrims from Munster, timing their pilgrimage to Cork to coincide with the feast of SS Finbar and Nessan on 25 July.[9] During the later medieval period, many of the indulgences granted to Irish churches were available to the faithful on the date of Church festivals such as Easter, or the feast day of a particular saint.[10]

In early modern Ireland, local devotion to the patron saint of the parish often manifested in group pilgrimage to a holy well or other landscape relics dedicated to that saint on the pattern day. 'Pattern', derived from the Irish word '*patrún*', meaning patron, developed from the medieval tradition of the honouring the feast of the patron saint of the parish. In many parishes around modern Ireland, pilgrimage still takes place on the saint's feast day. Similar pilgrimages were surely made to the relics and holy wells of patron saints in medieval Ireland.

Up until the 1980' the pattern days were regarded as public holidays in some parts of Ireland. People were expected to abstain from all work and children given the day off school. There are many folk tales of misfortune that befell those who flouted tradition and carried out any work, other than the most essential of farm tasks, such as milking cows. Those who did not obey the social norms often suffered terrible consequences, as recorded in the folklore relating to the feast of St Martin at Ballynacally, Co. Clare, or that of St Ciaran at Seir Kieran, in Co. Offaly. Abstaining from work on the saint's feast day may have much older roots. A miracle tale relating to the relic of the True Cross at Holycross Abbey recalls similar misfortune befalling a man of 'moderate means', named Terence from Roscommon who, on 3 May 1621, the feast of the Invention of the Holy Cross, carried out unnecessary work and lost his mind. This feast was a

> day the church forbids servile work, nevertheless he continued at his usual servile labour; but all of a sudden, he lost his senses, mind, and reason.[11]

Only pilgrimage to the relic of the True Cross at Holycross Abbey brought about a cure for the unfortunate man's affliction.

Church festivals such as Christmas and Easter or the feast of relics were also popular days of pilgrimage, as relics were often openly displayed, providing great opportunities for pilgrims to gaze upon and, if lucky enough, touch these holy objects.

In 1687, Sir Richard Cox, the Lord Chancellor of Ireland, described a pilgrimage to the relic of the True Cross at Tracton Abbey, during Easter week:

> and this is so firmly believed that on every Holy Thursday vast multitudes from far and near resort to pay their devotions to this relick.[12]

Many larger churches had collections of relics and multiple altars dedicated to different saints, all of whose feast days were celebrated with a special Mass and, in some cases, the display of relics, which helped attract pilgrims. Christ Church Cathedral in Dublin had between eight and nine altars, including the high altar. Several of these altars were dedications to saints whose relics were part of the cathedral's collection.[13] From the 12th century, Irish churches following the Sarum Rite, carried out reliquary processions to altars on the feast days of individual saints, as well as other important feast days such as the feast of relics. The Sarum Rite, also known as the Use of Sarum, was a highly elaborate pattern of worship that originated in Salisbury Cathedral in England. It governed the way churches organised their affairs and liturgy. Rituals involving relics were elaborate affairs and, given the opportunity they provided for close proximity to relics, they prompted many to be present on these occasions.

Special occasions such as the translation of the saint's body and the enshrinement of relics also resulted in pilgrimage. Translations were accompanied by great pomp and ceremony, with processions affording the observers a chance for close contact with their beloved saints. It was widely believed that miracles accompanied these events. There are numerous examples of the translation of Irish saints in the early medieval sources (see Chapter 1), all of which must have resulted in pilgrimage on the day or days or weeks following. Translation of the saints' bones was accompanied by a special liturgy and attended by the great and the good, as well as devoted pilgrims. Similar pomp and ceremony must have accompanied the placing of the bones of St Manchan in his elaborate house shrine at Lemanaghan, Co. Offaly, in the 12th century (see Chapter 1). Occasionally, the date of translations retained a special significance for pilgrims, and some developed into a special day of devotion. At Canterbury, the body of St Thomas à Becket was translated from his original burial place in the crypt to a new shrine in the Trinity Chapel in the cathedral, on 7 July 1220/1221. The anniversary of the translation went on to be celebrated as a second feast day and attracted large numbers of pilgrims.[14] This day also features in many surviving medieval liturgical calendars. The Calendar of Christ Church Cathedral in Dublin, which records the feast days celebrated by the cathedral, includes the date of the translation of SS Brigit, Patrick and Colmcille at Downpatrick, as well as that of the non-Irish saints Werburgh and Cyniburg.[15]

Worshipping Brigit in 7th-century Kildare

One of the earliest and most detailed accounts of early Irish pilgrimage is found in the 7th-century *Life of Brigit*, written by a monk at the monastery of Kildare called Cogitosus. According to tradition, Brigit had founded a monastery of nuns at Kildare in the 5th century. By the 7th century, Kildare had become a double monastery of monks and nuns overseen by an abbess and an abbot-bishop. It was also the head of a large paruchia or federation of churches that stretched across the province of Leinster.[16] The *Life of Brigit* provides a wonderful glimpse into what it was like to be a pilgrim in the 7th century.

> And who can count the different crowds and numberless peoples flocking from all the provinces – some for the abundant feasting, others for the healing of their afflictions, others to watch the pageant of the crowds, others with great gifts and offerings – to join in the solemn celebration of the feast of the saint Brigit.[17]

Cogitosus tells us the 'crowds' of pilgrims came from 'all provinces' of Ireland. It is unlikely that Kildare had a truly national appeal at the time. The numbers of pilgrims were probably exaggerated to support Kildare's attempts to become the pre-eminent church in Ireland. Most of the pilgrims came from Leinster and areas where Kildare held direct influence. Given its links with the Uí Dúnlainge dynasty, whose members held lands in north Leinster, along the Liffey Valley and the Kildare Plains, a large proportion of the pilgrims probably also came from Uí Dúnlainge territory.[18]

It is difficult to know what Kildare or contemporary monasteries looked like in the 7th century. A century later, at most Irish monasteries and ecclesiastical sites, the main church and graveyard were enclosed by a ditch, earthen bank or stone wall. Wealthy monasteries such as Clonmacnoise, Armagh and Glendalough were surrounded by several concentric boundaries, all defined by a ditch and bank, with each enclosure demarcating areas of decreasing holiness. The church and graveyard were at the centre and domestic and craft areas were located in the outer enclosures.[19] Kildare, after the 8th century, had at least two enclosing banks: the footprint of the outer enclosure is preserved in the modern streetscape of Nugent Street and White Abbey Street, while the wall that surrounds the medieval cathedral church and graveyard appears to preserve the extent of the inner enclosure.[20] Smaller monasteries had a single enclosing bank or stone wall. The internal space was divided with a dividing wall or bank, separating the church and graveyard from the domestic space used by the monks and religious.[21]

In winter and early spring, pilgrimages like those for Brigit's feast day were affected by the weather. February is a harsh month, with changeable weather, and dry crisp days are interchangeable with snow showers, biting wind or heavy frosts, all of which added to the difficulties of travel, regardless of the distance. All the pilgrims arrived relatively warm from the physical exertion of their journey but quickly cooled down. People would have wanted to move inside the monastery as quickly as possible. Pilgrimage rituals involved slow movement and there were no doubt many opportunities for standing still that would make people become cold. Could there have been areas with fires, where they could warm themselves? Was food provided for those who had travelled far? The crowds of pilgrims were all from different places and people may have mingled. Some perhaps sought out familiar faces in the crowd; others may have made small talk with the nearest stranger, exchanging news and gossip, talking about the weather and their journey. Pilgrims may have carried food with them, perhaps sharing with the less fortunate, or perhaps the monks and nuns provided hot drinks and bread.

For many, the pilgrimage was an annual event religiously repeated on the saint's day. Such pilgrims understood how they were expected to move around at

Kildare and how to participate in ritual activities and prayers. For others, this was a new experience; some first-timers may have asked their fellow pilgrims about rituals or the order of ceremonies. Others sheepishly copied the actions of their fellow pilgrims. Perhaps members of the religious community were on hand to provide guidance and give direction. However, all the pilgrims were drawn there to venerate the corporeal relics, the bones of Brigit and St Conláed, the first bishop of Kildare. The *Life* tells us that the remains of the two saints were housed separately in the main church, in elaborate containers, known as reliquary shrines. To encounter these precious objects, the pilgrims needed to move into the very heart of the monastery, an area normally off limits to lay people.[22] Scholars suggest that the *Life* was composed with a view of how contemporary pilgrims experienced Kildare. As the reader told the story of Brigit's life and death, those who listened could, in their mind's eye, move through a mental landscape of holy places consecrated by the saint, which corresponded to the physical world around them. The text allowed the reader to move mentally through the monastery, following the route or path taken by contemporary pilgrims at Kildare.[23]

Pilgrims first passed through the entrance or gateway into the outermost confines of the monastery; and from there they gradually moved closer to the most sacred area where the reliquary church lay. The entrance must have been substantial and imposing, designed to impress the visitor. Kildare was, after all, a very wealthy place.

A rare example of an outer entrance survives at the early medieval ecclesiastical site of Glendalough, Co. Wicklow. Dating to the 12th century, the entrance is a substantial stone gatehouse with round arches. It is still used as an access point by modern tourists who, when passing under the arches, follow the footsteps of earlier pilgrims. Just inside the inner gate, pilgrims passed by an enormous stone more than 1 metre high, incised with three large crosses. The crosses signalled to all who passed that they were now in a sacred space.[24]

To limit disruption and to stop people wandering off into the areas that were off limits, a member of the religious community may have acted as guide, helping to funnel pilgrims along a designated route and perhaps pointing out other holy locations in the monastery. The *Life* makes note of a miraculous millstone at the entrance, an enclosure that surrounded the reliquary church.[25] The millstone was a relic of St Brigit. It was moved by the saint, with a miraculous display of strength, from the top of a mountain to a mill in the valley below, a feat which many men had tried unsuccessfully. Following miracles at the mill, the stone was brought to Kildare and placed:

Left: Medieval gateway leading into the monastery of Glendalough.
Right: Stone cross inside monastic gateway at Glendalough.

> ... near the doorway of the ornate cashel which surrounds the church where many congregate out of veneration for the most blessed Brigit's miracles.[26]

The source goes on to say that the stone ' ... drives disease and afflictions from the faithful who touch' it. The *Life* suggests that both healthy and sick pilgrims were allowed physical contact with the stone, which acted as a ritual focal point in the sacred landscape of Kildare.[27] Any pilgrim who visited the reliquary church had to pass by this miraculous stone. As pilgrims moved into the inner enclosure, their eyes were immediately drawn to the reliquary church. We are told the church had been recently renovated to accommodate the increasing numbers of lay visitors. The building was made of wood, as were most contemporary Irish churches. At the time, wooden churches were made either of vertical staves set in sill beams and wall plates, or of vertical staves set in a groove in corner posts. The exterior and interior of these buildings may have been decorated with elaborate carvings and some were painted.[28] Historical sources often refer to early wooden churches by the name *dairthech* ('oak house'), suggesting that many were made from sturdy oak planks. Some early churches were roofed with shingles.[29] This roofing option afforded opportunities to add extra decoration and colour, as the shingles could be shaped, painted and laid out in decorative patterns.[30] Stone churches began to be built in the 8th to 10th centuries but they did not become common until the 11th to 12th centuries.[31] A wealthy foundation like Kildare could afford the best of craftsmen, so the church must have been a sight to behold. Before going inside the church, pilgrims would have marvelled at the building. How magnificent it must have seemed in comparison to their own homes. The *Life* tells us that the interior of the church had a high ceiling and

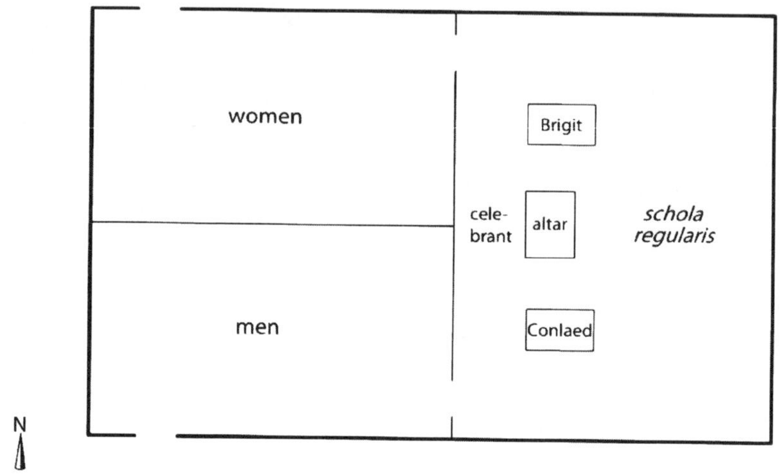

Conjectural plan of St Brigit's Church at Kildare. ©Tómas Ó Carragáin

the walls were adorned with pictures.[32] The internal space was divided by 'board walls under a single roof', and a longitudinal division with a low, waist-height screen.[33] It is clear that the pilgrims at Kildare were not all equal and once inside the church they were divided according to status and gender.[34] Women occupied the north side of the nave and men the south, with both groups entering through separate doorways in the north and south walls.[35]

This design differed from the majority of early medieval Irish churches, which had a simple rectangular plan with a single western doorway and were lit by a small window in the east wall.[36]

The chancel area at Kildare was divided from the nave by some sort of screen with two doors, in the north and south. There may have been a central space above the chancel rail that permitted the altar and reliquaries to be seen from the nave, as well as facilitating the distribution of the Eucharist.[37] The bones of the saints were found in reliquaries on either side of the altar.[38]

> … the glorious bodies of both – namely Archbishop Conleth and our most flourishing virgin Brigit - are laid on the right and left of the ornate altar and rest in tombs adorned with a refined profusion of gold, silver, gems and precious stones with gold and silver chandeliers hanging from above and different images presenting a variety of carvings and colours. [39]

The liturgy was central to the pilgrim experience at all churches during the early and late medieval periods.[40] At Kildare and at other contemporary churches, pilgrims joined the religious community in the liturgical celebration of their

Top: St David's holy well, Woodhouse, Co. Waterford.
Bottom: A modern pilgrim taking water from the holy well on Caher Island, Co. Mayo.
© Louise Nugent

saint.[41] Pilgrims felt a mix of emotions on such occasions: some were filled with excitement, expectations of longed-for miracles and curiosity, as well as feelings of pure devotion. These emotions were enhanced by the liturgy: the odours of burning wax and incense, the sounds of singing and the chanting of prayers all created a unique atmosphere. Pilgrims listened attentively to hymns about the saint, sung by the religious.[42] Many of the surviving early Irish hymns were written to be sung 'on special feast days or in extra-liturgical communal devotion'.[43] Great importance was attached to the singing of hymns in the Irish Office and collections of hymns of Irish saints such as Patrick and Comgall survive in later 7th- and early 12th-century texts.[44] During or after the Mass, the saint's *Life* and accounts of her miracles were read aloud. The Irish *Life of St Colmcille*, written between 1150 and 1182 at Derry, was composed in the style of a homily to be read aloud on the saint's feast day, 9 June, while the Tripartite Life of Saint Patrick was composed to be read in three parts over the three days of the saint's festival.[45] Those in search of healing listened carefully to stories of the saint's miracles, taking hope that they too would be lucky enough to be healed or find ease from their afflictions. We cannot under-estimate the sensory experience of such occasions. Flickering candles caused atmospheric shadows to dance across the walls of the church, highlighting painted pictures and wall-hangings.[46] Pilgrims inhaled smells from candle wax and incense, and in summer and spring, the scent of decorative flowers, and sometimes even the unpleasant odours of some of their fellow pilgrims.

At outdoor pilgrim destinations, the sensory experience was also a key part of the pilgrimage – the smells of aromatic plants and flowers that grew wild, and the light of the sun, as it moved through the day, illuminating areas briefly before they returned to shadow. Other natural events, such as rolling mist and fog, the gurgling sound of water, the chattering of birds and the lowing of cows, existed in the same moment in time as the prayers and rituals of the pilgrims, and these would have affected how they experienced holy places.

Communing with Relics in Early Medieval Ireland

The desire for contact with the holy was universal and not confined to a specific place or time period. The 7th-century pilgrims at Kildare desired to get as close as possible to the relics of their beloved saint. Unfortunately, we are not told how pilgrims interacted with the relics at Kildare. It is very possible they may never have been allowed to do more than gaze at the saint's shrine from the nave. How did contemporary and later Irish pilgrims interact with relics and burial places of the saints or landscape relics? Outside Ireland, the level of access to relics varied from place to place and time to time. Access to relics, statues and burial places was controlled by the keepers or guardians of the shrine and, while physical contact was very much desired by pilgrims, it was not always allowed. We must not overlook the importance of visual contact with relics or the power of being in relative proximity to the sacred. For pilgrims, the sanctity of a saints extended beyond the grave or relics and permeated into the church, monastery grounds and physical structures. Special displays of relics were significant events and, for some, 'just seeing the relic in its reliquary was judged to be thaumaturgically effective'.[47]

Pilgrimage is often depicted as the great leveller, where all were equal. While this is true in many respects, social status and wealth allowed for certain privileges. At Aachen, in Germany, the social status of the pilgrim influenced the level of access to the shrine's relics, with the more important members of society able to get closer to the relics than the poor.[48] Issues of access were less problematic at local shrines, due to the smaller numbers of pilgrims, or at landscape relics located away from churches and monasteries and where the robust nature of the spring or stone needed little protection and few restrictions on contact.

Pilgrimage places such as Kildare, under the direct control of the Church, had to balance a fine line between encouraging pilgrimage and preventing pilgrims from disrupting the monastic way of life. Pilgrimage generated an important income stream; it also fanned the flames of cults, resulting in the patronage of the wealthy, which, in turn, resulted in bequests of lands and money. On the other hand, pilgrims could disrupt daily prayer and the routine necessary for living a good monastic life. This dilemma was as true for large and small monastic sites during the early medieval period as it was on the eve of the Reformation. To facilitate pilgrimage, but maintain the monastic way of life, access to holy places and relics had to be controlled. Pilgrims may have been encouraged to follow designed routes or arrive at certain times during the day.

Kildare was unusual in its treatment of the saint's remains. At the majority of 7th-century Irish pilgrim sites, the patron saint rested in a special grave in the monastic graveyard. It may have been easier for pilgrims to get closer, too, and to spend time in prayer and even to touch these holy graves freely. *The Martyrology of Oengus* suggests that St Maelruain's grave at Tallaght was accessible to pilgrims in the 9th century.[49] The 12th-century *Life of St Flannan* tells of pilgrims flocking to the saint's grave and of the miracles that took place there.

> … after his death the fame of his sanctity attracted crowds to his tomb where, through his intercession, miracles took place: there the blind received sight; the lame, the use of their limbs; and every bodily ill was cured.[50]

Similar accounts are found in texts relating to St Ita's tomb at Killeedy, Co. Limerick, in the 12th century,[51] and the tomb of St Máedóc of Ferns.[52] These suggest that at some foundations, pilgrims came into close proximity with the saint's grave and may have even engaged in practices like incubation, fasting and vigils.

Pilgrims who visited Caherlehillan, in the Iveragh Peninsula, Co. Kerry, between the 6th and the early 8th centuries, had access to saints' graves in the monastic graveyard. Pilgrims could interact with the upper portions of the stone-lined grave, as well as the flat lintel stone that sealed it. The side stones, along with the lintel stone, show signs of polishing and wear as a result of prolonged

Killabuonia gable shrine, Co. Kerry.
© Amanda Clarke

human contact. The distinctive wear pattern points to ritual activity at the grave that involved the touching of the upper surface of the grave.[53]

A few outdoor stone reliquary shrines also point to direct physical contact with the saint's tomb. Three 8th-century gable-shrines from Co. Kerry (Killabuonia, Killoluaig and Kilpeacan) all have special openings called '*fenestellae*' cut into their gable stones. Similar openings existed in contemporary reliquary shrines from outside Ireland. The opening provided access to relics in the shrine and acted as a tiny window that allowed pilgrims to view the relics inside.[54] The Killabuonia shrine has a 15-centimetre opening, with a small simple Latin cross carved above it.

The aperture is positioned close to the base of the shrine, forcing the devotee to kneel or crouch down to place a hand inside or view the interior. Other outdoor reliquaries are also designed to be low to the ground, requiring the pilgrim to kneel to be at eye level with the shrine. The opening in the Killabuonia shrine is large enough to insert a hand, so pilgrims could have shoved pieces of cloth inside or a hand, to physically touch the holy bones of St Buonia.[55] During the 19th century, pilgrims there passed hairpins, buttons and the tassels from wool shawls through the hole as votive offerings, once they had completed their pilgrimage rounds.[56]

The physical appearance of the Kerry gable shrines is reminiscent of a 7th-century wooden reliquary shrine at Lichfield in England (it is possible that wooden reliquaries like this also existed at Irish churches). It held the bones of St Chad and had a similar opening from which pilgrims used to collect holy dust:

> Chad's burial place is covered by a wooden tomb made in the form of a little house with an aperture in the wall through which those who visit it out of devotion may insert their hand and take out some of the dust.[57]

Reconstruction of pilgrims praying at a gable shrine. Image by JG O'Donaghue

Levels of access to the saint's relics or grave could change over time. Areas that pilgrims freely accessed could become off limits or restricted. The excavations at Caherlehillan show that during the 8th century, the 6th-century saint's grave, worn smooth through the contact of early pilgrims, was surmounted by a later corner-post shrine. The original grave remained undisturbed but was now physically separated from pilgrims. The interior of the new shrine was filled with earth and small stones and sealed with three large flat slabs. The shrine introduced a degree of distance between the saint and the pilgrim. The presence of a small aperture in the surface one of the uppermost slabs appears to have been designed to allow access to the contents of the new shrine. The earth probably also became seen as sacred, through the direct contact with the founder's grave below. The aperture allowed the pilgrims a chance for a more intimate experience, while protecting the grave below.[58] Perhaps pilgrims shoved pieces of cloth into this opening to be taken away and used when needed for healing of the sick or to provide protection for the home.

Pilgrims who visited the monastic settlement on island of Illaunloughan, Co. Kerry, in the 8th/9th century, were also given access to the saint's shrine. The shrine, a gable shrine was built on a low rectangular *leacht*. It was the most prominent feature at the monastery and could be seen clearly by all passing sea traffic.[59] Pilgrims approached the shrine by climbing a series of sandstone steps set into the corner of the *leacht*. The surface of the *leacht* was divided into internal and external areas defined by upright stones.

A worn path led the pilgrim from the steps to a central paved area surrounding the shrine. The design suggests that pilgrims were allowed to move around the shrine and kneel before it.[60] The 12th/13th-century outdoor reliquary shrines known as mortuary houses were also designed to facilitate the physical

Top: Plan and section drawing from excavation of the early grave of saint found under corner-post shrine at Caherlehillan. **Bottom**: Photo of modern reconstruction of gable shrine following excavations. © John Sheehan

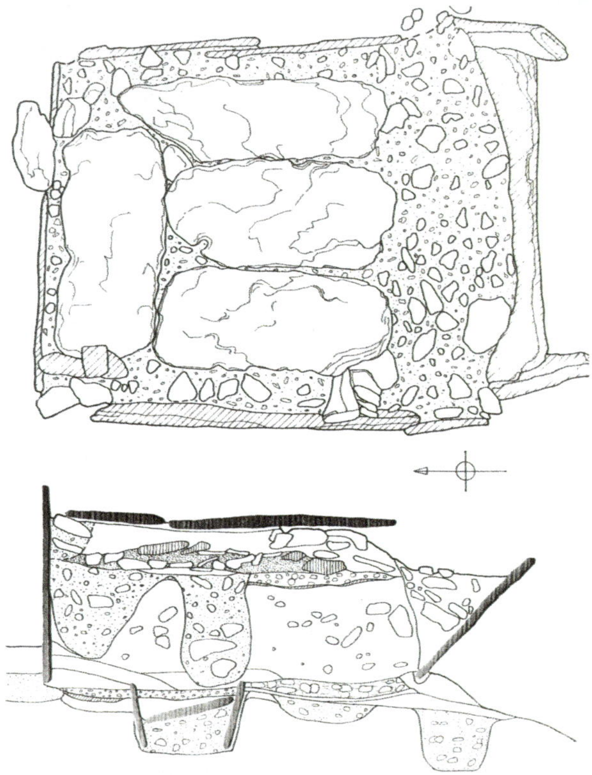

Aerial view of *leacht* and gable shrine at Illaunloughan. © National Monuments Service Department of Culture, Heritage, and the Gaeltacht

View of paved path leading to and around the gable shrine at Illaunloughan. © jim@megalithcireland.com

contact of pilgrims with the relics of the saints.[61] A small opening in the east gable of the early 13th-century shrine at Bovevagh allowed pilgrims to access part of a body-shaped cavity that may have held the remains of the saint. Smoothing of the stones on the exterior of the openings could be a result of 'the passing of innumerable hands, seeking to touch the skull, through an originally narrow slit'.[62] A similar opening was noted in the fabric of St Cadan's mortuary house at Tamlaght, Co. Down,[63] while the reliquary shrine at Cooley, Co. Donegal, known as 'the skull house', also has a small opening in its western end.[64]

Direct contact with the interior of the saint's tomb or shrine was discouraged at other Irish churches. The 9th-century *Martyrology of Oengus* tells us that St Cianán's remains were kept in a tomb at his monastery in Duleek. St Adomnán went into St

Cianán's tomb to 'behold and touch the body' of the saint. His actions resulted in the loss of his eye, a punishment for the violation of the saint's resting place. The text goes on to say, 'Thenceforward no one dares to enter the tomb.'[65]

Many Irish monasteries had extensive devotional landscapes. These consisted of churches, the burial place of the saint, their relics – corporeal, or items owned by the saint – and landscape relics. At 7th-century Kildare, the landscape consisted of the relics of Conláed and Brigit, and the miraculous millstone. From the 9th century, pilgrims to Clonmacnoise could visit the site of St Ciaran's grave, covered by a shrine chapel known as Temple Ciarán, two holy wells and a collection of secondary relics, some of which were displayed on the altars of individual churches.

The relic known as the Carracán, or 'model', of Solomon's Temple stood on the high altar of the great church at Clonmacnoise until it was stolen in 1129, along with a silver chalice decorated with burnished gold, a drinking horn, a silver cup and altar plate.[66]The Bearnán Chiaráin, 'the gapped bell of Ciarán', was housed in its own church in the 11th century.[67] Other relics of St Ciaran were kept in a treasury attached to a larger church known as the Erdamh Chiaráin.[68]

Glendalough also had a complex landscape of relics that the included, by the 12th century, the Priest House, a reliquary chapel and relics housed in other churches such as St Kevin's Kitchen.

Modern pilgrims praying on the pattern day at Teampall Ciaran, Clonmacnoise. © Louise Nugent

Top left: Bullaun stone known as the Deerstone at Glendalough © Louise Nugent.

Top right: St Kevin's Kitchen, Glendalough.

Bottom: The Priest House at Glendalough. Photos by Christiaan Corlett, courtesy of Culture Stock.

The landscape extended outside the monastic enclosure and included the large bullaun stone known as the Deer Stone and St Kevin's cave, located at the upper lake.[69] Other devotional points visited by post-medieval pilgrims at Glendalough, such as St Kevin's holy well and a series of crosses and penitential cairns, may also have been part of this early landscape.[70]

Unfortunately, we do know how pilgrims engaged with the landscape and how accessible individual components were. Most of the larger ecclesiastical foundations had multiple churches, all located in the inner enclosure or set in separate enclosures. The churches varied in size and had different functions: larger ones were used for big congregations and some of the smaller ones housed relics or catered for particular groups.[71] Early medieval churches were undivided buildings with a western doorway and, in some cases, they were too small to accommodate large numbers of pilgrims, but they only needed to be large enough to accommodate the priest and clerics officiating at the Mass. Lay attendees and pilgrims could join in the worship from the outside.[72]

Modern pilgrims attending Mass outside medieval church at St MacDara's Island on the saint's feast day.
© Louise Nugent

St Mella's Church Lemanaghan, Co. Offaly. An example of an early stone church.
© Louise Nugent.

When individual churches were not in use for religious ceremonies, pilgrims may have been able to access them under supervision. They stepped in to the early stone churches through a simple flat lintelled door in the west gable leading in to a small open and undivided space. The inside was lit with candles and lamps. A stone or wooden altar was positioned opposite the door in front of a small east wall. Windows were used sparingly in these buildings.

Lucky pilgrims might have seen displayed on the altar a precious item owned or touch by the saint. As early as the 7th century, the tunic and book of St Colmcille were displayed on the altar of one of the churches on Iona.[73] Perhaps a monk stood quietly in the shadows to stop pilgrims getting to close to the relics. The walls were embellished with wall hangings, the altar decorated with crosses, elaborate altar plate, embroidered cloths etc. Some churches were painted and render was found on the walls of the oratory and altar at High Island, Co. Galway.[74]

From the 12th century, larger and more elaborate buildings with a defined chancel and nave were a feature of bigger ecclesiastical sites like Clonmacnoise and Glendalough and some were built in the Romanesque style.

After the arrival of the new monastic orders and Anglo-Normans in the 12th century, many new pilgrim sites developed around churches. There was a great variety in the types of churches pilgrims visited from late 12th century onwards – parish, cathedral and monastic churches. Some parish churches had a rectangular plan with an undifferentiated chancel and nave, while others had a clearly demarcated chancel and nave. Rarer examples of parish churches with a transept occurred in medieval towns like New Ross. Transepts were also found in collegiate and cathedral churches.[75] Pilgrimage churches also belonged to new monastic orders. Most later monasteries had a claustral plan, with churches and domestic buildings arranged around a rectangular open space.[76] Pilgrims' experience of later monasteries would have been inside the church. They may also have stayed at their guesthouses or hospitals. The domestic space of the religious was seldom seen by a lay person.

The Augustinian canons were in charge of most of these new pilgrim sites. They had also taken control of established early medieval pilgrimages places like Glendalough, Devenish and Kilmacduagh.[77] There was no standard plan for an Augustinian church.

Romanesque church at Killeshin, Co. Laois. © Louise Nugent

Those built in Gaelic areas of Ireland often had a nave with a short chancel or were designed with transepts like most Cistercian churches. Others had long naves with narrow choirs, and some had a plan similar to that of the mendicant orders.[78] Mendicant churches for the Dominican, Franciscan, Carmelite and Augustinian friars tended to be long buildings, with the choir filling a third of the length. A belfry tower often marked the junction between the chancel and the un-aisled nave. After the 1400s, newly built mendicant churches were aisled on one side and accompanied by wings that led into small east-facing chapels.[79]

From the 13th century, the division between the nave and the chancel was commonly defined with the insertion of rood screens made of stone, wood or iron.[80] The pilgrims' experience in later churches need not have been linear, and there were often mini pilgrim landscapes inside, including side altars, rood screens and statues, as well as relics and reliquary shrines.

Pilgrims who made pilgrimages to monasteries founded by the new religious orders, such as the Augustinian canons entered the church nave through a door in the north or the west wall.[81] The naves of most churches were semi-open spaces and the design varied from place to place: some had pillars and arches that defined side aisles, while others were long, narrow rectangular spaces. As the pilgrims' eyes adjusted to lower levels of light, they darted between the rood screen, stained-glass windows, painted walls and coloured tiled floors. Flickering candles, torches and lamps were scattered throughout the church. At Kells priory, the rubble walls were plastered and painted, as were many of the carved architectural features of the church.[82] The walls of medieval churches were often whitewashed and painted with designs in red and yellow ochre.[83] A common technique called false ashlar – where a single colour was painted in a solid line, to imitate the joins of cut-stone masonry – was often used around doors and windows. The space above the chancel arches was often painted with scenes from the Bible, the lives of saints or the more awesome scene of the Last Judgement.[84]

As the pilgrims moved deeper into the nave, they noticed side altars positioned against pillars and walls or in transept chapels. The altars were decorated with altar cloths, candlesticks, a crucifix and statues and some were surrounded by wooden screens.[85] The elaborate tombs and more subtle grave slabs that marked the burial places of the elite were scattered in the nave and side chapels. These monuments acted as reminders of the fragility of life and impending death.[86]

The pilgrims' eyes were also drawn to windows filled with painted glass. Decorative windows depicted elaborate floral patterns on painted white glass, and ornate figurative windows, depicting scenes from the Bible or the lives of the saints, created with glass painted in hues of blue, red, green and brown, were found in many churches.[87] The imagery displayed often conveyed stories and meaning for pilgrims. For example, at Canterbury the elaborate 'Miracle Window' depicts images of pilgrims being healed by the saint, while at York Minster a panel in a 15th-century glass window in the choir depicts pilgrims at the tomb of St William of York. Glimpses of the types of visual imagery encountered by Irish pilgrims can be seen in surviving wall paintings at Holycross Abbey, Abbeyknockmoy, Co. Galway, and Clare Island Abbey, Co. Mayo,[88] as well as fragments of stained glass recovered from archaeological excavations at Holycross Abbey, the Rock of Cashel, Blacfriary, at Trim, Co. Meath, Kells Priory, Co. Kilkenny, and Boyle Abbey, Co. Roscommon.[89]

Fragment of medieval stained glass found during recent excavations at Blackfriary Abbey, Trim.
© Fionola O'Carroll

Medieval statue of Our Lady in a statue niche at Sailsbury Cathedral.
© Louise Nugent

The floors of wealthy churches were often covered with colourful glazed tiles set out in intricate patterns. The ceilings were also decorated.[90] The imagery on walls, windows, floors and ceilings were immediately recognised by the viewer and conveyed important messages relating to spiritual life and the pilgrimage.

The pilgrims found statues of all sizes placed on altars and in statue niches. Statues of the Blessed Virgin were often located in a special Lady Chapel. In 1538, Thomas Allen refers to the statue of Our Lady of Trim being located in its own chapel.[91] Other venerated statues, such as the 'venerable statue' of St Radegund at Rathkeale Abbey, Co. Limerick, may have been located on a side altar.[92]

Medieval statues were made from metal, stone, wood and alabaster. In the mid-15th century Lady Killeen gave a gift of a gilt image of the Virgin Mary worth £10 to the high altar at Christ Church Cathedral.[93] Many statues were brightly painted, adding pops of colour to their surroundings.[94] Popular statues were dressed in embroidered clothing and adorned with jewels. In England, the

Medieval statue of Our Lady of Monserrat, Spain.

statue of Our Lady of Lincoln wore a crown decorated with pearls and precious stones, while the statue of Our Lady of Walsingham wore a golden crown donated by Henry II (1133–189).[95] Some Irish statues were also dressed in elaborate and expensive robes. The robes belonging to the statue of St Catherine at Christ Church Cathedral were stolen during a robbery in 1311.[96] Alice Cassell (1472) bequeathed a robe to the image of the Blessed Virgin in the chapel of St Maurus in Lusk.[97]

Statues such as Our Lady of Trim and Navan were the focus of popular pilgrimages in late medieval Ireland. We know little of the Irish pilgrim rituals relating to holy statues during this period. Pilgrims surely offered prayers before the statues and performed vigils and fasts and made offerings of gifts and candles to miraculous statues, as they did elsewhere in Europe. In some cases, physical contact with the saint was allowed. In 1408, Archbishop Arudrel of Canterbury described the interactions of English pilgrims with miraculous crosses and statues, noting that when pilgrims approached these holy objects, they would often bend their knees, bow to the statue and, when allowed, kiss the statue.[98] Another example of ritual behaviour relates to a French couple who brought their child with walking problems to the statue of St Vaast at Woirel. The infant's foot was placed against a shoe held in the saint's hand. In north-eastern Spain, mothers desperate for a cure for their sick children passed them through a cloak that dressed a statue of the Virgen del Pilar at Zaragossa in Aragon.[99]

The earliest detailed description of Irish pilgrims interacting with a holy statue relates to St Gobnait at Ballyvourney, Co. Cork. Sir Richard Cox first mentions that the statue of St Gobnait was an object of veneration in 1687, which had caused 'many cures and other miracles'.[100]

Pilgrimage to the statue on Gobnait's feast day, 11 February 1731, is described in John Richardson's book *The Great Folly of Pilgrimage*. Pilgrimage rituals involved the pilgrims moving three times around the statue on their knees, while reciting a 'certain number of Aves, Paters and Credos'.[101] The pilgrims then kissed the statue, 'making an Offering to it everyone according to their Ability, which generally amounts in the whole to Five or Six Pounds'.[102] The statue was rubbed on aching limbs and handkerchiefs were tied about its neck, to be worn afterwards, as a preventative against sickness.[103] The description is reminiscent of modern interaction with the statue, which is displayed in the parish church at Ballyvourney on 11 February each year. The statue, which is only 68 centimetres high, is placed on a small table in the church, in front of the altar. Pilgrims queue to touch the statue, armed with handfuls of colourful ribbons. The pilgrims perform a ritual called 'St Gobnait's measure', whereby they use the ribbons to 'measure' the statue. The ribbons are held along the length of the statue and then wrapped around the neck, then the waist and, finally, the feet of the statue. Some pilgrims make the sign of the cross when this is done, some pick up the statue and kiss it and others bless themselves while holding the statue. The ribbons are then taken home and used to ward off or cure sickness. Some farmers still place these ribbons in outhouses and barns to protect livestock from disease.

Medieval statue of St Gobnait at Ballyvourney, Co. Cork. © Louise Nugent

In many cases, miraculous statues were displayed on altars, often in their own chapel. Outside Ireland, miraculous statues were often displayed on columns, an example being the statue of the virgin, known as Notre Dame du Pilier, at Chartres Cathedral.[104] These holy statues were illuminated by the many candles that burned before them. On the Continent, many of the surviving medieval statues of Mary have become darkened from centuries of candle smoke and are known as Black Madonnas. A very fine example is still visited by pilgrims to the abbey of Santa Maria de Montserrat in Spain.

In 1462, Edward IV made special grants to the abbot of the shrine of Our Lady of Trim, in return for

> perpetual continuance of a wax candle continually from day to day and from night to night burning before the image of Our Blessed Lady.[105]

Pilgrims interacting with the statue of St Gobnaits at Ballyvourney on the saint's feast day. © Louise Nugent

The grant also stipulated that four other wax candles should continually burn before the image at the Mass of St Mary, to petition 'the good estate' of the king and his family and the souls of his ancestors.

By the 13th century, the division between the nave and the chancel, normally off limits to lay people, was well defined in Irish churches. The separation of holy space could be achieved with a rood screen made of stone, wood or iron. Most screens, especially those made of wood, incorporated decorated openings that framed the view of the high altar, allowing pilgrims and lay people standing in the nave to gaze into this scared space. Obscuring the view of the chancel increased the mystery of the Mass. Some screens may have incorporated curtains and hangings that were closed to limit visibility at certain points in the liturgy, or carefully opened in dramatic fashion to reveal relics or the host. Rood screens were surmounted by a rood loft that carried a sculptural representation of the crucifixion, known as the rood. The crucifix was often flanked by figures of the Virgin Mary and St John. Rood screens with a solid construction hid the chancel completely from the nave, though most allowed access between the two areas via a central doorway.[106] This design did not prevent people in the nave from attending Mass. Solid and closed roods incorporated a bell called the 'Sacring-Bell', or consecration bell, which was rung at the time of the consecration of the host during the Mass, which allowed lay people to follow the ceremony.[107]

Left: Timber rood screen at church of St Peter and St Paul, Eye, Suffolk, England. ©Margaret Hilditch.

Right: Medieval stone rood screen at Sligo Abbey, Co. Sligo. © Louise Nugent

We have very little information from this period about how or where holy relics or miraculous statues were displayed in Irish churches. Little is known about how pilgrims accessed and engaged with these holy objects. Reconstructing the pilgrim activities in post-12th-century buildings from the archaeological record is very difficult. Many later medieval churches like the shrine of Our Lady of Navan and Tracton Abbey are no longer standing, while others survive in ruins, shells of their former selves.

Following earlier traditions, secondary relics continued to be kept in the church and, from the 12th century, a large portion of Irish corporeal relics were also kept in churches. Some relics were displayed openly, on or close to the high altar, making them visible from the nave; others were seen only on special occasions such as the feast of relics. Irish pilgrims who visited English churches and cathedral shrines, often encountered corporeal relics. These were kept in stone tomb shrines or in portable reliquaries known as feretories, displayed on supporting bases made either of columns or solid structures, at the eastern end of the church, beyond, but in close proximity to the high altar. Relics were also housed in chapels, also called feretories, set close to the main altar. [108] Many feretory stands and stone tomb shrines had modifications to allow close contact with pilgrims. Irish pilgrims to the shrine of

Some stone shrines like that of St Edward the Confessor had recesses in their bases where pilgrims could kneel and pray. © Dean and Chapter of Westminster Abbey

St Edward the Confessor could kneel and pray in special niches in the shrine's base.

Prior to the 15th century, Irish pilgrims to Winchester made pilgrimages to St Swithun's shrine, displayed on a feretory platform behind the high altar. An opening known as the 'Holy Hole' enabled the pilgrims to crawl underneath the reliquary, allowing for a very intimate experience, while avoiding direct contact with the shrine.[109] Irish pilgrims who might have stopped at Salisbury Cathedral while en route to London or Dover visited St Osmund's stone shrine. It had three circular openings, or *foramina,* that again allowed for closer contact with the interior of the tomb, with pilgrims squeezing their upper bodies into the space above the saint's grave.

There is little evidence to suggest that stone shrines were common in late medieval Ireland. To date, only a handful of stone shrines and feretory stands from the later medieval period have been identified, three of the most complete being found at the abbeys of Holycross and Claregalway.[110] A possible stone shrine associated with St Thomas's Abbey in Dublin may be represented by a single fragment of stone that was probably located inside the abbey's church.[111] When complete, the shrine may have held relics of its patron, St Thomas à Becket, acquired from Canterbury. A single stone records another such shrine at Clonfert but, as with the shrine fragment at St Thomas's Abbey, it is impossible to know if it was located inside or outside the church.

From the scattered historical references and surviving archaeological remains of stone tombs, its possible to make some observation as to where relics and shrines were kept or displayed on special occasions.

Irish pilgrims encountered some relics displayed in the chancel on or close to the high altar. After the translation of St Cianán's remains from his grave in the 14th century, pilgrims visited his new shrine at the Augustinian church at Duleek.[112] The shrine seems to have been incorporated into the north wall of the chancel, so pilgrims would either have looked at it from a distance while standing

St Osmund's Shrine at Salisbury Cathedral.
© Louise Nugent

in the nave, or may have been allowed into the chancel at set times.[113] Pilgrims who came to pray before the shrine of St Richard of Dundalk at St Nicholas's medieval parish church in Dundalk would also have needed to enter the chancel to be in close proximity to his tomb.[114] Reliquaries such as St Manchan's Shrine may have been displayed on the high altar or perhaps on a stand close to it. Outside Ireland, feretory stands and stone reliquaries were rarely kept in the naves of churches. Exceptions are found at some low-status pilgrim churches or at churches with unofficial cults.[115] At the Franciscan friary in Claregalway, Co. Galway, the remains of the base of a feretory stand is located in the nave, close to the entrance to the west transept. The stone shrines at the Cistercian Holycross Abbey were both located in the north and south transepts of the church.[116]

It is likely that the interactions of Irish pilgrims with non-landscape relics and graves in the early and later medieval period were supervised and monitored by individual religious at monastic and cathedral shrines. Many busy churches outside Ireland had special arrangements in place 'to enable the monks to continue to celebrate services in relative peace whilst admitting large number of pilgrims to the shrine'.[117] Durham Cathedral in England employed stewards to oversee pilgrims.[118]

Some relics could only be accessed by request. In the late 16th century, St Cuthbert's shrine at Durham Cathedral had a master of the feretory, so when pilgrims asked to pray before the shrine, the master was summoned by his clerk and accompanied them. He also supervised the drawing of curtains surrounding the shrine.[119] Specially appointed custodians guarded some miraculous images, such as the statues of Our Lady of Caversham and Our Lady of Walsingham. At Bury

St Edmunds, the relics of the saint were the responsibility of the sacristan. There is evidence for a more discreet observance of pilgrims at some English churches. Late medieval watching lofts survive at Durham Cathedral, Christ Church Cathedral in Oxford, St Frideswide Priory and St Alban's Cathedral. The lofts allowed clergy to keep a watchful eye on the shrine and altars below, while also keeping a distance from the pilgrims.[120] At St Albans, the shrine keeper kept vigil in the tower, while overlooking the tomb and the pilgrims below.[121] Possible evidence for the observation of Irish pilgrims is found at Claregalway Abbey, where there is a small blunt pointed opening in the wall of the transept beside the stone shrine. This opening or window would have allowed the religious to observe pilgrims as they approached the shrine.[122]

Processions: The Ritual of Movement in Early Medieval Ireland

Throughout the medieval period, pilgrims observed and participated in religious processions.[123] Recent archaeological studies of the landscapes of early medieval monasteries and hermitages on the west coast of Ireland suggest that they were influenced by religious processions of the early and later medieval church.

The phenomenon of the Catholic procession has a very long history, originating in the east in the early centuries of the Church. It was recorded in Jerusalem and Rome as early as the 4th century and went on to become a key component of Church ritual.[124] In the late medieval Church, processions in which relics were carried enabled lay people to get close to such items. There are numerous references from early medieval Ireland to reliquary processions taking place outside a pilgrimage setting. In the early Irish Church, relics were carried by church officials from place to place, to promulgate laws, collect tributes and ward off disease. Early Irish reliquary processions were often politically motivated and used by the Church to reaffirm bonds and re-enforce traditional rights to church land.[125] Many of the surviving early medieval reliquaries, such as bells and croziers, were designed to be portable and could easily be carried from place to place.

The movement of relics through the landscape could result in a type of inverted pilgrimage, whereby local people made short journeys to see the relics as they moved through their locality. In 9th-century Italy, when the relics of St Columbanus were carried around the lands attached to the monastery of Bobbio, local people made it their business to view the relics as they moved through their hamlets. The impressive procession was led by two presbyters who, for as long as the relics were being carried, rang two hand-bells, while the secondary relics, the cup of Columbanus and the leather satchel he used for his bible, were carried in front of the casket that contained his relics with crosses, candles and incense burners.[126]

When the relics came to the town of Pavia, the townspeople lined the streets and 'climbed on top of walls and on rooftops to try to get a glimpse of the holy body'.[127] Processions also seem to have been part of the foundation rituals of some early medieval Irish churches. The 7th-century text *Liber Angeli* refers to a weekly procession of the clergy reciting psalms (every Sunday), to the church of Na Ferta at Armagh, and by the 9th century, a reliquary procession was taking place at Armagh at Pentecost. Some argue that Armagh's reliquary procession was a symbolic re-enactment of the original monastic foundation rituals and was used ritually to reaffirm the sanctity of the Church and its physical limits.[128] The use of circular movement in monastic foundation rituals can also be seen in the *Life of St Senan*, where the saint consecrates Scattery Island, the location of his principal monastery, by walking clockwise around the edge of the island – the symbolic outer enclosure for monastery.[129]

When early medieval pilgrims arrived at pilgrim churches on important church festivals, they probably encountered, along with liturgical celebrations, some form of religious procession. Many of the surviving Irish vernacular litanies, some as early as the 9th century, were composed as processional liturgies, designed to be recited while moving, on special days such as the saint's feast day.[130] The 7th-century *Life of St Brigit* makes a curious reference to pilgrims who had come 'to watch the pageant of the crowds'. The term 'pageant' is open to interpretation, but one wonders if the author was referring to groups of pilgrims arriving at Kildare in family or tribal groups, or perhaps a reliquary or religious procession as rituals of the saint's feast day.[131]

Archaeological evidence for early medieval processional landscapes survives at several early medieval ecclesiastic and monastic sites in the west of Ireland. One of the best preserved is found on the windswept island of Inishmurray, off the coast of Co. Sligo. Historical sources tell us little of the island's history before the Reformation. A programme of archaeological excavation and survey has shed much light on the development of the monastic settlement and earlier pilgrim traditions.

The medieval pilgrimage at Inishmurray was focused on a monastery founded by St Molaise in the 6th century. Today, the monastery consists of a large stone-walled enclosure surrounding three churches, Templemolaise, Templenatinny and a shrine chapel called Tech Molaise; three dry-stone huts; a collection of cross-slabs; four *leachta* and a graveyard.

Aerial view of the monastery of Innishmurray, Co. Sligo.
©Neil Jackman, Abarta Heritage

Shrine chapel known as Tech Molaise at Inishmurray.
©Neil Jackman, Abarta Heritage.

Outside the enclosure are several buildings and structures associated with the monastic settlement. Additional buildings and monuments are found along the shoreline on the southern and south-eastern side of the island – a holy well, the Women's Church and graveyard, the burial ground of Relickoran and a horizontal water mill. Added to this are several isolated *leachta* scattered along the periphery of the island.

Inishmurray is a complex landscape that developed over an extended period of time. Some time between the 9th and 11th centuries, Tech Molaise was built over the grave of the saint or designed to house his relics. This suggests that the burial place of the saint and his relics were the main focus of devotional activity prior to and at this time. At the beginning of the first millennium, a series of *leachta*, surmounted by decorated cross slabs, were built inside and outside the monastery, extending the pilgrim landscape beyond the monastery walls.[132] During the 12th century, the island came under the control of the Augustinian canons, who continued to encourage pilgrimage. They maintained the existing churches and *leachta*, carrying out repairs and rebuilding works when needed. They also added new ritual features, such as a 13th-/14th-century statue of St Molaise and an artificial passage or chamber constructed as a penitential station (perhaps inspired by St Patrick's Purgatory in Co. Donegal).[133] Following the Reformation, pilgrimage continued to the island in various forms. Today, the island is the focus of a long-standing community pilgrimage on 15 August, the Feast of the Assumption. Unfortunately, recent access issues to the island have endangered the tradition.

Satellite *Leacht* on Inishmurray.
© Neill Jackman Abarta Heritage

Inishmurray had, by the first millennium, a complex processional landscape focused around the island's *leachta*. The size and shape of the *leachta* suggest that they were originally built as outdoor altars, where the Eucharist was celebrated on special occasions, such as the feast day of the saints to which they were dedicated.[134] The *leachta*, when combined with the altars in the island's three stone churches, amount to the same number of altars found at other important churches, such as Clonmacnoise or Glendalough.[135] During religious processional ceremonies, the churches and the *leachta* acted as stopping points or stations for religious processions organised for important days in the Church calendar, such as the feast day of the island's patron, St Molaise, or Easter, in a similar way to processions in large churches with multiple altars. Any pilgrim who arrived here on such occasions would have witnessed and perhaps even been involved in the procession.

The *leachta* also acted as stations for personal devotion and prayer and were visited by individual pilgrims throughout the year.[136] It is tempting to think that medieval pilgrims may have moved clockwise around them in a similar manner to 19th-century pilgrims to the island. Less complex, but similar stational routes surviving at other early medieval church sites like Innishark, Co. Galway, and Caher Island, Co. Mayo.[137] Archaeological evidence for a processional route can also be found at Glendalough. The route was defined by a series of early medieval crosses, cross slabs and *leachta* surmounted by crosses and a large bullaun stone known as the Deer Stone. The route linked the monastic core (with its churches that housed relics of St Kevin) to the upper lake, where Temple-na-Skellig Church and St Kevin's Cave were located.[138]

It is difficult to know how Irish pilgrims experienced processions during the early medieval period, as historical records provide little insight. It has been suggested that

> … communal rituals organised by a medieval community are likely to have been accompanied by psalms and especially litanies in which the crowd gives a short and unvarying response to invocations sung by one or more soloists.[139]

Processions: The Ritual of Movement in Later Medieval Pilgrimage

By the 13th century, processions had become an established part of the liturgical calendar and were encountered by Irish pilgrims in Ireland and when travelling abroad.[140] From the 12th century, most Irish churches had adopted the Sarum Rite and from this point processions were held with regularity, even at parish level. In these churches, processions took place before Sunday Mass, with a weekly procession to the rood, a practice that increased to twice weekly during Lent. Processions also took place at important feasts days such as Candlemas, Palm Sunday, Easter, Ascension, Pentecost, Corpus Christi and rogation days, the feast of relics and the feast days of certain saints.

Relics were carried as part of liturgical processions on Good Friday, Christmas, Epiphany, Corpus Christi, Palm Sunday, Rogationtide days,[141] the feast of the Ascension and the Feast of Relics.[142] Many pilgrims timed their visits to coincide with reliquary processions, as this gave them an opportunity to engage with and come into close contact with the saint outside the traditional feast day.[143]

Processions could take place inside the church or, less frequently, outside the church. Outdoor processions were known as extramural processions. Lay people experienced processions in different ways: inside the church they observed the clergy moving from the chancel and choir to a specific place in the nave, such as side altars, or to the rood cross. These stopping points were commonly known as stations. Participation was more interactive at processions outside the church. It was not unknown on the Continent for people to pass beneath relics while the procession was moving and such a scene is depicted in the carving on the tympanum of the south transept portal of Amiens Cathedral.[144]

Processions were elaborate ceremonies full of theatre and attracted large crowds of people. At the front of all processions was a large cross known as a processional cross. These crosses were elaborate items decorated with precious metals and gems. More than 40 medieval processional crosses survive from Britain and Ireland.[145] The Cross of Cong is one of the finest surviving Irish examples; made in the 1120s/1130s, it also enclosed a relic of the True Cross.[146] The cross was followed by clergy dressed in liturgical vestments. At wealthy churches, the vestments would have been decorated in rich embroidery, with some even using gold thread. They carried candles, lighted tapers, smaller crosses, aspergillums – liturgical implements used to sprinkle holy water – and censers, along with statues and banners bearing the emblem of the cross or images of the saints. During reliquary processions, relics and reliquaries were the star of the show. For dramatic effect, they were often framed by canopies or veils.[147]

Reliquary procession. Souvenir print of the opening in 1873 of the new Treasury of Saint Servatius in Maastricht, Netherlands (cropped) (unknown artist / public domain / Wikimedia Commons)
Source: Wikimedia Commons

The sensory experience of the processions was enhanced with the use of fragrant and beautiful flowers. The smells of lighted candles and smoking incense wafted through the church and drifted more subtly in outside environments. The sounds of instrumental music, mingled with the voices of the clergy chanting antiphons – a short sentence sung or recited before or after a psalm or a canticle sung by the group – interspersed with individual soloists reciting a versicle – a short sentence to which the congregation gives a response.[148]

Processions were complex rituals and to ensure that they were carried out correctly, each church had a type of manual, known as a 'processional', which detailed the chants, prayers and items required for each type of event.[149] Only two processionals survive from medieval Ireland, from the Church of St John the Evangelist in Dublin. The books, dating to c.1400, contain litanies and hymns to be sung for different religious processions and include processional hymns for the feasts of SS Patrick and Colmcille.[150]

As with earlier examples, a large proportion of the surviving late medieval Irish reliquaries were designed to be portable and some have fittings for the attachment of straps, thus enabling them to be easily carried in processions. Some Irish reliquary shrines could be hung around the neck or worn as a breastplate.[151] Examples of shrines with fittings for straps include the *Breac Maedhóg* and the St Patrick's bell shrine. During the 17th century, the relic of the True Cross at Holycross Abbey was often taken on procession, perhaps recalling or re-enacting older traditions.[152] A contemporary drawing of one of the processions shows the abbot on horseback carrying the relic in a bag that hung around his neck, followed by banners with a large cross.[153] The most splendid of Irish reliquaries, St Manchan's shrine had four metal loops at each corner of the base, to allow wooden poles to be inserted through when it needed to be moved.

St Manchan's Shrine was carried with poles passed through copper alloy rings attached to its base. © Louise Nugent

Processions are rarely recorded in historical sources for late medieval Ireland. The 1446 Dublin Assembly Rolls refer to people arriving for the feasts of SS George and Patrick and Corpus Christi, for 'procession and pilgrimage'.[154]

St Patrick's feast was a popular day for pilgrimage at the many holy places in Ireland. Relics of the saint are listed in the reliquary collection of Christ Church Cathedral, Dublin, but the procession mentioned in the Assembly Rolls concerns St Patrick's Cathedral, located just outside the walls of the medieval town of Dublin. Christ Church Cathedral would have had its own procession, perhaps only inside the church and it would have also made sure that its Patrician relics were on display. The procession at the nearby St Patrick's Cathedral was extramural and by this time had developed into a civic event.

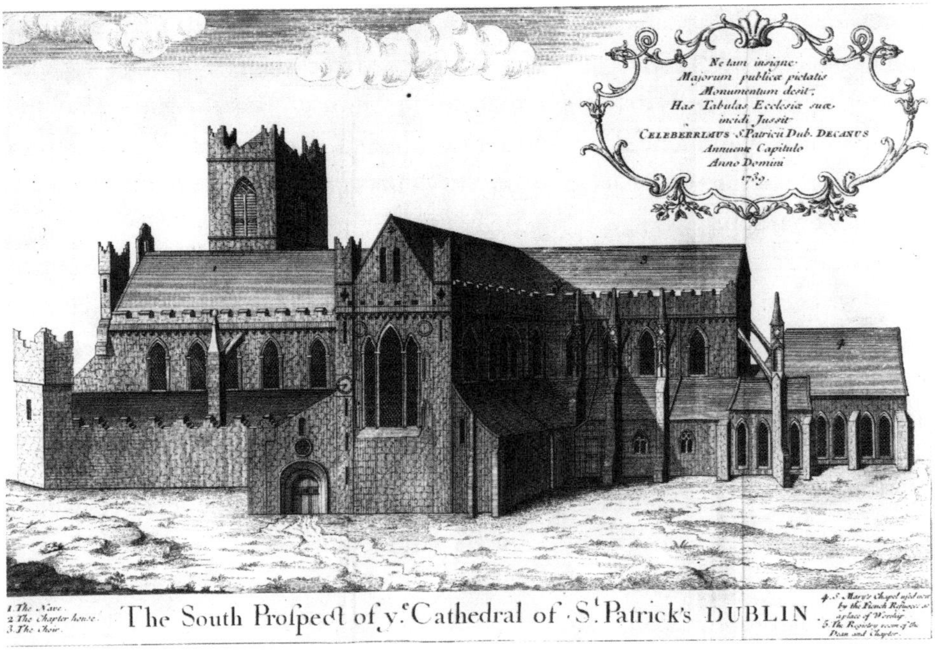

17th-century engraving of St Patrick's Cathedral, Dublin. © St Patrick's Cathedral Dublin

As a cathedral church, it would have had its own collection of relics, including some belonging to its patron. The St Patrick's day procession was first recorded in 1267, when it coincided with a day of public penances.[155] By the late 15th century, the St Patrick's day procession 'was an event established as much in the calendar of the city as in that of the cathedral'.[156] In 1509, the cathedral bells were rung to summon attendance, so that all could listen to sermons specially commissioned for St Patrick's day and the feast of relics, another day of procession.[157] On both occasions, the cathedral would have displayed its relics. Although there are no accounts of pilgrimage at St Patrick's Cathedral, people would have travelled there for the occasion.

A Palm Sunday procession at St Patrick's Cathedral is also mentioned in the historical sources. Palm Sunday was one of the more spectacular liturgies and there was an expectation of 'a larger than usual public attendance'.[158] As this was Ireland's largest cathedral, the Palm Sunday celebration would have been one of the most elaborate in Ireland and people would have travelled long distances to witness the spectacle and visit other pilgrim destinations in the town. In 1509, the proctor John Andowe noted that a type of reliquary known as a feretum/feretory was carried in the cathedral's processions on Corpus Christi, rogation days and Palm Sunday.[159] The consecrated host also played a central part in the Palm Sunday processions.[160] The ceremony was inspired by Christ's triumphal procession into Jerusalem detailed in the gospel for Palm Sunday. The procession began outside the walls of St Patrick's Cathedral church. It moved to several stations in the grounds before re-entering the church.[161] As the cathedral's liturgy was heavily influenced by Salisbury Cathedral, it is possible to reconstruct how the procession was enacted, using surviving accounts of Palm Sunday processions at Salisbury.

It began at a cross in the cemetery to the north of the choir. The Palm Sunday gospel was read aloud,[162] and the group was then joined by two boys who carried a feretory supported by two poles. The reliquary contained the consecrated host and the principal relics of the church. The feretory was often covered with a silken canopy.[163] Then there was a series of complex chants and responses and the group moved via the east gable to the second station at the southern side of the church. As the procession moved, all eyes were focused on the feretory, which was flanked on either side by two banners and accompanied by a lighted lantern and a thurifer (censer).[164] At the second station, seven boys, representing the Palm Sunday prophet, sang 'Glory, laud and honour be to thee, Christ king and redeemer, to whom the pious praise of children has uttered a Hosannah.'[165] The Palm Sunday hymn was then sung and the procession moved to the third station at the west door of the cathedral.[166] The, feretory which carried the host and relics, was raised aloft above the door. In some parishes, the priest struck the door with the processional staff in a symbolic act, demanding entry for Christ.[167] All present passed beneath the host and relics, entering into the nave. Once all were inside, the procession moved to the fourth station, the rood screen. The rood cross was then covered in a veil and all present knelt and sang the 'Ave Rex Noster'. Mass then began and the passion story from St Matthew's Gospel was sung in its entirety.[168] Variants of this ceremony took place on this day all over Ireland. The procession offered the participants, especially from lower classes, a chance for intimate contact with the relics as they passed beneath them at the third station.

The feast of Corpus Christi at Christ Church Cathedral was another religious ceremony that took on a civic importance in medieval Dublin. Corpus Christi is a festival that celebrates the transubstantiation or the presence of the body and blood of Jesus Christ, the Son of God, in the Eucharist. The celebration of Corpus Christi began after it was made an obligatory feast by Pope Clement V at the Council of Vienne in 1311. It was celebrated in England by the early 1300s and soon after was added to English liturgical books. It must have arrived in Ireland around this time. Typically, the celebration consisted of

Corpus Christi Procession.

Mass in the church, followed by a procession in which the consecrated host and the relics belonging to the church were carried through the streets as a public statement of the sacrifice of Christ for the salvation of the world. [169]

Christ Church Cathedral was the assembly point for the most elaborate Corpus Christi procession in Ireland and, by the 15th century, it had developed into a civic event that incorporated street drama and pageant wagons depicting scenes with religious and secular subject matter. The wagons were commissioned and wheeled through the streets by the city's trade guilds, many of which maintained altars in the cathedral.[170]

Corpus Christi was one of the feasts on which reliquary processions took place, and in the year 1542 it was recorded that a reliquary belonging to Christ Church cathedral was still part of the pageant procession.[171]

Victims of Success: The Problems of Mass Pilgrimage

Pilgrim sites run by religious orders had to balance encouraging pilgrimage and maintaining a monastic way of life. Sources relating to Melrose Abbey in Scotland point to this occasionally proving difficult. In the mid-13th century, the uncorrupted body of St Walter of Melrose was translated from his tomb to a new shrine in the monastic church. The translation coincided with the writing of the Life of the saint by Jocelin of Furness, and both events were part of efforts to revive his cult. The Life provides the usual accounts of the saint's birth, life and death, but also details the translation process and the tensions in the monastic community over how to accommodate the saint's growing cult, while maintaining the strict ethos of the Cistercian order.[172] Stories of miracles at the saint's shrine suggest that following the translation the sick had access and could stay in vigil overnight. There was a growing unease within the community regarding access by pilgrims and, as time passed, access became more and more restricted. Finally, Abbot William announced a completed ban on all but the sick at the saint's shrine,[173] so that

> monasteries of the Cistercian order be free from endless crowds flowing in upon them from every side.[174]

Apart from disrupting monastic routine, a criminal element among the pilgrims posed a threat to relics and the physical structures of the shrine. Some churches were reluctant to display relics, as theft and attempted theft of relics by pilgrims and opportunists were rife in medieval Europe.[175] There are countless accounts of relics being stolen from Irish churches in early medieval times. While many occurred during Viking raids, others can be attributed to Irish people. The *Life of St Flannan* tells of robbers entering the saint's tomb at Killaloe and stealing the gold from a gilded crozier belonging to the saint. That night, the saint appeared in a vision to the sacristan and told him the names of the men, who were duly punished.[176] As late as 1521, the head of St Boice was stolen from the parish church at Monasterboice.[177]

A close eye needed to be kept on offerings left before statues and relics. In the 12th century, Guibert de Nogent writes of canons from Laon in France arriving in England on a fund-raising mission, accompanied by relics from the cathedral collection. They stopped in an unnamed town and the relics were placed in the local church. Two local men short of money went to the church and one

> … pretending that he wished to show his reverence for [the relics] by kissing them, he put his mouth against them with his lips open and sucked up some coins that had been offered.[178]

Pilgrims sometimes damaged relics and tombs. Chipping pieces of stone shrines or even biting reliquary containers was recorded at busy European pilgrim shrines and at churches in the Holy Land. The 10th-century *Miracula Santi Columbani* recalls the theft of part of St Columbanus's reliquary shrine by a female pilgrim.

> She came and stretched herself out by the chest and with her teeth removed a small piece from a hidden place on the chest.[179]

The woman was punished for her actions and died that night in her sleep, with the stolen piece of wood lying by her head.[180] Closer to home, pilgrims to Bury St Edmunds in England, had to be prevented from biting off pieces of the gilt shrine that held the saint's remains. This type of activity may have encouraged the building of sturdier stone shrines.[181] However, even stone was not immune to damage. At Tours in France, a railing was placed around the tomb of St Martin to prevent pilgrims taking home pieces of the stone shrine,[182] while the *Life of William of Norwich* recalls that dust and chippings were scraped from the saint's stone tomb and drunk with holy water by the sick.[183]

Large numbers of pilgrims could be hard to control and there are accounts from outside Ireland of pilgrims fighting inside the churches. Fights were usually caused by people pushing to get as close as possible to the shrine and occasionally this type of behaviour resulted in pilgrims being crushed to death.[184] In 1018, 50 pilgrims were crushed during the vigil of the Feast of St Martial in Limoges in France.[185] More than a century later, in 1130, the abbot of the Abbey of Saint-Denis in Paris recalled another horrific crush resulting in many deaths.[186] This religious hysteria was no doubt heightened by the fact that many relics were displayed rarely.[187] It is doubtful that any Irish shrine attracted sufficiently large numbers to involve such crushes, but Irish pilgrims to foreign shrines could have found themselves in these situations.

Holycross Abbey

Outside Ireland, relics are known to have been displayed on altars or on stands, some even being hung on beams above the high altar.[188]

A relic of the True Cross at Holycross Abbey hung over the altar in the 17th century. Holycross, a Cistercian monastery, was one of the most popular places of pilgrimage in Munster. The earliest detailed accounts of pilgrim rituals there are found in the *Triumphalia Chronologica Monasterii Sanctae Crucis in Hibernia.* Written in the 1640s, the *Triumphalia* provides an account of the establishment of the abbey, with

View of cloister at Holycross Abbey, Co. Tipperary. © Louise Nugent

notices of its relics, administrators and miracle tales. The miracles provide a glimpse of how pilgrims behaved at Holycross in the 1600s. The text suggests that the relic of the True Cross was usually displayed over the high altar and under constant supervision by the monks. It was only taken down at the request of the sick, when it was applied to their ailing bodies.[189] One sick pilgrim waited in an 'appointed place', suggesting that the sick may have been kept apart. The text also tells of another pilgrim healed by the relic, making prayer in thanksgiving at the seven altars in the church.[190] Unfortunately, we cannot know if the behaviour of the 17th-century pilgrims mirrored the actions of earlier medieval pilgrims.

Before the Reformation, the abbey possessed between one and three relics of the Holy Cross.[191] If one of these had hung over the altar, as it did in the 17th century, it would have been visible to all pilgrims standing in the nave. The abbey was extensively remodelled between 1450 and 1500, partly financed by the wealth of pilgrim offerings. The earlier abbey church was much plainer in appearance, lacking the elaborately carved stone features of the second build. During the renovation works, two stone shrine-like structures were commissioned to display the abbey's relics.[192] The most elaborate of the shrines, known in folk tradition as the 'Waking Bier of the Monks', replaced the dividing wall between the two chapels of the south transept.

Curiously, when Malachy Harty describes this shrine in the 17th century, he appears to be unaware of its previous use as a reliquary shrine and suggests that it

Intact stone reliquary at Holycross Abbey. © Louise Nugent.

was used to wake the bodies of the monks.[193] The shrine base resembles a chest tomb and the upper half has a canopy with open arcades similar to those found at English reliquary shrines like St Albans at St Alban's Cathedral and St Swithun's at Winchester.[194] A second, less elaborate shrine of a similar design was located in the north-west angle of the north transept.[195] Today, it survives as a series of architectural fragments but is no longer on display. There are no accounts of how medieval pilgrims behaved when they arrived at Holycross, but some physical contact may have been allowed as parts of the canopy stone are polished smooth from the continuous contact with hands. Evidence from the unpublished archaeological excavations carried out in advance of modern restoration works show that the east window contained fragments of red, pink, blue and yellow glass.[196] The transept, chancel and choir were paved with small flagstones, while the nave had a clay floor.[197] The two stone shrines could not be accessed via the crossing arch without the consent of the monks, as the choir extended into this area.[198] Pilgrims who visited in the 15th century stepped into a nave with two aisles that opened into a north and south transept, entered through finely carved pointed and moulded arches.

It is possible that pilgrims may have been able to enter the reliquary areas via these aisles. The north transept may have been open, allowing the pilgrims free access through the junction of the ave aisle. It is unlikely the south transept was open, as stairs leading to the monks' domestic quarters, along with the door to the cloister, were on the south side of the church. Both transepts may have been closed off with screens from the nave, in which case pilgrims would have had to ask permission for closer contact with the abbey's shrines and relics.[199] Even if most pilgrims did not get past the nave, the importance of their physical proximity to the holy relics cannot be underestimated. Many pilgrims may have glimpsed these relics only during liturgical processions at Easter, Corpus Christi or the feast of the cross.

West doorway of church at Holycross Abbey.
© Louise Nugent

Pilgrims lucky enough to gain access to the shrine in the north transept would have gazed on what is now one of the few surviving medieval wall paintings in Ireland, depicting a hunting scene painted on plaster using a range of colours: red ochre, charcoal black, lime white and vermilion.[200] The shrine in the south transept may also have functioned as an Easter Sepulchre, or *Sepulchrum Domini* (the Lord's tomb), where, following the Good Friday liturgy, the relics of the cross and the consecrated host were covered in linen cloths and placed in a sepulchre that had been previously prepared. Candles were lit and a watch was kept until Easter Sunday, when the host and the relic of the cross were brought back to the main altar, to signify Christ's resurrection.[201] Perhaps the relics were only placed in the shrines on special occasions, like the feast of the exaltation, at which time pilgrims were allowed to view them through the open sides of the shrines. However, both shrines may have been less accessible at other times of the year.[202]

Pilgrimage Hotspot: Christ Church Cathedral

Dublin's Christ Church Cathedral was one of the most popular pilgrim destinations in late medieval Ireland. Pilgrims came from far and wide to pray before the cathedral's extensive collection of relics.

The cathedral was founded c.1030 by the Hiberno-Norse King Sitric Silkbeard after his return from a pilgrimage to Rome in 1028.[203] Originally a Benedictine priory and cathedral, by the 13th century it had become a house of Augustinian canons. The lives of the canons revolved around daily celebration of the divine office and completion of the seven canonical hours of the matins and lauds (each constituting a single hour): prime, terce, sext, nones, vespers and compline.[204] They were also involved in saying Mass at the cathedral's many altars, developing the pilgrimage and managing the cathedral's properties and granges.[205] The cathedral was more than just a place of religious worship, it played a key role in the civic life of Dublin as a venue for civic ceremonies, the swearing of oaths and to house parliament. The exchequer also used the priory as a safe place to store money outside of the castle, and the citizens of Dublin also stored some of their precious items here.[206]

Throughout its history the cathedral had a small community of canons. In 1300, it had eleven members, in 1468 only eight, and in 1540 ten. In religious communities at the time, there were seven essential offices: prior, sub-prior, steward, cellarer, kitchener, sacristan and precentor. The small size of the community at Christ Church meant that all the positions were filled but there was little time to fulfil duties of a parochial or secular nature.[207] Any investment in manpower to oversee pilgrims would have eaten into the time and resources of the community. Nevertheless, pilgrimage was encouraged, which is not surprising, given that pilgrim offerings helped to pay for the upkeep of the cathedral.

Christ Church Cathedral, also known as Holy Trinity, was located inside the town walls of medieval Dublin. Sitting on the brow of a hill, it had a prominent position on the city skyline. The pilgrims who came here can be split into two groups: those who lived within the medieval town walls and those who came from outside.

The names of most pilgrims have gone unrecorded. Thanks to legislation passed in the 15th century we know some pilgrims came from the parts of Ireland outside of English jurisdiction. Historical sources also suggest the cathedral was also an essential stop for foreign pilgrims travelling to St Patrick's Purgatory at Lough Derg. Both Ramon de Perellós in 1398 and Laurence Rathold of Pászthó in 1411 spent time here in prayer before travelling on to the purgatory.

It is difficult to reconstruct how Irish pilgrims during the medieval period truly experienced and moved around Christ Church. As with many buildings in continuous use, the fabric of the cathedral has undergone extensive alteration and rebuilding over the centuries and surviving historical sources provide little detail of the cathedral as a thriving centre of pilgrimage.

The modern building is much altered from medieval times, having undergone extensive restoration and renovation works, most notably by George Street in the late 19th century.[208] Between its foundation and the reformation the building was altered a number of times and pilgrims at different points in time had different experiences of the cathedral's exterior and interior. Little is known about the original Hiberno-Norse cathedral but, given the status of the church, it was probably built in stone. The *Liber Niger*, a medieval manuscript belonging to the cathedral, suggests its design was influenced by architectural fashions from outside Ireland and it was built in the style of a basilica, with a two-aisle nave. [209]

All traces of this building were swept away in a complete rebuild in the late 1180s. The building works were sanctioned by John Cumin, the first English archbishop of Dublin.

> The earliest parts of the cathedral (c.1185–1200) are the transepts and choir, with the crypt below. Apart from the westernmost bay, the choir is a nineteenth-century restoration. The transepts and choir were built in a late Romanesque style with a clear south-western English flavour … architectural detailing was rendered in fine, creamy limestone imported from Dundry, near Bristol.[210]

In the nave and chancel, pilgrims found elaborately carved historiated capitals and Romanesque arches. The nave was later rebuilt around 1230–40 in the Gothic style, in contrast with the chancel and transepts. The southern side of the nave is a modern restoration but the north elevation is almost entirely original.[211] Further works were carried out over the centuries, including the construction of a belfry with stone walls, crenellated with battlements in 1330.[212] Building works in the mid-14th century extended the chancel to the east and the choir under the crossing arch. The rood screen was moved to the eastern side of the crossing and formed an enclosed choir flanked on either side by aisles.[213] Originally the rood screen sat on the west side of the crossing, but east of the northern and southern entrance into the nave.[214] Surrounding the cathedral were the buildings used to house and feed the canons, and the medieval town.

Most pilgrims entered the cathedral via the nave. By the 15th century, there were several doors leading into the nave, and at least two entrances were found in the south walls connecting to the cloister and used almost exclusively by the canons. Access into the cathedral for the lay population was through doors in the west and north wall (in the fourth bay from the tower crossing) of the nave and a door in the north transept.[215] The western door was probably the preferred entrance for pilgrims especially those who arrived for church festivals and feast days. This door would have also been used during the cathedrals extra mural processions.

The 15th-century pilgrim stepped into an aisled nave with six bays. Each bay was defined by a wall shaft running vertically from floor to vaulted ceiling.[216] The upper portions had 'integrate triforium and clerestory elements' and 'deeply moulded' arcade arches. Dundry stone was used for architectural details and Purbeck marble, also brought from Southern England, was 'used in banded shafts which adorn the nave elevations'.[217]

Unlike in modern churches the nave was a relatively open space without chairs or seats. Light flooded into the building through windows in the west, east and side walls.[218] Historical references mention a number of individual glazed windows,[219] and although we cannot know for certain how many of the cathedral's windows were glazed, historical sources and archaeological evidence confirm the widespread use of glazing in Irish ecclesiastical buildings from the 13th century.[220] It is therefore probable that a large portion, if not all, of the windows were glazed. If glazed, figurative scenes would have been kept to the chancel area of the church and windows like those in the nave were probably filled with grisaille, a decorative patterned glass, very popular in Ireland from the 13th century onwards.[221] Grisaille had an ornamental design painted with black lines on uncoloured white or grey glass. It had the advantage of allowing more light into the building and it was also cheaper than coloured glass. By the 14th century, it became fashionable to add small panels of colour to the classic grisaille design.[222] Fragments of grisaille glass have been found at archaeological excavations at religious houses such as Boyle Abbey, Co. Roscommon, Duiske Abbey, Co. Kilkenny, Tintern Abbey, Co. Wexford, and Blackfriary, the Dominican friary at Trim, Co. Meath.[223]

When pilgrims moved into the nave they walked over colourful tiled floors. The modern cathedral floor still contains numerous original medieval floor tiles. The tiles include several different patterns, one of which depicts two foxes dressed as pilgrims, walking with staffs and satchels.[224] When these animal pilgrims were set in a circular arrangement, they depicted 'a complete circle of animal pilgrims walking one behind the other in a clockwise direction'.[225]

Throughout the day, the shifting light of the sun created coloured shadows from the glass that beamed across the floor, illuminating patches of floor and parts of the cathedral walls. Light was also provided by candles and torches that burned continuously, creating atmospheric shadows and giving off the comforting smell of melted beeswax. Along with colourful floors and window glass, additional colour was added by statues sitting in niches and on altars.[226] Finely carved stones defined the windows, doors and arches and accentuated the pillars and drew the gaze of all who walked by.

A 13th-century medieval grisaille glass window from Stodmarsh Church in Kent.
© Eleanor Parker

In 1430, the sub-prior, Richard Tristi, had the walls of church plastered and whitewashed.[227] It is possible that portions of the cathedral walls were also painted with more elaborate designs like those found at the nearby medieval church of St Audoen. Wall paintings or frescos were discovered in the 19th century on the south wall of the nave but they no longer survive. The first, found when stones were removed from a blocked-up window, was a design of 'cinquefoils and traverse bars'.[228] The second, found in a recess, depicted an elaborate scene of the Holy Trinity with angels kneeling in adoration below.[229]

A solid rood screen made of stone dominated the nave and immediately drew the gaze of all who entered the building. As noted above, prior to the mid-14th century works to extend the choir the rood screen was located on the western side of the crossing. Once moved, the rood screen concealed the chancel area with its high altar and choir from view.[230] In 1430, Richard Tristi had the high altar covered by some sort of tabernacle or canopy.[231] A locked door at the centre of the rood screen prevented curious visitors from wandering uninvited into this sacred area.[232] Historical sources provide little detail about what the screen looked like.

Solid rood screens were often painted with imagery of the saints or scenes from the Bible. A gallery or rood loft ran along the top of the screen under a large crucifix known as a rood cross.[233] The gallery provided access to the rood and allowed candles and lamps to be placed there too, illuminating this space. At Christ Church the rood cross hung between the two straight pillars of the eastern crossing arch. The arch above the rood loft was divided horizontally into two sections. The upper section acted as a form of tympanum and was filled with scenes of the Passion of Christ painted on timber boards. Peter Lewys, who oversaw building works to strengthen the arch above the rood on 24 November 1564, had the painted boards cut down and re-used in the building project.[234] The

Medieval tiles depicting foxes dressed as pilgrims at Christ Church Cathedral, Dublin. © Louise Nugent

imagery of the crucified Christ hanging above the screen along with the painted images of the Passion acted as reminders to pilgrims of the sacrifice of Christ for the salvation of humanity.

One of Christ Church's main attractions for pilgrims was its large and extensive reliquary collection. The 'speaking cross' was one of the stars in the cathedral's collection. The cross was mentioned in the *Life of St Laurence O'Toole* as being '... venerated by the people of Dublin and surrounding neighbourhoods'.[235] Unfortunately, the text provides no detailed descriptions of what the cross looked like or where it was located. Gerald of Wales, writing in the late 12th century, describes it in vague terms as 'a cross of most wonderful power. It bears a figure of the Crucified.'[236] He also noted that the cross 'earned everywhere respect and veneration' and listed four miracles associated with it.[237] The English chronicler Roger Howden described the cross as having a life-sized image of Christ,[238] which was the focus of a liturgical clamour ordered by Archbishop John Cumin in 1197.[239]

> There was in the cathedral-church of Dublin a certain cross on which a rather expressive figure of Christ was carved (incisa): all the Irish, and other people as

> well, held this cross in the greatest veneration. Now, while this image of the crucified one lay prostrate on the floor surrounded by thorns, it went into agony on the sixth day. Its face reddened vehemently as if it were close to a roaring fire, and it perspired freely. Drops fell from its eyes as if it were weeping.[240]

The clergy present reportedly collected this holy liquid and asked the archbishop to inform the pope.[241] The liquid became an additional relic in the cathedral's collection.

It may very well be that the Speaking Cross was the actual rood cross that hung above the cathedral's rood screen. Interestingly, in medieval Wales, a large number of rood crosses, such as d at Carmarthen, were associated with miraculous healing and visited by pilgrims.[242] In 1327, Thomas Fitz John FitzGerald, second earl of Kildare, retained a canon to celebrate a daily Mass at the altar before the Speaking Cross.[243] It was common for medieval churches to have altars built against the rood screen, often placed on either side of a central doorway, directly below the rood cross.[244] There are many accounts of bequests for lights to be kept burning before the Speaking Cross.[245] For example, in 1174, Richard FitzGilbert, second earl of Pembroke, provided a grant to maintain a candle before it.[246] Bequests to the Christ Church crucifix provide further glimpses of the cross and how it was treated and viewed by devotees. In 1335, a gold ring with a precious stone on a silver chain was gifted to the cross by John de Grauntsete, from which it was to be suspended perpetually.[247] Over time, the ring became a secondary relic, developing curative powers, and was applied to the sick by one of the canons, in return for prayers for the soul of John and his wife Alice de Grauntsete.[248]

> May from the same cross, with the said chain, firmly hang for the sick, that those whom Almighty God, by the virtue of the precious stone, shall have restored to health.[249]

As the rood cross the Speaking Cross was very accessible to pilgrims, and the canons needed to play an active part in devotions only if a sick person requested contact with the de Grauntsete ring.

Depending on the time of day pilgrims visited the nave, they may have participated in the Mass. After the second Synod of Cashel in 1172, the cathedral, like most Irish churches, followed the Sarum Rite.[250] Each day, the cathedral held several masses at the high altar, the side altars, in the chantry and the guild chapels, along with a Mass in honour of the Blessed Virgin. Despite the solid rood screen obscuring the view of the high altar, pilgrims still experienced part of the ceremony. The ringing of bells alerted all who stood in the nave to important stages of the Mass such as the consecration of the host and they could hear the words uttered by the priest. The divine office and the other Masses were sung in plain chant, and on special days with polyphony. The sounds of the canons' chants and song reverberated throughout the building. From the 1480s on, the voices of a choir of boys maintained by the cathedral also filled the ears of pilgrims.[251] A more intimate liturgical experience was to be found at the masses offered at the side altars, chantry and guild chapels scattered around the building. [252]

Pilgrims must have visited some, if not all, of the cathedral's chapels and side altars. In the nave the Holy Trinity chapel, supported by the merchant's guild, was found in the south aisle between Strongbow's tomb and the south transept. Mass was said in the chapel every Sunday and at the request of the guild members and their families.[253] As with the cathedral's other chapels, we know little about what it looked like but, given that the merchants were a wealthy guild, we can speculate that it was decorated with the best of materials.

The focal point of all the cathedral's chapels was the altar, which was made of wood or stone. The altar was dressed in candles, fine altar cloths, religious statues and painted altar screens. Many citizens of Dublin left bequests of statues, altar plate and linen cloths to adorn various altars in the cathedral. They also left elaborate vestments for the clergy.[254]

Guild chapels were extra busy on the feasts of their patrons. Throughout Dublin, guild members assembled for religious worship in their respective guild-chapels on the feast of their patron. They attended the Anthem or Vespers on the eve of the feast, and Mass on the following day. All guild members had to pay one penny as an offering or, in default of attendance, a half pound of wax. The offerings were used to maintain the lights of the chapel and to support the chantry.[255]

Many pilgrims, especially those undertaking a journey abroad, made a point of visiting the chapel of St Nicholas, set in the two western bays of the north aisle. The oldest chapel in the cathedral, it was dedicated to St Nicholas of Myra, who was a favoured saint of sailors and travellers.[256] A chapel known as the Barbers' Chapel, located in the east half of the nave aisle, was mentioned in the Proctor's Account of 1595, but we have no details as to when it was founded.[257]

Finely carved arches connected the nave with the north and south transepts and similarly designed arches connected the transepts to the chancel area of the church.[258] To access the chancel, pilgrims had to move through the transepts. There are no records to tell the order in which holy places were visited within the cathedral, but all visits probably started in the nave before moving deeper into the church. Additional chapels were found in the chancel area. From the second half of the 14th century, after the choir was extended and the stalls of the canons were closed off from the rest of the church,[259] aisles ran along either side of the choir. From the chancel aisles pilgrims could access at least two chapels established during the post-Invasion rebuilding of the cathedral. The two chapels sat on either side of the choir, St Edmund's Chapel at the east end of the north aisle, and the chapel of St Mary of Whitland (Alba Landi) on the south side.[260] The former was dedicated to the English royal saint, Edmund, king and martyr (d. 869) and was later under the care of the military guild of St Edmund.[261]

The chapel of St Mary, often referred to as the White Chapel, was said to have a statue carved from white stone called the Sancta Marie Alba.[262] The statue no doubt sat in a prominent position within. The Mary Chapel was rededicated in the 13th century to the Irish saint Laurence O'Toole. The rededication coincided with the building of a new Marian chapel called the Lady's Chapel or St Mary's Chapel at the north-east side of the cathedral on the site now occupied by the later Chapter House.[263] The new Lady Chapel was originally a separate building but, following the mid-14th-century choir extension, its southern wall became an integrated part of the fabric of the chancel serving as the north wall of choir.[264] The Lady Chapel was the largest chapel in the cathedral at 20 metres long. It had two entrances, one in the west, through a 13th-century arch, and the other through a door leading directly into the choir.[265] It was finely decorated – in the 15th century Thomas Sinott paid for the reglazing of four of the chapels windows and later sources suggest at least half the floor was tiled.[266] An 18th-century drawing shows it was a square building with two large round-headed windows. It had its own bell and, like the rest of the cathedral, a battlement roof.[267] The Lady Chapel was not only as a place of prayer, it was also used for civic functions. In 1314 it was the location of the appointment of the freeman, mayor and bailiffs, and during the 15th century it was the crown's venue for swearing in new governors in front of the Irish council.[268]

In the early decades of the 16th century, the number of chapels increased again, with the creation in the main body of the choir of the Kildare Chantry Chapel, built for the eighth earl of Kildare and dedicated to St Mary in 1512.[269] It contained the tomb of the earl and an altar dedicated to the Blessed Virgin and was surrounded by elaborate ornate wooden screens on the north-east and western sides, surmounted by canopies.[270] This chapel was linked to the Lady Chapel on the other side of the wall by door.[271]

The rededication of the chapel of St Mary to St Laurence O'Toole coincided with his canonisation in 1225.[272] The chapel of St Laurence would have been a popular destination for pilgrims in the years proceeding his canonisation. From the transept, pilgrims stepped into the chapel through a round arch, with an inner order of decorated roll moulding.[273] An altar within may have displayed one or more of the saint's relics throughout the year or on his feast day, 14 November. Historical records hint at how the chapel might have looked. A reference to a glazed image of the saint within the chapel is mentioned in a 1567 record that describes repairs made to a storm-damaged window of the saint housed within the chapel of the Holy Ghost. We know St Laurence's chapel had been rededicated to the Holy Ghost in the 15th century but the new chapel may have maintained an altar dedicated to St Laurence.[274] A decorative statue niche between the chapel's entrance and the arch leading into the cathedral choir may have held an image of the saint.[275] The niche also hints at the use of statues throughout the medieval church.

Many pilgrims came to the cathedral to be close to certain relics. The Speaking Cross could be found in the nave and was easily accessible. From the time of its foundation Christ Church had an extensive relic collection, much of which came from Cologne. The collection was added to over the years and by the 14th century it had the relics of Irish and foreign saints, along with a portion of the True Cross, a thorn from the Crown of Thorns and the Bachall Íosa. Marian relics were represented by a phial of the Virgin Mary's milk along with her belt or girdle. Apostolic relics included those of SS Paul and Andrew, along with the Cross and Chain of St Peter. Relics of SS Sylvester and Catherine of Alexandria and the vestments of St Olaf of Norway and St Herbert of Cologne, as well as the relics of English and Welsh saints like David, Oswald, Wulfstan and Edward the Confessor were included in the collection. Irish saints were represented by relics of SS Patrick, Brigit, Laurence O'Toole and Brendan, including a portable marble altar associated with St Patrick.[276] The Bachall Íosa is one of the better documented relics in the cathedral's collection. The Bachall was believed to be the pastoral staff or crozier given to St Patrick by Christ himself. Originally kept at Armagh, it came into the possession of Christ Church Cathedral during the 12th century and was venerated there until its destruction in 1538.[277] It was repeatedly mentioned in the annals and credited with numerous miracles, and oaths were frequently validated before the staff. It also featured frequently in medieval wills.[278] Its popularity was such that in 1493 offerings made by pilgrims to the Bachall were used to support the choirboys at Christ Church.[279] Although there are no descriptions of what the Bachall looked like it was probably not too dissimilar to the elaborate croziers covered in precious decorated metals that are on display in the National Museum of Ireland collections.

There are many unanswered questions as to where or how the cathedral's relics were stored or displayed over the centuries. There is also little evidence as to how pilgrims interacted with them or the level of contact with the relics that was allowed. In churches following the Sarum Rite, some relics would have been carried in liturgical processions on important Church feast days, such as Palm Sunday and Corpus Christi, allowing pilgrims visual contact with the relics. It is also possible that individual relics may have been displayed on the altars of chapels throughout the year or on special occasions such as the feast days of individual saints. Given the small number of canons at Christ Church the latter may have been more likely. By the 14th century, part, if not all, of the relic collection was housed close to, and possibly even displayed on or behind, the high altar. The extension of the choir in the 14th century seems to have been a deliberate attempt to make space behind the high altar for the display of the cathedral's relics and perhaps even to create a feretory space.[280] On 19 July 1461, a great storm blew in the east window and

> falling stones broke many chests containing jewels, relics, ornaments, and vestments of the altar, and muniments … By a miracle the Staff of Jesus, though the chest in which it was kept and other relics therein were destroyed, was found uninjured lying above the stones.[281]

Details of the event suggest that many of the relics were concealed from view in chests and reliquary containers. As there is no mention of damage to the high altar, we can assume it was located at a distance from the window, supporting the theory that a feretory existed at the time.[282] The damage caused by the window was very costly and the following year a royal protection was extended to all pilgrims visiting there,

> as the destruction of the two chief windows, commonly called Gabilles, cannot be restored without the aid of Christians and oblations of pilgrims.[283]

If a feretory existed pilgrims surely had some access to the sacred space. Pilgrims would have travelled from the nave through the transepts and along one of the aisles on either side of the choir to gain access to the feretory at the top of the chancel.

In the medieval world feretory chapels tended to be small, with limited space. If pilgrims to Christ Church were allowed access to see the relics it was surely under supervision and perhaps by appointment at set times. Pilgrims may have filed in one entrance, prayed before the relics/shrines, and have been ushered out through an opposite door. Alternatively, they may have been marshalled in small groups.[284] Even if close contact with the relics housed near the altar was not available to pilgrims, they could be viewed in a public setting on procession days, when relics were placed in elaborate portable containers. A glimpse of the elaborate reliquaries owned by the cathedral is found in 1344–5, when it is noted that John Savage was paid 17 shillings for carving and ornamenting 18 images for a shrine.[285]

NOTES

1 Sumption, 82.
2 *Life of St Brigit*, 7.
3 VC, 202, [II. 45].
4 Ludwig Bieler, *The Irish Penitentials* (Dublin: Dublin Institute for Advanced Studies, 1963), 167 [III.7 57. (I)].
5 Alfred P. Smyth, *Warlords and Holy Men, Scotland AD 80–1000* (London: Edward Arnold, 1984), 21–22.
6 AU.
7 AFM.
8 O'Sullivan and Ó Carragáin, *Inishmurray*, 319.
9 Meyer, *Aislinge Meic Conglinne*, xviii, 148.
10 Nugent, 'Pilgrimage in Medieval Ireland,' Vol.II, Appendix IX. A study of Irish indulgences has yet to be undertaken by Irish scholars, despite the ample references to this phenomenon in the CPL.
11 Malachy Harty, *Triumphalia Chronologica Monasterii Sanctae Crucis in Hibernia* (Dublin: Fallon, 1893), 141.
12 Robert Day, ed., 'Regnum Corcagiense, or a Description of the Kingdom of Cork, by Sir Richard Cox (Contd),' *JCHAS*, 2, 8, no. 55 (1902): 163.
13 Stalley, 'The Architecture of the Cathedral and Priory Buildings,' 104.
14 Bugslag, 'Performative Thaumaturgy,' 229.
15 Pádraig Ó Riain, 'The Calendar and Martrology of Christ Church Cathedral, Dublin,' in *The Medieval Manuscripts of Christ Church Cathedral, Dublin*, ed. Raymond Gillespie and Raymond Refaussé (Dublin: Four Courts Press, 2006), 40.
16 Halpin and Newman, *Ireland. An Oxford Archaeological Guide*, 308.
17 *Life of St Brigit*, 27.
18 Mark Zumbuhl, 'Uí Dúnlainge,' in *Medieval Ireland An Encyclopedia.*, ed. Séan Duffy (London: Routledge, 2005), 487.
19 Nancy Edwards, *The Archaeology of Early Medieval Ireland* (London: Routledge, 1999), 105–12.
20 Halpin and Newman, *Ireland. An Oxford Archaeological Guide*, 310.
21 Edwards, *The Archaeology of Early Medieval Ireland*, 114–21.
22 *Life of St Brigit*, 25.
23 Lisa M. Bitel, *Landscape with Two Saints: How Genovefa of Paris and Brigit of Kildare Built Christianity in Barbarian Europe* (Oxford: Oxford University Press, 2009), 145.
24 Christiaan Corlett, *Glendalough* (Wicklow: Coles Lane, 2017), 50.
25 *Life of St Brigit*, 24–25.
26 *Life of St Brigit*, 25.
27 *Life of St Brigit*, 25; Bitel, *Landscape with Two Saints*, 148.
28 Aidan MacDonald, 'Adomnán's Monastery of Iona,' in *Studies in The Cult of Saint Columba*, ed. Cormac Bourke (Dublin: Four Courts Press, 1997), 31; Tomás Ó Carragáin, *Churches in Early Medieval Ireland: Architecture, Ritual and Memory* (London: Yale University Press, 2010), 19.
29 Ó Carragáin, *Churches in Early Medieval Ireland*, 15–17.
30 MacDonald, 'Adomnán's Monastery of Iona,' 31.
31 Edwards, *The Archaeology of Early Medieval Ireland*, 112.
32 *Life of St Brigit*, 26.
33 Carol Neuman De Vegvar, 'Romanitas and Realpolitik in Cogitosus' Description of the Church of St Brigit, Kildare', in *The Cross Goes North: Processes of Conversion in Northern Europe, AD 300–1300*, ed. Martin Carver (Suffolk: The Boydell Press, 2003), 161: Ó Carragáin, *Churches in Early Medieval Ireland*, 172.
34 Neuman De Vegvar, 'Romanitas and Realpolitik,' 164; *Life of St Brigit*, 26.
35 Neuman De Vegvar, 'Romanitas and Realpolitik,' 156–59.
36 For an in-depth discussion of early Irish churches, see Ó Carragáin, *Churches in Early Medieval Ireland.*
37 Neuman De Vegvar, 'Romanitas and Realpolitik,' 164.
38 Neuman De Vegvar, 156–60, Fig. 10.4.
39 *Life of St Brigit*, 25.
40 Sumption, *Pilgrimage*, 212–13; Bugslag, 'Performative Thaumaturgy,' 219; Ann Buckley, 'From Hymn to Historia: Liturgical Veneration of Local Saints in the Medieval Irish Church,' in *Music, Liturgy, and the Veneration of Saint's of the Medieval Irish Church in a European Context*, ed. Ann Buckley (Turnhout: Brepols Press, 2017), 161–83.

41 Neuman De Vegvar, 'Romanitas and Realpolitik,' 164.
42 For excellent discussion early Irish hymns and liturgies see Buckley, 'From Hymn to Historia,' 161–83.
43 Buckley, 'From Hymn to Historia,' 169.
44 Buckley, 'From Hymn to Historia,' 167.
45 Brian Lacey, *Colum Cille and the Columban Tradition* (Dublin: Four Courts Press, 1997), 87; Buckley, 'From Hymn to Historia,' 172, 175–76.
46 *Life of St Brigit*, 25.
47 Bugslag, 'Performative Thaumaturgy,' 241.
48 Gerhard Lutz, 'Introduction to the Late Medieval Pilgrim Architecture,' *Peregrinations* no. 4 (2004): 5.
49 Stokes, *The Martyrology of Oengus the Culdee*, 92.
50 Malone, *Life of St. Flannan*, 51.
51 VSH, Vol.II, 130.
52 VSH Vol.II, 130; VSH Vol.II, 162–163.
53 Sheehan, 'A Peacock's Tale: Excavations at Caherlehillan, Kerry, Ireland,' 199.
54 Françoise Henry, 'Early Monasteries, Beehive Huts and Dry Stone Houses in the Neighbourhood of Caherciveen and Waterville (Co. Kerry),' *PRIA* 58 C (57 1956): 161.
55 Thomas, *The Early Christian Archaeology*, 141–42; Ann O'Sullivan and John Sheehan, *The Iveragh Peninsula: An Archaeological Survey of South Kerry* (Cork: Cork University Press, 1996), 296.
56 In the late 1800s, pilgrims to Killabuonia completed nine rounds or circuits of stations, such as the holy well, finishing at the gable shrine known, at the time, as the priest's grave. The pilgrims placed votive offerings inside it. A 'hair-pin, button, or generally the tassel from wool shawls, worn by the peasantry of Kerry, is passed through the hole in the end stone of the grave'. See P. J Lynch, 'Some of the Antiquities around St. Finan's Bay, County Kerry,' *JRSAI* 32 no.1 (1902): 46–47. Up to the 20th Century, pilgrims to the Templecronan poured water over the gable shrine and whatever water flowed out again was taken away for healing. Personal communication with Jim Higgins.
57 Bede, *Ecclesiastical History of the English People: With Bede's Letter to Egbert and Cuthbert's Letter on the Death of Bede*, trans. David Farmer (London: Penguin, 2003), Book IV Chapter 3, 347–348.
58 Sheehan, 'A Peacock's Tale,' 199.
59 White Marshall and Walsh, *Illaunloughan Island*, 66.
60 White Marshall and Walsh, *Illaunloughan Island*, 58–66.
61 Dudley Waterman, 'An Early Christian Mortuary House at Saul, Co. Down, with Notes on Similar Monuments in Ulster,' *UJA* 23 (1960) 82–88.
62 Waterman, 'An Early Christian Mortuary House,' 86; Edwards, The Archaeology of Early Medieval Ireland, 131.
63 Waterman, 'An Early Christian Mortuary House,' 84, 86.
64 Waterman, 'An Early Christian Mortuary House,' 83; Harbison, *Pilgrimage in Ireland*, 154.
65 Stokes, *The Martyrology of Oengus*, 245.
66 Raghnall Ó Floinn, 'Clonmacnoisee: Art and Patronage in the Early Medieval Period,' in *Clonmacnoisee. Studies. Seminar Papers*, ed. Heather King, vol. 1 (Dublin: The Heritage Council, 1998), 94.
67 Ó Floinn, 'Clonmacnoisee,' 93.
68 Ó Floinn, 'Clonmacnoisee,' 94.
69 Nugent, 'Pilgrimage in Medieval Ireland,' Vol. I, 235–236; Rachel Moss, 'Architectural Sculpture at Glendalough,' in *Glendalough :City of God*, ed. Charles Doherty, Linda Doran, and Mary Kelly (Dublin: Four Courts Press, 2011), 296.
70 Lorcan Harney, 'Medieval Burial and Pilgrimage within the Landscape of Glendalough the Evidence of the Crosses and the Cross-Slabs,' in *Glendalough: City of God*, ed. Charles Doherty and Mary Kelly (Dublin: Four Courts Press for the Royal Society of Antiquaries of Ireland, 2011), 112–36.
71 Edwards, *The Archaeology of Early Medieval Ireland*, 112.
72 Ó Carragáin, *Churches in Early Medieval Ireland*, 228.
73 VC 201 [II.45].
74 White Marshall and Rourke, *High Island*, 85.
75 Tadhg O'Keeffe, *Medieval Irish Buildings, 1100–1600* (Dublin: Four Courts Press, 2015), 135–39.

76 O'Keeffe, *Medieval Irish Buildings* 68–71.
77 Louise Nugent 'Pilgrimage and the Augustinians in Medieval Ireland,' in Martin, *Households of God: The Regular Canons and Canonesses of St Augustine and of Prémontré in Medieval Ireland* ed. Martin Browne & Colmán Ó Claibaigh (Dublin: Four Courts Press, 2019), 216–217.
78 O'Keeffe, *Medieval Irish Buildings*, 158–60.
79 O'Keeffe, *Medieval Irish Buildings* 154–58.
80 Higgins, *Claregalway*, 19–23.
81 Yeoman, 'An Archaeology of Pilgrimage,' 646; Nilson, 'The Medieval Experience of a Shrine,' 97.
82 Karena Morton, 'The Wall Painting Fragments,' in *Kells Priory, Co Kilkenny: Archaeological Excavations*, ed. Miriam Clyne (Dublin: Stationery Office, 2007), 216.
83 Jane Fawcett, *Historic Floors* (Oxford: Butterworth-Heinemann, 2001), 1; Michael Huxtable and Ronan O' Donnell, 'Medieval Colour,' in *The Oxford Handbook of Later Medieval Archaeology in Britain*, ed. Christopher Gerrard and Alejandra Gutiérrez (Oxford: Oxford University Press, 2018), 745.
84 Morton, 'The Wall Painting Fragments,' 212; Jon Cannon, *Medieval Church Architecture* (London: Bloomsbury Publishing, 2014), 15.
85 John Steane, *The Archaeology of Medieval England and Wales* (London: Routledge, 2014), 69.
86 Steane, *The Archaeology of Medieval England and Wales* 70; O'Keeffe, *Medieval Irish Buildings, 1100–1600*, 115–16.
87 Fawcett, *Historic Floors*, 1; Josephine Moran, 'The Shattered Image: Archaeological Evidence for Painted and Stained Glass in Medieval Ireland,' in *Art & Devotion in Late Medieval Ireland*, ed. Rachel Moss, Colmán Ó Clabaigh, and Salvador Ryan (Dublin: Four Courts Press, 2006), 128–30.
88 Morton, 'The Wall Painting Fragments.'
89 Josephine Moran, 'The Window Glass,' in *Kells Priory, Co. Kilkenny: Archaeological Excavations*, ed. Miriam Clyne (Dublin: Stationery Office, 2007), 261–316; Moran, 'The Shattered Image.'
90 Fawcett, *Historic Floors*, 2.
91 Potterton, *Medieval Trim*, 309.
92 Radegund was the patron saint of Poitiers in France. Her cult spread to England from Aquitaine and she was venerated at Evesham Abbey, Glastonbury and Worcester. The spread of her cult was no doubt aided by the close trading links of Ireland, England and Aquitane. See George Beech, 'England and Aquitaine in the Century before the Norman Conquest,' *Anglo-Saxon England* 19 (1990): 91.
93 Raymond Refaussé & Colm Lennon eds. *The Registers of Christ Church Cathedral, Dublin* (Dublin Four Courts Press), 20.
94 Catriona MacLeod, 'Mediaeval Wooden Figure Sculptures in Ireland, Mediaeval Madonnas in the West,' *JRSAI* 75, no. 3 (1945): 180–81; Catriona MacLeod, 'Some Medieval Wooden Figure Sculptures in Ireland. Statues of Irish Saints,' *JRSAI* 76 (1946): 164–70.
95 Gary Waller, *The Virgin Mary in Late Medieval and Early Modern English Literature and Popular Culture* (Cambridge: Cambridge University Press, 2011), 87.
96 James Lydon, 'The Text and Its Context,' in *The Account Roll of the Priory of the Holy Trinity, Dublin, 1337–1346*, ed. James Mills (Dublin: Four Courts Press, 1996), xv.
97 Henry Berry, ed., *Register of Wills and Inventories of the Diocese of Dublin in the Time of Archbishops Tregury and Walton, 1457-1483* (Dublin: The University Press, 1898), 53. Statues are often left to beneficiaries in bequests in Irish wills: xxxiii, 5, 12, 15, 30, 48, 64, 71, 76, 82, 94, 103, 122, 128, 153.
98 Finucane, *Miracles and Pilgrims*, 201.
99 Bugslag, 'Performative Thaumaturgy,' 247–48.
100 D.M.A Ó hÉaluighthe, 'Saint Gobnet of Ballyvourney,' *JCHAS* 57 (1952), 48.
101 John Richardson, *The Great Folly, Superstition, and Idolatry, of Pilgrimages in Ireland* (Dublin: J. Hyde, 1727), 71.
102 Richardson, *The Great Folly*, 72.
103 MacLeod, 'Some Medieval Wooden Figure Sculptures,' 165.
104 Bugslag 'Performative Thaumaturgy,' 247–248.
105 Stat. Ire., 12–22 Edw. IV , xli, 42–47; James Hardiman, ed., *A Statute of the Fortieth Year of King Edward III: Enacted in a Parliament Held in Kilkenny, A.D. 1367, Before Lionel Duke of Clarence*, vol. 2 (Dublin: Irish Archaeological Society, 1843), 51.

106 Kate Giles and Aleksandra McClain, 'The Devotional Image in Late Medieval England,' in *The Oxford Handbook of Later Medieval Archaeology in Britain*, ed. Christopher Gerrard and Alejandra Gutiérrez (Oxford: Oxford University Press, 2018), 662–63.

107 Satis N. Coleman, *Bells: Their History, Legends, Making, and Uses* (New York: Rand, McNally & Company, 1928), 97.

108 J. Patrick Greene, *Medieval Monasteries* (London: Continuum, 2005), 96.

109 Webb, *Pilgrimage in Medieval England*, 83.

110 Higgins, *Claregalway*, 16.

111 Paul Duffy and Tadhg O'Keeffe, 'A Stone Shrine for a Relic of St Thomas Becket in Dublin?' *Archaeology Ireland* 31, no. 4 (2017):,18–23.

112 Susan Leigh Fry, *Burial in Medieval Ireland 900–1500: A Review of the Written Sources* (Dublin: Four Courts Press, 1999), 164–65; Hughes, *Church and Society In Ireland*, 355 V.

113 E. St. John Brooks, '14th Century Monastic Estates in Meath. The Llanthony Cells of Duleek and Colp,' *The JRSAI* 83, no. 2 (1953): 145.

114 Katherine Walsh, *Richard FitzRalph in Oxford, Avignon, and Armagh* (Oxford: Clarendon Press, 1981), 465; Robert Chambers, *The Book of Days: A Miscellany of Popular Antiquities in Connection with the Calendar, Including Anecdote, Biography, & History, Curiosities of Literature and Oddities of Human Life and Character*, vol. 2 (Edinburg: W. & R. Chambers, 1872), 186; James Ware, *The Whole Works*, vol. I, 83.

115 Nilson, 'The Medieval Experience,' 97.

116 Higgins, *Claregalway*, 16.

117 Greene, *Medieval Monasteries*, 96.

118 Sumption, *Pilgrimage*, 213.

119 Webb, *Pilgrimage in Medieval England*, 85.

120 Huitson, *Stairway to Heaven*, 60; Webb, *Pilgrimage in Medieval England*, 84.

121 Roger Rosewell, *The Medieval Monastery* (Shire Publications, 2012), 28–29.

122 Higgins, *Claregalway*.

123 The movement of people in an organised manner as part of organised ritual or as an expression of popular piety.

124 Elisa A. Foster, 'Moveable Feasts: Processions as Multimedia Performance in Le Puy-En-Velay,' *Peregrinations* 5, no. 1 (2015), 43.

125 Charles Doherty, 'The Use of Relics in Early Ireland,' in *Irland Und Europa: Die Kirche in Frühmittelalter*, ed. Próinséas Ní Chátháin and Michael Richter (Stuttgart: Klett-Cotta, 1984), 89–104; Edel Bhreathnach, *Ireland in the Medieval World, AD 400–1000: Landscape, Kingship and Religion* (Dublin: Four Courts Press, 2014), 69–70.

126 Alexander O'Hara and Faye Taylor, 'Aristocratic and Monastic Conflict in Tenth-Century Italy: The Case of Bobbio and the Miracula Sancti Columbani,' *Viator* 44 no. 3 (2013), 50.

127 O'Hara and Taylor, 'Aristocratic and Monastic Conflict,' 51.

128 Bieler, *The Patrician Texts*, 190–191 XI.3(31); Nicholas, Boyeter, Aitchson, *Armagh and the Royal Centres in Early Medieval Ireland: Mounuments,Cosmology, and the Past* (Woodbridge: Boydell & Brewer, 1994), 266–81.

129 Whitley Stokes, *Lives of Saint's from the Book of Lismore* (Oxford: Clarendon Press, 1890), 214. See also Celeste Ray, *The Origins of Ireland's Holy Wells* (Oxford: Archaeopress, 2014), 97.

130 O'Sullivan and Ó Carragáin, *Inishmurray*, 328.

131 *Life of St Brigit*, 27.

132 O'Sullivan and Ó Carragáin, *Inishmurray*, 320.

133 O'Sullivan and Ó Carragáin, *Inishmurray*, 341–42.

134 O'Sullivan and Ó Carragáin, *Inishmurray*, 321.

135 O'Sullivan and Ó Carragáin, *Inishmurray*, 320. A 'plurality of altars with different dedications was regarded as basic requirements for important ecclesiastical establishments.' See also O'Sullivan and Ó Carragáin, *Inishmurray* 323

136 O'Sullivan and Ó Carragáin, *Inishmurray*, 325.

137 Ryan Lash et al., " Differing in Status, but One in Spirit': Sacred Space and Social Diversity at Island Monasteries in Connemara, Ireland,' *Anitquity* 92 (2018), 437–55; Ryan Lash, 'Pebbles and Peregrinatio: The Taskscape of Medieval Devotion on Inishark Island, Ireland,' *Medieval Archaeology* 62 (2018), 82–103; Herity, 'The Antiquity of an Turas,'; Gibbons and Gibbons, 'Inishglora.'

138 Harney, 'Medieval Burial and Pilgrimage.'

139 O'Sullivan and Ó Carragáin, *Inishmurray*, 317–18.

140 Foster, 'Moveable Feasts,' 43.

141 Rogationtide was a communal procession to emphasise the unity of parish and parishio-

ners. It was held on special days of fasting and prayer that took on 25 April (the Major Rogation) and the Monday, Tuesday and Wednesday before the feast of the Ascension. It was common practice for relics to be part of some procession, especially extramural ones.

142 Tekippe, 'Pilgrimage and Procession,' 698; Catholic Church, *Processionale Ad Usum Insignis Ac Praeclarae Ecclesiae Sarum* (Leeds: Printed by M'Corquodale, 1882), xiii.

143 Tekippe, 'Pilgrimage and Procession,' 694.

144 Bugslag, 'Performative Thaumaturgy,' 237–38.

145 C Hourihane, "Holye Crossys', a Catalogue of Processional, Altar, Pendant and Crucifix Figures for Late Medieval Ireland,' *PRIA* 100C no.1 (2000), 1–85.

146 For a detailed discussion of the cross, see Griffin Joseph Murray, *The Cross of Cong and Church Metalwork from Romanesque Ireland* (NUI, 2007, at Department of Archaeology, UCC., 2007).

147 Foster, 'Moveable Feasts,' 48; Tekippe, 'Pilgrimage and Procession,' 700, 703–4.

148 Tekippe, 'Pilgrimage and Procession,' 704; Foster, 'Moveable Feasts,' 45.

149 Anon, 'Sarum Customary Online – Context – The Medieval Church – Medieval Liturgy,' http://www.sarumcustomary.org.uk/context/medievalchurch/liturgy.php. Accessed 31 January 2019,

150 Buckley, 'From Hymn to Historia,' 179.

151 Hilary Richardson, 'Visual Arts and Society,' in *A New History of Ireland. Prehistoric and Early Ireland*, ed. Donnchadh Ó Cróinín (Oxford: Oxford University Press, 2005), 696.

152 Harty, *Triumphalia Chronologica Monasterii*, 164–67.

153 Raghnall Ó Floinn, *Irish Shrines & Reliquaries of the Middle Ages* (Dublin: Town House and Country House, 1994), 37.

154 Alan Fletcher, 'The Civic Pageantry of Corpus Christi in Fifteenth- and Sixteenth-Century Dublin,' *Irish Economic and Social History*, 23 (1996): Appendix 1, 86.

155 Alan Fletcher, 'The Liturgy and Music of the Medieval Cathedral,' in *A History of St Patrick's Cathedral*, ed. John Crawford and Raymond Gillespie (Dublin: Four Courts Press, 2009), 138.

156 Fletcher, 'The Liturgy and Music,' 138.

157 William Monck Mason, *The History and Antiquities of the Collegiate and Cathedral Church of St. Patrick near Dublin, from Its Foundation in 1190, to the Year 1819* (Dublin: Printed William Monk Mason by W. Folds, 1820), xxviii.

158 Fletcher, 'The Liturgy and Music,' 138.

159 Fletcher, 'The Liturgy and Music,' 138; Mason, *The History and Antiquities*, xxviii–xx.

160 William Peter Mahrt, 'The Role of Old Sarum in the Processions of Salisbury Cathedral,' in *Study of Medieval Manuscripts of England: Festschrift in Honor of Richard W. Pfaff*, ed. Linda Doran and George Brown (Tempe, Arizona: Arizona Center for Medieval and Renaissance Studies with Brepols, 2010), 139.

161 Fletcher, 'The Liturgy and Music,' 140.

162 Fletcher, 'The Liturgy and Music,' 141.

163 Fletcher, 'The Liturgy and Music,' 140; Duffy, *The Stripping of the Altars*, 23.

164 Fletcher, "The Liturgy and Music,' 141–42.

165 Fletcher, 'The Liturgy and Music,' 142.

166 Fletcher, 'The Liturgy and Music,' 142.

167 Duffy, *The Stripping of the Altars*, 24–25.

168 Fletcher, 'The Liturgy and Music,' 142.

169 Miri Rubin, *Corpus Christi: The Eucharist in Late Medieval Culture* (Cambridge: Cambridge University Press, 1991), 203; Elisa A. Foster, "This Is My Body": Devotion to the Corpus Christi Shrine in Late Medieval York,' in *Devotional Interaction in Medieval England and Its Afterlives*, ed. Elisa A. Foster, Julia Perratore, and Steven Rozenski (Leiden: Brill, 2018), 245.

170 Fletcher, 'The Liturgy and Music,' 140; John J. Webb, 'The Guilds of Dublin,' *The Irish Montly* 45 (530) (1917):,510.

171 Fletcher, 'The Liturgy and Music,' 140.

172 Helen Birkett, 'The Struggle for Sanctity: St Walther of Melrose, Cistercian in-House Cults and Canonization Precedured at the Turn of the Thirteenth Century,' in *The Cult of Saint's and the Virgin Mary in Medieval Scotland*, ed. Steve Boardman and Eila Williamson (London: The Boydell Press, 2010), 44–45.

173 Birkett, 'The Struggle for Sanctity,' 47–48.

174 Birkett, 'The Struggle for Sanctity,' 49.

175 Sumption, *Pilgrimage*, 31–35.

176 Malone, *Life of St. Flannan*, 52–53.

177 Laurence P. Murray, 'Archbishop Cromer's Register (Continued),' *JLAS* 8 no. 2 (1934), 187, no. 92; Raymond Gillespie, 'Who Stole St Buite's Head? Gossip and Guilt in Sixteenth-Century Louth,' in *A Carnival of Learning. Essays to Honour George Cunningham and His 50 Conferences on Medieval Ireland Cistercian Abbey of Mount St Jospeh, Roscrea, 1987–2012*, ed. Peter Harbison and Valerie Hall (Roscrea: Cistercian Press, 2012), 74–86.
178 Finucane, *Miracles and Pilgrims*, 44.
179 Alain Dubreucq and Alessandro Zironi, eds., *Miracula Sancti Columbani. La Reliquia e Il Giudizio Regio. La Relique et Le Jugement Royal. Relic and Royal Judgment. Ediz. Multilingue* (Firenze: Edizioni del Galluzzo per la Fondazione Ezio Franceschini, 2015), 65, Chapter XVIIII.
180 Dubreucq and Zironi, *Miracula Sancti Columbani*, 65.
181 Webb, *Pilgrimage in Medieval England*, 84–5.
182 Ruth A Johnston, *All Things Medieval: An Encyclopedia of the Medieval World, Volume 1* (California: Greenwood Publishing Group, 2011), 563.
183 Thomas of Monmouth, *The Life and Miracles of St. William of Norwich*, ed. M.R. James and Augustus Jessopp (Cambridge: Cambridge University Press, 1896), 163–64.
184 Sumption, *Pilgrimage*, 213.
185 Bernard Iterii, 'The Chronicle and Historical Notes of Bernard Itier,' ed. Andrew W. Lewis (Oxford: Oxford University Press, 2013), 217.
186 Sumption, *Pilgrimage*, 213–14.
187 Sumption, *Pilgrimage*, 214–15.
188 Toby Huitson, *Stairway to Heaven: The Functions of Medieval Upper Spaces* (Oxford: Oxbow Books, 2014), 63–64.
189 Harty, *Triumphalia Chronologica Monasterii*, lxiv, 125—3. Miracles were also brought about when water the relics, was plunged into was sprinkled on crops.
190 Harty, *Triumphalia Chronologica*, 143, 149.
191 Colmcille Ó Conbhuidhe, *The Cistercian Abbeys of Tipperary*, ed. Finbarr Donovan (Dublin: Four Courts Press, 1999), 166.
192 Roger Stalley, *The Cistercian Monasteries of Ireland: An Account of the History, Art and Architecture of the White Monks in Ireland from 1142–1540* (London: Yale University Press, 1987), 116.
193 Harty, *Triumphalia Chronologica*, lv; Dagmar Ó Riain-Raedel, 'Holy Cross, Co Tipperary: Pilgrimage Site and Boon to Antiquarians,' unpublished article supplied by author.
194 Stalley, *The Cistercian Monasteries of Ireland*, 116–17.
195 It was recorded in this position in 1913 and moved after restoration of the abbey.
196 William J. Hayes, *Holycross: The Awakening of the Abbey* (Lisheen Publications, 2011), 88.
197 Hayes, *Holycross*, 102.
198 Harbison, *Pilgrimage in Ireland*, 305.
199 Harbison, *Pilgrimage in Ireland*, 305.
200 Mary McGrath, 'The Materials and Techniques of Irish Medieval Wall-Paintings,' *JRSAI* 117 (1987): 123.
201 Ó Riain-Raedel, 'Holy Cross, Co Tipperary.'
202 Ó Riain-Raedel, 'Holy Cross, Co Tipperary.'
203 His pilgrimage was made in the company of Flannacán ua Cellaig, king of Brega, *AU*.
204 Boydell, *Music at Christ Church*, 12. Although details of the internal structure of prayers and liturgy varied between monastic and secular practice, the broad outline of the divine office was common throughout Europe.
205 At one point the cathedral held 10,500 acres along with properties in Dublin, Kildare, Meath and Louth, see M. J. McEnery and Raymond Refaussé, eds., *Christ Church Deeds* (Dublin: Four Courts Press, 2001), 20–21.
206 Raymond Refaussé, *The Registers of Christ Church Cathedral, Dublin* (Dublin Four Courts Press, 1998), 21; McEnery & Refaussé, *Christ Church Deeds*, xiv–xv.
207 Mills, *Account Roll of Holy Trinity*, xix–xx.
208 Raymond Refaussé, 'Introduction,' in *Christ Church Cathedral Dublin: a History*, ed. Kenneth Milne (Dublin: Four Courts Press, 2000), 7.
209 Stalley, 'Construction of the Medieval Cathedral,' 56.
210 Halpin and Newman, *Ireland. An Oxford Archaeological Guide*, 284.
211 Halpin and Newman, *Ireland. An Oxford Archaeological Guide*, 284.
212 McEnery & Refauss, *Christ Church Deeds*, no. 223, 76.

213 Stuart Kinsella, 'An Architectural History of Christ Church Cathedral Dublin c.1540–1870,' Unpublished PhD Thesis, Department of History of Art and Architecture of Trinity College (2009), 77; Stalley 'Architecture of the Cathedral and Priory Buildings,' 95–96.
214 Kinsella, 'Architectural History of Christ Church Cathedral,' 88.
215 Kinsella, 'Architectural History of Christ Church Cathedral,' 76.
216 Halpin and Newman, *Ireland. An Oxford Archaeological Guide*, 284.
217 Halpin and Newman, *Ireland. An Oxford Archaeological Guide*, 284.
218 Myles Ronan, 'Religious Life in Old Dublin,' *Dublin Historical Record*, no. 2 (1939): 49.
219 Kinsella, 'Architectural History of Christ Church Cathedral,' 107–108.
220 Josephine Moran 'Glass from Bective Abbey' in *The Bective Abbey Project, Co Meath: Excavations 2009–12*, Geraldine Stout and Matthew Stout (eds.) (Bray: Wordwell Press 2016), 90.
221 Personal communication with Josephine Moran, archaeological stained glass specialist.
222 Moran, 'The Window Glass,' 262.
223 Moran 'Glass from Bective Abbey,' 90.
224 Elizabeth S. Eames and Thomas Fanning, *Irish Medieval Tiles* (Dublin: Royal Irish Academy, 1988), 5, 79, 98.
225 Eames and Fanning, *Irish Medieval Tiles*, 21.
226 Kinsella 'Architectural History of Christ Church Cathedral,' 107.
227 Refaussé and Lennon, *Registers of Christ Church Cathedral*, 44; Stalley, 'Architecture of the Cathedral and Priory Buildings,' 103.
228 Mary McMahon, *St Audoen's Church, Cornmarket, Dublin: Archaeology and Architecture.* (Dublin: The Stationary Office, 2006) 45.
229 Mc Mahon, *St Audoen's Church*, 47.
230 Kinsella 'Architectural History of Christ Church Cathedral,' 98.
231 Stalley 'Architecture of the Cathedral and Priory Buildings,' 103; Refaussé and Lennon, *Registers of Christ Church Cathedral*, 44
232 Stalley, 'Construction of the Medieval Cathedral,' 101.
233 Stalley, 'Architecture of the Cathedral and Priory Buildings,' 101; Berry, *Register of Wills, Dublin*, 7; Ronan, 'Religious Life in Old Dublin,' 47.
234 Kinsella, 'Architectural History of Christ Church Cathedral,' 98; Raymond Gillespie, ed., *The Proctor's Accounts of Peter Lewis, 1564–1565* (Dublin: Dublin Four Courts Press, 1997), 15, 38–39.
235 Albert Legris, *Life of St. Laurence O'Toole: Archbishop of Dublin (1128–1180)* (Dublin: Catholic Truth Society of Ireland, 1914), 36.
236 John O'Meara, *The History and Topography of Ireland by Giraldus Cambrensis* (Portlaoise: Dolmen Press, 1982), 85–86.
237 Stuart Kinsella, 'From Hiberno-Norse to Anglo-Norman, *c.*1030–1300', in *Christ Church Cathedral Dublin: a History*, ed. Kenneth. Milne, (Dublin: Four Courts Press, 2000), 46; Giraldus Cambrensis, *The Topography of Ireland. Translated by Thomas Forester. Revised and Edited with Additional Notes by Thomas Wright* (Cambridge, Ontario: In parentheses Publications, 2000), 58.
238 Stalley, 'Architecture of the Cathedral and Priory Buildings,' 108.
239 Flanagan, *Transformation of the Irish Church*, 234.
240 Flanagan, *Transformation of the Irish Church*, 234; William Stubbs, ed., *Chronica Roger de Houedone*, vol. iv, (London: Longman, Green, Reader & Dyer, 1868), 29–30.
241 Flanagan, *Transformation of the Irish Church*, 234. For discussion of the clamour and tradition of ritual humiliation of relics in Gaelic Ireland see pp 235–37.
242 Hurlock, *Medieval Welsh Pilgrimage*, 66–67.
243 Alan. J Fletcher, 'Liturgy in the Late Medieval Cathedral Priory,' in *Christ Church Cathedral Dublin: a History.*, ed. Kenneth Milne (Dublin: Four Courts Press, 2000), 134.
244 Stalley, 'Architecture of the Cathedral and Priory Buildings,' 105.
245 McEnery and Refaussé, *Christ Church Deeds*, nos.1–3, 36.
246 Fletcher, 'Liturgy in the Late Medieval Cathedral Priory,' 133.
247 Fletcher, 'Liturgy in the Late Medieval Cathedral Priory,' 135.
248 Raghnall Ó Floinn, 'The Foundation Relics of Christ Church Cathedral and the Origins of the Diocese of Dublin' in *Medieval Dublin VII, Proceedings of the Friends of Medieval Dublin Symposium 2005*, ed. Sean Duffy

(Dublin: Four Courts Press, 2006), 89–102.; James Mills, ed., T*he Account Roll of the Priory of the Holy Trinity, Dublin, 1337–1346* (Dublin: Four Courts Press, 1996), 150–51.

249 Mills, *Account Roll of Holy Trinity*, 151.

250 Colmán Ó Clabaigh, 'The Church, 1050–1460,' in *The Cambridge History of Ireland*, ed. Brendan Smith (Cambridge: Cambridge University Press, 2018), 361.

251 McEnery & Refaussé, *Christ Church Deeds, 101, no. 357*; Boydell, *Music at Christ Church*, 30.

252 Boydell, *Music at Christ Church*, 12.

253 Stalley, 'Architecture of the Cathedral and Priory Buildings,' 105–6.

254 Mills, *Account Roll of Holy Trinity*, xvii–xvii; John Clarke, Crosthwaite, *The Book of Obits and Martyrology of the Cathedral Church of the Holy Trinity, Commonly Called Christ Church. Dublin*, (Dublin: Irish Archeolog. Soc., 1844), 27; Kinsella 'Architectural History of Christ Church Cathedral,' 80, fn 26.

255 Ronan, 'Religious Life in Old Dublin,' 46–54, 52.

256 For a discussion of the cult of St Nicholas see Eoin Bairéad, 'Nicholas and Dublin,' in eds. M. Davies, U. MacConville & G. Cooney, A *Grand Gallimaufry: Collected in Honour of Nick Maxwell* (Dublin: Wordwell, 2010). 152–154.

257 Stalley, 'Architecture of the Cathedral and Priory Buildings,' 106; James Mills, 'Sixteenth Century Notices of the Chapels and Crypts of the Church of the Holy Trinity, Dublin,' *JRSAI*, fifth series, 10 no. 3 (1900), 200.

258 Kinsella, 'Architectural History of Christ Church Cathedral,' 103.

259 Stalley, 'Architecture of the Cathedral and Priory Buildings,' 101.

260 Lydon 'Christ Church in the Later Medieval Irish World, 1300–1500,' 78–80; Stalley, 'Architecture of the Cathedral and Priory Buildings,' 104.

261 Francis Young, *Athassel Priory and the Cult of St. Edmund in Medieval Ireland* (Dublin: Four Courts Press, 2020).

262 Stalley, 'Architecture of the Cathedral and Priory Buildings,' 104; Crosthwaite, *The Book of Obits*, 33.

263 Mills, 'Sixteenth Century Notices,' 198–99; Kinsella, 'Architectural History of Christ Church Cathedral,' 80, 83–84.

264 Kinsella, 'Architectural History of Christ Church Cathedral,' 77; Stalley 'Architecture of the Cathedral and Priory Buildings,' 98.

265 Stalley 'Architecture of the Cathedral and Priory Buildings,' 107

266 Crosswaite, *The Book of Obits*, 10.

267 Stalley 'Architecture of the Cathedral and Priory Buildings,' 107.

268 Kinsella, 'Architectural History of Christ Church Cathedral,' 84–85.

269 Stalley, 'Architecture of the Cathedral and Priory Buildings,' 104.

270 Stalley, 'Architecture of the Cathedral and Priory Buildings,' 105.

271 Kinsella 'Architectural History of Christ Church Cathedral,' 87–88

272 Stalley, 'Architecture of the Cathedral and Priory Buildings,' 104. Kinsella 'Architectural History of Christ Church Cathedral,' 80.

273 Stalley, 'Construction of the Medieval Cathedral,' 57–58.

274 Lydon 'Christ Church in the Later Medieval Irish World, 1300–1500,' 82.

275 Stalley, 'Construction of the Medieval Cathedral,' 58.

276 Nugent 'Pilgrimage and the Augustinians in Medieval Ireland,' 215–234, 231; Ó Floinn 'The Foundation Relics of Christ Church Cathedral and the Origins of the Diocese of Dublin,' 89–102.

277 Lucas, 'The Social Role of Relics and Reliquaries in Ancient Ireland,' 9; Bourke, *Patrick: the Archaeology of a Saint*, 18–20, 49.

278 Lydon, 'Christ Church in the Later Medieval Irish World, 1300–1500,' 93.

279 Barra Boydell, 'The Establishment of the Choral Tradition, 1480–1647', in *Christ Church Cathedral Dublin: a History*, ed. Kenneth Milne (Dublin: Four Courts Press, 2000), 238; Raymond Gillespie, 'The Crisis of Reform, 1625–60', In *Christ Church Cathedral, Dublin: a History*, 160.

280 Stalley, 'Architecture of the Cathedral and Priory Buildings,' 101.

281 Hugh J. Lawlor, 'A Calendar of the Liber Niger and Liber Albus of Christ Church, Dublin,' *PRIA* 27 (1908): 56, no. 100.

282 Stalley, 'Architecture of the Cathedral and Priory Buildings,' 99–100, 103; Kinsella, 'Architectural History of Christ Church Cathedral,' 89–91.
283 Stalley, 'Architecture of the Cathedral and Priory Buildings,' 100.
284 Nilson, 'The Medieval Experience of a Shrine,' 101.
285 Mills, *Account Roll of Holy Trinity*, 98. The term *'depictandis pro feretro'* implies that the shrine was a feretory portable container.

CHAPTER 8

Pilgrim Prayers: The Individual Rituals of Irish Pilgrims

Private Prayer at the Shrine

Outside Mass and processions, there were also opportunities for pilgrims to pray as individuals. Medieval accounts of pilgrimage from outside Ireland show that pilgrims used a wide variety of postures, gestures, movements and prayers, when in the presence of relics and holy statues.[1]

The most intimate form of prayer was direct contact through touch. If permitted, pilgrims would have touched and kissed relics, reliquary containers, tombs and miraculous statues. It was widely believed that these actions allowed for a deeper connection with the saint.[2] Kissing was an especially favoured way of expressing a person's devotion to relics of the True Cross.[3]

Many accounts of pilgrims from outside Ireland engaging physically with relics have survived, but what of medieval Ireland?[4] Contact seems to have been allowed in some cases but how widespread this was is difficult to know. The Lives of the early Irish saints mention several instances of clothing relics, such as girdles, being physically placed on the bodies of pilgrims during healing rituals (see Chapter 1). The *Topography of Ireland* by Gerald of Wales also suggests that the kissing of relics was practised by Irish pilgrims in the 12th century. Gerald tells a tale of St Patrick's brass horn, in the care of a mendicant cleric in Wales. No one was allowed to sound the horn out of reverence to the saint but on one occasion, when, 'having handed round the horn, according to the custom in Ireland, to be kissed by the bystanders',[5] the horn came into the hands of a foolish priest, who sounded the instrument and immediately suffered a stroke. The priest was restored to health, 'having crossed over to Ireland, on a pilgrimage to St Patrick'.[6] William of Malmesbury, writing in the early 12th century, noted that Irish pilgrims to Glastonbury, 'according to their unsavoury national custom, throng to kiss the remains of their favourite saint'.[7] A 16th-century manuscript detailing the sale of chattels from the suppressed Irish monasteries states that John Aleyn, Chancellor, George, Archbishop of Dublin, along with Robert Cowley, Master of the Rolls of Chancery, and Thomas Cusack Esquire were sent to Ireland to search out relics and put an end to pilgrimage and the kissing of holy objects.

> … amongst other things, to investigate, inquire and search where within the said land of Ireland there were any notable images or relics to which the simple people of the said lord the king were wont to assemble superstitiously and as vagrants to walk and roam in pilgrimage, or else to lick, kiss or honour contrary to God's honour. [8]

If direct contact with the relics was not allowed, there were ways around this, as shown in an early 17th-century miracle tale from Holycross Abbey. The story tells that in 1609, a woman under a malicious spell was healed after Abbot Bernard placed a girdle round her body, that had touched the relic of the True Cross.[9] Evidence detailed in Chapter 1 also suggests that some Irish relics were washed and dipped in the water, and the liquid then used to wash the diseased limbs and bodies of the sick.

Pilgrims also made offerings before relics. The Paternoster (Our Father), one of the oldest Christian prayers, features in accounts of pilgrim ritual at foreign shrines. For example, the Anglo-Saxon manuscript *The Lacnunga* (c.1050) tells of a healing ritual at a holy well that required the sick to recite the Creed and the Paternoster beside the well.[10] A medieval pilgrim to the tomb of St Hugh at Lincoln Cathedral recited nine Paternosters, while placing his hand inside an aperture in the saint's shrine.[11] Irish pilgrims surely uttered this prayer. The Ave or Hail Mary, as we know it today, is one of the most popular prayers said at modern Catholic pilgrim shrines. The prayer did not assume it's modern form until the 16th century,[12] but earlier forms were widely known in Ireland. The *Liber Exemplorum*, a collection of preachers' tales, compiled c.1275 by an English Franciscan working in Ireland, tells the story of a monk who became possessed by a demon. In passing, the story mentions that the monk 'had been accustomed to say an Ave Maria whenever he passed by a statue of the Virgin Mary'.[13] It is very likely that Irish pilgrims to Marian statues like Our Lady of Trim or Navan said this prayer.[14]

Physical prayers could include genuflection, a practice that was very popular with the early Irish saints.[15] The 9th-century *Martyrology of Óengus* records three different postures to be used in prayer: kneeling on both knees, kneeling with the arms stretched out, and prostration – lying outstretched on the ground.[16] The design of many of the Irish early medieval outdoor reliquary shrines (gable shrines, corner post shrines) are low to the ground and would have encouraged pilgrims to kneel and even lie prostrate before them. In 1408, Arudrel, Archbishop of Canterbury, describes the type prayer recited by English pilgrims before crosses and statues, including 'bending of knees, bowing of the body ... kissings, offerings, lighting of candles'.[17] Similar behaviour was described in 1415 by Lollard John Clayton, who appeared before the court of the archbishop and stated:

> ... images are not to be sought in pilgrimage nor should Christians bend the knee before images or kiss them or venerate them in any way.[18]

Carving of man with his hands clasped in prayer at Holycross Abbey, Co. Tipperary. © Louise Nugent

The practice of clasping hands together in prayer, so familiar to modern pilgrims, appears only from the 11th/12th centuries and could have been practised by Irish pilgrims, especially when petitioning the saints.

Another prayerful attitude was prostration. It was practised as a form of penance or an act of submission by the early Irish saints.[19] Outside Ireland, the position was popular with those petitioning the saints for cures.[20]

Singing and dancing, and the acting out of the legends associated with the pilgrim shrine, are recorded outside Ireland during the later medieval period.[21] In 1445, the Scottish pilgrim Alexander Stephenson, who had travelled to Canterbury for a cure for worms and sores on his feet, danced joyously for three days after being miraculously cured.[22] Singing and dancing were also part of the pilgrim rituals on St Cuthbert's day in northern England and for the feast day of St Eluned of Brecon in Wales.[23] We can only wonder if similar scenes occurred in Ireland.

Moving in Circles: Doing the Rounds at Pilgrimage Sites

In modern Ireland, a number of active places of pilgrimage, such as holy wells, are surrounded by ritual points in the landscape, including holy stones, penitential cairns or *leachta*, church ruins, early medieval crosses and bullaun stones. Modern pilgrims follow routes that incorporate these sacred points. They visit each holy place in a set order while performing set prayers and rituals. The pilgrim route is known as a '*turas*' and the devotional points are known as stations. The route of the *turas* is unique to each place and can vary in length. For example, at Glencolmcille in Co. Donegal, it is spread over a 4–5 kilometre area and takes many hours to complete, while the one at St Caillin's holy well at Ballyconnelly encompasses two penitential cairns and a holy well and can be completed in 20–30 minutes. A common ritual at these sites is walking clockwise round pilgrim stations, while reciting set prayers, usually the Creed, Hail Mary and Our Father, recited in sets of 3, 5, 7 and 9. This circular movement was a common part of 18th- and 19th-century pilgrim rituals and is known by the word 'circumambulation'. The word comes from the Latin *circum* (around) and *ambulare* (to walk). In the Irish language it is called *an deseil* (sunwise). Many modern Irish pilgrims refer to these actions as 'doing the rounds'. Traditionally, those making the rounds did so barefoot.

Some scholars believe that circumambulation can be traced back to early medieval times and would have been practised by Irish pilgrims.[24] The *Vita Sancti Cuthberti* (the *Latin Life of St Cuthbert*), completed soon after the saint's body was translated in the year 698, refers to a paralysed youth, brought to the monastery for healing. As part of the young man's pilgrimage, he spent the night asleep before the tomb of Cuthbert, while wearing the saint's shoes upon his crippled feet. The following day, he awoke to find himself cured. In celebration of his healing, he performed prayers of thanksgiving:

> On the day he went round the places of the sacred martyrs (*circuibat loca sanctorum martyrum*) giving thanks to the Lord because he had been restored to his former health, according to his faith, through the merits of the holy bishop.[25]

Some argue that the 'places of the sacred martyrs' in the graveyard at Lindisfarne are stations or devotional points in the landscape and that the youth moved around them in the fashion of modern pilgrims.[26]

The Lives of Irish saints also suggest that circumambulation was practised in cemeteries attached to churches, as part of the individual devotions of monks and penitents.[27] These stories suggest that in early and late medieval Ireland, the act of walking in prayer in a clockwise motion was practised at some church sites in Ireland and Britain, as part of individual and group prayer during ritual and penance. However, it is difficult to know how widespread the practice was. It is tempting to think it may have been part of the penitential rituals engaged in by Heneas Mac Nichaill, at least at some of places in his itinerary.

Holy Dust, Stones and Bark

The bodies and relics of the saint were thought to infuse their surroundings, turning them into sacred spaces, so it is not surprising that some pilgrims desired to take away something physical from the shrine. They could do this in a number of ways: by touching relics or the saint's tomb with pieces of cloth, thus creating a secondary relic;[28] by collecting oil from lamps that burned close to these holy objects; or collecting dust, stones or earth.[29]

There are many accounts from outside Ireland of sick pilgrims applying to their bodies dirt, stones and scraps of paper or cloth that had been in contact with the saint's tomb or relic.[30] It was common practice for pilgrims to the Holy Land to collected dust from the Holy Sepulchre and the Tomb of St Theodore.[31] Closer to home, English pilgrims travelling to the spot where St Oswald died in 642, fighting the Mercians, carried away earth and dust to be mixed with water and given to the sick, who 'received great benefit'. The practice became so popular that a great hole was created.[32] Contemporary pilgrims to the shrine of St Chad removed dust from the interior. The dust was mixed with water and ingested, 'by which means their ailment is quickly relieved'.[33] The collection of dust and clay was also important to Irish pilgrims.

Right: Tomb of martyred priest Fr. Nicholas Sheehy, Shanrahan, Co. Tipperary.
Left: Hatch in tomb that allows pilgrims to remove earth from within.
© Louise Nugent

The *Annals of Connacht* recall that following the death of St Ciarán in 530, King Diarmuid was so grief-stricken that he went deaf. St Colmcille advised him to travel to Clonmacnoise, where he was miraculously cured when earth from the saint's grave was mixed with holy water in the bell known as the White Bell and poured into his ear. It is unlikely that the story originated from such an early date. However, the account does suggest that at the time it was written, there was a belief that earth from the saint's grave could bring about healing.[34] The *Life of St Máedóc* of Ferns tells how earth from Máedóc's grave brought about the miraculous healing of the blind, deaf and lame

> by the earth [of his sepulchre], by his clothing, and by his relics healed blind and deaf and lame and all other diseases.[35]

The *Martyrology of Óengus*, when referring to the tombs of the holy souls, refers to the belief that dew on the graves had healing properties, which tentatively suggests that pilgrims were able to get close to the graves to collect the dew:

> The soul without striving, into with brightness: after him, when attained it, the dew of his grave will heal.[36]

The removal of holy earth from the graves of saints and healing priests was certainly part of the modern pilgrim tradition in Ireland. The tomb of Fr Nicholas Sheehy at Shanrahan, Co. Tipperary, even has a hatch in the side to facilitate the process. As with the English medieval accounts described above, 19th-century Irish pilgrims also mixed holy earth with water to be ingested or applied to the body as a poultice. At Ardmore, earth from the saint's grave was sold to pilgrims as part of the pattern-day rituals during this period. Each year, the grave, in St Declan's Oratory, an early reliquary shrine, was refilled with new earth, where it absorbed the healing power of the saint. The earth, known as Declan's Ashes, was believed to have curative powers and was often made into poultices.[37]

St Declan's grave at Ardmore. © Louise Nugent

Earth was also taken by pilgrims from the shrine chapel of Temple Ciaran at Clonmacnoise and the grave of St Colman Mac Duagh at Kilmacduagh.[38] Similar activity was noted at Downpatrick, where contemporary pilgrims took earth from the supposed site of St Patrick's grave.[39]

Medieval pilgrims to the Holy Land often brought home small stones and pebbles as mementos.[40] Irish pilgrims may also have taken stones as mementos and contact relics from Irish pilgrim sites. The 14th-century text *The Miracles of St Senan* mentions the saint creating a lime kiln to help in the rebuilding of a church at Killnagalliach. The kiln, apart from supplying a never-ending supply of lime, was also used to cure disease, either by applying the lime to the body or by using a stone from it.

> ... every kind of disease in man or beast, if only (the patient) were rubbed with the lime, would be healed at once, or if a stone taken thence were heated and put in their drink, it would cure everyone.[41]

During the 19th century, stones taken from holy places were used as talismans. One Limerick woman sent stones from the holy well at Barrigone, Co. Limerick, to her son fighting in the Crimean War as a defence against enemy bullets.[42] At St Olcan's well at Cranfield, Co. Antrim, it was customary for pilgrims to remove pebbles from the holy well as healing aids. They were believed to be especially beneficial for women during childbirth, but also acted as talismans against drowning, fire and burglary.[43] Nineteenth-century pilgrims to Scattery Island, Co. Clare, took stones from St Senan's grave. They were used as talismans against disease and drowning. Sometimes, a hole was drilled into the pebbles and they were worn around the neck as a charm.[44]

Irish medieval pilgrims who visited holy trees also occasionally took mementos home. The 12th-century Latin *Life of St Columba of Terryglass* relates how the leaves and bark of a miraculous hazel tree created by saint were taken away to be used for healing by the sick.[45]

The fourth *Life of St Brigit*, written in the 10th century, tells of a miraculous tree at Kildare associated with healing. By the time the *Life* was written the tree, was no more then a decayed trunk. It says: 'through the miracles of St Brigid, many miracles have been performed by that wood'.[46] This line suggests that the tree may have died from pilgrims removing pieces of its bark and wood to take home with them. Parallels to this kind of ritual behaviour can be found in medieval sources relating to continental healing shrines, where trees played a significant role.[47] For example, pilgrims were in the habit of taking away pieces of a holy tree at the Marian shrine at Scherpenheuvel, in Belgium. The tree was a focus of pilgrimage from 1304 until the 17th century.[48]

During the 19th century, Irish pilgrims took twigs and bark from certain holy trees. In living memory, twigs and bark from St Moling's tree at Mullenakill, Co. Kilkenny, were used as a protection against fire and lightning.[49] Wood from holy trees was used in a similar way as protection against lightning, drowning and fire. Emigrants to America often took pieces of wood from holy trees with them.[50]

Medieval sources from the Continent suggest that some holy trees functioned as vehicles for transference of sickness. St Maur's Chapel at Vatteville-la-Rue, Normandy, was associated with cures for rickets and arrested growth. Parents in search of healing for their children left supplications for cures written on leaves on the

St Columba's holy well, Terryglass, Co. Tipperary.
© Louise Nugent

Top: Holy tree at St Patrick's well Ballyshannon.
Below: Pilgrims tying rags to holy tree dedicated to St Inion Buí at Duhallow on the saint's feast day.
© Louise Nugent

altar of the church. As part of the ritual, they also visited a tree close to the chapel and worked a branch of the tree into a knot. When the knot worked itself out, the child would be cured.[51] In modern Ireland, pilgrims carry out a similar practice of tying rags to holy trees, believing that, as the rag rots, the sickness will disappear.

Offerings to the Saints: Votive Worship by Irish Pilgrims

Pilgrims, especially those who needed to curry favour with the saint, arrived at the pilgrim churches with gifts or offerings. These items were turned into income for the shrine, used to buy wax and put towards essential repairs and renovation of buildings.[52] The earliest reference to gifts and offerings in Ireland is found in the 7th-century *Life of Brigit*, where pilgrims to Kildare arrived 'with great gifts and offerings'. The 8th-century *Vita Prima Sanctae Brigita* makes reference to sick pilgrims giving 'food and clothing' in return for healing and contact with the saint's girdle.[53]

Further evidence of this tradition is found in the Irish *Life of St Máedóc* of Ferns. SS Máedóc and Brigit appeared to St Finian Lobar on the eve of St Máedóc's feast, on 30 January. Máedóc proceeded to tell Finian that he and Brigit will bless all pilgrims who bring gifts and offerings on both of their feast days:

> And to-morrow is my festival, and the day after to-morrow is the festival of yonder virgin [Brigit]. And we have come on purpose to bless everyone who shall honour the days and festivals of our earthly decease with alms and offerings.[54]

Offerings were also made in thanks for healing or prayers answered. In 1611, a deaf and dumb teenager 'made an offering' of thanks to the relic of the True Cross at Holycross Abbey, following his miraculous cure.[55]

Pilgrim offerings recorded outside Ireland included precious metals, jewels, wax, foodstuffs, livestock and coins. A Welsh soldier who had been shot in the head with an arrow arrived at the shrine of St Thomas de Cantilupe at Hereford with a wax replica of his head and promised to return with his best cow, if a cure was obtained.[56]

Offerings left at St James's Cathedral at Santiago de Compostela in the year 1250 were wide-ranging and included candles, wax, cloth and incense, pilgrim staffs, crosses, swords, bells and candelabra.[57] In 1307, the offerings left before the shrine of St Thomas de Cantilupe included 170 silver ships, 41 wax ships, 1,200 wax images of body parts, along with linen shifts, walking sticks, carts and candles, 450 gold rings, 65 gold brooches, rings of silvers, iron chains and anchors, lances, spears and knives.[58]

Stained glass image of a pilgrim presenting wax offerings at the shrine of St William of York. © Chapter of York: Reproduced by kind permission.

Some pilgrims left more unusual offerings. Sources from the Continent tell of penitential pilgrims leaving behind symbols of their sins, such as murder weapons and chains.[59] In medieval England, coins were offered to relics and holy statues. Coins were first introduced into Ireland by the Vikings, but it was not until after the 12th century that the usage of coins became more common.[60] From this time onwards, coins may have been given as offerings. Gerald of Wales mentions a Norman archer leaving a penny before the Speaking Cross at Christ Church Cathedral.[61] It was customary for Cork merchants to make offerings of pennies to the friars of Red Abbey in the medieval town of Cork, before embarking on trading trips,[62] and similar offering were made by Waterford merchants to Christ Church Cathedral in Waterford.[63] Pilgrims travelling abroad may have made similar offerings to statues or altars before setting sail. A single 11th-century coin found under the paving surrounding the gable shrine at Illaunloughan and six silver pennies of 13th- and 14th-century date, found near the door of the neighbouring oratory, may also represent coin offerings left by pilgrims.[64]

Outside Ireland, busy pilgrim shrines often had special collection boxes placed in front of the saint's tomb/reliquaries and holy statues, in which pilgrims could place their offerings.[65] By the 15th century, Holycross Abbey had 'special collectors' – men employed to collect offerings made by the large numbers of pilgrims to the 'wood of the Holy Cross'.[66]

The shrine of St Thomas de Cantilupe at Hereford Cathedral.

Wax in various forms – raw, candles or replicas of body parts – was a common offering. At Canterbury, the volume of wax offerings was so great they were stored for recycling in a room known as the Wax Chamber.[67] Sailors who visited pilgrim shrines in England and Wales often presented boats made of wax and silver. In 1307, a group of Irish sailors who survived a treacherous storm at sea presented a silver ship to the shrine of St Thomas de Cantilupe of Hereford.[68]

Those too sick to undertake a pilgrimage often sent a candle in their stead, carried by a relative or friend. A rare letter written in 1443 by Englishwoman Margaret Paston to her sick husband provides a glimpse into this process and shows how families were prepared to do all they could to obtain a positive outcome for a loved one:

> My mother promised another image of wax of the weight of yourself to Our Lady of Walsingham and she sent 4 nobles to the 4 orders of friars at Norwich to pray for you: and I have promised pilgrimages to be made for you to Walsingham and to St Leonard's [Priory, Norwich]. By my troath, I have had so heavy a season from the time that I knew of your sickness, until I knew of your amending, and still my heart is not at great ease, nor shall be until I know that you are truly well.[69]

There are no accounts of Irish pilgrims presenting wax at Irish shrines but, given how widespread the practice was outside Ireland, it must have taken place. Supporting this theory is the fact that wax candles feature in many accounts relating to penance in late medieval Ireland. Accounts of public penance from the 16th century often recall the penitent, clothed in white linens, presenting wax to an altar, statues or church, as part of his or her penance.[70] As punishment for as-

Wax candles burning before holy image at Holycross Abbey. © Louise Nugent

sault and perjury, Nicholas of Strabannan, Co. Louth, was ordered in 1522 to burn two pounds of wax before the statue of Our Lady at Stabannan Church.[71] Wax was a valuable commodity: it was needed to produce candles need to light the church and to be burned before altars and statues. On average, a pound of wax was needed to make a single candle and 32 pounds were needed for a torch. In the early 15th century, wax cost about 2d per pound and in 1484, it was 5d per pound.[72]

Pilgrims who had received healing were known to leave behind evidence of disease that passed from their bodies, such as kidney stones, tapeworms, human hair and bone.[73] In 1851, pilgrims to St Cuan and St Brogan's holy well at Mothel, Co. Waterford, left rags and nails, buttons and human hair tied to a tree beside the well.[74] The practice was also recorded at Kilterney, near Kesh, Co. Fermanagh, and the *Londonderry Sentinel* on 22 August 1851 tells of pilgrims to an unnamed holy well, who were seen 'often tearing their hair from their heads knotting it … to the branches' of a tree beside the well.[75]

There are many medieval accounts from outside Ireland of pilgrims with disabilities and poor mobility making pilgrimage, hobbling on crutches or pulling themselves along with hand-trestles. Those few who were lucky enough to be healed left behind crutches as a sign of faith in their cure.

The late 10th-century *Life of St Swithun* describes the saint's church at Winchester as

> completely hung round, from one end to the other and on either wall, with crutches and with the stools of the cripples who had been healed: and nevertheless they couldn't hang half of them up.[76]

Pilgrim offerings were highly valued. The shrine of Our Lady of Trim and Christ Church Cathedral and the church of St Catherine at Fieldstown petitioned the Crown to protect pilgrims arriving from areas of Gaelic Ireland during the 15th century.[77] The pilgrim offerings left at Christ Church Cathedral were used to repair the east window that had fallen in 1461, while offerings to the Bachall

Íosa in 1493 were used to support a choir of boys.[78] Pilgrim offerings helped to pay for the extensive 15th-century renovations and rebuilding works at Holycross Abbey, Co. Tipperary.[79] The offerings made by 16th-century Irish pilgrims are mentioned in passing in sources relating to the destruction of Irish shrines during the Reformation. Sir James Ware, when describing the burning of the Blessed Virgin of Trim, noted that 'the gifts of the pilgrims were taken away … and subsumed into the coffers of the King'.[80]

Pilgrim offerings rarely survive in the archaeological record. Foodstuffs were consumed, precious metals turned into income, and wax melted down. There are a few exceptions. An interesting example is a small stone with the inscription + OR [ÓIT] AR BRAN NAILITHER 'Pray for Bran the pilgrim', discovered in the 1820s under a grave slab at Temple Brecan, on Inis Mór. The gravestone had the inscription S[AN]C[T]I BRE[CA]NI and may have marked the grave of a holy person or saint. Perhaps the stone was left as a gift by a visiting pilgrim.[81]

Three decorated pebbles were found placed at the foot of a special grave, dating to the 10th to 12th centuries on Ardoileán/High Island, in the period after the abandonment of the monastery. White Marshall and Rourke (2000) suggest these stones were made and left by pilgrims as offerings on the grave, as were quartz stones.[82] Quartz pebbles have been found at several early medieval Irish pilgrim sites. Pilgrims who visited Tem-

Offerings left by modern pilgrims at Doon holy well, Co. Donegal.
© Louise Nugent

Water-rolled pebbles left by pilgrims at Templeteenaun. © Aidan O'Sullivan, UCD School of Archaeology, September 2006

pleteenaun, Co. Wicklow, left water-rolled pebbles on top of one of the *leachta* in the monastic graveyard. These stones were carried onto the site and may have been deposited on the leacht as a prayer offering.

Medieval pilgrims to the Clochán Congleo complex, dedicated to the early Pope St Leo the Great (d. AD 461), on the island of Inishark, Co. Galway, also donated offerings of quartz. Pilgrims to Inishark may be responsible for the 700 or so water-rolled quartz pebbles placed on the top of two early medieval *leachta* and on the surrounding pavement.[83] Further deposits of quartz were found during excavation of a *leacht* at the Clochán Congleo complex on Inishark.[84] Also of interest are two rounded stones, a cross-inscribed granite stone and a dark, dense pebble with an incised Maltese cross of similar appearance to the Ardoileán/High Island examples.[85] These stones, also found during excavation on Inishark, may have been used by pilgrims in rituals for swearing oaths, blessings or curses.[86]

The Clochán Congleo complex at Inishshark during excavation carried out by Dr Ryan Lash and Dr Ian Kuijt. Quartz pebbles were found on top of the flagstone pavement surrounding the *leacht* perhaps offerings left by pilgrims. Photograph by Alessandro Martellaro

Modern offerings of quartz left by pilgrims at St Colmcille's holy well, Co. Donegal.
© Louise Nugent

Stones left by modern pilgrims on penitential stations at St Patrick's holy well, Ballyshannon, Co. Donegal.
© Louise Nugent

Self-Sacrifice: Pilgrim Fasting and Vigils

It was not unusual for some pilgrims to spend days and weeks in prayer at pilgrim churches, but for many others the visit was much shorter. Many performed fasts and kept vigils before statues and relics. Prayer vigils were a common ritual, and there are numerous accounts from the Continent of pilgrims arriving the day before the feast and spending the night in vigil in the church.[87] In 1113, the annals record a freak act of nature that killed 30 pilgrims at Croagh Patrick.

> A ball of fire came on the night of the feast of Patrick 17 March on Cruacháin Aighle, and destroyed thirty of those fasting.[88]

When the tragedy struck, the pilgrims were all performing a prayer vigil, while fasting on the eve of the saint's feast.

Pilgrims also engaged in a practice called incubation-sleeping at a holy place, in the hope of experiencing a divinely inspired dream or cure. There are many accounts of foreign pilgrims with poor health spending the night in very close proximity to holy statues, the saint's tomb or relics. Sometimes a single night was not enough for a cure, so pilgrims spent weeks or even months in prayer.[89] One miracle tale associated with the shrine of St Thomas à Becket tells of a Hiberno-Norse pilgrim called Sitricius, 'from the middle region of Ireland', keeping vigil before the saint's shrine at Canterbury. Having fallen asleep, Sitricius had a vision of St Thomas striking him with his pastoral staff and addressing him in Irish: 'Get up, Irishman, you are healed.'[90] In an Irish context, the 7th-century *Life of Brigit* suggests that vigils may have also taken place in the reliquary church at Kildare. When the chief craftsman was remodelling the church, he encountered difficulties accommodating the old door into the new door frame. He spent the night in prayer by the saint's shrine to pray for a solution, which duly came to him.

> And so he passed the night praying by the glorious tomb of Brigit and getting up in the morning after that night, having completed his prayer with faith, he had the old door pushed in and placed on its hinges and it filled the whole doorway.[91]

Incubation was part of the pilgrim rituals at many holy places in 19th-century Ireland. At Labbamolaga in Cork, people in search of a cure for rheumatism spent the night beneath a stone slab said to mark the saint's grave in the early medieval shrine chapel.[92] In Co. Mayo, pilgrims trying to find a cure for epilepsy travelled by boat to Caher Island, where they spent the night on an early medieval cross slab known as the Leabaidh Phadruig (Patrick's Bed).[93] Similarly, 19th-century accounts mention that pilgrims to Inishark slept in the Clochán Leo, having completed the *turas*.[94]

Many pilgrims fasted during their time at a holy place or prior to arrival. In the medieval church, fasting could be undertaken as an act of ritual purification and, along with going to Confession, was a key part of spiritual preparations for any who hoped to come in contact with the saint's tomb or relics.[95] The 12th-century text *Aislinge Meic Conglinne* mentions pilgrims ' … going to Cork to fast on the feast of Finbarr and Nessan'.[96] Fasting was also used to increase the penitential aspects of pilgrimage. At Croagh Patrick, fasting allowed pilgrims to imitate St Patrick, who was said to have fasted for 40 days and nights on the summit.[97] The *Annals of Tigernach*, in 758, record that Abbot Gorman of Louth fasted for a year at St Fingen's holy well at Clonmacnoise, presumably as a form of penance. The

Martyrology of Oengus tells that after Adamnán lost an eye for entering the tomb of St Cianán of Duleek, his sight was restored when he repented his actions and fasted at the tomb.[98]

Leabaidh Phadruig 'Patrick's Bed' at Caher Island.
© Louise Nugent

There are many accounts from outside Ireland of fasting connected to healing. In the 6th century, Gregory of Tours mentions that a man called Leunnast of Bruges was cured of a cataract after he fasted and prayed in the church of St Martin at Tours.[99] Collections of miracles from foreign shrines frequently refer to pilgrims fasting and performing vigils before being healed by the saint.[100] Fasting was also used by Irish pilgrims seeking healing. The 12th-century Irish *Life of St Colmáin maic Lúacháin* tells of a holy well created by the saint in the land of Dun Carraig, where pilgrims could be healed of disease if they fasted next to it.[101] In later medieval Ireland, fasting continued to be practised by Irish pilgrims. In AD 1397, Hugh Mac Mahon recovered his sight by fasting before the miraculous statue of Our Lady of Trim and the Holy Cross of Raphoe.[102] He probably also performed a night vigil and many have spent days at each place in prayer.

Facing Your Sins: St Patrick's Purgatory

St Patrick's Purgatory is located at Lough Derg, a freshwater large lake with 46 islands in the southeast corner of Co. Donegal. The medieval pilgrimage revolved around two of the lake islands – Saints Island and Station Island. According to tradition, a monastery was founded on Saints Island in the 5th century by St Patrick, who later appointed St Davog as the first abbot. A semicircular enclosure may represent part of an early medieval ecclesiastical settlement. Little else is known about the early history of the lake or its islands.

Sometime in the 1130s, a priory of Augustinian canons dedicated to St Patrick was established on Saints Island. The priory was a dependant of the Augustinian Abbey of SS Peter and Paul at Armagh.[103] The Purgatory Cave was located a short distance away on Station Island, today the focus of a thriving modern pilgrimage. From the 12th century, the cave was promoted in Ireland and Europe as an earthly

Aerial view of Station Island, Lough Derg, Co. Donegal. © Lough Derg Sanctuary

access point to Purgatory. The main function of the priory on Saints Island was to minister to the needs of the pilgrims and to maintain and facilitate access to St Patrick's Purgatory on Station Island.

There are varying descriptions of what the cave looked like. In 1411, Florentine merchant Antonio Mannini described it as:

> three feet wide, nine feet long and high enough for a man to kneel but not to stand upright. It is exactly like a sepulchre, for it is vaulted overhead and lies towards the south.[104]

An earlier pilgrim in 1353 described the cave as 'two miles' long, and in 1430 another pilgrim said that it was a:

> hole … nine feet from east to west and turns towards south-west and as a whole is fourteen to fifteen feet long. It was built with black stones and is about two feet wide and three feet high.[105]

The cave was destroyed and rebuilt on several occasions between the 16th and 18th centuries. It was closed for good in the 1780s, although its former location is still pointed out on Station Island.

Souterrain at Pipers Hill, Naas, Co. Kildare. © by Ian Russell, Archaeological Consultancy Services Unit Ltd

The medieval and 16th-century descriptions of the cave suggest that it was a man-made structure built in the style of a souterrain – an underground chamber and passage found at Irish ring forts and early medieval ecclesiastical sites.[106]

We know the names of a handful Irishmen who made the pilgrimage – presumably only the tip of the iceberg. English or AngloIrish, John Bonham and Guidu Cissy made a pilgrimage to this place in 1366,[107] the priest Thomas O'Callachan in 1470,[108] the priest Nylanus O'Ledan in 1507,[109] and Heneas Mac Nichaill in 1543. There are no written accounts of Irish experiences there, but a sizeable collection of 16th- and 17th-century Irish bardic poetry relating to the Island and pilgrimage has survived. These poems show the significance of the cave in Ireland at the time and provide insight into how the Irish elite viewed this pilgrimage, as well as sin and penance during this period.[110] As noted in Chapter 5, 29 accounts of European pilgrims from 1185–1517 survive, all detailing the experiences of pilgrimage to St Patrick's Purgatory. All the foreign pilgrims were male and from wealthy aristocratic backgrounds. Interestingly, there is only one, medieval references from Irish or foreign sources to a woman making pilgrimage to this place.

The accounts left by the European pilgrims are focused on the visions of Purgatory that they claim to have experienced while in the cave. This is in contrast with how the cave is portrayed in Irish poetry, where the island is shown as a

Image of pilgrim entering St Patrick's Purgatory from Morgan-Mâcon' Golden Legend. © New York Library Morgan Library, M.672-5, II, fol.178v.

place of intensive prayer and penance.[111] For example, the 16th-century Irish Poet Tuileagna Ó Maol Chonaire wrote:

> Of Patrick's Cave I read that, for one who would
> cleanse his soul, no better penance-cell exists;
> it ceases not to wash away his sin.[112]

Lough Derg was not freely accessible. As shown in Chapter 5, all foreign pilgrims had to seek permission from the Archbishop of Armagh before making their way to the lake. Irish pilgrims probably did likewise. Pilgrims arrived at the edge of the lake at a spot looking across to Saints Island. From here they took a canoe or small hide boat out to the island. Having landed on Saints Island, the pilgrims walked up a gentle slope to the interior where the priory was located.

The community living there was small and its numbers varied over the centuries. Unfortunately, the monastic buildings are long gone, but perhaps their foundations endure under the grass. The buildings would have included a church, domestic buildings and possibly some form of guest accommodation. Today, Saints Island is uninhabited, but semicircular and rectangular enclosures point to a complex history of human settlement that has yet to be fully understood.[113]

View of medieval embarkation point for pilgrims to Saints Island.
© Louise Nugent

The pilgrims presented to the prior any letters of safe conduct and written permission to undertake the pilgrimage obtained from the Archbishop of Armagh. At this point, the prior tried to dissuade them from entering the cave, explaining the dangers they faced. If the pilgrims held steadfast, they began a series of preparatory rituals. Most scholars agree these that rituals were made on Saints Island before they took a boat to Station Island, where the Purgatory Cave was located.[114]

The 12th-century pilgrim Owain spent 15 days in the church, where he prayed and fasted to prepare himself for the spiritual ordeal ahead. In 1353, Hungarian pilgrim George Grissaphan, first made Confession and performed penance before fasting for 15 days 'on limited quantities of bread of the coarsest sort and water'.[115] At the end of his fast, the Office of the Dead or Requiem Mass was said for him:

> … a bier is set up in the middle of the choir of the church, covered with black cloth and the pilgrim is placed in it as though dead, with priest, deacon, subdeacon and acolytes in funeral vestments and carrying cross, thurible and holy water. In the morning, the Office of the Dead is followed by requiem Mass, after which the pilgrim is absolved as though before burial and bells are rung for the dead.[116]

The next step for pilgrims was to leave Saints Island by boat or canoe to travel to nearby Station Island. Both islands are inter-visible and, as pilgrims climbed into the canoe and looked across at Saints Island, expectation and anticipation began to build up. Italian pilgrim Antonio Mannini was rowed to Station Island by Canon John. He describes his boat as:

> made like a kind of hollow tree trunk, roughly dug out and where four people would hardly have fitted.[117]

He probably left from the north of Saints Island at the site of 'an old quay', marked on the 1st edition Ordnance Survey map of 1836.

The lake's waters are normally calm and still. On a very still day the lake was like a mirror reflecting the surrounding mountains. As the boat moved off, the pilgrim's ears were filled with the sounds of the boat's oars slicing through the water. The journey was quite short and would have taken no more than 15-20 minutes in a modern rowboat. On cloudy days, the lake's water had a dark murky appearance, perhaps emitting a sense of foreboding to the apprehensive pilgrims. During the summer months pilgrims had to contend with the irritating and constant nipping by midges – creatures that still torment modern pilgrims to Station Island.

Most of what we know about Station Island in medieval times relates to the cave, so it is hard to know what the island the pilgrims landed on looked like. The Hungarian pilgrim George Grissaphan (1363) mentions that a small chapel was built over the entrance to the cave. The cave was sealed by three great stones.[118] It is difficult to know how reliable his account of the pilgrimage is, as descriptions of the pilgrimage become more fanciful from this point onwards. However, in 1411, Antonio Mannini also prayed in the chapel on Station Island before entering the cave.[119]

Quay where medieval pilgrims left Saints Island to travel by boat to Station Island. © Louise Nugent

Once on Station Island, the pilgrims underwent further preparations to enter the cave. We are told that some were taught a prayer by the prior to be reiterated when encountering the terrors in Purgatory. In 1406, English pilgrim William Stanton was taught the prayer 'Jhesu, filii Dei, miserere mei' ('Jesus Son of God have mercy on me') before entering the cave. In 1397, Catalan pilgrim Ramon de Perellós recited a similar prayer, 'Christi filii Dei vivi miserere mei' ('Christ son of the living God, have mercy on me')[120] As noted above, some of the pilgrims prayed in a chapel on station island before entering the cave. Antonio Mannini's description of the chapel and altar with a crucifix and images of St Patrick and the Blessed Virgin provides a glimpse as to what it may have looked like and how it was decorated.[121]

Most of the pilgrims spent 24 hours in the cave. The majority of surviving accounts suggest that they felt they had experienced the horrors of Purgatory. For many, this must have been a truly harrowing experience. In the 12th century, Gerald of Wales describes the pilgrim's experience as follows:

> … he is seized immediately by malignant spirits, and is crucified all night with such severe torments, and so continuously afflicted with many unspeakable punishments of fire and water and other things, that, when morning comes, there is found in his poor body scarcely even the smallest trace of life surviving. [122]

When the knight Owain entered Purgatory, he was confronted by souls suffering the consequences for serious sins such as pride, lechery, gluttony, covetousness and usury. For example, the slothful were nailed to the ground and the gluttonous eaten by demons.[123] Englishman William of Stanton (c. 1406) experienced equally terrifying otherworldly tortures. For example, he meets eight fires described as

> hot out of measure and black as any pitch, and small sparkling lights of blue like unto brimstone came out thereof. In that fire were many souls, both men and women, some hanging by their privy members with chains of iron burning, and some by the heart and some by their eyes, and fiends beating on them with burning hammers.[124]

Not every pilgrim experienced these horrors. For example, the English knight Sir William de Lisle in 1395 recounted:

> In the morning we were awakened, they opened the bolt, for so we had ordered, and we issued out and within a short season clean forgot our dreams and visions; wherefore we thought and think all that matter was but a phantasy.[125]

In 1494, a Dutch Augustinian monk from Eymstadt Abbey made a pilgrimage to the cave. After being sealed in for 24 hours, he emerged from the cave, frustrated and disappointed at having experienced nothing remotely supernatural. Given the graphic accounts of the island circulating at the time, his expectations must have been high. Later, he made an official complaint to Rome, [126] prompting Pope Alexander VI to order the closure of the cave in 1497. The closure is described in the *Annals of Ulster* by Cathal Mac Manus, Dean of Loch Erne, who was present on the occasion.

> The cave of the Purgatory of Patrick... was broken this year by the Guardian of Dun-na-Gall and by the representatives of the bishop in the deanery of Loch-Erne, by authorization of the Pope, about the feast of Patrick of this year; it being understood by everyone in general from the History of the Knight and other old Books that this was not the Purgatory Patrick got from God, although they were, everyone, visiting it.[127]

Modern pilgrims praying at penitential beds as part of their pilgrimage on Station Island at Lough Derg.
© Fr Robert

One or two bad 'customer reviews' were not enough to end this lucrative pilgrimage and the cave was reopened by 1507, when priest Nylanus O'Ledan made his pilgrimage 'on the Island of the said Purgatory and … stayed in the ditch of the same St. Patrick'.[128] Pilgrimage continued after the Reformation, despite many attempts to destroy it. After this time, Station Island was the sole focus of pilgrims. The modern pilgrimage still retains its penitential nature with a three-day visit in which the pilgrims fast and walk barefoot and take part in a prayer vigil. An interesting change to the demographic of pilgrims is that while men dominated and appear to have been the only pilgrims to the island in medieval times, women now outnumber their male counterparts.[129]

Immersed in Worship: Penitential Bathing at Tigh Moling

Tigh Moling, a monastery on the banks of the River Barrow in Co. Carlow, is one of the best-documented medieval outdoor pilgrimages in Ireland. Founded in the 7th century by St Moling Luachra, it sits in the centre of the village of St Mullins. The ruins of the monastery Tigh Moling consist of six post-12th-century churches, the base of a 10th–12th-century round tower and a 9th-century granite high cross, all located at the centre of the early monastery.

The early pilgrimage was probably focused on the grave of St Moling, who died and was buried there on 17 June 696/697.[130] Within a few centuries, Tigh Moling had grown in status and power and was the chosen burial place for the kings of South Leinster.[131] From the 10th century, an extensive pilgrim landscape that included a spring well and a millrace, filled by water diverted from the Aughavard River, had developed around it.

Pilgrims were well aware of the many miracles the saint had performed during his lifetime. It was said that he healed the blind and crippled and had even resurrected the dead.[132] His grave must surely have been sought out in the early centuries. We do not know exactly where the saint was buried, but it must have been in the monastic graveyard. Modern folk tradition locates it in the chancel of Tempall Mór, marked by a large flat stone. Could folk memory recall a much earlier translation of the saint?

Such an event is not recorded in historical sources but in 1170, Maurice de Prendergast and Donal Mac Giolla Patrick pledged oaths on the shrine of St Moling. It is impossible to know if the shrine housed corporeal remains or a collection of secondary relics. In 1323, we are told that the church of Tigh-Moling and its relics were burnt by Edmund Butler.[133] The loss of these relics did not affect pilgrimage, as the sturdier relics – the millrace and holy well – remained unharmed and have survived to the present.

Medieval church known as Teampall Mór at St Mullins, Co. Carlow. © Louise Nugent

St Moling's holy well is a large pool filled by a natural spring. Its waters flow into a small early stone chapel. The well's water flows through the east gable of the church from two holes in large granite slabs. The holy waters cascade onto a stone font, before falling directly onto the paved granite floor. The water runs across the floor out of the door and into an artificial channel connected to the Aughavard River.

The well chapel is a very rare early medieval baptismal chapel. Its primary function was the sacrament of Baptism.[134] The waters of the well are associated with healing, and the 10th-century Irish *Life of St Moling* recalls that the saint's eye was healed with water from the well brought to him by an angel, who blessed the well and its waters.[135]

St Moling's millrace can be traced in the landscape as a depression running along the northern edge of the modern graveyard from the site of an old mill building across the village green, heading roughly north east, parallel to the modern road out of the village, following a line parallel to the townland boundary of Glebe, ending more than a mile away at a building known as the Sluiceman's Hut. This building, located at the confluence of Aughavard River and St Mullins millrace, is a drystone structure of post-medieval date, of which only

St Moling's holy well, St Mullins, Co. Carlow. © Louise Nugent

Plan of medieval pilgrim landscape at St Mullins showing the extent of St Moling's mill race. Created by Johnny Ryan

the base of the walls survives. Folklore suggests that the building was the residence of the person in charge of the millrace.

The Latin *Life of St Moling*, written in the late 12th/early 13th century, recalls how the saint single-handedly dug the millrace over seven years. When his work was completed, he consecrated it by walking through it. More importantly, the Life tells us that the saint promised to intercede on behalf of all who subsequently walked through the water:

> Saint Molyng assembled very many saints to the consecration of that rivulet, and they blessed that water, walking through it 'against the flood' as far as that place in which the rivulet was separated from the river.[136]

It is unsurprising that the text tells us of large numbers of pilgrims arriving there, walking along the banks of the millrace and ritually bathing in its water to cleanse themselves of sins.

> … numerous crowds of both sexes assemble from all parts of Ireland, at all times to this rivulet and walk on its shores … and wash themselves in the water, hoping – not now doubting that the filth of their sins in the very washing will, by the grace of God, through the solicitations of the most blessed father Molyng be washed away. Many miracles and prodigies are performed there by God.[137]

Wading in the waters of the millrace also brings about physical healing. A poem in the 10th-century Irish *Life and Birth of St Moling* tells us of the benefits:

> Whoever went to my millrace,
> From every disease it will heal him;
> It will be communion, it will be sacrifice
> To everyone who shall drink it.
> It were well for me, then, said he,
> To drink my fill of the water of the Barrow,
> and through it be well, may my Lord
> to consecrate it
> and hallow my millrace;
> May there be cleansing and consecration
> And communion and sacrifice
> To everyone who may drink it and go from it.[138]

In 1348, the millrace was the focus of a mass pilgrimage, in response to the Black Death, with men and women desperately washing and praying in the waters of St Moling's millrace and holy well.[139] The wading and walking through water seem to have been part of the pilgrim rituals at other Irish sites.[140] The second Irish *Life of St Kevin* refers to sick pilgrims bathing and walking in the waters of the Upper Lake at Glendalough:

> And [by)] driving them through the lough to cleanse them,
> They do carry their sickness away with them.[141]

Wading was part of the rituals at a handful of holy wells during the 19th and 20th centuries. At Toureen Peakaun, the ruins of an early medieval monastery in Co. Tipperary, pilgrims walked a portion of the Toureen stream barefoot until the 1950s, before commencing the rounds at the medieval church and other peniten-

Surviving section of the medieval mill race at St Mullins. © Louise Nugent

tial stations.[142] Modern pilgrims to at SS Cuan and Brogan's holy well at Mothel, Co. Waterford, still walk barefoot nine times through a stream that flows from the holy well. Similar activity occurred at Tobar Íosa, on the outskirts of the town of Cahir, Co. Tipperary, in the 19th century.[143]

For medieval pilgrims, the narrative of the millrace at Tigh Moling was more than its association with St Moling. In two Irish Lives of St Moling, the saint's millrace is equated with the 'locus of Christ's baptism', and identified as a 'branch of the river Jordan'.[144] The wading or ritual washing undertaken at Tigh Moling may be inspired or even modelled on the rite of baptism administered by John the Baptist in the River Jordan to the people from Jerusalem. Bathing here could be seen as a form of baptism for the cleansing of sin and the curing of physical disease as distinct from baptism of the individual into the Church.[145] In the wider medieval world, there was a great desire for spiritual renewal. Penitential pilgrimage took place in the context of the sacrament of penance. Confession of sins provided the pilgrim with absolution and reconciliation with the Church. Although confession expunged sin, the punishments to be suffered in Purgatory remained.[146] To avoid or lessen their time in Purgatory, medieval people did all in their power during their lifetime to obtain remission of sin through good works, by obtaining indulgences and by performing pilgrimage.[147] Concern for purification of the soul gave rise to the use of baptismal imagery in devotional literature and iconography and, over time, spiritual renewal became equated with a 'second baptism'.[148] One of the earliest representations of ritual purification or 'second baptism' as a part of pilgrimage is found in the *Life of St Mary of Egypt*. The saint had led a sinful life as a prostitute but was purified and cleansed of all her past sins after she visited the Holy Land, when she bathed in the River Jordan, in imitation of Christ. Her story was very popular in Western

View of the upper lake at Glendalough. Photo by Christiaan Corlett Courtesy of Culture Stock

Pilgrims wading in stream as part of the pilgrimage rounds in 2016, at St Cuan and Brogan's holy well, Mothel, Co. Waterford. © Louise Nugent

Europe during the later medieval period. In imitation of St Mary, medieval pilgrims travelled to the River Jordan to be wiped clean of past sins by washing in its waters.[149] In the 9th-century *Life of St Silvan*, the saint walked into the Jordan and emerged with his 'spiritual ills cured, and his life's desire fulfilled'.[150]

Stories like those of St Mary of Egypt and St Silvan resulted in ritual bathing in the River Jordan becoming an essential part of the pilgrim's rituals in the Holy Land.[151] Over time, the idea of the 'second baptism' came to be seen as a spiritual cleansing that went as far as to offer a remission for past sins. This can be clearly seen from the pilgrimage of Håkon Paulsson, Earl of Orkney, who made a pilgrimage to the Holy Land in 1117, and bathed in the Jordan to expiate his sin for his part in the martyrdom of St Magnus at Egilsay.[152]

In common with the millrace at Tigh Moling, the River Jordan was also a place of physical healing. Many believed that bathing in the river cured a multitude of diseases. In the late 11th century, Jacinthus the Presbyter noted:

> On the feast of the Epiphany cripples and sick people come and, using the rope to steady themselves, go down to dip themselves in the water: women who are barren also come here.[153]

The belief in the healing power of the River Jordan's waters stem from the biblical tale of Naaman the Syrian, whose leprosy was cured after he had bathed in it several times. In the 15th century, Irish leper John Bellew died en route to the Holy Land. He probably hoped, like many of his contemporaries, to wash away his disease in the waters of Jordan.[154]

18th Century Gravestone at St Mullins showing Christ's baptism in the River Jordan.
© Louise Nugent

The religious of Tigh Moling now placed the River Jordan in their own landscape, allowing Irish pilgrims to have similar experiences of physical healing and spiritual rebirth without travelling halfway across the world.

Washing Away Sins at Struell

The washing away of sins was also a concern for pilgrims to the holy wells of Struell in Co. Down. The wells were part of a cluster of Patrician pilgrim places, which include Patrick's grave and relics at Downpatrick and the nearby Saul Abbey, places that were visited by medieval pilgrims. Struell was once a bustling pilgrim destination in summer months, until the time of its suppression in the late 19th century. Thousands of people are said to have made a pilgrimage to this place for midsummer, in the 19th century.

Today, Struell is a quiet peaceful spot, with the ruins of a small church, two holy wells called the Drinking Well and the Eye Well, two bathhouses – the Women's and Men's Bathhouses – all overlooked by a rock outcrop known as St Patrick's Chair. A series of penitential cairns was also noted there in the 19th century .[155]

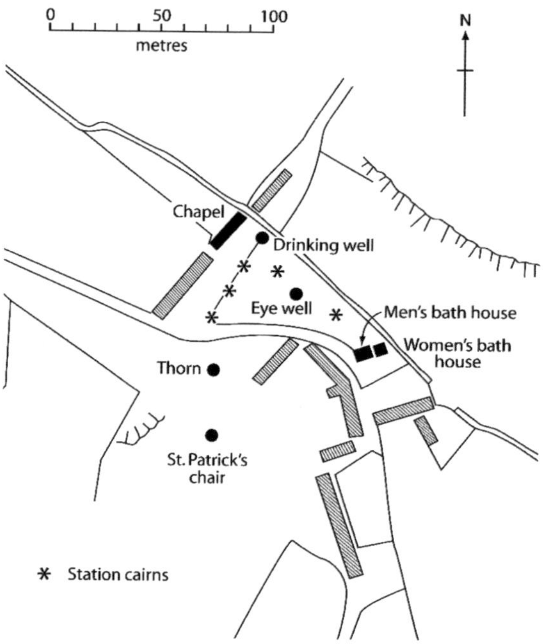

Map of the pilgrimage landscape at Struell, Co. Down. © Findbarr McCormick

The Drinking Well is a spring covered by an oval-shaped well house with a corbelled roof. It is one of the oldest structures at the site. Traces of wickerwork in its mortared roof and a fragment of carved door moulding suggest that it was built between the 13th and 15th centuries, but in later centuries the building was altered and repaired.[156] The well was regarded as the most important one at Struell, being described in antiquarian accounts as the mother well or the 'well of life'. One account from the 17th century insists it was the place where St Patrick spent the night in prayer.[157]

The Eye Well is a small square windowless structure built in a style local to the region. The well is fed by a culvert that flows under its walls and two steps lead into its interior. The Eye Well is mentioned in historical sources no earlier than the mid-18th century.[158]

To the south-east of the well and chapel are two stone bathhouses. The Women's Bathhouse, the older of the two, is a rectangular unroofed building.

A doorway in the west wall allowed pilgrims access to the bathing area. The interior is largely unchanged and water channelled from the wells flows in through an opening in the north wall, before cascading onto the floor. It flows across the floor through an open drain that extends under the south gable. Parts of the building, such as the doorway, date to the 13th to 15th centuries. The structure was also mentioned in a historical account of the pilgrimage left by the papal nuncio, Bishop Chiericati, who visited Struell in 1515.[159] Dixon Hardy makes note of a statue of St Patrick in the north gable venerated by pilgrims in the 19th century.[160]

Near the top of the gable of the building that encloses the principal well was a carved figure of the saint's face, now almost worn away, but penitents seem to think it necessary to put their fingers in the wall connected with it. They then touch the remnant of the figure with their hands, which they then kiss devoutly.

The Men's Bathhouse, with its vaulted stone roof, was built around 1700. Pilgrims entered the building through doorways in each gable.[161] In the 19th century, the western doorway was used by male pilgrims, who followed a series of steps, worn smooth by centuries of footsteps, passing through a simple doorway in the west gable. They entered a small room lined with stone benches. It was here that the male pilgrims undressed before entering the adjoining room with its sunken bath. A series of inbuilt steps allowed the pilgrims to climb down into the bath, which was filled by a pipe in the wall.

Female pilgrims in the 18th and 19th centuries also used this building. They entered through a door in the east gable, moving into a small room closed off from the men's areas. When the women had undressed, they left the building and entered the Women's Bathhouse, whose entrance was directly opposite the women's changing area in the Men's Bathhouse.[162]

The ruins of a small unfinished rectangular church overlooks the wells in the north. 'The record of the taxation of 1306 indicates that at that time Struell was a separate parish and by implication must have had a parish church.'[163] A chapel dedicated to the saint mentioned in 18th-century sources is probably the medie-

The Drinking Well, Struell. © Findbarr McCormick

Eye Well & Women's Bathhouse at Struell. © Findbarr McCormick

The interior of the Women's Bath House at Struell . © Findbarr McCormick

Men's Bathhouse at Struell.
© Louise Nugent

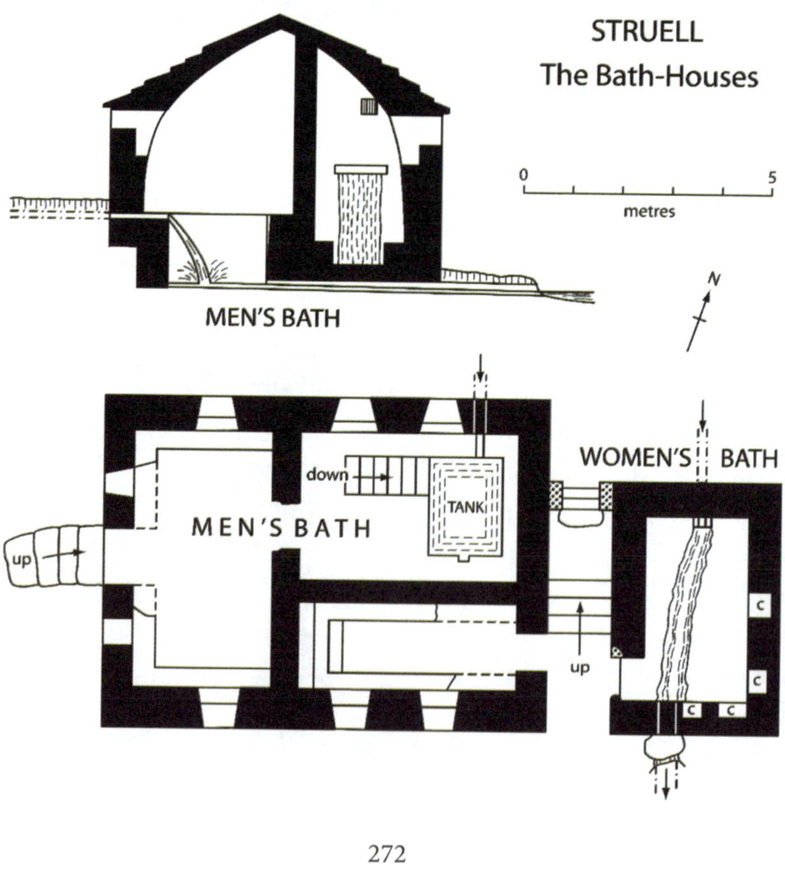

Plan of the Struell bathhouses.
© Findbarr McCormick

val church, which was demolished to build the current (ruined) church. A few architectural carved stones survive, having been incorporated into a modern wall next to the Drinking Well. In medieval times, pilgrims and local people would have prayed in the old church.[164]

To the south, these buildings are overlooked by St Patrick's Chair, a natural outcrop of rock. An important station on the modern pilgrimage, it is covered by large amount of graffiti left by pilgrims. One of the oldest dates to 1711.

The earliest detailed description of the chair is found in the writings of Fr MacCana in 1642:

> The bed of St Patrick on the hill opposite the above-mentioned stream, consisting of two large rocks, as it were the sides of a couch, and another large rock for the bolster. Upon this the most holy man used, towards the close of the night, in the open air, and under the cold sky, to seek a little rest for his wearied body.

Evidence for Medieval Pilgrimage at Struell

Struell first appeared in the early Irish poem know as 'Fiacc's Hymn', written in honour of St Patrick, c.800, and recorded in an 11th–12th-century text called the *Liber Hymnorum*. The poem tells the origin story of the holy wells. St Patrick was said to have prayed at one of the wells and to have immersed himself in its waters while reciting psalms. He then slept on a stone, perhaps an early reference to the outcrop known as St Patrick's Chair.

St Patrick's Chair at Struell, Co. Down. © Louise Nugent

> The cold of the weather used not to keep him from spending the night in pools:
>
> He strove after his kingdom in heaven; he preached by day on heights.
>
> In Slane [Struell] north of the Benna Bairche – neither drought nor flood used to seize it – he sang a hundred psalms every night, he was a servant to the King of angels.
>
> He slept on a bare flagstone then, with a wet quilt about him:
> His bolster was a pillar-stone; he left not his body in warmth.[165]

The fact that the wells and holy stone are mentioned in the hymn suggests that both had a religious significance and were seen as holy places at the time the poem was composed. In more recent centuries, the Drinking Well still retained a folk tradition that it was the very the spot in which Patrick had immersed himself in the water.

Praying and keeping word vigil while being immersed in water was a common activity for the Irish saints. There are numerous accounts of saints, including Ciarán of Saighir, Comgall of Bangor and Kevin of Glendalough, mortifying their flesh through long periods of immersion in cold water. These saintly immersions were often accompanied by the recitation of psalms or by cross-vigils – the practice of holding arms outstretched during devotions.[166] It is possible that these stories may have inspired pilgrims to imitate the saints in some form, but we can never know for sure.

The earliest account of how pilgrims act at Struell is found in an 11th/12th-century commentary on Fiacc's Hymn. It notes:

> Because every sick person over whom the water passed used to be whole (slán).[167]

This single sentence suggests that the sick immersed themselves in the well's waters or poured water over themselves to be healed. Given Struell's later association with penance, it is possible to infer that the process cleansed those laden with sins, making their souls whole again. The Irish *Life of St Finnian of Clonard*, found in the *Book of Lismore* and compiled in the second half of the 15th century, suggests that immersion was part of the healing rituals undertaken by pilgrims to St Finian's holy well and stones at Achonry, Co. Sligo. At Achonry, pilgrims seeking healing first immersed themselves in the water and then recited a Paternoster

St Finnian's holy well, Achronry, Co. Sligo. © Louise Nugent

on the flagstone beside the well. Interaction with both the well and the stone was essential for the pilgrimage to be successful.[168]

> Findian's well and his flagstone are there. Whatsoever sick man shall go into the well will come healthy out of it. Though a troublesome party shall come to the prior, his honour will not be taken away provided he repeat his pater-noster at that flagstone: *sic* Tipra Fhinnein [Findian's Well'] and Lec in Pupaill ['the Flagstone of the Tent'] at Acad Abla.[169]

Similar themes of washing to obtain healing are seen in 17th-century Lives of Irish saints. In the second Irish *Life of Ciaran of Saighir*, the saint asks God for a well to heal every disease for all who washed in it:

> After Ciaran asked of God a fountain, and the angel showed one to him, and it would heal every disease if washed in.[170]

The *Life of St Ruadan* also records the miraculous healing of 12 lepers who washed in the waters of another holy well that was miraculously created by St Ruadan.[171]

Rituals for healing and prevention of disease that involved the immersion of small children are associated with several 19th-century holy wells, such those at St Mullins and Glendalough.

St Ciarán's holy well Seir Kieran, Co. Offaly.
© Louise Nugent

Little else is known about the early pilgrimage at Struell, but it seems to have endured and in 1515 was important enough to warrant a visit from the then papal nuncio, Bishop Chiericati. His visit provides further details about how pilgrims behaved there. His account implies that pilgrims entered what is now the Women's Bathhouse and, kneeling in the water, recited the familiar Paternoster and Ave Maria, along with a prayer to Saint Patrick.

> … in the village of Calvano [Streull] a stream gushes out under a mountain and falls down into a small open building the pilgrims enter it [the Women's Bathhouse] and say a Pater noster and an Ave Maria as well as prayer to St Patrick. They remain there on their knees with the water falling all the time on top of them; and this, they say was done by.[172]

It is unlikely that the rituals had changed much since Heneas McNichaill went there as part of his penitential pilgrimages in 1543. As with Tigh Moling, the pilgrimage at Struell seems to have been aimed at those in search of physical and spiritual cures, but in later centuries it was very much a place of penance.

The rituals of 18th- and 19th-century pilgrimages are recorded in much more detail, especially those of the 19th century. By this time, the pilgrim landscape was more extensive, including the wells, St Patrick's chair, the two bathhouses and a number of penitential cairns, as well as the statue of St Patrick. Pilgrims made rounds of certain holy points in the landscape, while reciting set prayers. They also bathed naked in the bathhouses. The pilgrimage at this time was very much seen as a penitential exercise, with thousands arriving there each year for midsummer. While we must allow for the evolution and development of pilgrim rituals and traditions, Struells's association with penance and penitential bathing stretches back to medieval times, as does devotion focused on the Drinking Well, the Women's Bathhouse and St Patrick's Chair. There is no doubt that medieval ideas of penance and immersion influenced the more recent pilgrimage rituals at Struell.

Pilgrimage: A Good Day Out

Time spent at busy pilgrim churches was not all prayer and penance; there was also, especially for pilgrims who arrived on the saint's feast day, time for fun and socialising.[173] Historical accounts from outside Ireland detail how vendors sold items like shoes, clothing, wax candles and souvenirs at fairs and markets held on busy feast days. Here, pilgrims mingled with local people, jugglers and conjurers, stall owners and even unsavoury pickpockets.[174] Many fairs were held to coincide with times of pilgrimage. At the end of the 13th century, at Amiens, in France, the head of St John the Baptist was displayed over a three-week period, coinciding with his feast, 24 June. The week of the feast became the focus of a great fair that attracted large number of pilgrims and merchants.[175] Irish pilgrims to Santiago de Compostela made purchases of souvenirs sold at stalls in front of the cathedral, some of which have survived in archaeological excavations. These small objects are clear evidence of consumer tendencies of Irish pilgrims when travelling abroad.

We are clearly told that pilgrims to Kildare in the 7th century came not only to pray and honour their saint but also 'for the abundant feasting'. Is it possible that food and communal eating played a part of pilgrim traditions at other early medieval religious sites? As early as the 9th and 10th centuries, many larger Irish monasteries were associated with fairs and markets. For example, Armagh, Kildare and Glendalough had all developed fixed marketplaces, defined by crosses.[176] The fair at Lynally, an early medieval monastery and place of pilgrimage founded by St Colmán Ela, is listed in the 9th-century *Triads of Ireland*, alongside the great secular fairs/*óenaig* of Teltown and Croghan. The feast day of St Colmán Ela was 26 September, followed exactly a week later, on 3 October, by the feast of his birth. The fair at Lynally was held during the week between these two feasts and lasted several days, taking advantage of the increased numbers of pilgrims visiting on either holy day.[177] Seventeenth-century records relating to Holycross Abbey mention two fair days on 1 May and 14 September, the feast of the Exaltation of the Holy Cross, one of the most important days of pilgrimage at the abbey.

Gatherings of large groups of pilgrims could be problematic and there was the potential for conflict and violence. Brawls and improprieties at and around pilgrim shrines were far from uncommon in medieval Europe and some pilgrim churches even had to be re-consecrated because instances of violence, rape or bloodshed had occurred in them.[178] The presence of boisterous pilgrims attending the holy wells of Struell are hinted at in the 11th/12th-century commentary on Fiacc's Hymn. The text alludes to confusion over the exact true location of the wells, as a direct result of the wells being stopped up or filled in by the Ulstermen because of their annoyance with the crowds going out to them.[179] It is unlikely the Struell wells were closed for long, as the pilgrimage continued. Although an isolated reference, there are many parallels to the blocking up of wells in 18th- 19th- and 20th-century Ireland, to prevent pilgrimage. There are also many accounts from the 19th century of unruly behaviour among pilgrims, such as fighting and drinking to excess.

Large gatherings of pilgrims were also prime targets for thieves, and there are numerous accounts from European shrines of cut-purses stealing from pilgrims, even when inside churches. It is very likely that some Irish pilgrims fell victim to pickpockets at home and abroad. In later medieval periods well-to-do pilgrims carried money about their persons, to cover travel costs, offerings for the shrine and alms, and were especially favoured targets. Popular shrines were very crowded, making pilgrims, who were overwhelmed by devotion or in awe of their surroundings, easy targets. One miracle tale from Worcester tells of a pilgrim targeted by a husband and wife pickpocket team. The husband would cut purses from the unsuspecting pilgrim and immediately pass them to his wife, as she walked out of the church.[180] Although not recorded, Irish pilgrims to Christ Church or other busy church sites may have had to contend with similar behaviour.

NOTES

1 Davies, *Pilgrimage Yesterday*, 56.
2 Hurlock, *Medieval Welsh Pilgrimage*, 92.
3 Davies, *Pilgrimage Yesterday*, 55–56.
4 Eric Johnson, 'Interaction with Relics,' in *Encyclopaedia of Medieval Pilgrimage*, ed. Larissa Taylor et al. (Leiden: Brill, 2010), 288; Hurlock, *Medieval Welsh Pilgrimage*, 92; Webb, *Pilgrimage in Medieval England*, 43.
5 Giraldus Cambrensis, *The Topography of Ireland*. Translated by Thomas Forester. Revised and Edited with Additional Notes by Thomas Wright (Cambridge, Ontario: In parentheses Publications, 2000), 82.
6 Giraldus Cambrensis, *The Topography of Ireland*, 82.
7 William Wells Newell, 'William of Malmesbury on the Antiquity of Glastonbury,' *PMLAA*, 1903, 489 (2).
8 Charles McNeill, 'Accounts of Sums Realised by Sales of Chattels of Some Suppressed Irish Monasteries,' *JRSAI* 12, no. 1 (1922): 11–12.
9 Harty, *Triumphalia Chronologica Monasterii*, 127.
10 Bugslag, 'Performative Thaumaturgy,' 252–53.
11 Finucane, *Miracles and Pilgrims*, 63.
12 O'Sullivan and Ó Carragáin, *Inishmurray*, 317–-8.
13 Salvador Ryan and Anthony Shanahan, 'How to Communicate Lateran IV in 13th Century Ireland: Lessons from the Liber Exemplorum (c.1275),' *Religions* 9 (3) (2018):11.
14 All prayers uttered by Irish pilgrims were recited in Latin, the language of public and private prayer for Catholics in most Western European countries up to the Reformation. Cathal Ó Háinle, 'The Pater Noster in Irish: The Pre-Reformation Period',' *Celtica* 21 (1990): 470–74.
15 The 10th-century *Miracula Sancti Columbani* tells of Irish monks genuflecting up to a hundred times a day in Dubreucq and Zironi, *Miracula Sancti Columbani*, 19 Chapter III.
16 Stokes, *The Martyrology of Oengus*, xlviii: attach, urgaiss, dubart, ernaigthe, guide, itge, diprecóit.
17 Finucane, *Miracles and Pilgrims*, 201.
18 Webb, *Pilgrims and Pilgrimage in Medieval Europe*, 245.
19 BNÉ Vol. II 37, 40.
20 Aimé Georges Martimort, ed., *The Church at Prayer*, vol. 1 (Shannon: Irish University Press, 1968), 188. Dawn Marie Hayes, *Body and Sacred Place in Medieval Europe, 1100–1389* (London: Routledge, 2003), 88.
21 James Bugslag, 'Local Pilgrimages and Their Shrines in Pre-Modern Europe,' *Pereginations* 2, no. 1 (2005), 24.
22 David Ditchburn and Marjory Harper, 'Aberdeen and the Outside World,' in *Aberdeen before 1800: A New History*, ed. E. Patricia Dennison, David Ditchburn, and Michael Lynch (East Linton: Tuckwell Press, 2002), 385.
23 Hurlock, *Medieval Welsh Pilgrimage*, 91.
24 Herity, 'The Antiquity of an Turas,' 95–143.
25 Bertram Colgrave, trans., *Two Lives of Saint Cuthbert: A Life by an Anonymous Monk of Lindisfarne and Bede's Prose Life: Texts, Translation and Notes* (Cambridge: Cambridge University Press, 2007), 139 (xvii). A second life by Bede provides another version of the story of the youth, 'when morning came he went to the church and, with everyone watching and congratulating him, he went round the holy places (circuituit loca santa) praying and offering the sacrifice of praise to his Saviour in Colgrave.' *Two Lives of Saint Cuthbert,* 301 (xlv).
26 Michael Herity, 'Early Irish Hermitages in the Light of the Lives of Cuthbert,' in *Studies in the Layout, Buildings and Art in Stone of Early Irish Monasteries*, ed. Michael Herity (London: Pindar Press, 1995), 80–81.
27 Kuno Meyer, ed., *Liadain and Cuirithir. An Irish Love-Story of the Ninth Century*, trans. Kuno Meyer (London: D-Nutt, 1902), 18. See also O'Sullivan and Ó Carragáin, *Inishmurray*, 328; Kuno Meyer, ed., *Betha Colmáin Maic Lúachaín: The Life of Colman Son of Luachan* (Dublin: Hodges & Figgis & Co. Ltd, 1911), 54≠55. For additional references to individuals 'going around' a cemetery, which may refer to the practice of 'doing rounds at the burial ground' in the modern sense, see Máire Herbert and Pádraig Ó Riain (eds), *Betha Adamnáin: The Irish life*

of Adamnán, Irish Texts Society 54 (London, 1988), p. 55. 76; BNÉ Vol.II. 274.

28 Sumption, *Pilgrimage*, 24.

29 Limor, 'Earth, Stone, Water and Oil: Object of Veneration in Holy Land Travel Narratives,' in *Natural Materials of the Holy Land and the Visual Translation of Place, 500–1500*, ed. Renana Bartal, Neta Bodner, and Bianca Kuhnel (London: Routledge Press, 2017), 7.

30 Sumption, *Pilgrimage*, 82.

31 Sumption, *Pilgrimage*, 24–25; Ora Limor, 'Earth, Stone, Water and Oil,' 7.

32 Bede, *Ecclesiastical History of the English People*, 206, III.9.

33 Bede, *Ecclesiastical History of the English People*, 109. IV.3.

34 530 ALC.

35 BNÉ Vol. II, 183.

36 Stokes, *The Martyrology of Oengus*, 274.

37 Stiofán Ó Cadhla, *The Holy Well Tradition. The Pattern of St Declan, Ardmore, County Waterford, 1800–2000* (Dublin: Four Courts Press, 2002), 24–25; Thomas Johnson Westropp, 'Notes on the Antiquities of Ardmor,' *JRSAI* 13 (1903): 366.

38 Jerome Fahey, *The History and Antiquities of the Diocese of Kilmacduagh* (Dublin: M. H. Gill & Son, 1883), 99.

39 Eugene Vetromile, *Travels in Europe, Egypt, Arabia Petræa, Palestine and Syria* (New York: D. & J. Sadlier & Company, 1871), 63.

40 Limor, 'Earth, Stone, Water and Oil,' 7.

41 Charles Plummer, 'The Miracles of Senan,' *Zeitschrift Für Celtische Philologie* 10 (1914): 17.

42 Louise Nugent, 'Barrigone Holy Well and the Crimean War: An Unlikely Connection,' *NMAJ* 56 (2016), 121–126.

43 Ben Simon, *Tales, Traditions & Folklore of Ireland's Trees* (Kildare: Crann Publication, 2012), 102; P., 'Petrification and Pebbles', *BMLJ* 1 (1825): 493.

44 Clare Local Studies Project, 'Scattery Island: Folklore and Customs,' http://www.clarelibrary.ie/eolas/coclare/places/folklore_customs.html. Accessed June 3, 2016. Twentieth-Century pilgrims to St Berrihert's holy well in Co. Tipperary took stones from the well to protect against fire (personal communication with Liam Quirke) and at St Bartholomew's holy well, Bartlemy Co. Cork, pilgrims seeking a cure for eye problems would take a pebble from the well stream home and return the stone when healing had occurred (personal communication with John Arnold).

45 Ó Riain, *Four Tipperary Saints*, 12.

46 John O'Hanlon, ed., *Life of St. Brigid, Virgin : First Abbess of Kildare, Special Patroness of Kildare Diocese, and General Patroness of Ireland* (Dublin: Joseph Dollard, 1877), 97; Patrick Logan, The Holy Wells of Ireland (Gerrards Cross: Smythe, 1980), 91.

47 Bugslag, 'Performative Thaumaturgy,' 245.

48 Bugslag, 'Performative Thaumaturgy,' 245.

49 The tree was first mentioned in the 17th-century poem 'Tobar Deas Chrann Moling.' Dáithí Ó hÓgáin, ed., *Duanaire Thiobraid Árann : Cnuasach d'fhilíocht Ndaoine ó Oirdheisceart an Chontae* (Baile Átha Cliath [Dublin]: An Clóchomhar, 1981), 61.

50 Logan, *The Holy Wells of Ireland*, 89–96; Simon, *Tales, Traditions*, 106–8.

51 Bugslag, 'Performative Thaumaturgy,' 245.

52 Davies, *Pilgrimage Yesterday*, 57; Ben Nilson, *Cathedral Shrines of Medieval Europe* (Woodbridge: The Boydell Press, 1998), 105.

53 V Prima, 25, no. 44.

54 BNÉ Vol. II 266–267.

55 Harty, *Triumphalia Chronologica*, 131.

56 Davies, *Pilgrimage Yesterday*, 58; Harpur, *Sacred Tracks*, 87.

57 Gitlitz and Davidson, *The Pilgrimage Road to Santiago*, 345.

58 Finucane, *Miracles and Pilgrims*, 98.

59 Sumption, *Pilgrimage*, 158.

60 Downham, *Medieval Ireland*, 55–57.

61 O'Meara, *The History and Topography of Ireland*, 85–86.

62 Ó Clabaigh, *The Friars*, 19.

63 Niall Byrne, ed., *The Great Parchment Book of Waterford. Liber Antiquissimus Civitatis Waterfordiae* (Dublin: Irish Manuscript Commission, 2007), xix.

64 White Marshall and Walsh, *Illaunloughan Island*, 133, 176.

65 Diana Webb, *Pilgrimage in Medieval England*, 72.

66 CPL, Vol. XIV 225–226.

67 Bugslag, 'Performative Thaumaturgy,' 223.

68 O'Neill, *Merchants and Mariners*, 46.

69 Diane Watt, *The Paston Women: Selected Letters* (Woodbridge: DS Brewer, 2004), 46–47.
70 Aubrey Gwynn, 'Archbishop Cromer's Register (Continued),' *JLAS* 10, no. 2 (1942), 120; Laurence P. Murray, 'Archbishop Cromer's Register,' *JLAS* 7 no. 4 (1932): 517.
71 Laurence P. Murray, 'Archbishop Cromer's Register (Continued),' *JLAS* 8 no. 4 (1936), 332, no. 146.
72 Myles Ronan, 'Religious Life in Old Dublin,' *Dublin Historical Record* 2, no. 2 (1939), 49.
73 Davies, *Pilgrimage Yesterday*, 58; Sumption, *Pilgrimage*, 157.
74 W Blackett, 'Antiquities of Waterford,' *TKAS* Vol. L, no. III (1851), 500.
75 Simon, *Tales, Traditions*, 103.
76 Michael Lapidge, *The Cult of St Swithun* (Oxford: Oxford University Press, 2003), 606–7.
77 M. J. McEnery and Raymond Refaussé, eds., *Christ Church Deeds* (Dublin: Four Courts Press, 2001), 90. no. 291.
78 *Christ Church Deeds*, 100, no.357.
79 CPL, 1484–1492, Vol. XIV, 225–226.
80 James Ware, *The Antiquities and History of Ireland* (Dublin: printed by A. Crook for E. Dobson and M. Gunne, 1705), 99.
81 John Waddell, 'An Archaeological Survey of Temple Brecan, Aran,' *JGAHS Vol.* 33 (73, 1972): 23.
82 White Marshall and Rourke, *High Island*, 161; Georgina Scally, High Island (Ardoileán), Co Galway. Excavations of an Early Medieval Monastery (Dublin: Stationery Office), 144, 212.
83 Ryan Lash et al., "Differing in Status, but One in Spirit': Sacred Space and Social Diversity at Island Monasteries in Connemara, Ireland,' *Anitquity* 92 (2018): 449.
84 Ryan Lash, 'Pebbles and Peregrinatio: The Taskscape of Medieval Devotion on Inishark Island, Ireland,' *Medieval Archaeology*, 62.1 (2018), 90.
85 Ryan Lash 'Pebbles and Pereginatio' 95.
86 Ryan Lash et al., 'Differing in Status, but One in Spirit,' 451.
87 Sumption, *Pilgrimage*, 212; Irina Metzler, *Disability in Medieval Europe: Thinking about Physical Impairment in the High Middle Ages, c. 1100–c. 1400* (New York: Routledge Press, 2006), 180.
88 AU.
89 Bugslag, 'Performative Thaumaturgy,' 231.
90 Colmán Ó Clabaigh and Michael Stanton, 'Thomas Becket and Ireland,' in *Listen, O Isles, unto Me: Studies in Medieval Word and Image in Honour of Jennifer O'Reilly*, ed. Elizabeth Mullins and Diarmuid Scully (Cork: Cork University Press, 2011), 92.
91 *Life of St Brigit*, 26.
92 Harbison, *Pilgrimage in Ireland*, 149.
93 Logan, *The Holy Wells of Ireland*, 73.
94 Ryan Lash et al., 'Differing in Status, but One in Spirit,' 444.
95 Patrick J. Geary, *Living with the Dead In The Middle Ages* (Ithaca and London: Cornell University Press, 1994), 170; Finucane, *Miracles and Pilgrims*, 48.
96 Meyer, *Aislinge Meic Conglinne*, xvii, 114, 148.
97 Bieler, ed., *The Patrician Texts*, 153.
98 Stokes, *The Martyrology of Oengus*, 245.
99 IMetzler, *Disability in Medieval Europe: Thinking about Physical Impairment*, 142, fn. 116.
100 Christine Walsh, *The Cult of St Katherine of Alexandria in Early Medieval Europe* (Burlington, VT: Ashgate Press, 2007), 95; Benedicta Ward, *Miracles and the Medieval Mind: Theory, Record and Event 1000–1215* (Aldershot: Scolar, 1987), 64, 86, 166.
101 Meyer, ed., *Betha Colmáin Maic Lúacháin: The Life of Colman Son of Luachan*, 17, 52-53.
102 AFM.
103 Aubrey Gwynn and Richard Neville Hadcock, *Medieval Religious Houses: Ireland: With an Appendix to Early Sites* (Dublin: Irish Academic Press, 1988), 218.
104 Shane Leslie, *Saint Patrick's Purgatory: A Record From History and Literature* (London: Burns Oates & Washbourne, 1932), 38.
105 Harbison, *Pilgrimage in Ireland*, 59.
106 A. T. Lucas, 'Souterrains: The Literary Evidence,' *Béaloideas* 39/41 (1971): 189–91.
107 Lawlor, 'A Calendar of the Register,' 274, no. 193.
108 Anthony Lynch, 'A Calendar of the Reassembled Register of John Bole, Archbishop of Armagh, 1457–71,' *Seanchas Ardmhacha* 15, no. 1 (1992): 148.

109 Ludwig Bieler, 'Letter of Credence by Donatus Magrahe, Prior of Lough Derg, for Nylanus O Ledan, Priest and Pilgrim,' *Clogher Record* 2, no. 2 (1958), 257–59.

110 Leslie, *Saint Patrick's Purgatory*, 163–83; Seosamh Ó Dufaigh, 'Two Poems on St Patrick's Purgatory,' in *History of the Diocese of Clogher*, by Henry A. Jefferies (Dublin: Four Courts Press, 2005); Tadhg Ó Dúshláine, 'Lough Derg in Native Irish Poetry,' *Clogher Record* 13, no. 1 (1988): 76–84.

111 Fiona Rose McNally, 'The Evolution of Pilgrimage Practice in Early Modern Ireland. Thesis for the Degree of MLitt. Department of History National University of Ireland Maynooth,' (MLitt., 2012), 13.

112 Harbison, *Pilgrimage in Ireland*, 55.

113 Upstanding remains have yet to be dated securely, so it is difficult to know what period of history they belong to.

114 Ó Dufaigh, 'Two Poems on St Patrick's Purgatory,' 115; Haren and de Pontfarcy, *The Medieval Pilgrimage to St Patrick's Purgatory*, 132, 182; Leslie, *Saint Patrick's Purgatory*, 36.

115 Haren and de Pontfarcy, *The Medieval Pilgrimage to St Patrick's Purgatory*, 132.

116 Haren and de Pontfarcy, *The Medieval Pilgrimage to St Patrick's Purgatory*, 132.

117 Haren and de Pontfarcy, *The Medieval Pilgrimage to St Patrick's Purgatory*, 182.

118 Haren and de Pontfarcy, *The Medieval Pilgrimage to St Patrick's Purgatory*, 132.

119 Leslie, Saint Patrick's Purgatory, *The Medieval Pilgrimage to St Patrick's Purgatory*, 38.

120 Haren and de Pontfarcy, *The Medieval Pilgrimage to St Patrick's Purgatory*, 68, 115.

121 Haren and de Pontfarcy, *The Medieval Pilgrimage to St Patrick's Purgatory*, 183–84.

122 Meara, *The History and Topography of Ireland*, 61.

123 Haren and de Pontfarcy, *The Medieval Pilgrimage to St Patrick's Purgatory*, 63.

124 Haren and de Pontfarcy, *The Medieval Pilgrimage to St Patrick's Purgatory*, 72.

125 Leslie, *Saint Patrick's Purgatory*, 22.

126 Haren and de Pontfarcy, *The Medieval Pilgrimage to St Patrick's Purgatory*, 190–92.

127 AU.

128 Bieler, 'Letter of Credence,' 259.

129 Personal communication with Fr La Flynn, Prior of Station Island, Lough Derg.

130 AU, AFM.

131 Conleth Manning, 'St Mullin's: An Early Ecclesiastical Site and Medieval Settlement in County Carlow,' *Archaeology Ireland Heritage Guides No. 5*, 1999.

132 Whitley Stokes, *The Birth and Life of St. Moling Edited, from a Manuscript in the Royal Library, Brussels, with a Translation and Glossary, by Whitley Stokes* (London: Privately printed [by Harrison and Sons], 1907), 58.

133 Williams, *The Annals of Ireland*, 176.

134 Tomás Ó Carragáin, 'Archaeology of Early Medieval Baptism at St Mullin's, Co Carlow,' *Peritia* 21 (2010): 290.

135 De Paor, *Saint Moling Luachra*, 182–83.

136 Patrick O'Leary, trans., *The Ancient Life of Saint Molyng. Being Translation of an Old Manuscript at Marsh's Library, Dublin. With Notes and Translation by P. O'L.* (Dublin: James Duffy and Sons, 1887), 9.

137 O'Leary, trans., *The Ancient Life of Saint Molyng*, 10.

138 De Paor, *Saint Moling Luachra*, 212–13.

139 Williams, *The Annals of Ireland*, 246; see also section on 'Crisis', in Chapter 4.

140 Ó Carragáin, 'Archaeology of Early Medieval Baptism,' 293.

141 BNÉ Vol. II, (iiib), 131; The first Life of St Coemgen notes of the lake: 'Therefore men and cattle, and all kinds of sick folk come to be healed and cured in the water of the lesser lake in honour of God and Coemgen,' BNÉ Vol. II, ii(4), 121.

142 Ó Carragáin, 'Archaeology of Early Medieval Baptism,' 293. In 2014 I Interviewed Ellen Morranes who lived close to the holy site and remembered the tradition of walking the stream being practised in the 1950s.

143 The Schools' Collection, Volume 0569, 119.

144 Ó Carragáin, 'Archaeology of Early Medieval Baptism,' 295. De Paor, *Saint Moling Luachra*, 210-11.

145 Ó Carragáin, 'Archaeology of Early Medieval Baptism,' 293.

146 Naoë Kukita Yoshikawa, *Margery Kempe's Meditations: The Context of Medieval Devotional Literature, Liturgy and Iconography* (Cardiff: University of Wales Press, 2007), 47–48.

147 Kukita Yoshikawa, *Margery Kempe's Meditations*, 48.
148 Kukita Yoshikawa, *Margery Kempe's Meditations*, 48. Sumption, *Pilgrimage*, 128–29.
149 Kukita Yoshikawa, *Margery Kempe's Meditations*, 48.
150 Sumption, *Pilgrimage*, 129.
151 Sumption, *Pilgrimage*, 129.
152 Pringle, *Pilgrimage to Jerusalem and the Holy Land*, 12.
153 Francesca de Châtel, 'Baptism in the Jordan River: Immersing in a Contested Transoundary Watercourse,' *Wiley Interdisciplinary Reviews: Water* 1 (2014): 1.
154 Kenny, *Anglo-Irish and Gaelic Women*, 100.
155 For a detailed discussion of the pilgrimage – medieval and modern – see Finbar McCormick, 'Struell Wells: Pagan Past and Christian Present,' *JRSAI* 139 (2009): 45–62.
156 McCormick, 'Struell Wells,' 46.
157 McCormick, 'Struell Wells,' 46–47
158 McCormick, 'Struell Wells,' 47
159 McCormick, 'Struell Wells,' 49.
160 Philip Dixon Hardy, *Holy Wells of Ireland* (Dublin: Hardy and Walker, 1840), 39.
161 McCormick, 'Struell Wells,' 50.
162 McCormick, 'Struell Wells,' 50.
163 McCormick, 'Struell Wells,' 51.
164 McCormick, 'Struell Wells,' 50–51.
165 Whitley Stokes and John Strachan, *Thesaurus Palæohibernicus: A Collection of Old-Irish Glosses, Scholia, Prose, and Verse* (Cambridge: Cambridge University Press, 1903), 315.
166 Colin Ireland, 'Penance and Prayer in Water: An Irish Practice in Northumbrian Hagiography,' *Cambrian Medieval Celtic Studies* 34 (1997): 51–53. Ulster Society for Medieval Latin Studies, 'The Life of Saint Monenna by Conchubranus: Part I,' *Seanchas Ardmhacha* 9 no. 2 (1979), 269.
167 'Slana iarsindi ba slán cech imlobor tarateg int uisc ocus ic Sabull ata,' in Stokes and Strachan, *Thesaurus Palæohibernicus*, fn. 25, 315.
168 Ray, *The Origins of Ireland's Holy Wells*, 99.
169 Stokes, *Lives of Saints from the Book of Lismore*, 228.
170 BNÉ Vol. II, 118
171 BNÉ Vol. II, 317.
172 Mahaffy 'Two Early Tours in Ireland,' *Hermathea* 18(40) (1914): 14.
173 Sumption, *Pilgrimage*, 211.
174 Sumption, *Pilgrimage*, 211.
175 Annemarie Weyl Carr, 'The Face Relics of John the Baptist in Byzantium and the West,' *Gesta* 46 no. 2 (2007): 167.
176 Charles Doherty, 'Exchange and Trade in Early Medieval Ireland,' *JRSAI* 110 (1980), 67–89.
177 Thomas Charles-Edwards, *Early Christian Ireland* (Cambridge: Cambridge University Press, 2000), 557.
178 Webb, *Medieval European Pilgrimage*, 39.
179 Latin gloss '*(sed) repleurerunt Ulaid illum propter molestiam turbarum exeuntium ad illam*' attached to the hymn. See Stokes and Strachan, *Thesaurus Palæohibernicus*, 315.
180 Finucane, *Miracles and Pilgrims*, 44.

Conclusion: The Pilgrim's Return

For most pilgrims, whether they had performed penance, prayed for healing or simply enjoyed the hustle and bustle of the shrine, there came a time to return home and pick up the threads of their everyday life. Those away from home for a long time must have been eager to see loved ones. Some pilgrims were filled with a new spiritual purpose; and penitents who had atoned for their sins or gained an indulgence felt relief that the full horrors of Purgatory would not be visited upon them.

The return home mirrored the journey to the shrine, as described in Chapters 5 and 6. Some pilgrims retraced their exact steps, while others embarked on a new route that allowed them to stop at new pilgrim destinations. Those who had travelled longer distances endured the same risks and hardships of the initial journey and they were aware that just because the first half of the pilgrimage had been successful, there was no guarantee that the final stage would be plain sailing. The journey home was of little concern to pilgrims who lived locally; it took little time and brought them through familiar territory.

Some pilgrims never got the chance to leave the pilgrim shrine, succumbing to ill health, disease and even exhaustion. In 1445, the *Annals of Lecale* record the deaths of a number of wealthy Irish pilgrims who died in Spain after making pilgrimage in the jubilee year to Santiago de Compostela:

> Gerott, son of Thomas, one of the Momonian Geraldines, died in Spain, and Evilin, daughter of Edmond Fitz Thomas O'Feargail, wife of Pier Dalton, had also died.[1]

Some pilgrims set off for home hale and hearty, only to become infirm or contract a disease during the journey. This was the case with Hugh, son of Conor Moinmoy [O'Conor], who died in 1224 while returning home from Jerusalem and the River Jordan.[2] Any pilgrims who had the misfortune to die away from home (in Ireland and outside Ireland) could expect to be given a Christian burial in the grounds of a church or hospital. The Church, which had long fulfilled a role of caring for travellers, considered it a duty to bury travellers. In 1128, Archbishop Diego Gelmírez of Santiago de Compostela donated land to the pilgrim hospice to be used as a pilgrim burial ground.[3] Almost a century before, in 1053, Pope Leo IX had issued a bull confirming the responsibility of those who served the church of St Salvatore in Terrione to continue to bury pilgrims who died in Rome. The bull stated that any 'pilgrims or strangers, rich or poor, noble or commoners' who had the misfortune to die beyond the Alps, were to be buried at the Church of St Salvatore or another suitable church.[4] The annals record the deaths of several Irish pilgrims in Rome over the centuries, including Donnchad O Brien of Munster, in 1064,[5] and Muirchertach Ua Flannagain of Tuath-Rath, in Magheraboy, Co. Fermanagh, who died of plague in 1450.[6] As compensation for the expense of the burial, the church was entitled to all the deceased pilgrim's belongings.[7] From the 12th century, confraternities also helped to bury pilgrims. Beyond the main pilgrim centres, pilgrims were laid to rest in parish graveyards or special burial grounds for pilgrims. Designated burial grounds for Jacobean pilgrims existed at Roncesvalles, León and Oviedo.[8] By about 1177, the port of Wissant, frequently traversed by Irish pilgrims and merchants travelling between France and England, had a special burial ground attached to its pilgrims' hostel especially for Irish and English pilgrims.[9] Likewise, pilgrims who died in Ireland could expect burial at Irish churches.

Aside from death, other misfortunes could also befall the returning pilgrim. Some people ran out of funds and could not afford to meet the costs of the journey home. Letters written by Irish pilgrims returning from Rome to Bishop Franco of Liège (854–901), illustrate this point very clearly. In one letter, the writer asks for financial assistance, referring to himself as 'a poor Irish pilgrim'. Another letter asks the bishop to receive an old Irish priest who can no longer continue to Rome because of infirmity and the third letter refers to a pilgrim whose property had been stolen.[10]

No pilgrimage was ever truly complete until the travellers were home in their own beds. Pilgrimage could put a lot of stress on the body, particularly if the pilgrim was elderly or infirm. In 1428, a group of pilgrims that included Hugh (Aedh) Maguire landed at Kinsale. Even though Hugh was on Irish soil, his pilgrimage was far from over, as he now faced a 290-kilometre journey across Ireland to his home in Fermanagh. The strain of the journey seems to have been too much – he died 'the very night he landed' and his body was taken to Cork for burial.

> Hugh the Hospitable, son of Philip Maguire, the most famous and illustrious man of his time for hospitality, died at Kinsale, the first night after his arrival in Ireland, after performing the pilgrimage of St James, on the third of the Ides of August, and after rigid penance for his sins. Thomas Oge Maguire, who was along with him, conveyed his body to Cork, where he was interred.[11]

Baltimore Castle, the home of Irish Chieftain Fineen O'Driscoll.
© Louise Nugent

Irish chieftain Fineen O'Driscoll 'died in his own house' at Baltimore immediately after 'having performed the pilgrimage of St. James', in 1472.[12] One month later, his son Teige, 'having returned from the same pilgrimage', also died.[13]

In the year 1518, Felim, son of Conor Oge Maguire, died after his return from 'the city of St James', where he had performed pilgrimage in the year of grace, a time when a plenary indulgence was offered to pilgrims. His family may have taken some comfort in his having received a plenary indulgence. He was later buried at the monastery of Monaghan.[14]

Remembering the Experience

Before setting forth, pilgrims stocked up on essentials like food and perhaps a new pair of shoes. Like modern tourists, many pilgrims felt the need to bring a memento of their pilgrimage home. From the 12th century, souvenirs were manufactured and sold to pilgrims at churches and monasteries in England, Scotland and continental Europe. The practice of acquiring a memento has a long history dating back to the early centuries of the Church, with accounts of pilgrims to the Holy Land collecting a variety of items like dust from the saints' graves, pebbles and water from the River Jordan, along with oil from the lamps that burned at shrines and palm leaves.[15] Early pilgrims also brought home pieces of cloth that had been pressed against the relics, turning them into treasured contact relics. This non-invasive practice continued into the late medieval period.[16]

Pilgrim badge from Rome, depicting SS Peter and Paul, found during excavations at High Street, Dublin. Illustrated by John Murray © National Musuem of Ireland

The process of obtaining a memento could be destructive, and there are many accounts of pilgrims deliberately chipping bits of stone from the Holy Sepulchre. Such acts of pilfering and the creation of graffiti at shrines in the Holy Land was heartily condemned by the Church. Franciscans who controlled most of the holy places from the mid-14th century were at pains to prevent such practices and pilgrims were under threat of excommunication if they took stones from the Holy Sepulchre building or other monuments. Spiritual sanctions were complemented by the building of a wall around the Holy Sepulchre.[17]

By the 11th and 12th centuries, manufactured souvenirs were available for purchase at pilgrim sites across Christendom. Pilgrim souvenirs consisted of small metal badges and *ampullae* filled with water or oil from the shrine. In the 15th century, additional objects like bells, whistles and mirrors were also for sale.[18]

Most souvenirs were made of pewter or lead, mass-produced from stone moulds, which made them very affordable. Pilgrims with deeper pockets and more discerning tastes could also purchase souvenirs made of precious metals. A gold badge cost up to 300 times more than its lead or pewter equivalent.[19] Pilgrim badges were also made from less durable materials, and there are accounts of badges made from painted or embroidered strips of leather, along with wax and printed paper.[20] Perforated scallop shells were sold as badges at Santiago de Compostela from the 12th century, and in later centuries they were sold alongside metal replicas of the shell. Badges from continental shrines had rings at the corners or edges and could be stitched to the pilgrim's clothing (scrip, cloak or hat), while badges from English shrines were attached to clothing with a pin at the back of the badge. *Ampullae* were often worn high up on the chest, suspended by a chain or cord around the neck. They were filled with holy oil or water from the shrine and, once sealed, they became devotional objects as well as personal ornaments. The scallop shell was associated primarily with the cult of St James and his shrine at Santiago de Compostela. Roman badges often had a double image of St Peter (with a key) and St Paul (with a sword), along with the inscription *Signa Apostolorum Petri et Pauli.*[21]

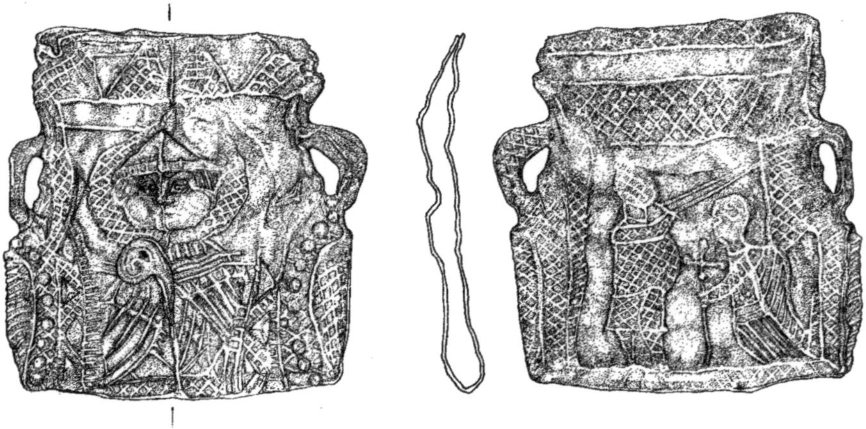

Ampulla of St Thomas à Becket from John's Lane at Wood Quay, Dublin. Illustrated by Patricia Johnson © National Museum of Ireland

The shrine of St Thomas at Canterbury had various types of design for it badges and *ampullae*, all depicting different aspects of the cult of the saint, such as his mitred head, his exile to France or the scene of his martyrdom.[22]

Pilgrim souvenirs were much more than just pretty baubles. They provided a physical and portable link to the saint. They could also be presented to employers, lords, bishops and spouses as proof of completion of pilgrimage.[23] Badges could become holy objects, if pressed by the owner against the saint's relics, thus being transformed from mere souvenirs into much-coveted secondary relics.[24] Once filled with oil or holy water, *ampullae* fulfilled a similar function. As secondary relics, the badge and the *ampulla* were thought to have the power to ward off danger and even cure sickness and disease.[25]

Despite their popularity, not all pilgrim destinations produced souvenirs. There are no known badges or *ampullae* from Welsh or Irish pilgrim sites, although example may have existed. Did Irish pilgrims have the opportunity to purchase or acquire mementos at Irish shrines? The practice is not recorded in the historical sources. Could Irish souvenirs have been produced from natural materials like wood or leather?

Pilgrim badges found during excavations in Waterford City. © Waterford Treasures Museums in the Viking Triangle

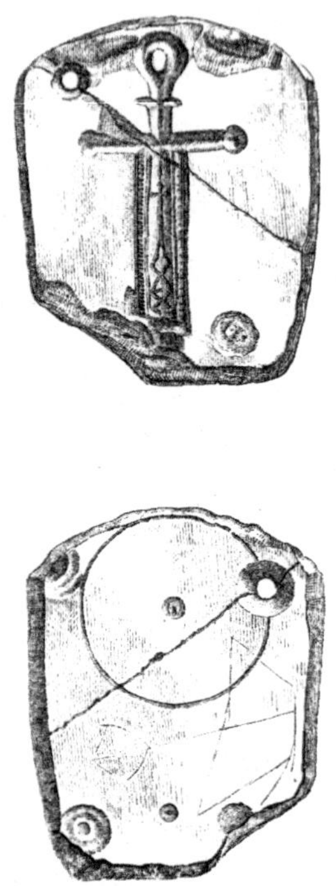

Drawing of the the stone mould, known as the Duivhin-Deglain, found in the grave of St Declan, used to treat headaches and sore eyes. © Royal Society of Antiquaries of Ireland

In Chapter 7, we saw that 18th- and 19th-century pilgrims were in the habit of taking home pieces of bark from holy trees, soil from the graves of saints or holy persons, and pebbles from holy wells. Unfortunately, we don't know if this was a continuation or a reinvention of an older tradition or if it began spontaneously during this period. If medieval pilgrims carried out similar practices, the survival of and ability to identify such items in the archaeological record is very limited.

Tentative evidence for the production of Irish souvenirs comes from two stone moulds associated with the pilgrim churches of Devenish Abbey, Co. Fermanagh, and St Declan's Monastery at Ardmore, Co. Waterford. The Devenish mould dates to the 15th century and was recovered from excavations at St Mary's Abbey on Devenish Island. The island was the cult centre of St Molaise from early medieval times, and in the later medieval period it was a wayside shrine for pilgrims heading to Lough Derg. The mould was used to manufacture lozenge-shaped medals with a central figure of the Blessed Virgin grasping a floral spray in each hand.[26] While it is possible that the mould could have been used to produce souvenirs, no medals from the mould have yet been found; it is equally possible that it was created to make a one-off piece. The second mould was kept as a relic of St Declan at Ardmore, known as the Duivhin-Deglain. It disappeared in the mid-19th century but antiquarian descriptions and drawings of the object still survive.[27] The mould seems to have been used to produce a small cross-shaped badge or pendant.[28] Again, no badges produced from the mould have been found and it is difficult to know if it was used to produce a one-off piece or to produce souvenirs for pilgrims commercially.

Irish pilgrims who travelled to England, Scotland and the Continent had the opportunity to purchase souvenirs, and a small number have been recovered from excavations in Ireland. They confirm Irish pilgrimages to Rome, Canterbury and Santiago, as well as identifying pilgrimages to Worcester, Amiens and

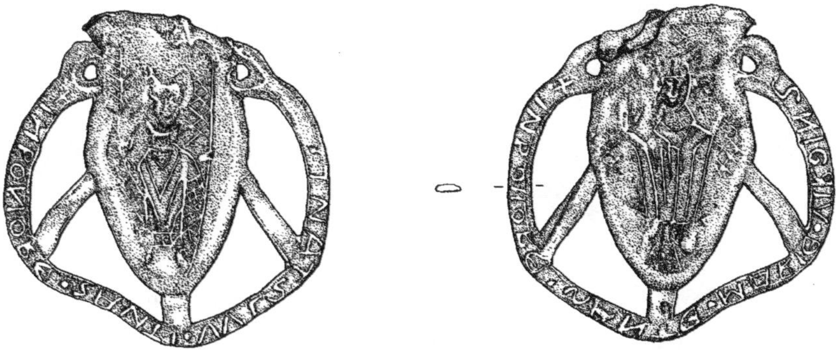

Ampulla from shrine of St Wulfstan at Worcester, from High Street, Dublin. Illustrated by John Murray. © National Museum of Ireland.

Rocamadour.[29] These tiny objects represent the purchases of real Irish pilgrims, who browsed stalls close to or outside the entrance to the pilgrim churches and cathedrals.[30] Irish pilgrims to Santiago de Compostela had ample opportunity to purchase souvenirs sold at the market in the square in front of the cathedral. The market was described in the 11th-century *Pilgrims Guide to Santiago De Compostela* and lists a wide variety of items for sale, from medicinal herbs to items of clothing like sandals and souvenirs, along with scallop shell badges:

> The small scallop shells which are the insignia of the Blessed James are sold to pilgrims and wine flasks, sandals, deerskin scrips, pouches, straps, belts and all sorts of medicinal herbs and spices.[31]

The majority of metal souvenirs purchased by Irish pilgrims were recovered from excavation in the medieval towns of Dublin, Waterford and, most recently, Cork.[32] All were port towns in which pilgrims from the east and south of Ireland departed and arrived back from foreign pilgrimages. The souvenirs all date to the 13th century. They are fascinating objects, owned and worn by real Irish pilgrims, and represent not only individual journeys but also evidence of personal devotion and belief. Three *ampullae* were found in Dublin, two from the shrine of St Thomas at Canterbury and a third from the shrine of St Wulfstan of Worcester.

Two even have the impression of their owners' teeth, where they sealed the top of the *ampulla* shut by biting. This technique, known as crimping, kept the contents of the flask from spilling. All three have evidence of attachment loops near the neck of the vessel and were purchased during the 13th century. *Ampullae* were by far the most popular pilgrim souvenirs sold at Canterbury and there was great variety in the designs available. The Dublin *ampullae* include a rectangular

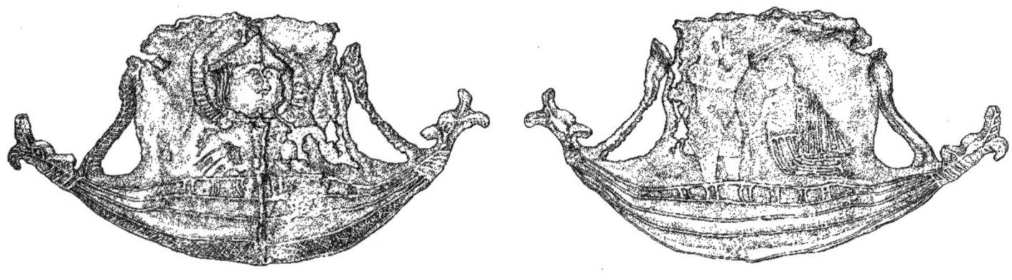

Ampulla of St Thomas à Becket from Wood Quay, Dublin. Illustrated by Patricia Johnson © National Museum of Ireland.

vessel with an image of the saint dressed as a bishop, with mitre and crozier on one side and his martyrdom on the other. Found during excavations at the John's Lane end of Wood Quay, it may have been discarded by its owner. Wear on the surface suggests that it was worn for a while before it was disposed of, unopened. The second Canterbury *ampulla* is in the form of a double-ended, crescent-shaped ship. One side depicts St Thomas standing on the ship's deck, while the reverse depicts the saint's martyrdom. Its design suggests that it was made to celebrate the *Regressio Sancti Thomae*, an annual festival to commemorate the saint's return from exile in France, in December 1170. The owner of the *ampulla* may have made his or her pilgrimage to coincide with the festival celebrated on 2 December. Damage to the object tells us that the owner deliberately cut away the top of the vessel to access the holy contents. With the water or oil gone, the flask was disposed of and eventually ended up amid dumped material placed behind the 13th-century waterfront revetment.[33]

The Worcester pilgrim flask or *ampulla* dates to the 13th century and represents a third pilgrimage. The flask is set in a narrow circular band of metal and has two attachment loops to close the neck. Images of St Wulfstan and the Blessed Virgin are found on either side. The mouth of the flask was bitten shut by its owner. Given that it was found on High Street, one of medieval Dublin's busiest thoroughfares, it was perhaps lost when the string suspending it from its owner's neck broke.[34] Excavations at High Street also produced a badge from Rome, dated to the 13th century. The badge, a solid rectangular plaque, depicts SS Peter and Paul. All four attachment loops are in place and it may represent a casual loss by a newly returned pilgrim, while walking down this busy street.[35] Three other souvenir badges from excavations in Waterford and Cork were found in association with houses, perhaps suggesting that the owners were inhabitants of the towns.

At Waterford, a circular badge with the image of St John the Baptist was purchased at the cathedral shrine of Amiens. Three of the four attachment loops were missing. As the badge was recovered from the back garden of a 13th-century sill beam house, it was probably discarded by the owner after it broke. The second badge came from an unidentified shrine. Its style suggests it was made on the Continent, possibly in France. The badge is rectangular and depicts the rather violent death scene of an unknown saint. The saint is tied to a tree, while a man beats him with a hooked stick. The badge bears the inscription + SIGL/LVM: IONANNI/S: CRVCIFIX/I: A IVDEIS: P (the seal (or sign) of John, crucified by the Jews at P). Perhaps the badge was purchased by pilgrim at minor shrine on his or her way to Santiago or returning from Rome. It was recovered from a 13th-century refuse pit. The four attachment were missing, suggesting that it was also deliberately discarded by its owner because it was broken.[36]

Pilgrim badge from the shrine of Thomas à Becket at Canterbury discovered during recent excavations in Cork City. ©Maurice Hurley

Recent excavations at South Main Street in Cork have identified a boat-shaped badge from Canterbury, discovered in a 13th-century deposit associated with a house.[37] It may simply have been lost or discarded by its owner.

Not all souvenirs were lost or discarded, and many were treasured by their owners long after their return home. Medieval wills from England record bequests of pilgrim badges – some attached to rosary beads – to family members.[38] Several shell pilgrim badges were so precious to their owners that they were taken to the grave. Some pilgrims also kept part of their clothing, such as the staff or the scrip, as mementos. This is the case, in a story in the *Liber Exemplorum* (c. 1275), of the wife of publican, who had been to the Holy Land and used her husband's pilgrim staff to test if a wine barrel was empty.[39]

Pilgrim Returned: Arriving Home

Having arrived home safely long-distance pilgrims presented pilgrim souvenirs, letters and certificates from the shrine to the relevant parties. Pilgrims to local and regional shrines, especially for pilgrimage events focused on the saint's feast day, would not have needed proof as they were gone only a short time and often in the company of friends and neighbours. A letter written as proof of completion of pilgrimage to St Patrick's Purgatory has survived. It was written by Prior

Donatus Magrahe, for the priest and pilgrim, Nylanus Ledan, and is dated 12 August 1507. It states:

> Be it known to you all that the bearer of these presents, Nylan Oledan, a devout priest and pilgrim, has done all the pilgrimages of the island of the said Purgatory, and has stayed in the ditch of the same St Patrick for a natural day; if he has seen or experienced any punishments or torments he did so bodily ...[40]

The penitential pilgrim Heneas Mac Nichaill, having completed his epic pilgrimage around Ireland, returned to Armagh in 1543 and presented Archbishop Dowdall with proofs and certificates from the 18 shrines he had visited.[41]

A Lasting Benefit: The Long-term Impact of Pilgrimage

Those who visited a local pilgrim place strengthened existing bonds with their saint. If relief was gained for minor sickness, word spread quickly among family and friends and the wider community. Such occurrences reinforced the belief in saints as intercessors and miracle workers in the community. For some, pilgrimage was life changing. Pilgrims who travelled abroad were exposed to different types of food, people with different traditions and customs and different styles of architecture. Pilgrimage, like trade, was a means for new ideas and fashions to reach Ireland. Irish pilgrims may even have indirectly influenced art and architecture, bringing back ideas of styles encountered in their travels, such as Romanesque architecture. Leask suggests that the 'stepped battlements' at Kildare Cathedral were inspired by similar features found in the Roussillon and Catalonian districts of Northern Spain.[42] Some pilgrims were inspired to commemorate their pilgrimage through pious acts. King Sitric of Dublin, following his return from pilgrimage to Rome in 1028, founded Christ Church Cathedral and appointed Bishop Dúnán as the first bishop of Dublin.[43] In 1188 Ailred Palmer, who went on pilgrimage to the Holy Land in 1179, set up the Hospital of St John the Baptist in Dublin, after receiving papal confirmation from Pope Clement III.[44] Centuries later, Thomas Óg Maguire, following a successful pilgrimage to Santiago in 1450, endowed the church at Inishkeen, Co. Fermanagh, with a new window. Part of the window still survives and displays a carved scallop shell, along with a scene from legend of an angel conveying the body of the saint in a stone boat to Santiago de Compostela.[45]

In 1510, James Lynch FitzStephen built, at his own expense, a chapel dedicated to St James at Newcastle, Co. Galway, shortly after his wife had returned from a

Medieval window commissioned by Thomas Óg Maguire from Inishkeen, Co. Fermanagh.

pilgrimage to the shrine of St James in Spain.[46] The chapel went on to have a special devotional significance for local people and, in 1684, it as reported that it 'was wont to be visited on St James eve and day yearly by the people of Galway for devotion'.[47] Finally, the Earl of Antrim paid for the reconstruction of the bathhouse at St Brigit's holy well at Bridewell, Co. Roscommon, following his pilgrimage there in 1625.[48]

Some pilgrims who received healing went on to do good deeds in thanksgiving. The priory of St Wulfstan at Celbridge, in Co. Kildare, was founded in 1205 by Adam de Hereford, one of the first generation of Norman colonisers in Ireland. Although not Irish by birth, he had been cured of dropsy by the intercessions of St Wulfstan at Worcester, which prompted him to establish the priory of St Wulfstan at Celbridge.[49]

Local and regional pilgrimages were regular events in the lives of Irish people but long-distance pilgrimages, especially those outside Ireland, were often a once-in-a-lifetime experience. Pilgrimage was such a transformative experience that it had to be repeated. For some individuals, the initial pilgrimage to Rome or the shrine of St James at Santiago inspired them to undertake additional pilgrimages. Others were spurred on to visit other holy places by the desire to obtain more indulgences. In Chaucer's *Canterbury Tales*, the wife of Bath had travelled thrice to Jerusalem and once to Cologne. The English pilgrim Margery Kempe made numerous pilgrimages throughout her lifetime. As well as visiting local pilgrim sites, she visited the Holy Land, Rome and Santiago de Compostela. The Irish pilgrim Gilla Míchíl made seven pilgrimages to Rome and one to the shrine of St Edward the Confessor, in the 11th century, despite his physical impairments.[50] The obituary of Thomas Óg Maguire (1480) tells us that he had been once to Rome and twice to Santiago de Compostela,[51] while the priest Christin Oferagaid/Giolla-Chríost Ó Feradhaigh, who was about to head for Jerusalem in 1413, had already visited 'Rome and other shrines'.[52] Finally, James Rice, Lord Mayor of Waterford, is known to have made two pilgrimages to Santiago de Compostela in the years 1473 and 1483.[53]

Death and Pilgrimage

Pilgrimage to high-status destinations like the Holy Land, Rome and the shrine of St James in Spain could be transformative in other ways, changing how the local community and the pilgrim saw themselves. It could elevate social standing and, in some cases, men and women were forever more identified by their peers as pilgrims. For example, pilgrims to the Holy Land in the 12th and 13th centuries continued to be referred to as 'palmer' long after their pilgrimage was completed. This change in identity to 'pilgrim' can be seen in Irish burials with symbols of pilgrimage – scallop shells from the shrine of St James.

Throughout the medieval period, most Christians were buried naked, wrapped only in a shroud. Archaeological excavations have discovered a small but significant number of burials dating from the 12th century to the Reformation, believed to be the graves of pilgrims. They are identified as such because of the inclusion of pilgrimage-related artefacts, or through imagery on their grave markers. A handful are known from elaborate grave markers that depict the deceased dressed as a pilgrim, with satchel, staff and other symbols of pilgrimage. They are found in England, Wales, Italy and Denmark.[54] Several Irish chest tombs dating to the 15th century display religious imagery that implies that the deceased had been a pilgrim. At Kilconnell Friary, Co. Galway, a 15th-century chest tomb depicts St James and the figures of St Louis of Toulouse and St Denis. The choice of these saints suggests a strong devotion to them and perhaps also indicates that the deceased had made a pilgrimage to the Abbey of Saint-Denis in Paris, the tomb of St Louis at Toulouse, and the shrine of St James at Santiago de Compostela.[55] A similar 15th-century chest tomb at Strade Abbey, Co. Mayo, displays the images of the Three Wise Men, St Thomas à Becket and SS Peter and Paul, along with what appears to be a figure of a pilgrim kneeling.

As at Kilconnell, the iconography may commemorate a pilgrimage to the relics of the Three Wise Men at Cologne, Canterbury and Rome – three very important pilgrim destinations in the late medieval world.[56]

Some medieval people were buried with their staff, scrip or pilgrim souvenirs marking them as former pilgrims. Scallop shell badges have been found in burials from France, Spain, Germany, Scandinavia, Britain, Ireland and as far east as Lithuania and Turkey.[57] The presence of the shell that points to the deceased having made a pilgrimage to the shrine of St James.

In Ireland, burials containing scallop shells and a metal badge from the shrine of St James have been found in graves in the graveyards of both monastic and parish churches, with smaller numbers associated with disturbed burials.

Pilgrim's tomb at Strade Abbey, Co. Mayo.
© Louise Nugent

In 2016, a scallop shell was found during excavations of the medieval parish church of St Mary's in Kilkenny. The shell has a single hole and was designed to be worn as a pendant. Unfortunately, it is not possible to know if the shell was originally included in a burial, having been found in a disturbed context.[58]

During excavations in the medieval cathedral church at Ardfert, Co. Kerry, a 15th-century pewter shell badge with a gilt figure of St James was found in the north wall of a narrow tomb that contained two burials. The tomb was located in the nave of the church. Both the Ardfert and Kilkenny souvenirs represent an individual pilgrimage to Santiago de Compostela. The Ardfert pilgrim probably set sail from the nearby port town of Tralee, while the Kilkenny pilgrim could have followed the Barrow to sail from New Ross or Waterford, or alternatively travelled to Dublin to find a ship. Given the locations at which both shells were discovered, it is difficult to know for certain if they were deliberately included in the burials. In the case of Ardfert, the badge could also have been left by a family member who completed pilgrimage on behalf of one of the deceased, or it may have been left as an offering of thanksgiving for a safe return.[59]

The remaining scallop shells were all found in burials. At the Augustinian abbey of St Thomas the Martyr in Dublin two pilgrim burials were uncovered from 13th/14th-century levels in the monastic graveyard. Each burial contained a sin-

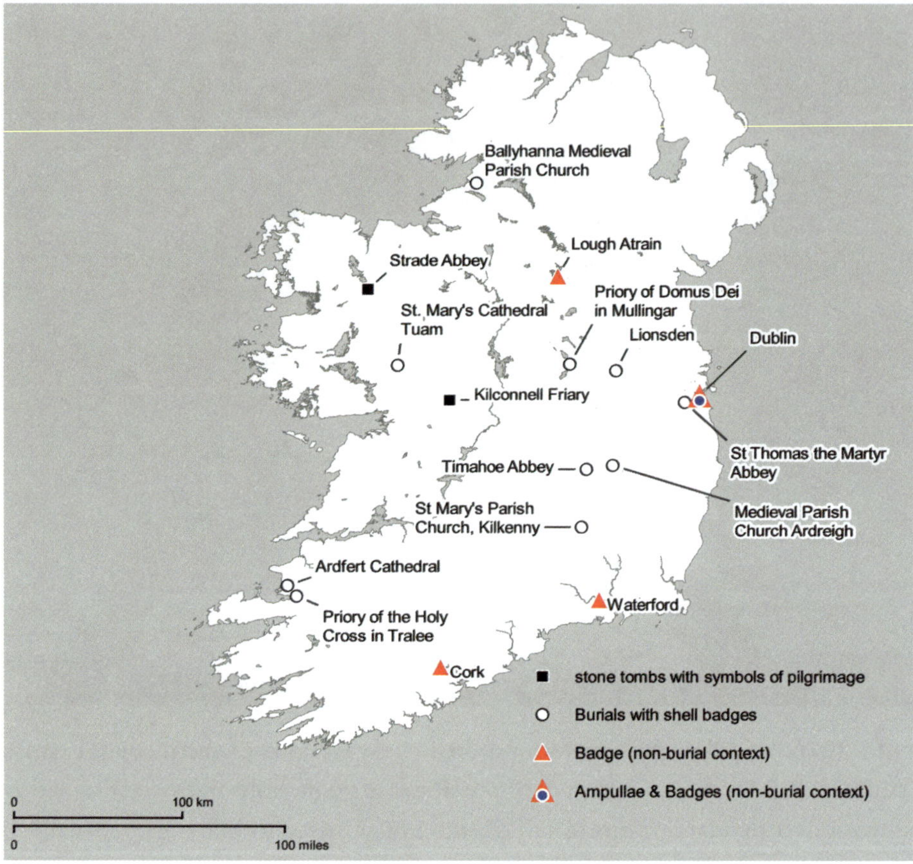

Map showing the findspots of all known pilgrim souvenirs and burials from Ireland. Created by Richard Clutterbuck

gle scallop shell. One had been placed on the abdomen of the deceased and the other on the right arm of the second body. Both skeletons are adult males aged approximately 30 years at the time of death. It is not certain that they were canons, as the graveyard was also used for lay burials. The abbey was located close to the St James's pilgrim hostel at St James's Gate, and it may have taken responsibility for the burial of unfortunate pilgrims who died while in residence.[60]

The burial of a 45-year-old male pilgrim was found during excavations outside the north wall of Tuam Cathedral, Co. Galway. The pilgrim was 1.79 metres tall and his bones showed evidence of arthritis in the back, hip and shoulder. This would have made walking long distances difficult.[61] A single scallop shell badge was found on his right hip. Given his health at death, perhaps the pilgrimage was carried out when the man was younger, or if completed later in life, he may have offered up all the pain and discomfort of the pilgrimage as penance. A second scallop shell was found with a disturbed burial and represents a second pilgrimage, but unfortunately little can be said about this pilgrim.[62]

A female pilgrim was found during the excavation of the medieval parish graveyard at Ballyhanna, Co. Donegal. At the time of burial, a single scallop shell had been placed on her right breast and a piece of quartz was placed in both her hands. The woman probably left Ireland from the nearby port of Ballyshannon. We do not know if she undertook the journey alone, like the medieval pilgrim Margery Kempe, or in the company of her husband or other male relative or as part of a group from her parish.[63]

Burial with inclusion of scallop shell, found during excavations at the Augustinian Abbey of St Thomas the Martyr, Dublin City. © Paul Duffy.

Two pilgrims, probably male, were found during excavations at the Augustinian Priory of *Domus Dei* in Mullingar, Co. Westmeath, in the 1990s. One burial had a perforated scallop shell and a piece of burnished bone, possibly a relic, placed under his chin. The second pilgrim had a perforated scallop shell on his left arm. The excavator suggests that both were members of the monastic community.[64] Another medieval pilgrim was discovered during archaeological works to find the extent of the Dominican Priory of the Holy Cross in Tralee. The pilgrim, an adult of unknown sex, had a scallop shell badge placed at the neck when laid to rest in the grave. The burial was recorded and left undisturbed. It is possible that the deceased was a member of the medieval Dominican community.[65]

Scallop shell from pilgrim burial at Ardreigh, Co. Kildare. © Louise Nugent

Three burials, all with inclusions of shells, were found during excavations of the medieval parish church and graveyard at Ardreigh, Co. Kildare. They date to a phase of activity in the graveyard spanning from the 12th to the 15th centuries. Only one of the burials contained a scallop shell but the excavator has interpreted the other shells as evidence of pilgrimage. The youngest pilgrim at Ardreigh was a female child aged 8 to 12 years. A single perforated cockle shell was found on her neck, suggesting that it was worn as a necklace.[66] Cockle shells have been found in a few other burials identified as pilgrims. The cockle shell seems to have acted occasionally as a substitute for a scallop shell, as was the case with the burial of an adult male found at Worcester Cathedral, with a cockle shell attached to his walking staff.[67]

The second burial was an adult female aged 40 to 50. A fossil shell was placed on her chest during the burial process.[68] The third burial, a young male adult who stood 1.70 metres tall, was buried with the more traditional scallop shell badge. This was found near his neck/shoulder, suggesting that it was worn around the neck as a pendant.[69]

A few pilgrim burials have been uncovered outside archaeological excavation. During the 1940s, council workers in Laois uncovered a burial with a large fossilised scallop shell, while carrying out drainage works in the village of Timahoe. The burial was found at the centre of the village, on the east bank of the Bauteogue River, close to the ruins of monastery. Originally founded by St Mochua, in the 7th century, all that remains of this once important early foundation is an imposing round tower. In the later medieval period, the lands and church of Timahoe were granted to the Augustinian priory of Great Connell, near Newbridge, Co. Kildare, and the church seem to have formed the focus of a grange or outfarm for the priory.[70] Folk memory recalls that the workmen dug up the burial and and had a wake for the skeleton in the local pub before reburial.[71]

Evidence for one, if not two pilgrim burials was uncovered at Lionsden, near Longwood, Co. Meath, in 2006. Human remains were identified by the National Museum of Ireland, after a 'dwelling house had been built and heavily disturbed human bone was found throughout the topsoil'. [72] Two perforated scallop shells were found alongside the disturbed bones, suggesting the presence of one if not two pilgrim burials among the dead.

The Irish pilgrim burials described here represent 9 medieval pilgrims, 15 if we include the shells found in disturbed contexts associated with the burials. The shells and burials are all physical evidence of real people who went on pilgrimage to Santiago de Compostela during the later medieval period. Unfortunately, not all the burials have been radiocarbon dated, so it is difficult to tie the pilgrims into a narrower time period than the 12th to 16th centuries. This small group of burials represents all members of society, a child (Ardreigh), members of the clergy (Tralee, Mullingar, St Thomas's), as well as laymen (Tuam, Ardreigh) and laywomen (Ballyhanna, Ardreigh).

The presence of a child burial with a pilgrim souvenir is very unusual and only a handful of examples are known from outside Ireland.[73] The Ardreigh child burial raises the question of whether the child had gone on pilgrimage. It is possible that her parents may have taken her with them. There are records of children accompanying their mothers on pilgrimage from outside Ireland. For example, the *Acta Sanctorum* of St James tells a story of a mother pushing her crippled son in a cart to view the relics of St James at the Basilica of St Zeno in Verona. Once inside the church, the boy's bones were healed and he was able to walk back to Florence with his mother.[74] Given the length and difficulty of the journey to Santiago, it may be more likely that someone in the Irish child's family had been on pilgrimage. Could the shell be a precious family heirloom buried with the child by a grieving parent, as a talisman to protect her in the afterlife?[75]

Irish shell badges have wide geographical distribution when compared to the metal souvenirs described above. Burials with shells are found in the west of Ireland (Ballyhanna, Co. Donegal; Tuam, Co. Galway, Tralee and Ardfert, Co. Kerry) in the east (Dublin; Kilkenny; Ardreigh, Co. Kildare) and the midlands (Lionsden, Co. Meath, Mullingar, Co. Westmeath).

Many of the badges were deliberately placed on the body of the deceased, either prior to or during the early stages in the funeral and burial ceremony. The shells found around the necks of the burials at Mullingar, Ardreigh and Tralee indicate that they were worn as a medallion and the deceased may have been dressed in pilgrim clothing prior to burial. In this group, one of the burials at Mullingar and another from Ardreigh also wore a piece of worked bone around the neck, perhaps representing a relic of an unknown saint or another type of pilgrim souvenir. Placing the scallop shell on the right hip of the burial at Tuam and on the abdomen of the St Thomas's Abbey burial may tentatively suggest that it was attached to a scrip or satchel and that the deceased was dressed in his pilgrim attire prior to burial. St James is often depicted in medieval iconography with a scallop shell attached to a satchel or hat, and a fine carving of the saint depicted in this manner can be found on a 15th-century tomb at Kilconnell, Co. Galway. Studies of European burials have shown that this position for the shell was very common until the mid-14th century, when it fell out of fashion.[76]

The second pilgrim burial at Mullingar had the shell placed on his arm, as did one of the burials at St Thomas the Martyr Abbey in Dublin, while the female pilgrims from Ballyhanna and Ardreigh had shells placed on the right chest. The presence of shells on the arm and chest in the burial suggests that they were sewn onto the burial shroud or placed on the shroud before the burial was covered in.

This small group of Irish burials represents only a fraction of the pilgrims who travelled to Santiago from the 12th century to the Reformation. One cannot help but wonder why some people were dressed or buried with symbols of pilgrimage, while the majority of pilgrims were not. It is also interesting that pilgrim badges from other pilgrim shrines were not included in the Irish burials, perhaps implying a special status for pilgrimage to Santiago de Compostela over other pilgrim destinations.[77]

What was the purpose of placing items of pilgrimage, such as shell souvenirs, the pilgrim staff or the satchel into a burial? One answer might be that the dead people or their loved ones had chosen to be identified in this way, hoping that their pilgrimage would count in their favour on Judgement Day. In medieval literature, pilgrimage was often presented as an allegory of the soul's journey through life and death. The inclusion of pilgrim badges in the burials may relate both to the honouring of pilgrimages undertaken in the lifetime of the deceased and the more complex concept of the long journey that each soul must make to achieve its rewards in the next life.[78]

Conclusion

This book demonstrates that pilgrimage was a central part of devotional life in medieval Ireland. The stories and names of the individuals recorded in the book make up only a fraction of the true numbers of Irish pilgrims. The vast majority have gone unrecorded, as was the case across the Christian world. Archaeological evidence, such as burial and pilgrim souvenirs, brings us face to face with small numbers of those anonymous pilgrims who travelled outside Ireland in search of indulgences and out of devotion to favoured saints like James and Thomas à Becket. Irish pilgrims came from all classes of society and included men and women, old and young, sinners, sick and healthy, religious and lay people.

Local pilgrimage was almost certainly the preferred option for most and was regularly practised by the majority of the population throughout this period. Yet it has left almost no trace in the historical or archaeological records. In smaller numbers Irish pilgrims also visited foreign shrines and surviving pilgrim souvenirs and burials are testament to these journeys. While pilgrimage in modern Ireland may seem like a world apart from medieval pilgrimage, there continue to be threads that bind the two, such as the pilgrim's journey. Many of the medieval motivations for pilgrimage such as indulgences are no longer the driving force behind modern pilgrimages, but some, like the quest for healing and relief from suffering are as relevant to many modern pilgrims as they were a thousand years ago. Irish people still travel to holy wells around the country for themselves and on behalf of loved one; some even fly to the shrine of Lourdes in France, seeking cures, relief and the strength to cope with sickness. Modern Irish people follow in the footsteps of their medieval ancestors when making journeys along pilgrim paths and caminos in Ireland and abroad. While most are no longer motivated by concerns for their soul or Purgatory, many still seek adventure as well as spiritual experience and the physical essence of the journey remains unchanged. Although not as obvious, devotion to the local saints and a focus on the saint's feast are still important parts of the spiritual lives of communities around Ireland, whose members still gather at hundreds of holy wells for pattern days. Holy places, which can be empty, quiet, contemplative places during the year can be transformed on these days to areas of busy activity, where pilgrims make traditional prayer rounds, and catch up with friends and acquaintances. Although modern pilgrimage has evolved and changed through time, in today's age of phones and laptops, it continues to have relevance.

NOTES

1 Cunningham, *Medieval Irish Pilgrims*, 143.
2 AFM.
3 Linda Kay Davidson, 'Reformulations of the Pilgrimage to Santiago de Compostela,' in *Redefining Pilgrimage: New Perspectives on Historical and Contemporary Pilgrimages*, ed. Antón M Pazos (Farnham: Ashgate Publishing Limited, 2014), 161–62.
4 Birch, *Pilgrimage to Rome*, 146.
5 AI.
6 AU, other examples include 'Imhar Ua hAedhagain, by whom the church of Paul and Peter at Ard-Macha was erected, died at Rome on his pilgrimage,' in 1134 AFM and 'Eachdonn Mac Gilluire, Coarb of St Patrick and Primate of Ireland, died at Rome, after a well-spent life,' in 1216 AFM.
7 Chris Wickham, *Medieval Rome: Stability and Crisis of a City, 900–1150* (Oxford Studies in Medieval European History. (Oxford: Oxford University Press, 2015), 138.
8 Davidson, 'Reformulations of the Pilgrimage to Santiago de Compostela,' 161–62.
9 Flanagan, *The Transformation of the Irish Church*, 152; Griffith Hartwell Jones, *Celtic Britain and the Pilgrim Movement* (London: Honourable Society of the Cymmrodorion, 1912), 525.
10 Kenney, *The Sources for the Early History of Ireland*, 601.
11 AFM. See also ALC & AU (1428).
12 AFM.
13 AFM.
14 AFM. See also AU.
15 Hopper, *To Be a Pilgrim*, 131–32.
16 Sumption, *Pilgrimage*, 24–25.
17 Spencer, 'Pilgrim Souvenirs,' 34; Spencer, *Pilgrim Souvenirs and Secular Badges*, 3.
18 Spencer, *Pilgrim Souvenirs and Secular Badges*, 3.
19 Spencer, *Pilgrim Souvenirs and Secular Badges* 12.
20 Spencer, *Pilgrim Souvenirs and Secular Badges* 7.
21 Birch, *Pilgrimage to Rome*, 78.
22 Spencer, *Pilgrim Souvenirs and Secular Badges*, 38–133.
23 Spencer, *Pilgrim Souvenirs and Secular Badges*, 3, 16.
24 Spencer, *Pilgrim Souvenirs and Secular Badges*, 16.
25 Ester Cohen, 'In Haec Signa. Pilgrim Badge Trade in Southern France,' *JMH* 2 (3) (1976): 195.
26 Dudley Waterman, 'St Mary's Priory, Devenish: Excavations of the East Range, 1972-4,' *UJA* 42 (1979): 45.
27 E. Fitzgerald, 'On Lugud's Leacht, and the "Duivhin-Deglain",' *JKSEIAS* 3 no.1 (1860): 51.
28 Ó Floinn, *Irish Shrines & Reliquaries*, 41, Fig. 6.7.
29 A badge from an unidentified French shrine was also recovered from excavations in Waterford.
30 Spencer, *Pilgrim Souvenirs and Secular Badges*, 15.
31 Alison Stones et al., eds., *The Pilgrim's Guide to Santiago de Compostela: A Critical Edition*, vol. II (London: Harvey Miller Publishers, 1998), 73.
32 A small metal shell from Ardfert Cathedral, which has been excluded from this discussion, it is instead discussed as part of the section of pilgrim burial. A badge from Rocamadour, found in the 19th century, has also been excluded from the discussion due to the lack of information about the context in which it was found.
33 Spencer, 'Pilgrim Souvenirs,' 35–39.
34 Spencer, 'Pilgrim Souvenirs,' 39–43.
35 Spencer, 'Pilgrim Souvenirs,' 43–45.
36 Brian Spencer, 'Pilgrim Signs,' in *Late Viking Age and Medieval Waterford: Excavations 1986–1992*, ed. Maurice F. Hurley et al. (Waterford: Waterford Corporation, 1997), 33–48.
37 This information was kindly provided by the excavator Maurice Hurley.
38 Spencer, *Pilgrim Souvenirs and Secular Badges*, 18.
39 Salvador Ryan and Anthony Shanahan, 'How to Communicate Lateran IV in 13th-century Ireland: Lessons from the Liber Exemplorum (c.1275),' *Religions* 9 (3) (2018): 6.
40 Bieler, 'Letter of Credence,' 259.
41 Gwynn, *The Medieval Province of Armagh*, 268–69.
42 Harold Leask, *Irish Churches & Monastic Buildings: II: Gothic Architecture A.D. 1400* (Dundalgan Press, 1958), 99.
43 Sitric had made pilgrimage in the company of Irish king, Flannacán ua Cellaig, king of

Brega Barra; see AU, 467; Boydell, 'Music in the Medieval Cathedral Priory,' in *Christ Church Cathedral Dublin: A History*, ed. Kenneth Milne (Dublin: Four Courts Press, 2010), 4.

44 Grace O'Keeffe, 'The Hospital of St John the Baptist in Medieval Dublin: Functions and Maintenance,' in *Medieval Dublin IX. Proceedings of the Friends of Medieval Dublin Symposium 2007*, ed. Séan Duffy (Dublin: Four Courts Press, 2009), 166, 168.

45 Claire Foley, Ronan McHugh and Brian Scott, eds., *An Archaeological Survey of County Fermanagh.* (Northern Ireland Environment Agency, n.d.), Vol. II, 660–662, 684. Accessed 28 July 2018.

46 Stalley, 'Sailing to Santiago,' 415.

47 Raymond Gillespie, *Devoted People: Belief and Religion in Early Modern Ireland* (Manchester University Press, 1997), 88.

48 Logan, *The Holy Wells of Ireland*, 31.

49 Arthur Spears, *The Cult of Saint Catherine of Alexandria in Ireland* (Rathmullen: Rathmullan District Local Historical Society, 2006), 58.

50 Dutton, *Aelred of Rievaulx,* 162–65.

51 AFM; AU.

52 Lawlor, 'A Calendar of the Register,' 158 no. 229.

53 McEneaney, 'Politics and the Art of Devotion,' 35–38.

54 Mark Hall, 'Roman Pilgrim,' *Pereginations,* 2 no. (2009); John Adair and John Eric Adair, *The Pilgrims' Way: Shrines and Saints in Britain and Ireland* (London: Thames and Hudson, 1978), 140–141,170–173; P. Quaife, 'Stone Pilgrims in England and Wales,' *Confratenity of St James Bulletin* 7 (1984): 6–8; Nona Ree and Terry John, *Pilgrimage. A Welsh Perspective* (Llandysul: Gomer Press, 2002), x–xi, 11, 191-92; *Santiago de Compostela: 100 Ans de Pèlerinage Européen, Europalia 85.* (Gent: Ausstellungskat, 1985), 202.

55 Roger Stalley, 'The End of the Middle Ages: Gothic Survival in Sixteenth-Century Connacht,' *JRSAI* 133 (2003): 17.

56 Ó Clabaigh, *The Friars*, 194–95.

57 Kurt Köster, 'Les Coquilles et Ensigns de Pèlerinage de Saint-Jacques de Compostelle et Les Routes de Saint-Jacques En Occident,' in *Santiago de Compostela; 100 Ans de Pèlerinage Européen, Europalia 8.5*, ed. Anon (Gent: Ausstellungskat, 1985), 85–95.

58 The shell was found in a trench excavated against the south-west wall of the graveyard. The soil (deposit) surrounding the shell produced fragments of a glass bottle and clay pipe dating to the early 18th century. It is possible that the shell came from an earlier burial that was disturbed but this cannot be proved (personal communication with Cóilín Ó Drisceoil).

59 Fionnbarr Moore, *Ardfert Cathedral. Summary of Excavation Results* (Dublin: Stationery Office, 2007), 107.

60 Personal communication with Paul Duffy, excavator.

61 The burial had 'osteophytosis of the spinal column and moderate osteoarthritis in both hip and shoulder joints, with a slight degree in the right knee.' See Miriam Clyne, 'A Medieval Pilgrim: From Tuam to Santiago de Compostela,' *Archaeology Ireland* 4 no. 3 (1990): 22.

62 Miriam Clyne, 'Excavation at St. Mary's Cathedral, Tuam, Co. Galway,' *JGAHS* 41 (1987): 99-101.

63 MacDonald and Carver, 'Archaeological Excavations at Ballyhanna Graveyard – Chronology,' in *The Science of a Lost Medieval Gaelic Graveyard: The Ballyhanna Research Project*, ed. Catriona J. McKenzie, Eileen M. Murphy and Colm J. Donnelly (Dublin: Transport Infrastructure Ireland (TII), 2015), 83, 163–64.

64 Personal communication with Michael Gibbons.

65 Michael Connolly, 'Medieval Tralee Uncovered,' The Kerry Magazine 15 (2005): 18–22; Michael Connolly, 'Investigations in the Abbey, Tannery & Tesco Car Parks, Tralee, Co. Kerry. Excavations Carried out in 2000 under License 00E0433. Unpublished Excavation Report.' Unpublished report 2000, 74–75, Figures 28 and 29.

66 The shell (00E0156:1703:001) was found on the 2nd/3rd vertebrae of the skeleton No.1703. Colm Maloney, Louise Baker, and Carmelita Troy, 'R417 Ardreigh Road Realignment. Final Report on Archaeological Investigations at Site 00E0156, in the

Medieval Borough of Ardreigh, Athy, Co. Kildare. Report Kildare County Council,' Excavation Report, 2012, 43,120.

67 Helen Lubin, *The Worcester Pilgrim. Cathedral Publications, No. 1* (Worcester: Cathedral Publications, 1990).

68 Burial No. 541. Maloney, Baker, and Troy, 'R417 Ardreigh Road Realignment. Final Report on Archaeological Investigations at Site 00E0156, in the Medieval Borough of Ardreigh, Athy, Co. Kildare. Report Kildare County Council,' 44, 120.

69 Maloney, Baker, and Troy: 120855 was buried with a shell and bone pendant (00E0156:855:001, Appendix 14). The burial at Mullingar was also buried with a bone pendant.

70 Christiaan Corlett, 'Teach Mo Chua – An Early Ecclesiastical Site at Timahoe, Co. Laois,' *Archaeology Ireland Heritage Guides, No. 83*, 2018.

71 Personal communication with Mr Hayden of Timahoe.

72 Mary Cahill and Maeve Sikora, eds., *Breaking Ground, Finding Graves – Reports on the Excavations of Burials by the National Museum of Ireland, 1927–2006*, vol. 2 (Bray: Wordwell Press in association with the National Museum of Ireland, 2012), 503.

73 Roberta Gilchrist, 'Magic for the Dead? The Archaeology of Magic in Later Medieval Burials,' *Medieval Archaeology* 52 (2008): 129 Table 1; D. A Sherlock and H Woods, *St Augustine's Abbey: Report on Excavations 1960–78. Monograph Series of the Kent Archaeological Society 4* (Kent: Kent Archaeological Society, 1988), 66, Fig. 69; Lars Andersson, *Pilgrimsmärken Och Vallfart: Medeltida Pilgrimskultur i Skandinavien, (Lund Studies in Medieval Archaeology 7)* (Stockholm: Almqvist & Wiksell International, 1989), 144, Grave 11.

74 Hopper, *Mothers, Mystics and Merrymakers*, 7–8.

75 Roberta Gilchrist and Barney Sloane, *Requiem. The Medieval Monastic Cemetery in Britain* (London: Museum of London Archaeological Service, 2005), 161.

76 Clyne, 'A Medieval Pilgrim: From Tuam to Santiago de Compostela,' 22.

77 Christopher Daniell, *Death and Burial in Medieval England 1066–1550* (London: Routledge, 1997), 148-49; Lubin, *The Worcester Pilgrim*, 11; Gilchrist and Sloane, *Requiem. The Medieval Monastic Cemetery in Britain*, 97.

78 Daniell, *Death and Burial*, 152–56; Gilchrist and Sloane, *Requiem. The Medieval Monastic Cemetery*, 98.

Abbreviations

AC	*The Annals of Clonmacnoise, being Annals of Ireland from the Earliest Period to A.D. 1408.* (Murphy, 1896, 1993).
ACon	*Annála Connacht: The Annals of Connacht (AD 1224–1544).* (Freeman, 1944.)
Acc. Roll. H.T	*The Account Roll of the Priory of the Holy Trinity, Dublin, 1337–1346* (Mills, 1891, 1996).
AFM	*Annals of the Kingdom of Ireland from the earliest times to the year 1616/the Four Masters* (O'Clery, 1856, 1990).
AI	*The Annals of Inisfallen* (Mac Aairt, 1951).
ALC	*The Annals of Loch Cé. A chronicle of Irish affairs from A.D. 1014 to A.D. 1590,* (Hennessy, 1871).
Anal. Hib.	Analecta Hibernica Journal
AU	*The Annals of Ulster, to AD 1131.* (Mac Airt, and Mac Niocaill, 1983).
BNÉ	*Bethada Náem nÉrenn.* (Plummer 1922, 1997).
BMLJ	Belfast Magazine and Literary Journal.
Cal. pat. rolls, 18–45 Eliz.	*Calendar of the Patent and Close Rolls of Chancery in Ireland, from the 18th to the 45th of the Queen Elizabeth.* (Morrin,1862).
Cal. pat. rolls, Hen. VIII–Eliz	*Calendar of the Patent and Close Rolls of Chancery in Ireland, Henry VIII to 18th Elizabeth,* (Morrin, 1861).
Cal. pat. rolls,1232–47[etc]	*Calendar of the Patent Rolls 1232–47 [etc].*
CDI	*Calendar of Documents Relating to Ireland* (Sweteman, 1875–81).
CJR Ed. I	*Calendar of the Justiciary Rolls, or Proceedings in the Court of the Justiciar of Ireland Preserved in the Public Record Office of Ireland* (Mills, 1905).
CJR Ed. II	*Calendar of the Justiciary Rolls, or, Proceedings in the Court of the Justiciar of Ireland, I to VII Years of Edward II* (Wood and Langman, 1952).
CS	*Chronicum Scotorum: A Chronicle of Irish Affairs, from the Earliest Times to AD 1135.* (Hennessy, 1866).
COD	*Calendar of Ormond Deeds* (Curtis, 1935–1943).
CPL	*Calendar of the Entries in the Papal Registers Relating to Great Britain and Ireland. Papal Letters.*
CSPI	*Calendar of State Papers, Ireland.*
HE	*Bede's Ecclesiastical History of the English People.* (Colgrave, and Mynors (1969).
Heist VSH	*Vitae Sanctorum Hiberniae Ex Codice Olim Salmanticensi Nunc Bruxellensi.* (Heist, 1965).
HMSO	His/Her Majesty's Stationery Office
IEP 1270–1446	*Irish Exchequer Payments, 1270–1446.* (Connolly, 1998).
IHS	Irish Historical Studies.
ILCC	'The Life of Colum Cille'. In *Iona, Kells and Derry: The History and Hagiography of the Monastic Familia of Columba.* (Herbert, 1996).
ITA	Irish Tourist Authority Survey [1941–45] Topographical and General Survey.
JCHAS	Journal of the Cork Historical and Archaeological Society.

JEH	Journal of Ecclesiastical History.
JGAHS	Journal of the Galway Archaeological and Historical Society.
JIA	Journal of Irish Archaeology.
JKAS	Journal of the Kildare Archaeological Society.
KAJ	Kildare Archaeological Journal.
JKAHS	Journal of the Kerry Archaeological and Historical Society.
JKSEIAS	The Journal of the Kilkenny and South-East of Ireland Archaeological Society.
JLAS	Journal of the Louth Archaeological Society.
JMH	Journal of Medieval History.
JOAS	Journal of the Ossory Archaeological Society.
JRSAI	Journal of the Royal Society of Antiquaries of Ireland.
JWAH	Journal Wicklow Archaeology and History.
JWSEIAS	Journal of the Waterford and South East of Ireland Archaeological Society.
Med. Arch.	Medieval Archaeology.
Life of St Brigit	Seán Connolly and Jean-Michel Picard, eds. 'Cogitosus's "Life of St Brigit" Content and Value.' *JRSAI* 117 (1987): 5–27.
MIA	*Miscellaneous Irish Annals (A.D.1114–1437), Fragment Vol I–III.* (Ó hInnse, 1947).
NMAJ	North Munster Antiquarian Journal
OSL	Ordnance Survey Letters, Mss. At Ordnance Survey Office, reprinted – O'Flanagan, Rev. M. (Compiler). Bray: Typescript.
OSNB	Ordnance Survey Name Books, Mss. At Ordnance Survey Office.
Peregrinations	Peregrinations: The Journal of the International Society for the Study of Pilgrimage Art.
PMLAA	Proceedings of the Modern Language Association of America.
PRIA	Proceedings of the Royal Irish Academy.
PSAS	Proceedings of the Society of Antiquaries of Scotland.
Seanchas Ardmhacha	Seanchas Ardmhacha: Journal of the Armagh Diocesan Historical Society.
Stat. Ire., 1–12 Edw. IV	Henry. F. Berry ed. Statute Rolls of the Parliament of Ireland, 1st to 12th Years of the Reign of King Edward IV. HMSO. Dublin: 1914.
Stat. Ire., 12–22 Edw. IV	Henry. F. Berry ed. Statute Rolls of the Parliament of Ireland, 12th and 13th to the 21st and 22nd Years of the Reign of King Edward IV. Dublin: The Stationery Office 1939.
Stat. Ire. Hen. VI	Henry, F. Berry ed. *Statute Rolls of the Parliament of Ireland, Reign of Henry VI*, HMSO. Dublin: 1910.
Stat. Ire. John- Hen. V	Henry, F. Berry ed. Statutes and Ordinances, Acts of the Parliament of Ireland, King John to Henry V.HMSO. Dublin: 1907.
Stat. Ire. Ric. III–Henry VIII	Philomena Connolly, ed. Statute Rolls of the Parliament of Ireland Richard III–Henry VIII. Four Courts Press. Dublin: 2002.
'Stat Ire., Hen. VI & VIII'	D.B. Quinn. 'The Bills and Statutes of the Irish Parliaments of Henry VII Henry VIII,' edited by D. B. Quinn. *Anal. Hib.* 10, 1941.
SMR	Sites and Monuments Files in the National Monuments Section, Heritage and Planning Division, Department of the Environment, Heritage and Local Government.
Tipp. Hist. Jour	Tipperary Historical Journal.

TRHS	Transactions of the Royal Historical Society.
TRIA	Transactions of the Royal Irish Academy.
TKAS	Transactions of the Kilkenny Archaeological Society.
UJA	Ulster Journal of Archaeology.
V Prima	Seán Connolly. 'Vita Prima Sanctae Brigitae Background and Historical Value.' *JRSAI 119 (1989),* 5–49.
VSH	Charles Plummer, ed. *Vitae Sanctorum Hiberniae.* 2 vols. Clarendon Press: Oxford: 1910. Reprint 1968.
WAJ	World Archaeology Journal.

Bibliography

Adair, John, and John Eric Adair. *The Pilgrims' Way: Shrines and Saints in Britain and Ireland.* London: Thames and Hudson, 1978.

Africa, Dorothy. *Life of St Ita* (translation). http://monasticmatrix.usc.edu/cartularium/article.php?-textId=32. Accessed 9 July 9 2018.

Ainsworth, John, and Edward MacLysaght. 'Survey of Documents in Private Keeping, Second Series.' *Anal. Hib.*, no. 20 (1958): 1–393.

Aitchson, Nicholas Boyeter. *Armagh and the Royal Centres in Early Medieval Ireland: Monuments, Cosmology, and the Past.* Woodbridge: Boydell & Brewer, 1994.

Anderson, Alan, and Marjorie Anderson, eds. *Adomnan's Life of Columba.* London: Thomas Nelson, 1961.

—. *Adomnán's Life of Columba. Oxford Medieval Texts*, revised ed. (1961). Oxford: Oxford University Press, 1991.

Andersson, Lars. *Pilgrimsmärken Och Vallfart: Medeltida Pilgrimskultur i Skandinavien (Lund Studies in Medieval Archaeology 7).* Stockholm: Almqvist & Wiksell International, 1989.

Anon. 'Historical Notes on Downpatrick Cathedral.' *JRSAI* 41 (1911): 293–300.

—. 'Sarum Customary Online – Context – The Medieval Church – Medieval Liturgy.' http://www.sarumcustomary.org.uk/context/medievalchurch/liturgy.php. Accessed 31 January 2019.

—. *Tóchar Phádraig. A Pilgrim's Progress.* Ballintubber: Ballintubber Publications, 1989.

Arnold, Thomas. *Memorials of St. Edmund's Abbey.* London: HMSO, 1967.

Bairéad, Eoin. 'Nicholas and Dublin', In A *grand gallimaufry: collected in honour of Nick Maxwell*, edited Mary Davies, Una MacConville, & Gabriel Cooney, 152–154. Dublin: Wordwell, 2010.

Bale, Anthony, trans. *The Book of Margery Kempe.* Oxford: Oxford University Press, 2015.

Ball, Francis Elrington, 'Descriptive Sketch of Clondalkin, Tallaght, and Other Places in West County Dublin.' *JRSAI* 9, no. 2 (1899): 93–108.

Barber, Richard. *Pilgrimages.* Woodbridge: Boydell Press, 1991.

Barrow, Lennox. *Glendalough and St. Kevin.* Dunzzdalk: Dundalgan Press, 1972.

Barry, Terry. *The Archaeology of Medieval Ireland.* London: Routledge, 1987.

—. 'Transport and Communication in Medieval and Tudor Ireland.' In *Travel and Transport in Ireland*, edited by Kevin Nowlan, 32–46. Dublin: Gill & Macmillan, 1973.

Bartal, Renana, Neta Bodner, and Bianca Kuhnel, eds. *Natural Materials of the Holy Land and the Visual Translation of Place, 500–1500.* New York: Routledge, 2017.

Bartlett, Robert. *Why Can the Dead Do Such Great Things?: Saints and Worshippers from the Martyrs to the Reformation.* New Jersey: Princeton University Press, 2013.

Bateson, J.D. 'Four Post–Medieval Coin Hoards from Ulster.' *UJA* 39 (1976): 56–61.

BBC. 2015 'Pilgrim completes "medieval" journey from Southampton to Canterbury' https://www.bbc.com/news/uk–england–35197493. Accessed 08/01/2018

BBC. 2015. 'Man sets off on medieval' pilgrimage from Southampton to Canterbury' https://www.bbc.com/news/uk–england–35108393 accessed 08/01/2018.

Bede. *Ecclesiastical History of the English People: With Bede's Letter to Egbert and Cuthbert's Letter on the Death of Bede.* Translated by David Farmer. London: Penguin, 2003.

Beech, George. 'England and Aquitaine in the Century before the Norman Conquest.' *Anglo-Saxon England* 19 (1990): 81–101.

Berry, Henry. 'Ecclesiastic, Cathedral & Bridge Builder and His Company of Masons.' *Ars Quatuor Coronatorum* 15 (1902): 4–22.

Berry, Henry, ed. *Register of Wills and Inventories of the Diocese of Dublin in the Time of Archbishops Tregury and Walton, 1457–148: From the Original Manuscript in the Library of Trinity College, Dublin*. Dublin: The University Press, 1898.

—, ed. *Statutes and Ordinances, Acts of the Parliament of Ireland, King John to Henry V.* Dublin: HMSO, 1907.

—, ed. *Statute Rolls of the Parliament of Ireland, Reign of Henry VI.* Dublin: HMSO,1910.

—, ed. *Statute Rolls of the Parliament of Ireland, 1st to 12th Years of the Reign of King Edward IV.* Dublin: HMSO, 1914

—, ed. *Statute Rolls of the Parliament of Ireland, 12th and 13th to the 21st and 22nd Years of the Reign of King Edward IV.* Dublin: The Stationery Office ,1939

Bhreathnach, Edel. *Ireland in the Medieval World, AD 400–1000: Landscape, Kingship and Religion.* Dublin: Four Courts Press, 2014.

Bieler, Ludwig. 'Letter of Credence by Donatus Magrahe, Prior of Lough Derg, for Nylanus O Ledan, Priest and Pilgrim.' *Clogher Record* 2, no. 2 (1958): 257–59.

—. *The Irish Penitentials*. Dublin: Dublin Institute for Advanced Studies, 1963.

—, ed. *The Patrician Texts in the Book of Armagh/Edited with an Introduction, Translation and Commentary by Ludwig Bieler; with a Contribution by Fergus Kelly*. Dublin: Dublin Institute for Advanced Studies, 2000.

Birch, Debra. *Pilgrimage to Rome in the Middle Ages: Continuity and Change*. Woodbridge: Boydell Press, 1998.

Bird, Jessalynn. 'Penance.' In *Encyclopaedia of Medieval Pilgrimage*, edited by Larissa J. Taylor et al., 498–501. Leiden: Brill, 2010.

Birkett, Helen. 'The Struggle for Sanctity: St Walthe of Melrose, Cistercian In-House Cults and Canonization Procedure at the Turn of the Thirteenth Century.' In *The Cult of Saints and the Virgin Mary in Medieval Scotland*, edited by Steve Boardman and Eila Williamson, 43–60. Woodbridge: Boydell Press, 2010.

Birt, Henry. 'Abbey.' In *The Catholic Encyclopedia*. New York: Robert Appleton Company, 1907. http://www.newadvent.org/cathen/01010a.htm. Accessed 18 December 2018.

Bishop, Morris. *The Middle Ages*. New York: Houghton Mifflin Company, 2001.

Bitel, Lisa. *Landscape with Two Saints: How Genovefa of Paris and Brigit of Kildare Built Christianity in Barbarian Europe*. Oxford: Oxford University Press, 2009.

Blackett, W. 'Antiquities of Waterford.' *Transactions of the Kilkenny Archaeology Society*, 1, no. 3 (1851): 486–500.

Bleeke, Marian. 'The Eve Fragment from Autun and the Emotionalism of Pilgrimage.' In *Crying in the Middle Ages: Tears of History*, edited by Elina Gertsman, 16–34. New York: Routledge, 2012.

Blindheim, Martin. 'A House–Shaped Irish–Scots Reliquary In Bologna, and Its Place among the Other Reliquaries.' *Acta Archeologica* 55 (1984): 1–53.

Bliss, William Henry, ed. 'Volume III: 2 Clement VI.' In *Petitions to the Pope 1342–1419*, 18–39. London: Eyre and Spottiswoode, 1896, British History Online http://www.british–history.ac.uk/no–series/petitions–to–pope/1342–1419 accessed 1 September 2019.

Bolster, Evelyn. *A History of the Diocese of Cork: From the Earliest Times to the Reformation*. Shannon: Irish University Press, 1972.

Bond, James. *Monastic Landscapes*. Gloucestershire: Tempus, 2004.

Bonner, Gerald, David Rollason and Clare Stancliffe, eds. *St Cuthbert, His Cult and His Community to AD 1200*. Woodbridge: Boydell Press, 1989.

Booker, Sparky. *Cultural Exchange and Identity in Late Medieval Ireland: The English and Irish of the Four Obedient Shires*. Cambridge: Cambridge University Press, 2018.

Bourke, Cormac. 'Irish Croziers of the Eighth and Ninth Centuries.' In *Ireland and Insular Art A.D. 500–1200*, edited by Michael Ryan, 166–73. Dublin: Royal Irish Academy, 1987.

—. 'Medieval Ecclesiastical Metalwork from the Diocese of Clogher.' In *History of the Diocese of Clogher*, edited by Henry A. Jefferies, 25–40. Dublin: Four Courts Press, 2005.

—. *Patrick: The Archaeology of a Saint*. Belfast: HMSO, 1993.

—. 'Peregrinatio Columbae.' In *The Island of St. Patrick. Church and Ruling Dynasties in Fingal and Meath, 400–1148*, edited by Ailbhe Mac Shamhráin, 79–88. Dublin: Four Courts Press, 2004.

—. 'Shrine (St Patrick's Hand).' *Irish Arts Review* 4, no. 3 (1987): 25–27.

—. 'What the Pilgrim Saw." In *Down Survey 2000: The Yearbook of Down County Museum*, edited by Bryan Stanley Turner, 7–11. Downpatrick: Down County Museum, 2000.

Bourke, Cormac, Richard Warner, and Michael Ryan. 'From Blackwater to Bobbio – A Coincidence of Shrines.' *Archaeology Ireland* 5, no. 2 (1991): 16–17.

Boydell, Barra. *A History of Music at Christ Church Cathedral, Dublin*. Woodbridge: Boydell Press, 2004.

—. 'Music in the Medieval Cathedral Priory.' In *Christ Church Cathedral Dublin: A History*, edited by Kenneth Milne, 142–50. Dublin: Four Courts Press, 2010.

—. 'The Establishment of the Choral Tradition, 1480–1647.' In *Christ Church Cathedral Dublin*, edited by Kenneth Milne, 237–51. Dublin: Four Courts Press, 2000.

Bracken, Gerry, and Patrick A. Wayman. 'A Neolithic or Bronze Age Alignment for Croagh Patrick.' *Cathair Na Mart* 12 (1992): 1–12.

Bradley, Ian. *Water: A Spiritual History*. London: Bloomsbury Publishing, 2012.

Bradley, John. 'Bridges.' In *Medieval Ireland: An Encyclopedia*, edited by Séan Duffy. London: Routledge, 2005.

—. 'The Topography and Layout of Medieval Drogheda.' *JLAS* 19, no. 2, (1978): 108–9.

Bradley, John, and Andy Halpin. 'The Topographical Development of Scandinavian and Anglo–Norman Waterford City.' In *Waterford History and Society: Interdisciplinary Essays on The History of an Irish County*, edited by William Nolan and Thomas Power, 105–30. Dublin: Geography Press, 1992.

Bradley, John, Andy Halpin and Heather King. *Cork Urban Archaeology Survey*. Dublin: National Monuments Service, Department of the Environment, Heritage and Local Government, 1985.

Branigan, Gary. *Ancient and Holy Wells of Dublin*. Dublin: History Press Limited, 2012.

Breen, Thaddeus, Hilda Parkes and Richard Bradshaw. 'Excavation of a Roadway at Bloomhill Bog, County Offaly.' *PRIA* 88C (1988): 321–39.

Bremer, William. 'Note on the Hollywood Stone.' *JRSAI* 16, no. 1 (1926): 51–54.

Brindley, Anna, and Jan Lanting. 'Radiocarbon Dates for Irish Trackways.' *JIA* 9 (1998): 45–67.

Broderick, David. *The First Toll-Roads. Ireland's Turnpike Roads 1729–1858*. Cork: The Collins Press, 2002.

Brown, Andrew. *Civic Ceremony and Religion in Medieval Bruges c.1300–1520*. Cambridge: Cambridge University Press, 2011.

Browne, Charles R. 'The Ethnography of Inishbofin and Inishark, Co Galway.' *PRIA* 3 (1893): 317–70.

Brundage, James. 'Cruce Sigari: The Rite for Taking the Cross in England.' *Traditio* 22 (1966): 289–310.

Buckley, Ann. 'From Hymn to Historia: Liturgical Veneration of Local Saints in the Medieval Irish Church.' In *Music, Liturgy, and the Veneration of Saints of the Medieval Irish Church in a European Context*, edited by Ann Buckley, 161–83. Turnhout: Brepols Press, 2017.

—. 'Music and Musicians in Medieval Irish Society.' *Early Music* 28, no.2 (2000): 165–90.

Bugslag, James. 'Local Pilgrimages and Their Shrines in Pre-Modern Europe.' *Peregrinations* 2, no. 1 (2005): 1–26.

—. 'Material and Theological Identities: A Historical Discourse of Constructions of the Virgin Mary.' *Théologiques* 17, no. 2 (2009): 19–67.

—. 'Performative Thaumaturgy: The State of Research on Curative and Spiritual Interaction at Medieval Pilgrimage Shrines.' In *The Sacred and the Secular in Medieval Healing Sites, Objects and Texts*, edited by Barbara S. Bowers and Linda Migl Keyser, 219–65. London: Routledge, 2016.

—. 'Relics of the Virgin Mary.' In *Encyclopedia of Medieval Pilgrimage*, edited by Larissa J. Taylor et al., 603–10. Leiden: Brill, 2010.

Burke, John, and Sir Bernard Burke. *Burke's Genealogical and Heraldic History of Peerage, Baronetage and Knightage.* Vol. 3. London: Burke's Peerage Limited, 1830.

Butterworth, Philip, and Katie Normington. *European Theatre Performance Practice, 1400–1580.* London: Routledge, 2014.

Bynum, Caroline Walker. *Wonderful Blood: Theology and Practice in Late Medieval Northern Germany and Beyond.* Philadephia: University of Pennsylvania Press, 2007.

Byrne, Joseph Patrick. *Encyclopedia of the Black Death*. Oxford: ABC–CLIO, 2012.

Byrne, Niall, ed. *The Great Parchment Book of Waterford. Liber Antiquissimus Civitatis Waterfordiae.* Dublin: Irish Manuscript Commission, 2007.

Cahill, Mary, and Maeve Sikora, eds. *Breaking Ground, Finding Graves – Reports on the Excavations of Burials by the National Museum of Ireland, 1927–2006*, 2 vols. Dublin: Wordwell, in Association with the National Museum of Ireland, 2012.

Calendar of State Papers, Ireland, 24 vols, *London:* HMSO, 1860–1911.

Calendar of Entries in the Papal Registers Relating to Great Britain and Ireland: Papal Letters, 18 vols. London, 1893– , Dublin, 1978– .

Calendar of Entries in the Papal Registers Relating to Great Britain and Ireland: Papal Letters, A.D. 1427–1447. Vol. 8. London: HMSO, 1909.

Calendar of the Patent Rolls 1232–47 [etc]. HMSO: 1908.

Campbell, Kieran. 'Drogheda James's Street.' *Med. Arch* 27 (1983): 218–19.

—. 'Drogheda, James's Street and South Quay.' *Med. Arch* 28 (1984): 256.

Cannon, Joanna. *Religious Poverty, Visual Riches: Art in the Dominican Churches of Central Italy in the Thirteenth and Fourteenth Centuries*. New Haven: Yale University Press, 2013.

Cannon, Jon. *Medieval Church Architecture*. London: Bloomsbury Publishing, 2014.

Cardwell, Peter. 'Excavations of the Hospital of St Giles by Bromton Bridge, North Yorkshire.' *Archaeology Journal* 152 (1995): 109–245.

Carr, Annemarie Weyl. 'The Face Relics of John the Baptist in Byzantium and the West.' *Gesta* 46, no.2 (2007): 159–77.

Carrigan, William. *History and Antiquities of the Diocese of Ossory*. 4 vols. Dublin: Sealy, Bryers and Walker, 1905.

Carroll, Michael P. *Irish Pilgrimage: Holy Wells and Popular Catholic Devotion*. London: JHU Press, 1999.

Carson, Robert, Andrew Glendinning, and Claire O'Kelly. 'A Catalogue of the Roman Coins from Newgrange, Co. Meath and Notes on the Coins and Related Finds.' *PRIA* 77 (1977): 35–55.

Carville, Geraldine. *The Heritage of Holy Cross*. Belfast: Blackstaff Press, 1973.

Catholic Church. *Processionale Ad Usum Insignis Ac Praeclarae Ecclesiae Sarum*. Leeds: Printed by M'Corquodale & Co., 1882.

Cavan County Council. 'Conservation and Management Plan of St Mogue's Island, Templeport, Bawnboy, Co Cavan.' Cavan: Cavan County Council, 2013.

Chalmers, Alexander. *The General Biographical Dictionary Containing an Historical and Critical Account of the Lives and Writings of the Most Eminent Persons*. Vol. XXVI. London: J. Nichols, 1816.

Chalmers, George. *Calendonia: Or, An Account, Historical and Topographic, of North Britain; from the Most Ancient to the Present Times: With a Dictionary of Places, Chorographical and Philological. In Four Volumes*. London: T. Cadell and W. Davies, 1824.

Champion, Matthew. 'Medieval Graffiti Inscriptions.' In *The Oxford Handbook of Later Medieval Archaeology in Britain*, edited by Christopher Gerrard and Alejandra Gutiérrez, 626–40. Oxford: Oxford University Press, 2018.

Chareyron, Nicole. *Pilgrims to Jerusalem in the Middle Ages*. New York: Columbia University Press, 2005.

Charles-Edwards, Thomas. *Early Christian Ireland*. Cambridge: Cambridge University Press, 2000.

—. 'Érlam: The Patron–Saint of an Irish Church.' In *Local Saints and Local Churches in the Early Medieval West*, edited by Alan Thacker and Richard Sharpe, 267–90. Oxford: Oxford University Press, 2002.

—. 'The Social Background to Irish Peregrinatio.' *Celtica* 11 (1976): 43–59.

De Châtel, Francesca 'Baptism in the Jordan River: Immersing in a Contested Transboundary Watercourse.' *Wiley Interdisciplinary Reviews: Water* 1 (2014): 219–27.

—. 'Baptized in the Jordan: Restoring a Holy River.' *Origins Current Events in Historical Perspective* 7, issue 12 (2014). http://origins.osu.edu/article/baptized–jordan–restoring–holy–river accessed 30/04/19.

—. 'Vanishing Water Landscapes in the Middle-East: Public Perceptions, Political Narratives and Traditional Beliefs Surrounding Water and Scarcity in an Arid Region. PhD thesis, Radboud University, Nijmegen, 2014. https://repository.ubn.ru.nl/handle/2066/127594 accessed 30/04/19.

Childs, Wendy. 'The Perils, or Otherwise, of Maritime Pilgrimage to Santiago de Compostela in the Fifteenth Century.' In *Pilgrimage Explored*, edited by Jennie Stopford, 123–43. York: York Medieval Press, 1999.

Clare Local Studies Project. 'Scattery Island: Folklore and Customs.' http://www.clarelibrary.ie/eolas/coclare/places/folklore_customs.html. Accessed 3 June 2016.

Clark, J. M. *The Abbey of St. Gall as a Centre of Literature and Art*. Cambridge: Cambridge University Press, 2013.

Clyne, Miriam. 'A Medieval Pilgrim: From Tuam to Santiago de Compostela.' *Archaeology Ireland* 4, no. 3 (1990): 21–22.

—. 'Excavation at St. Mary's Cathedral, Tuam, Co. Galway.' *JGAHS* 41 (1987): 90–103.

Cogan, Anthony. *The Diocese of Meath: Ancient and Modern*. 3 vols. Dublin: John F. Fowler, 1862.

—. *The Diocese of Meath: Ancient and Modern*. 3 vols. Dublin: John F. Fowler, 1862.

Cogan, Rev. Anthony. *Ecclesiastical History of the Diocese of Meath: Ancient and Modern*. 3 vols. Dublin: John Fowler, Joseph Dollard, 1862.

Cohen, Ester. 'In Haec Signa. Pilgrim Badge Trade in Southern France.' *JMH* 2 no.3 (1976): 193–214.

Coleman, Satis N. *Bells: Their History, Legends, Making, and Uses*. New York: Rand, McNally & Company, 1928.

Coleman, Simon, and John Elsner. *Pilgrimage: Past and Present in the World Religions.* Massachusetts: Harvard University Press, 1995.

Colgrave, Bertram, trans. *Two Lives of Saint Cuthbert: A Life by an Anonymous Monk of Lindisfarne and Bede's Prose Life: Texts, Translation and Notes.* Cambridge: Cambridge University Press, 2007.

Bertran Colgrave, and R.A. Mynors (eds). *Bede's Ecclesiastical History of the English People.* Oxford: Claredon Press, 1969

Comerford, Rev. M. *Collections Relating to the Diocese of Kildare and Leighlin.* 3 vols. Dublin: Duffy Brothers, 1886.

Conbhuidhe, Colmcille Ó. *The Cistercian Abbeys of Tipperary.* Edited by Finbarr Donovan. Dublin: Four Courts Press, 1999.

Connolly, Dan. 'At the Centre of the World: The Labyrinth Pavement of Chartres Cathedral.' In *Art and Architecture of Late Medieval Pilgrimage in Northern Europe and the British Isles,* edited by Sarah Blick and Rita Tekippe, 285–314. Leiden: Brill, 2005.

Connolly, Michael. 'Investigations in the Abbey, Tannery & Tesco Car Parks, Tralee, Co. Kerry. Excavations Carried out in 2000 under License 00E0433.' Unpublished Excavation Report, 2000.

—. 'Medieval Tralee Uncovered.' *The Kerry Magazine* 15 (2005): 18–22.

Connolly, Philomena, ed. *Irish Exchequer Payments, 1270–1446.* Dublin: Irish Manuscripts Commission. 1998.

—, ed. *Medieval Record Sources.* Dublin: Four Courts Press, 2002.

—, ed. *Statute Rolls of the Irish Parliament, Richard III–Henry VIII.* Dublin: Four Courts Press, for the National Archives of Ireland, 2002.

—. 'The Enactments of the 1297 Parliament.' In *Law and Disorder in Thirteenth–Century Ireland. The Dublin Parliament of 1297,* edited by James Lydon, 139–62. Dublin: Four Courts Press, 1997.

Connolly, Philomena, and Geoffrey Haward Martin, eds. *The Dublin Guild Merchant Roll, c. 1190–1265.* Dublin: Dublin Corporation, 1992.

Connolly, Sean. J. *Contested Island: Ireland 1460–1630 Oxford Press.* Oxford. Oxford University Press, 2007.

Connolly, Seán. 'Vita Prima Sanctae Brigitae Background and Historical Value.' *JRSAI* 119 (1989): 5–49.

Connolly, Sean, and Jean-Michel Picard, eds. 'Cogitosus's "Life of St Brigit": Content and Value.' *JRSAI* 117 (1987): 5–27.

Constable, Olivia Remie. 'Storms at Sea on a Voyage between Rhodes and Venice, November 1470.' In *Medieval Christianity in Practice,* edited by Miri Rubin, 81–85. Princeton and Oxford: Princeton University Press, 2009.

Cooke, Thomas. 'On Ancient Irish Bells.' *TKAS* 2, no. 1 (1852): 47–63.

Corlett, Christiaan. 'A Font of Majuscule Proportions at Tallaght.' *Archaeology Ireland* 26, no. 3 (2012): 6.

—. *Antiquities of West Mayo.* Dublin: Wordwell, 2001.

—. *Beneath the Poulaphuca Reservoir: The 1939 Poulaphuca Survey of Lands Flooded by the Liffey Reservoir Scheme.* Dublin: Stationery Office, 2008.

—. 'Cursing Stones in Ireland.' *JGAHS* 64 (2012): 1–20.

—. *Glendalough.* Wicklow: Coles Lane, 2017.

—. 'Prehistoric Pilgrimage to Croagh Patrick.' *Cathair Na Mart* 16 (1996): 54–61.

—. 'Teach Mo Chua – An Early Ecclesiastical Site at Timahoe, Co. Laois.' *Archaeology Ireland Heritage Guides, No. 83.* Dublin: Wordwell, 2018.

—. 'The Prehistoric Ritual Landscape of Croagh Patrick, Co. Mayo.' *JIA* 9 (1998): 9–26.

Corlett, Christiaan, and John Medlycott, eds. *The Ordnance Survey Letters: Wicklow*. Roundwood: Roundwood District Historical & Folklore Society and Kestrel Books, 2000.

Corlett, Christiaan, and Mairéad Weaver, eds. *The Liam Price Notebooks: The Placenames, Antiquities and Topography of County Wicklow*. Dublin: Wordwell, 2002.

Costello, Michael A. *De Annatis Hiberniae: A Calendar of the First Fruits' Fees Levied on Papal Appointments to Benefices in Ireland. A.D. 1400 to 1535*. Maynooth: Saint Patrick's College for the Catholic Record Society of Ireland, 1912.

Cotter, Claire. '1990:021 Skeam West Early Church Site.' 1990. http://excavations.ie accessed 12/06/2018.

Cowan, Mairi. *Death, Life, and Religious Change in Scottish Towns c. 1350–1560*. Oxford: Oxford University Press, 2012.

Coyne, Frank. *Islands in the Clouds. An Upland Archaeological Study on Mount Brandon and The Paps, County Kerry*. Kerry: Kerry County Council with Aegis Archaeology Limited, 2006.

Coyne, Frank, and Tracey Collins. *Mount Brandon: Dingle's Holy Mountain. Heritage Guides, No. 29*. Dublin: Wordwell, 2005.

Crawford, Ciara. 'Disease and Illness in Medieval Ireland.' PhD thesis, Department of Anthropology, National University of Ireland, Maynooth, 2011. http://eprints.maynoothuniversity.ie/3573/1/CrawfordPhD.pdf. Accessed 24/11/2018

Crawford, H. 'The Round Tower and Castle of Timahoe.' *JRSAI* 54 (1924): 31–45.

Crawford, John, Raymond Gillespie and Alan Fletcher, eds. 'Liturgy and Music in the Medieval Cathedral.' In *St Patrick's Cathedral, Dublin: A History*, edited by John Crawford and Raymond Gillespie, 120–48. Dublin: Four Courts Press, 2009.

Crosthwaite, John Clarke. *The Book of Obits and Martyrology of the Cathedral Church of the Holy Trinity, Commonly Called Christ Church. Dublin. Ed. from the Original Manuscript. With an Introd. by James Henthorn Todd*. Dublin: For the Irish Archaeological Society, 1844.

Cunniffe, Christy. 'Medieval Clonfert: The Genesis, Development and Decline of a Gaelic Cathedral Town.' Unpublished PhD thesis, Department of Archaeology, NUI Galway, 2010.

Cunningham, Bernadette. *Medieval Irish Pilgrims to Santiago de Compostela*. Dublin: Four Courts Press, 2018.

Cunningham, John B. *Lough Derg Legendary Pilgrimage*. Monaghan: Davog Press, 1984.

Cuppage, Judith. *Archaeological Survey of the Dingle Peninsula. A Description of the Field Antiquities from the Mesolithic Period to the 17th Century A.D.* Ballyferriter: Oidhreacht Chorca Dhuibhne, 1986.

Curley, Michael J. 'The Miracles of Saint David: A New Text and Its Context.' *Traditio* 62 (2007): 135–205.

Curtis, Edmund, ed. *Calendar of Ormond Deeds*. Dublin: Irish University Press for the Irish Manuscripts Commission, 1935–1943.

Curran, Olive C, Olive Sharkey and Paul Connell. *History of the Diocese of Meath 1860–1993*. Mullingar: Catholic Church, Diocese of Meath, 1995.

Curtayne, Alice. *Lough Derg: St Patrick's Purgatory*. Omagh: Graham & Sons, 1976.

Daniell, Christopher. *Death and Burial in Medieval England 1066–1550*. London: Routledge, 1997.

Darlington, Reginald, ed. *The Vita Wulfstani of William of Malmesbury*. London: Royal Historical Society, 1928.

Davey, Francis, ed. *The Itineraries of William Wey*. Oxford: Bodleian Library, 2010.

Davidson, Linda Kay. 'Reformulations of the Pilgrimage to Santiago de Compostela.' In *Redefining*

Pilgrimage: New Perspectives on Historical and Contemporary Pilgrimages, edited by Antón M Pazos, 159–82. Farnham: Ashgate Publishing Limited, 2014.

Davies, John. *Pilgrimage Yesterday and Today. Why? Where? How?* London: SCM Press Ltd, 1988.

Day, Robert, ed. 'Regnum Corcagiense, or a Description of the Kingdom of Cork, by Sir Richard Cox (Contd).' *JCHAS*, 2, 8, no. 55 (1902): 156–79.

Day, Robert, ed. 'Regnum Corcagiense, or a Description of the Kingdom of Cork, by Sir Richard Cox (Contd)', CHAS Ser. 2, 8, no. 55 (1902): 156-179.

De Latocnaye, Bougrenet. *A Frenchman's Walk through Ireland, 1796–7*. Edited by John Stevenson. Belfast: McCaw, 1917.

De Paor, Máire B. *Saint Moling Luachra: A Pilgrimage from Sliabh Luachra to Rinn Ros Broic above the Stream-Pools of the Barrow: Geinemain Molling Ocus a Bhetae (The Birth and Life of St. Moling)*. Dublin: Columba Press, 2001.

Delehaye, Hippolytus. 'La Pèlerinage de Laurent de Paszthо Au Purgatoire de S. Patrice.' *Analecta Bollandiana* 27 (1908): 35–60.

Dickson, Gary. 'The Crowd at the Feet of Pope Boniface VIII: Pilgrimage, Crusade and the First Roman Jubilee (1300).' *JMH*, 25 (1999): 279–307.

Ditchburn, David. '"Saints at the Door Don't Make Miracles?" The Contrasting Fortunes of Scottish Pilgrimage, c. 1450–1550.' In *Sixteenth-Century Scotland: Essays in Honour of Michael Lynch*, edited by Julian Goodare and Alasdair A. MacDonald, 93–95. Leiden: Brill, 2008.

Ditchburn, David, and Marjory Harper. 'Aberdeen and the Outside World.' In *Aberdeen before 1800: A New History*, edited by E. Patricia Dennison, David Ditchburn and Michael Lynch, 377–407. East Linton: Tuckwell Press, 2002.

Doherty, Charles. 'Exchange and Trade in Early Medieval Ireland.' *JRSAI* 110 (1980): 67–89.

—. 'Kingship in Early Ireland.' In *The Kingship and Landscape of Tara*, edited by Edel Bhreathnach, 3–31. Dublin: Four Courts Press for The Discovery Programme, 2005.

—. 'The Basilica in Early Ireland.' *Peritia* 3 (1984): 303–15.

—. 'The Earliest Cult of Molaisse.' In *History of the Diocese of Clogher*, edited by Henry A. Jefferies, 13–24. Dublin: Four Courts Press, 2005.

—. 'The Use of Relics in Early Ireland.' In *Irland und Europa: Die Kirche in Frühmittelalter*, edited by Próinséas Ní Chátháin and Michael Richter, 89–104. Stuttgart: Klett-Cotta, 1984.

Dolan, Brian. 'Bedrocks and Bullauns: More than One Use for a Mortar?' *Archaeology Ireland* 23, no. 1 (2009): 16–19.

Doran, Linda. 'Medieval Communication Routes through Longford and Roscommon and Their Associated Settlements.' *PRIA* 104, no. 3 (2004): 57–80.

Douglas, Dale. *Dunstan: Saint and Statesman*. Cambridge: James Clarke & Co., 2013.

Dowd, Marion. *The Archaeology of Caves in Ireland*. Oxford: Oxbow Books, 2015.

Downham, Clare. *Medieval Ireland*. Cambridge: Cambridge University Press, 2018.

Dubreucq, Alain, and Alessandro Zironi, eds. *Miracula Sancti Columbani. La Reliquia e Il Giudizio Regio. La Relique et Le Jugement Royal. Relic and Royal Judgment. Ediz. Multilingue.* Firenze: Edizioni del Galluzzo per la Fondazione Ezio Franceschini, 2015.

Duffy, Eamon. *The Stripping of the Altars: Traditional Religion in England, c.1400–c.1580*. London: Yale University Press, 2005.

Duffy, Paul, and Tadhg O'Keeffe. 'A Stone Shrine for a Relic of St Thomas Becket in Dublin?' *Archaeology Ireland* 31, no. 4 (2017): 18–23.

Duffy, Séan. 'A Site for Sore Eyes: A Hiberno-Roman Curative Cult at Golden, Co. Tipperary.' *Archaeology Ireland* 16, no. 2 (2002): 8–9.

Duignan, Michael. 'The Moylough (Co. Sligo) and Other Irish Belt-Reliquaries.' *JGAHS* 24, no. 3/4 (1951): 83–94.

Dukelow, Natasha, and Beatrix Färber, eds. *The Journey of Symon Semeonis from Ireland to the Holy Land*: Author: Symon Semeonis (Simon FitzSimon). Electronic edition 2017. CELT: Corpus of Electronic Texts: a project of University College, Cork College Road, Cork, Ireland. https://celt.ucc.ie//published/T300002–001/index.html accessed 20/02/2019.

Dumville, David. *A Palaeographer's Review: The Insular System of Scripts in the Early Middle Ages. 2 vols. Suita, Institute of Oriental and Occidental Studies.* Osaka: Kansai University, 1999.

Dunne, Michael. 'Richard FitzRalph of Dundalk (c. 1300–1360) and the New World.' *Archivium Hibernicum* 58 (2004): 243–58.

Dutton, Hely. *Statistical Survey of the County of Clare.* Dublin: Graisberry and Campbell, 1808.

Dutton, Marsha, ed. *Aelred of Rievaulx: The Historical Works.* Translated by Jane Freeland. Cistercian Fathers Series: Number 56. Minnesota: Liturgical Press, 2005.

Eadmer. *The Life of St Anselm, Archbishop of Canterbury. Edited with Introduction, Notes and Translation by R.W. Southern.* Oxford: Clarendon Press, 1962.

Eames, Elizabeth S., and Thomas Fanning. *Irish Medieval Tiles.* Dublin: Royal Irish Academy, 1988.

Edgecomb, Richard. *The Voyage of Sir Richard Edgecomb into Ireland, in the Year 1488.* privately published, 1747–1750.

Edwards, Nancy. 'Celtic Saints and Early Medieval Archaeology.' In *Local Saints and Local Churches in the Early Medieval West*, edited by Alan Thacker and Richard Sharpe, 225–66. Oxford: Oxford University Press, 2002.

—. *The Archaeology of Early Medieval Ireland.* Philadelphia: University of Pennsylvania Press, 1990.

—. *The Archaeology of Early Medieval Ireland.* London: Routledge, 1999.

Ellington, Donna Spivey. *From Sacred Body to Angelic Soul: Understanding Mary in Late Medieval and Early Modern Europe.* Washington: Catholic University of America Press, 2001.

Erskine, Sarah. 'Is the Cloc Ind Édachta St Patrick's Oldest and Most Important Medieval Bell-Relic?' *JRSAI* 142/143 (2012): 74–85.

Erskine, Sarah Christine. 'St. Patrick's Bachall Ísu: Its Origins, Traditions, and Rise to Prominence as Armagh's Premier Relic.' *JASIMS* 6 (2013): 41–67.

Esposito, E, ed. *Itinerarium Symonis Semeonis Ab Hybernia Ad Terram Sanctum.* Dublin: Dublin Institute for Advanced Studies, 1960.

Esposito, Mario, ed. 'Conchubrani Vita Sanctae Monennae.' *PRIA* 28 (1910): 202–51.

Etchingham, Colmán. *Church Organisation in Ireland, A.D. 650 to 1000.* Maynooth: Laigin Publications, 1999.

Evenou, Jean. 'Processions, Pilgrimages, Popular Religion.' In *The Church at Prayer: An Introduction to the Liturgy*, edited by Georges Martimort, translated by Matthew J. O' Connell, Vol. 3. London: The Liturgical Press, 1987.

Fahey, Jerome. *The History and Antiquities of the Diocese of Kilmacduagh.* Dublin: M. H. Gill & Son, 1883.

Farmer, David, ed. *The Oxford Dictionary of Saints, 5th edition revised.* Oxford: Oxford University Press, 2011.

Farrelly, Jean, and Camin O'Brien. *Archaeological Inventory of County Tipperary/Compiled by Dúchas, The Heritage Service. Vol. 1, North Tipperary.* Dublin: Stationery Office, 2002.

Fawcett, Jane. *Historic Floors.* Oxford: Butterworth-Heinemann, 2001.

Finucane, Ronald C. *Miracles and Pilgrims: Popular Beliefs in Medieval England.* London: J. M. Dent and Sons, 1977.

Fisher, Jonathan. *Scenery of Ireland Illustrated in a Series of Prints of Select Views, Castles and Abbies Drawn and Engraved in Aquatinta by Jonathan Fisher, Volume the First Containing Sixty Prints with a Letter Press Description to Each*. Vol. 1. London: Published by J. Debrett for the author, 1795.

Fitzgerald, E. 'On Lugud's Leacht, and the Duivhin-Deglain.' *JKSEIAS* 3, no. 1 (1860): 47–53.

FitzPatrick, Elizabeth. 'On the Trail of the Ancient Highway: Rediscovering Dála's Road.' In *Lost and Found: Discovering Ireland's Past*, edited by Joe Fenwick, 164–74. Dublin: Wordwell, 2003.

—. 'Roads and Routes.' In *Medieval Ireland: An Encyclopaedia*, edited by Séan Duffy, 413–14. Abingdon: Routledge, 2005.

—. *Royal Inauguration in Gaelic Ireland c. 1100–1600: A Cultural Landscape Study*. Woodbridge: Boydell Press, 2004.

FitzPatrick, Elizabeth, and Camin O'Brien. *The Medieval Churches of County Offaly*. Dublin: Government of Ireland, 1998.

FitzPatrick, Elizabeth, Madeleine O'Brien, and Paul Walsh, eds. *Archaeological Investigations in Galway City, 1987–1998*. Dublin: Wordwell, 2004.

Flanagan, Marie Therese. *The Transformation of the Irish Church in the Twelfth and Thirteenth Centuries*. Woodbridge: Boydell & Brewer, 2013.

Fleming, John. *Gille of Limerick (c. 1070–1145): Architect of a Medieval Church*. Dublin: Four Courts Press, 2001.

Fletcher, Alan. 'Playing and Staying Together: Projecting the Corporate Image in Sixteenth-Century Dublin.' In *Civic Ritual and Drama*, edited by Alexandra F. Johnston and Wim Hüsken, 15–37. Amsterdam/Atlanta: Rodopi Press, 1997.

—. 'Performing Medieval Irish Communities.' In *Drama and Community: People and Plays in Medieval Europe, Medieval Texts and Cultures of Northern Europe 1*, edited by Alan Hindley, 179–99. Turnhout: Brepols, 1999.

—. 'The Civic Drama of Old Kilkenny.' *Records of Early English Drama* 13, no. 1 (1988): 12–30.

—. 'The Civic Pageantry of Corpus Christi in Fifteenth- and Sixteenth-Century Dublin.' *Irish Economic and Social History* 23 (1996): 73–96.

—. *Drama, Performance and Polity in Pre-Cromwellian Ireland*. Cork: Cork University Press, 2000.

—. 'Liturgy in the Late Medieval Cathedral Priory.' In *Christ Church Cathedral Dublin. A History*, edited by Kenneth Milne, 129–41. Dublin: Four Courts Press, 2000.

—. 'The Liturgy and Music of the Medieval Cathedral.' In *A History of St Patrick's Cathedral*, edited by John Crawford and Raymond Gillespie, 120–48. Dublin: Four Courts Press, 2009.

—. *Late Medieval Popular Preaching in Britain and Ireland: Texts, Studies, and Interpretations*. Turnhout: Brepols, 2009.

Foley, Claire, Ronan McHugh and Brian Scott, eds. *An Archaeological Survey of County Fermanagh*. 2 vols. Northern Ireland Environment Agency, 2018.

Foley, Ronan. *Healing Waters: Therapeutic Landscapes in Historic and Contemporary Ireland*. Farnham: Ashgate Press, 2010.

Forbes, Alexander Penrose. *Lives of S. Ninian and S. Kentigern. Compiled in the Twelfth Century*. Edinburgh: Edmonston and Douglas, 1874.

Foster, Elisa A. 'Moveable Feasts: Processions as Multimedia Performance in Le Puy-En-Velay.' *Peregrinations:* 5, no. 1 (2015): 37–67.

—. "This Is My Body': Devotion to the Corpus Christi Shrine in Late Medieval York.' In *Devotional Interaction in Medieval England and Its Afterlives*, edited by Elisa A. Foster, Julia Perratore and Steven Rozenski, 241–67. Leiden: Brill, 2018.

Freeman Alexander. Martin ed. *Annála Connacht: The Annals of Connacht (AD1224–1544),* Dublin: Dublin Institute for Advanced Studies, 1944.

French, Noel. *Meath Holy Wells.* Trim: Meath Heritage Centre, 2012.

Fry, Malcolm. *Coití: Logboats from Northern Ireland.* Antrim: Greystone Press on Behalf of the Environment and Heritage Service, Dept. of the Environment, 2000.

Fry, Susan Leigh. *Burial in Medieval Ireland 900–1500: A Review of the Written Sources.* Dublin: Four Courts Press, 1999.

Furnivall, Frederick, ed. *The Stacyons of Rome OS 25.* London: Early English Text Society, 1867.

Gaposchkin, Cecilia. 'Portals, Processions, Pilgrimage, and Piety: Saints Firmin and Honoré at Amiens.' In *Art and Architecture of Late Medieval Pilgrimage in Northern Europe and the British Isles,* edited by Sarah Blick and Rita Tekippe, 217–42. Leiden: Brill, 2005.

Garcia, Michael. 'Medieval Medicine, Magic, and Water: The Dilemma of Deliberate Deposition of Pilgrim Signs.' *Peregrinations* 1, no. 3 (2002): 1–13.

Geary, Patrick J. *Furta Sacra: Theft of Relics in the Central Middle Ages.* New Jersey: Princeton University Press, 1978.

—. *Living with the Dead In The Middle Ages.* Ithaca and London: Cornell University Press, 1994.

Gem, Richard. 'St Flannan's Oratory at Killaloe: A Romanesque Building of c. 1100 and the Patronage of King Muirchertach Ua Briain.' In *Ireland and Europe in the Twelfth Century. Reform and Renewal,* edited by Damian Bracken and Dagmar Ó Riain-Raedel, 74–105. Dublin: Four Courts Press, 2006.

Gibbons, Michael. 'Croagh Patrick and Prehistoric Mountain Pilgrimage.' In *Mayo History & Society,* edited by Gerard Moran and Nollaig Ó Muraíle, 45–66. Dublin: Geography Press, 2014.

Gibbons, Michael, and Myles Gibbons. 'Inishglora – 'The Western Threshold Between Land and Wave.'' In *Recent Explorations and Discoveries in Irish Heritage,* edited by Jim Higgins, 24–40. Galway: Rock Crow's Press, 2017.

Gilchrist, Roberta. 'Cemetery: Requiem for a Lost Age.' *British Archaeology* 84 (2005): 28–33.

—. 'Magic for the Dead? The Archaeology of Magic in Later Medieval Burials.' *Medieval Archaeology* 52 (2008): 119–59.

—. *Medieval Life: Archaeology and the Life Course.* Woodbridge: Boydell Press, 2012.

—. 'The Intimacy of Death: Interpreting Gender and the Life Course in Medieval and Early Modern Burials.' In *Interpreting the Early Modern World: Transatlantic Perspectives,* edited by Mary Baudry, and James Symonds, 159–73. New York: Springer, 2011.

Gilchrist, Roberta, and Barney Sloane. *Requiem. The Medieval Monastic Cemetery in Britain.* London: Museum of London Archaeological Service, 2005.

Gillespie, Raymond. *Devoted People: Belief and Religion in Early Modern Ireland.* Manchester: Manchester University Press, 1997.

—. 'The Coming of Reform, 1500–58.' In *Christ Church Cathedral, Dublin: A History,* edited by Kenneth Milne, 151–73. Dublin: Four Courts Press, 2000.

—. 'The Crisis of Reform, 1625–60.' In *Christ Church Cathedral, Dublin: A History,* edited by Kenneth Milne, 195–217. Dublin: Four Courts Press, 2000.

—, ed. *The Proctor's Accounts of Peter Lewis, 1564–1565.* Dublin: Dublin Four Courts Press, 1997.

—. 'Who Stole St Buite's Head? Gossip and Guilt in Sixteenth-Century Louth.' In *A Carnival of Learning. Essays to Honour George Cunningham and His 50 Conferences on Medieval Ireland. Cistercian Abbey of Mount St Joseph, Roscrea, 1987–2012,* edited by Peter Harbison and Valerie Hall, 74–86. Roscrea: Cistercian Press, 2012.

Giraldus Cambrensis. *The Topography of Ireland.* Translated by Thomas Forester, Revised and Edited with Additional Notes by Thomas Wright. Medieval Latin Series. Cambridge, Ontario: In parentheses Publications, 2000.

Gitlitz, David M., and Linda Kay Davidson. *The Pilgrimage Road to Santiago: The Complete Cultural Handbook.* New York: St. Martin's Press, 2000.

Gittos, Helen. *Liturgy, Architecture, and Sacred Places in Anglo–Saxon England.* Oxford: Oxford University Press, 2013.

Gowan, Margaret. '1986:41. Boherygeela (BGE). 'Ancient? Road/Trackway.' Database of Irish Excavation Reports, 1986. Http://excavation.ie accessed 14/02/2018.

Greene, J. Patrick. *Medieval Monasteries.* London: Continuum, 2005.

Gregory of Tours. *Glory of the Martyrs.* Edited by Raymond Van Dam. Liverpool: Liverpool University Press, 1988.

Grigsby, Byron Lee. *Pestilence in Medieval and Early Modern English Literature.* London: Routledge, 2004.

Groeneveld, Leanne. 'A Theatrical Miracle: The Boxley Rood of Grace as Puppet.' *Early Theatre* 10.2 (2007): 11–50.

Grogan, Eoin, and Annaba Kilfeather. *Archaeological Inventory of County Wicklow.* Dublin: The Stationery Office, 1997.

Guinness, Henry. 'Dublin Trade Guilds.' *JRSAI* 12 no. 2 (1922): 14–63.

Gwynn, Aubrey. 'Archbishop Cromer's Register. (Continued).' *JCLAS* 10, no. 2 (1942): 116–127.

—. 'Richard Fitzralph, Archbishop of Armagh.' *Studies: An Irish Quarterly Review 22 no. 87* (1933): 389–405.

—. 'The Cult of St Martin in Ireland.' *The Irish Ecclesiastical Record,* 105 (Ser 5), (1966): 353–64.

—. *The Irish Church in the Eleventh and Twelfth Century.* Dublin: Four Courts Press, 1992.

—. *The Medieval Province of Armagh 1470–1545.* Dundalk: Dundalgan Press, 1946.

Gwynn, Aubrey, and Richard Neville Hadcock. *Medieval Religious Houses: Ireland: With an Appendix to Early Sites.* Dublin: Irish Academic Press, 1988.

Hahn, Cynthia Jean. *Strange Beauty: Issues in the Making and Meaning of Reliquaries, 400–circa 1204.* University Park: Penn State University Press, 2012.

Hall, D. J. *English Medieval Pilgrimage.* London: Routledge & Kegan Paul, 1965.

Hall, Dianne. *Women and the Church in Medieval Ireland, c.1140–1540.* Dublin: Four Courts Press, 2003.

Hall, Mark. 'Crossing the Pilgrimage Landscape: Some Thoughts on a Holy Rood Reliquary from the River Tay at Carpow, Perth and Kinross, Scotland.' In *Beyond Pilgrim Souvenirs and Secular Badges. Essays in Honour of Brian Spencer,* edited by Sarah Blick, 75–91. Oxford: Oxbow Books, 2007.

—. 'Play and Playfulness in Late Medieval Britain: Theory, Concept, Practice.' In *Later Medieval Archaeology in Britain,* edited by Christopher Gerrard and Alejandra Gutiérrez, 530–42. Oxford: Oxford University Press, 2018.

—. 'Roman Pilgrim.' *Peregrinations* 2 no. 4 (2009).

Hallinan, Michael. *Tipperary County: People and Places: An Anthology of the Evolution of County Tipperary, Some Historic Events and the History of the Principal Towns in the County.* Dublin: Kincora Press, 1993.

Halpin, Andy, and Conor Newman. *Ireland. An Oxford Archaeological Guide to Sites from the Earliest Times to AD 1600.* Oxford: Oxford University Press, 2006.

Hamlin, Ann. 'The Early Irish Church: Problems of Identification.' In *The Early Church in Wales and the West. Oxbow Monograph 16*, edited by Nancy Edwards and Alan Lane, 138–44. Oxford: Oxbow Books, 1992.

Hanks, Patrick, and Flavia Hodges. *A Dictionary of Surnames*. Oxford: Oxford University Press, 1988.

Harbison, Peter. 'A Labyrinth on the Twelfth-Century High Cross Base on the Rock of Cashel, Co. Tipperary.' *JRSAI* 128 (1998): 107–11.

—. 'Early Irish Pilgrim Archaeology in the Dingle Peninsula.' *World Archaeology* 26, no.1 (1994): 90–103.

—. *Guide to the National Monuments in the Republic of Ireland*. Dublin: Gill & Macmillan, 1970.

—. *Pilgrimage in Ireland. The Monuments and the People*. London: Syracuse University Press, 1991.

—. 'Pilgrims and Pilgrimage.' In *Medieval Ireland: An Encyclopaedia*, edited by Séan Duffy, 374–75. Abingdon: Routledge, 2005.

—. 'The Clones Sarcophagus: A Unique Romanesque-Style Monument.' *Archaeology Ireland* 13, no. 3 (1999): 12–16.

—. 'The Date of the Moylough Belt-Shrine.' In *Irish Antiquity: Essays and Studies Presented to Professor M.J. O'Kelly*, edited by Donnchadh Ó Corráin, 231–39. Cork: Tower Books, 1981.

—. *The High Crosses of Ireland: An Iconographical and Photographic Survey*. 3 vols. Bonn: Habelt, 1992.

—. 'The Otherness of Irish Art in the Twelfth Century.' In *From Ireland Coming*, edited by Colum Hourihane, 103–20. Princeton: Princeton University Press, 2001.

Harbison, Peter, and Joss Lynam. *St Kevin's Way. Hollywood to Glendalough, Co. Wicklow*. Kilkenny: The Heritage Council, 2002.

Hardiman, James, ed. *A Statute of the Fortieth Year of King Edward III: Enacted in a Parliament Held in Kilkenny, A. D. 1367, Before Lionel Duke of Clarence*. Vol. 2. Dublin: Irish Archaeological Society, 1843.

—. *The History of the Town and County of the Town of Galway*. Dublin: W. Folds and sons, 1820.

Hardy, Philip Dixon. *The Holy Wells of Ireland*. Dublin: Hardy and Walker, 1840.

Haren, Michael. 'The Religious Outlook of a Gaelic Lord: A New Light on Thomas Óg Maguire.' *IHS* 25, no. 98 (1986): 195–97.

Haren, Michael, and Yolande de Pontfarcy. *The Medieval Pilgrimage to St Patrick's Purgatory: Lough Derg and the European Tradition*. Clogher Historical Society, 1988.

Harney, Lorcan. 'Glendalough: Power, Politics and Religion in an Ecclesiastical Landscape.' Unpublished MA thesis, School of Archaeology, University College Dublin, 2006.

—. 'Imitatio Romae: High Status Recumbent Crossslabs, High Crosses and the Organisation of the Early Monastic Landscape of Glendalough.' In *Proceedings of The Association of Young Irish Archaeologists Annual Conference 2007*, edited by Kim Rice and Brian Dolan, 31–46. Dublin: The Association of Young Irish Archaeologists, 2008.

—. 'Medieval Burial and Pilgrimage within the Landscape of Glendalough: the Evidence of the Crosses and the Cross-Slabs.' In *Glendalough: City of God*, edited by Charles Doherty and Mary Kelly, 112–36. Dublin: Four Courts Press for the Royal Society of Antiquaries of Ireland, 2011.

Harpur, James. *Sacred Tracks: 2000 Years of Christian Pilgrimage*. London: Frances Lincoln Ltd, 2002.

Harris, Nicholas. *Proceedings and Ordinances of the Privy Council of England*. Vol. VI. The Commission of Public Records, 1837.

Harrison, Martin. 'Penitenital Pilgrimage.' In *Encyclopedia of Medieval Pilgrimage*, edited by Larissa J. Taylor et al., 501–3. Leiden: Brill, 2010.

Hartwell Jones, Griffith. *Celtic Britain and the Pilgrim Movement*. London: Honourable Society of the Cymmrodorion, 1912.

Harty, Malachy. *Triumphalia Chronologica Monasterii Sanctae Crucis in Hibernia. De Cisterciensium Hibernorum Viris Illustribus. Edited, with a Translation, Notes, and Illustrations, by the Rev. Denis Murphy.* Dublin: Fallon, 1893.

Hawkes, William. 'The Liturgy in Dublin, 1200–1500: Manuscript Sources.' *Repertorium Novum* 2 (1958): 33–67.

Hayes, Dawn Marie. *Body and Sacred Place in Medieval Europe, 1100–1389. [Studies in Medieval History and Culture]*. London: Routledge, 2003.

Hayes, William J. *Holycross: The Awakening of the Abbey*. Lisheen Publications, 2011.

Healy, John. *History of the Diocese of Meath*. 2 vols, 1908.

Heist, William W., ed. *Vitae Sanctorum Hiberniae Ex Codice Olim Salmanticensi Nunc Bruxellensi*. Brussels: Société des Bollandistes, 1965.

William Hennessy, W. ed. *Chronicum Scotorum: A Chronicle of Irish Affairs, from the Earliest Times to AD 1135*. London: Published by the authority of the lords commissioners of Her Majesty's Treasury, under the direction of the master of the rolls, 1866.

—. ed. *The Annals of Loch Cé. A chronicle of Irish affairs from A.D. 1014 to A.D. 1590*, 2 vols, Rerum Britannicarum Medii Aevi Scriptores 54. London: Longman, 1871.

Hennig, John. 'Irish Saints in Early German Literature.' *Speculum* 22, no. 3 (1947): 358–74.

—. "St. Leonard in Ireland." *Journal of the County Louth Archaeological Society* 10, no. 4 (1994): 297–301.

Henry, Françoise. 'Early Monasteries, Beehive Huts and Dry Stone Houses in the Neighbourhood of Caherciveen and Waterville (Co. Kerry).' *PRIA* 58 C (1956): 45–166.

Herbert, Máire, *Iona, Kells and Derry: The History and Hagiography of the Monastic Familia of Columba*. Dublin: Four Courts Press, 1996.

Herbert, Máire, and Pádraig Ó Riain, eds. *Betha Adamnáin: The Irish Life of Adamnán, Irish Texts Society 54*. London: Irish Texts Society, 1988.

Herity, Michael. 'Cathair Na Naomh and Its Cross–Slabs.' *Cathair Na Mart* 9 (1989): 91–100.

—. 'Early Christian Decorated Slabs in Donegal: An Turas and The Tomb of The Founder Saint.' In *Donegal, History and Society*, edited by William Nolan, Liam Ronayne, and Mairead Dunlevy, 25–49. Dublin: Geography Press, 1995.

—. 'Early Irish Hermitages in the Light of the Lives of Cuthbert.' In *Studies in the Layout, Buildings and Art in Stone of Early Irish Monasteries*, edited by Michael Herity, 72–90. London: Pindar Press, 1995.

—. ed. *Ordnance Survey Letters Galway. Letters Relating to the Antiquities of the County of Galway Containing Information Collected during the Progress of the Ordnance Survey in 1838 and 1839 [Written by John O'Donovan and Thomas O'Conor]*. Dublin: Four Masters Press 2009.

—, ed. *Ordnance Survey Letters Mayo: Letters Relating to the Antiquities of the County of Mayo Containing Information Collected during the Progress of the Ordnance Survey in 1838 [Written by John O'Donovan and Thomas O'Conor]*. Dublin: Four Masters Press, 2009.

—, ed. *Studies in the Layout, Buildings and Art in Stone of Early Irish Monasteries*. London: Pindar Press, 1995.

—. 'The Antiquity of an Turas (the Pilgrimage Round) in Ireland.' In *Lateinische Kultur Im VIII. Jahrhundert. Traube-Gedenkschrift*, edited by Albert Lehner and Walter Berschin, 95–143. St Ottilien: EOS, 1989.

—. 'The Forms of the Tomb-Shrine of the Founder Saint in Ireland.' In *The Age of Migrating Ideas: Early Medieval Art in Northern Britain and Ireland: Proceedings of the Second International*

Conference on Insular Art Held in the National Museums of Scotland in Edinburgh, 3–6 January 1991, edited by Michael Spearman and John Higgitt, 188–96. Edinburgh: National Museums of Scotland, 1993.

—. 'The Hermitage on Ardoileán, County Galway.' *JRSAI* 20 (1990): 65–101.

—. 'The Layout of Irish Early Christian Monasteries.' In *Irland Und Europa, Die Kirche in Frühmittelalter*, edited by Próinséas Ní Chátháin and Michael Richter, 105–16. Stuttgart: Klett-Cotta, 1984.

—. 'The Ornamented Tomb of the Saint at Ardoileán, Co. Galway.' In *Ireland and Insular Art A.D. 500–1200*, edited by Michael Ryan, 141–43. Dublin: Royal Irish Academy, 1987.

Herwaarden, Jan Van. *Between Saint James and Erasmus: Studies in Late-Medieval Religious Life: Devotions and Pilgrimages in the Netherlands*. Leiden: Brill, 2003.

Higgins, Jim. *Claregalway Its Architecture, Archaeology and Its History*. Galway: Crow's Rock Press, forthcoming.

—. *St. James's Church & Cemetery, Gleninagh Heights, Galway*. Galway: Crow's Rock Press, 1996.

Hindle, Paul. 'Roads and Tracks.' In *The English Medieval Landscape*, edited by Leonard Cantor, 193–217. London: Croom Helm, 1982.

—. *Roads and Tracks for the Historian*. London: Philmore, 2001.

—. 'Seasonal Variation in Travel in Medieval England.' *Journal Transport History New Series* IV (78 1977): 170–78.

Holton, Karina. 'From Carters: Aspects of Fairs and Markets in Medieval Leinster.' In *Irish Fairs and Markets. Studies in Local History*, edited by Denis Cronin, Joe Gilligan and Karina Holton, 18–44. Dublin: Four Courts Press, 2001.

Hopper, Sarah. *Mothers, Mystics and Merrymakers. Medieval Women Pilgrims*. Stroud: Sutton Publishing, 2006.

—. *To Be a Pilgrim. The Medieval Pilgrimage Experience*. Stroud: Sutton Publishing, 2002.

Hore, Herbert F. 'Particulars Relative to Wexford and the Barony of Forth: By Colonel Solomon Richards, 1682.' *JKSEIAS*, 4, no.1 (1862): 84–92.

Horrox, Rosemary. *The Black Death*. Manchester: Manchester University Press, 1994.

Houlden, James Leslie. *Jesus in History, Thought, and Culture: An Encyclopedia*. Oxford: ABC-CLIO, 2003.

Houlihan, Michael. *The Holy Wells of County Clare*. Castleisland: Walsh Colour Print, 2015.

Hourihane, C. "Holye Crossys', a Catalogue of Processional, Altar, Pendant and Crucifix Figures for Late Medieval Ireland.' *PRIA* 100C no.1 (2000): 1–85.

Hughes, Harry. *Croagh Patrick (Cruach Phádraig – The Reek): An Ancient Mountain Pilgrimage*. Westport: Harry Hughes, 1991.

Hughes, Kathleen. *Church and Society in Ireland A.D. 400–1200*. Edited by David Dumville. London: Variorum Reprints, 1987.

—. *Early Christian Ireland: Introduction to the Sources*. Ithaca, NY: Cornell University Press, 1972.

—. 'The Changing Theory and Practice of Irish Pilgrimage.' *JEH* 11, no. 2 (1960): 143–51.

—. *The Church in Early Irish Society*. London: Methuen & Co Ltd, 1966.

Hughes, Kathleen, and Ann Hamlin. *The Modern Traveller to the Early Irish Church*. London: SPCK, 1977.

Huitson, Toby. *Stairway to Heaven: The Functions of Medieval Upper Spaces*. Oxford: Oxbow Books, 2014.

Hurley, Rev. Anthony. 'Blessed Thaddeus McCarthy, Bishop of Cork and Cloyne, 1490–1492.' *JCHAS* 2, no. 24 (1896): 497–509.

—. 'Blessed Thaddeus McCarthy, Bishop of Cork and Cloyne, 1490–1492 (Contd).' *JCHAS* 3, no. 27 (1897): 94–100.

Hurlock, Kathryn. *Medieval Welsh Pilgrimage, c.1100–1500*. Palgrave MacMillan, 2018.

Huxtable, Michael, and Ronan O'Donnell. 'Medieval Colour.' In *The Oxford Handbook of Later Medieval Archaeology in Britain*, edited by Christopher Gerrard and Alejandra Gutiérrez, 742–55. Oxford: Oxford University Press, 2018.

Ireland, Colin. 'Penance and Prayer in Water: An Irish Practice in Northumbrian Hagiography.' *Cambrian Medieval Celtic Studies* 34 (1997): 51-66.

Irish Manuscripts Commission. *Calendar of Entries in the Papal Registers Relating to Great Britain and Ireland. Papal Letters, Vol. XV: Innocent VIII: Lateran Registers 1484–1492*; Stationery Office for the Irish Manuscripts Commission, 1978.

Iterii, Bernard. *The Chronicle and Historical Notes of Bernard Itier*, edited by Andrew W. Lewis. Oxford: Oxford University Press, 2013.

Jacoby, David. 'Evolving Routes of Western Pilgrimage to the Holy Land, Eleventh to Fifteenth Century: An Overview.' In *Unterwegs Im Namen Der Religion/On the Road in the Name of Religion. Pilgern Als Form von Kontingenzbewältigung Und Zukunftssicherung in Den Weltreligionen/Pilgrimage as a Means of Coping with Contingency and Fixing the Future in the World's Major Religions*, edited by Klaus Herbers and Hans Christian Lehner, 2:75–97. Stuttgart: Franz Steiner Verlag, 2016.

James, David W. *St. David's and Dewisland: A Social History*. Cardiff: University of Wales Press, 1981.

Jefferies, Henry A. 'Erenaghs and Termonlands: Another Early Seventeenth-Century Account." *Seanchas Ardmhacha* 19, no. 1 (2002): 55–58.

—. The Armagh Registers and the Re-interpretation of Irish Church History on the Eve of the Reformation.' *Seanchas Ardmhacha* 18, no. 1 (1999): 81–99.

Johnson, Eric. 'Interaction with Relics.' In *Encyclopedia of Medieval Pilgrimage*, edited by Larissa J. Taylor et al., 287–90. Leiden: Brill, 2010.

Johnston, Ruth A. *All Things Medieval: An Encyclopedia of the Medieval World, Volume 1*. California: Greenwood Publishing Group, 2011.

Johnston, William M. *Encyclopedia of Monasticism*. London: Routledge, 2013.

Jones, G.H. *Celtic Britain and the Pilgrim Movement*. London: Honourable Society of Cymmrodorion, 1912.

Jones, Graham. 'Imaging Sant Magí: Souvenirs of a Catlan Pilgrimage' In *Beyond Pilgrim Souvenirs and Secular Badges. In Essays in Honour of Brian Spencer*, edited by Sarah Blick, 108–30. Oxford: Oxbow Books, 2007.

—. *Saints in the Landscapes*. Stroud: Tempus, 2007.

Jordan, Kieran, and Tom O'Connor. 'Archaeological Sites of Interest Surrounding The Turoe Stone.' *JGAHS* 55 (2003): 110–16.

Keats-Rohan, K.S.B. *Domesday Descendants: A Prosopography of Persons Occurring in English Documents, 1066–1166. Vol. II: Pipe Rolls to Cartae Baronum*. Woodbridge: Boydell Press, 2002.

Kehnel, Annette. *Clonmacnois – the Church and Lands of St. Ciarán. Change and Continuity in an Irish Monastic Foundation (6th to 16th Century)*. Münster: LIT Verlag, 1995.

Kelly, Eamonn P. 'Antiquities from Irish Holy Wells and Their Wider Context.' *Archaeology Ireland* 16, no. 2 (2002): 24–28.

Kelly, Fergus. *Early Irish Farming*. Dublin: Dublin Institute for Advanced Studies, 1997.

Kelly, Maria. *A History of the Black Death in Ireland*. Stroud: Tempus, 2001.

Kenney, James F. *The Sources for the Early History of Ireland: Ecclesiastical. An Introduction and Guide*. Dublin: Four Courts Press, 1993.

Kenny, Gillian. *Anglo-Irish and Gaelic Women in Ireland c. 1170–1540*. Dublin: Four Courts Press, 2007.

Kessler, Herbert L., and Johanna Zacharias. *Rome 1300. On the Path of the Pilgrim*. New Haven and London: Yale University Press, 2000.

Killanin, Lord, and Michael Duignan. *The Shell Guide to Ireland*. London: Ebury Press, 1967.

Kinsella, Stuart. 'From Hiberno-Norse to Anglo-Norman, c.1030–1300.' In *Christ Church Cathedral Dublin: A History*, edited by Kenneth Milne, 25–52. Dublin: Four Courts Press, 2000.

—. 'An architectural history of Christ Church Cathedral Dublin c.1540–1870' PhD thesis, Department of History of Art and Architecture of Trinity College Dublin 2009. http://www.tara.tcd.ie/handle/2262/77187 accessed 23/11/2019.

Klein, Holger. 'Relics of the Passion.' In *Encyclopedia of Medieval Pilgrimage*, edited by Larissa J. Taylor et al., 599–601. Leiden: Brill, 2010.

Koopmans, Rachel. *Wonderful to Relate: Miracle Stories and Miracle Collecting in High Medieval England*. Pennsylvania: University of Pennsylvania Press, 2011.

Köster, Kurt. 'Les Coquilles et Ensigns de Pèlerinage de Saint-Jacques de Compostelle et Les Routes de Saint–Jacques En Occident.' In *Santiago de Compostela; 100 Ans de Pèlerinage Européen, Europalia 85*, 85–95. Gent: Ausstellungskat, 1985.

Krasnodebska-D'Aughton, Malgorzata. 'Inflamed with Seraphic Ardor: Franciscan Learning and Spirituality in the Fourteenth-Century Irish Pilgrimage Account.' *Franciscan Studies* 70 (2012): 283–312.

—. 'Relics and Riches: Familiarising the Unknown in a Fourteenth-Century Pilgrimage Account from Ireland.' In *The Art, Literature and Material Culture of the Medieval World. Transition, Transformation and Taxonomy*, edited by Meg Boulton, Jane Hawkes and Melissa Herman, 111–24. Dublin: Four Courts Press, 2015.

Kupfer, Marcia. 'Symbolic Cartography in a Medieval Parish: From Spatialized Body to Painted Church at Saint-Aignan-Sur-Cher.' *Speculum* 75, no. 3 (2000): 615–67.

Lacey, Brian. *Archaeological Survey of County Donegal: A Description of the Field Antiquities of the County from the Mesolithic Period to the 17th Century A.D.* Lifford: Donegal County Council, 1983.

—. *Colum Cille and the Columban Tradition*. Dublin: Four Courts Press, 1997.

—ed. *The Life of Colum Cille by Manus O'Donnell*. Dublin: Four Courts Press, 1998.

Lanigan Wood, Helen. 'The Monastery of St Molaisse in Devenish from Early Christian Period until the End of the Medieval Period.' In *An Archaeological Survey of County Fermanagh. Volume 1. Part 2 The Early Christian and Medieval Periods*, edited by Claire Foley, Ronan McHugh and Brian Scott, 2 vols. Belfast: HMSO, 2014.

Lapidge, Michael. *The Cult of St Swithun*. Oxford: Oxford University Press, 2003.

Lash, Ryan. 'Pebbles and Peregrinatio: The Taskscape of Medieval Devotion on Inishark Island, Ireland.' *Med. Arch* 62 (2018): 82–103.

Lash, Ryan, Ian Kuijt, Elise Alonzi, Meredith Chesson and Tommy Burke. "Differing in Status, But One in Spirit': Sacred Space and Social Diversity at Island Monasteries in Connemara, Ireland.' *Antiquity* 92 (2018): 43–55.

Lawlor, Hugh Jackson. 'A Calendar of the Register of Archbishop Fleming.' *PRIA* 30 (1912): 94–190.

—. 'A Calendar of the Register of Archbishop Sweteman.' *PRIA* 29 (1911): 213–310.

—. 'A Calendar of the Liber Niger and Liber Albus of Christ Church, Dublin'. *PRIA* 27 (1908): 1–93.

Le Goff, Jacques. *The Birth of Purgatory*. Chicago: The University of Chicago Press, 1984.

Leask, Harold G. 'The Collegiate Church of St. Nicholas, Galway.' *JGAHS* 17 no. 1/2 (1936): 2–23.

—. *Irish Church Churches & Monastic Buildings: II: Gothic Architecture A.D. 1400*. Dundalgan Press, 1958.

Ledwich, Edward. *Antiquities of Ireland*. Dublin: Printed for Arthur Grueber, no. 59, Dame Street, 1790.

Lee John, *Cambridge and Its Economics. Studies in Regional and Local History, 3 vols*. Hatfield: University of Hertfordshire Press, 2005.

Lees, Clare A., and Gillian R. Overing, eds. *A Place to Believe In: Locating Medieval Landscapes*. University Park: Penn State University Press, 2006.

Legris, Albert, ed. *Life of St. Laurence O'Toole: Archbishop of Dublin (1128–1180)*. Dublin: Catholic Truth Society of Ireland, 1914.

Leslie, Shane. *Saint Patrick's Purgatory: A Record From History and Literature*. London: Burns Oates & Washbourne, 1932.

Lewis, Peter. *The Proctor's Accounts of Peter Lewis, 1564–1565*. Dublin: Four Courts Press, 1996.

Lewis, Samuel. *A Topographical Dictionary of Ireland, 2 vols*. London: Lewis and Co, 1837.

Limor, Ora. 'Earth, Stone, Water and Oil: Objects of Veneration in Holy Land Travel Narratives.' In *Natural Materials of the Holy Land and the Visual Translation of Place, 500–1500*, edited by Renana Bartal, Neta Bodner and Bianca Kuhnel, 3–18. London: Routledge Press, 2017.

Logan, Patrick. *The Holy Wells of Ireland*. Gerrards Cross: Smythe, 1980.

Lopez, Robert. 'The Evolution of Land Transport in the Middle Ages.' *Past and Present* IX (1956): 17–29.

Luard, Henry Richards, ed. *Lives of Edward the Confessor*. London: Longman, Brown, Green, Longmans, and Roberts, 1858. http://archive.org/details/livesedwardconf00luargoog.

Lubin, Helen. *The Worcester Pilgrim. Cathedral Publications, No. 1*. Worcester: Cathedral Publications, 1990.

Lucas, Anthony T. 'The Social Role of Relics and Reliquaries in Ancient Ireland.' *JRSAI* 116 (1986): 5–37.

—. 'Souterrains: The Literary Evidence.' *Béaloideas* 39/41 (1971): 165–91.

—. 'The Plundering and Burning of Churches in Ireland, 7th to 16th Century.' In *North Munster Studies. Essays in Commemoration of Monsignor Michael Moloney*, edited by Eitenne Rynne, 172–229. Limerick, 1967.

—. 'The Sacred Trees of Ireland.' *JCHAS* 68 (1963): 16–54.

—. 'Toghers or Causeways: Some Evidence From Archaeological, Literary, Historical and Place–Name Sources.' *PRIA* 85C (1985): 37–60.

Lutz, Gerhard. 'Introduction to the Late Medieval Pilgrim Architecture.' *Peregrinations* 1, no. 4 (2004): 1–14.

Lydon, James. 'Alexander Bicknor: Archbishop and Peculator.' *History Ireland* 1 (2) (1993): 14–17.

—. 'Parliament and the Community of Ireland.' In *Law and Disorder in Thirteenth-Century Ireland. The Dublin Parliament of 1297*, edited by James Lydon, 125–39. Dublin: Four Courts Press, 1997.

—. ed. *The Account Roll of the Priory of the Holy Trinity, Dublin, 1337–1346*. Dublin : Four Courts Press, 1996.

—. 'The Text and Its Context.' In *The Account Roll of the Priory of the Holy Trinity, Dublin, 1337–1346*, edited by James Mills, ix–xxii. Dublin: Four Courts Press, 1996.

—. 'Christ Church in the Later Medieval Irish World, 1300–1500.' In *Christ Church Cathedral Dublin: A History*, edited by Kenneth Milne, 75–94. Dublin: Four Courts Press, 2000.

—, ed. *Law and Disorder in Thirteenth-Century Ireland: The Dublin Parliament of 1297*. Dublin: Four Courts Press, 1997.

Lynch, Anthony. 'A Calendar of the Reassembled Register of John Bole, Archbishop of Armagh, 1457–71.' *Seanchas Ardmhacha* 15, no. 1 (1992): 113–85.

—. 'The Administration of John Bole, Archbishop of Armagh, 1457–71.' *Seanchas Ardmhacha* 14, no. 2 (1991): 39–108.

Lynch, Joseph, and Philip Adamo. *The Medieval Church: A Brief History*. 2nd ed. London: Routledge, 2014.

Lynch, P. J. 'Some of the Antiquities around St. Finan's Bay, County Kerry.' *JRSAI* 32, no. 1 (1902): 42–63.

Lyne, Ed. 'Lives through Time.' *Archaeology Ireland* 22 (2008): 17–21.

Lynn, Chris. 'Excavations at 46–48 Scotch Street, Armagh, 1979–80.' *UJA* 51 (1988): 69–84.

—. 'Some Fragments of Exotic Porphyry Found In Ireland.' *JIA* 2 (1984): 19–32.

Lyons, Mary Ann. *Church and Society in County Kildare, 1480–1547*. Dublin: Four Courts Press, 2000

Mac Airt Seán, ed. and tr, *The annals of Inisfallen: MS. Rawlinson B. 503,* revised ed. 1944. Dublin: Dublin Institute for Advanced Studies, 1951.

Mac Airt, Seán and Gearóid Mac Niocaill, eds. *The Annals of Ulster, to AD 1131*. Dublin: Dublin Institute for Advanced Studies, 1983.

Mac an Bhaird, Alan, ed. *The Journey of Viscount Ramon De Perellós to Saint Patrick's Purgatory.* CELT Cork, 2012. https://celt.ucc.ie/published/T100079A.html. Accessed 6 October 2017

Mac Carthy, B., ed. *Annala Uladh. Annals of Ulster, Otherwise, Annala Senait, Annals of Senait; A Chronicle of Irish Affairs A.D. 1379–1541*. Dublin: Stationery Office, 1895.

Mac Shamhráin, Ailbhe. *Church and Polity in Pre-Norman Ireland: The Case of Glendalough. Monographs 7*. Maynooth: An Sagart, 1996.

Macalister, Robert Alexander Stewart. *The Latin and Irish Lives of Ciarán*. London/New York: Society for Promoting Christian Knowledge & The Macmillan Company, 1921.

MacDonald, Aidan. 'Adomnán's Monastery of Iona.' In *Studies in The Cult of Saint Columba*, edited by Cormac Bourke, 24–44. Dublin: Four Courts Press, 1997.

MacDonald, Fiona. *The Plague and Medicine in the Middle Ages*. Milwaukee, WI: Gareth Stevens Pub Secondary Lib, 2005.

MacDonald, Philip, and Naomi Carver. 'Archaeological Excavations at Ballyhanna Graveyard – Chronology.' In *The Science of a Lost Medieval Gaelic Graveyard: The Ballyhanna Research Project*, edited by Catriona J. McKenzie, Eileen M. Murphy and Colm J. Donnelly, 47–84. Dublin: Transport Infrastructure Ireland (TII), 2015.

MacLeod, Catriona. 'Mediaeval Wooden Figure Sculptures in Ireland, Mediaeval Madonnas in the West.' *JRSAI* 75, no. 3 (1945): 167–182.

—. 'Medieval Wooden Figure Sculpture in Ireland. The Kilcorban St. Catherine and Calvary Figure.' *JRSAI* 75 no.4 (1945): 195–203.

—. 'Some Late Medieval Wood Sculptures in Ireland.' *JRSAI* 77, no.1 (1947): 53–62.

—. 'Some Medieval Wooden Figure Sculptures in Ireland. Statues of Irish Saints.' *JRSAI* 76, no.4 (1946): 155–70.

MacNeill, Máire. *The Festival of Lughnasa: A Study of the Survival of the Celtic Festival of the Beginning of Harvest*. Dublin: Folklore of Ireland Council, 2007, reprint 1962.

Magee, P. 'An Ancient Route to Lough Derg.' *Clogher Record* 7, no.3 (1971): 480–81.

Maggioni, Giovanni Paolo. 'The Tradition of Saint Patrick's Purgatory between Visionary Literature and Pilgrimage Reports.' *Studia Aurea* 11 (2017): 151–77.

Magoun, Francis P. 'The Pilgrim-Diary of Nikulas of Munkathvera: The Road to Rome.' *Journal of Mediaeval Studies* 6 (1944): 314–54.

Mahaffy, John. 'Two Early Tours in Ireland.' *Hermathea* 18 (40) (1914): 1–16.

Mahrt, William Peter. 'The Role of Old Sarum in the Processions of Salisbury Cathedral'. In *Study of Medieval Manuscripts of England: Festschrift in Honor of Richard W. Pfaff*, edited by Linda Doran and George Brown, 129–41. Tempe, Arizona: Arizona Center for Medieval and Renaissance Studies with Brepols, 2010.

Malone, Rev. Sylvester, trans. *Life of St. Flannan. Translated and Annotated by the Very Rev. S. Malone, V. G., M.R.I.A.* Dublin: James Duffy & Co, 1902.

Maloney, Colm, Louise Baker and Carmelita Troy. 'R417 Ardreigh Road Realignment. Final Report on Archaeological Investigations at Site 00E0156, in the Medieval Borough of Ardreigh, Athy, Co. Kildare. Report Kildare County Council.' Excavation Report, 2012.

Manning, Conleth. 'A Cross-Inscribed Pillar Stone on Tonelagee Mountain, Co. Wicklow.' *Wicklow Archaeology and History* 11 (1998): 26–28.

—. 'Rock Shelters and Caves Associated with Irish Saints.' In *Above and Beyond: Essays in Honour of Leo Swan*, edited by Tom Condit and Christiaan Corlett, 109–20. Dublin: Wordwell, 2005.

—. 'St Mullin's: An Early Ecclesiastical Site and Medieval Settlement in County Carlow.' *Archaeology Ireland Heritage Guides, No. 5*. Dublin: Wordwell, 1999.

Mant, Richard. *History of the Church of Ireland, from the Reformation to the Revolution.* London: John W. Parker, 1840.

Marshall, Jenny, White, Claire, Walsh, Grellan D. Rourke, E. V. Murray and Finbar McCormick. *High Island: An Irish Monastery in the Atlantic*. Dublin: Town House and Country House, 2000.

Marshall, Jenny White, and Claire Walsh. 'Illaunloughan, Co. Kerry: An Island Hermitage.' In *Early Medieval Munster Archaeology, History and Society*, edited by John Sheehan, 102–11. Cork: Cork University Press, 1998.

—. *Illaunloughan Island: An Early Medieval Monastery in County Kerry*. Dublin: Wordwell, 2005.

Martimort, Aimé Georges, ed. *The Church at Prayer*. Vol. 1. Shannon: Irish University Press, 1968.

Mason, William Monck. *The History and Antiquities of the Collegiate and Cathedral Church of St. Patrick near Dublin, from Its Foundation in 1190, to the Year 1819: Comprising a Topographical Account of the Lands and Parishes Appropriated to the Community of the Cathedral, and to Its Members, and Biographical Memoirs of Its Deans*. Dublin: Printed for William Monk Mason by W. Folds, 1820.

Matthew, E.A.E. 'The Governing of the Lancastrian Lordship of Ireland in the Time of James Butler, Fourth Earl of Ormond c. 1420–1452.' PhD thesis, Department of History, University of Durham,1995. https://core.ac.uk/download/pdf/109152.pdf accessed 24/09/2018.

McCormick, Finbar. 'Struell Wells: Pagan Past and Christian Present.' *JRSAI* 139 (2009): 45–62.

McDermott, Conor. 'A Paved Way In Bloomhill Bog in Counties Westmeath and Offaly.' In *Blackwater Survey and Excavations: Artefact Deterioration in Peat Lands, Lough More, Co. Mayo*, edited by Aonghus Moloney, 4:59–66. Dublin: Crannóg Publications, 1995.

McDermot, Conor and Louise Nugent. 'Preliminary Site Investigation at St. Kevin's Road Brockagh Townland, Co. Wicklow.' Unpublished Report, 2005.

McDermot, Conor, Brendan Fagan, Louise Nugent and Kim Rice. 'Preliminary Site Investigation at St. Kevin's Road, Brockagh Townland, Co. Wicklow.' Unpublished Report, 2006.

McEneaney, Eamonn. 'Politics and the Art of Devotion in Late Fifteenth-Century Waterford.' In *Art and Devotion In Late Medieval Ireland*, edited by Rachel Moss, Colmán Ó Clabaigh and Salvador Ryan, 33–50. Dublin: Four Courts, 2006.

McEnery, M J., and Raymond Refaussé, eds. *Christ Church Deeds*. Dublin: Four Courts Press, 2001.

McGrath, Mary. 'The Materials and Techniques of Irish Medieval Wall-Paintings.' *JRSAI* 117 (1987): 96–124.

McGuinness, David. 'Some Antiquities of the Early Christian Period on Three Rock Mountain, Co. Dublin.' *Wicklow Archaeology and History* 2 (2002): 45–60.

McMahon, Mary. St Audoen's Church, Cornmarket, Dublin: Archaeology and Architecture. Dublin: The Stationery Office, 2006.

McNally, Fiona Rose. 'The Evolution of Pilgrimage Practice in Early Modern Ireland.' MLitt thesis, Department of History, National University of Ireland, Maynooth, 2012. http://mural.maynoothuniversity.ie/3997/ accessed 18/10/2018.

McNeill, Charles. 'Accounts of Sums Realised by Sales of Chattels of Some Suppressed Irish Monasteries.' *JRSAI* 12, no. 1 (1922): 11–37.

Meek, Christine. 'Beyond the Frontier: Irishmen and Irish Goods in Lucca in the Later Middle Ages'. In *Colony and Frontier in Medieval Ireland*, edited by Terry Barry, Robin Frame, and Katherine Simms, 229–41. London: Hambledon Press, 1995.

Meigs, Samantha A. *The Reformation in Ireland: Tradition and Confessionalism, 1400–1690*. London: Macmillan Press, 1997.

Melman, Billie. 'The Middle East/Arabia: "The Cradle of Islam".' In *The Cambridge Companion to Travel Writing. Cambridge Companions to Literature*, edited by Peter Hulme and Tim Youngs, 105–21. Cambridge: Cambridge University Press, 2002.

Merrifield, Ralph. *The Archaeology of Ritual and Magic*. London: Batsford, 1987.

Metzler, Irina. *Disability in Medieval Europe: Thinking about Physical Impairment in the High Middle Ages, c. 1100–c. 1400*. New York: Routledge Press, 2006.

Meyer, Kuno. *Aislinge Meic Conglinne: The Vision of MacConglinne, a Middle-Irish Wonder Tale.* London: D. Nutt, 1892.

—, ed. *Betha Colmáin Maic Lúacháin: The Life of Colman Son of Luachan*. Dublin: Hodges & Figgis & Co. Ltd, 1911.

—, ed. *Liadain and Cuirithir. An Irish Love-Story of the Ninth Century*. Translated by Kuno Meyer. London: D–Nutt, 1902.

—. *The Triads of Ireland. Royal Irish Academy Todd Lecture Series*. Vol. XIII. Dublin: Hodges & Figgis & Co. Ltd, 1906.

Mills, James. 'Sixteenth-Century Notices of the Chapels and Crypts of the Church of the Holy Trinity, Dublin.' *JRSAI*, 10, no. 3 (1900): 195–203.

—, ed. *Calendar of the Justiciary Rolls, or Proceedings in the Court of the Justiciar of Ireland Preserved in the Public Record Office of Ireland/Edited by James Mills, under the Direction of the Master of the Rolls in Ireland. XXIII to [XXXV] Years of Edward I*. Dublin: HMSO, 1905.

—, ed. *The Account Roll of the Priory of the Holy Trinity, Dublin, 1337–1346*. Dublin: Four Courts Press, 1996.

Milne, Kenneth, ed. *Christ Church Cathedral Dublin: A History*. Dublin: Four Courts Press, 2010.

Modesti, Paola. 'Venice.' In *Encyclopedia of Medieval Pilgrimage*, 784–90. Leiden: Brill, 2010.

Moore, *Fionnbarr. Ardfert Cathedral. Summary of Excavation Results*. Dublin: Stationery Office, 2007.

Moore, Thomas. *The History of Ireland*. 3 vols. London: Longman Press, 1851.

Morahan, Leo. 'A Wealth of Monuments from Croagh Patrick Archaeological Survey.' *Cathair Na Mart* 18 (1998): 143–50.

—. *Croagh Patrick, Co. Mayo – Archaeology, Landscape and People*. Westport: Croagh Patrick Archaeological Committee, 2001.

Moran, Josephine. 'The Shattered Image: Archaeological Evidence for Painted and Stained Glass in Medieval Ireland.' In *Art and Devotion in Late Medieval Ireland*, edited by Rachel Moss, Colmán Ó Clabaigh and Salvador Ryan, 121–41. Dublin: Four Courts Press, 2006.

—. 'The Window Glass.' In *Kells Priory, Co. Kilkenny: Archaeological Excavations*, edited by Miriam Clyne, 261–316. Dublin: Stationery Office, 2007.

Morrin, James. ed. *Calendar of the Patent and Close Rolls of Chancery in Ireland, Henry VIII to 18th Elizabeth.* Dublin: HMSO, 1861.

—. *Calendar of the Patent and Close Rolls of Chancery in Ireland, from the 18th to the 45th of the Queen Elizabeth.* Dublin: Alexander Thom, 1862

Morris, Bridget, ed. *The Revelations of St. Birgitta of Sweden: Liber Caelestis, Books VI–VII. Introduction & Notes by Bridget Morris.* Translated by Denis Searby. 3 vols. Oxford: Oxford University Press, 2006.

Morris, Colin. *The Papal Monarchy: The Western Church from 1050 to 1250 (Oxford History of the Christian Church).* Oxford: Oxford University Press, 1991.

Morrison, Susan. *Women Pilgrims in Late Medieval England.* London: Routledge, 2002.

Morrissey, James, ed. *Statute Rolls of the Parliament of Ireland, 12th and 13th to the 21st and 22nd Years of the Reign of King Edward IV.* Dublin: Stationery Office, 1939.

Morton, Karena. 'The Wall Painting Fragments.' In *Kells Priory, Co Kilkenny: Archaeological Excavations,* edited by Miriam Clyne, 206–24. Dublin: Stationery Office, 2007.

Moss, Rachel. 'Architectural Sculpture at Glendalough.' In *Glendalough City of God,* edited by Charles Doherty, Linda Doran and Mary Kelly, 278–301. Dublin: Four Courts Press, 2011.

Mullins, Edwin. *The Pilgrimage to Santiago.* Devon: Readers Union Ltd, 1975.

Mulveen, Jack. 'Tóchar Phádraic: Mayo's Penitential and Sculptured Highway.' *JGAHS* 51 (1999): 167–81.

Murphy, Rev. Denis, ed. *The Annals of Clonmacnoise, Being Annals of Ireland from the Earliest Times to A.D. 1408.* Felinfach (Ceredigion): Llanerch Press, 1896.

Murphy, Richard. 'Omey Island.' *Irish University Review* 22, no. 1 (1992): 179.

Murray, Griffin. 'The Aghadoe and River Laune Crosiers.' In *Medieval Treasures of County Kerry,* edited by Griffin Murray. Tralee: Kerry County Museum, 2010.

—. *The Cross of Cong: A Masterpiece of Medieval Irish Art.* Dublin: Irish Academic Press, 2014.

—, ed. *The Medieval Treasures of County Kerry.* Tralee: Kerry County Museum, 2010.

Murray, Griffin Joseph. *The Cross of Cong and Church Metalwork from Romanesque Ireland.* Dublin: Irish Academic Press in Association with the National Museum of Ireland, 2007.

Murray Jones, Peter. 'Amulets: Prescriptions and Surviving Objects from Late Medieval England.' In *Beyond Pilgrim Souvenirs and Secular Badges. Essays in Honour of Brian Spencer,* edited by Sarah Blick, 92–107. Oxford: Oxbow Books, 2007.

Murray, Laurence P. 'A Calendar of the Register of Primate George Dowdall, Commonly Called the "Liber Niger" or "Black Book".' *JLAS* 6 no. 2 (1926): 90–100.

—. 'A Calendar of the Register of Primate George Dowdall, Commonly Called the 'Liber Niger' or 'Black Book.' (Continued)'. *JLAS* 6 no. 3 (1927): 147–58.

—. 'Archbishop Cromer's Register.' *JLAS* 7 no. 4 (1932): 516–24.

—. 'Archbishop Cromer's Register. (Continued).' *JLAS* 8 no. 2 (1934): 169–88.

—. 'Archbishop Cromer's Register. (Continued).' *JLAS* 8 no. 3 (1935): 257–74.

—. 'Archbishop Cromer's Register. (Continued).' *JLAS* 8 no. 4 (1936): 322–51.

—. 'Archbishop Cromer's Register. (Continued).' *JLAS* 9 no. 1 (1937): 36–41.

Neuman De Vegvar, Carol. 'Romanitas and Realpolitik in Cogitosus' Description of the Church of St Brigit, Kildare.' In *The Cross Goes North: Processes of Conversion in Northern Europe, AD 300–1300,* edited by Martin Carver, 153–70. Woodbridge: Boydell Press, 2003.

Newell, William Wells. 'William of Malmesbury on the Antiquity of Glastonbury.' *PMLAA,* 18, no. 4 (1903): 459–512.

Newett, Mary Margaret, ed. *Canon Pietro Casola's Pilgrimage to Jerusalem in the Year 1494.* Manchester: Manchester University Press, 1907.

Nicholls, Kenneth. 'The Register of Clogher.' *Clogher Record* 72, no. 3 (1971): 361–431.

Nicolas, Harris, ed. *Proceedings and Ordinances of the Privy Council of England: 22 Henry VI MCCCCXLIII TO 39 Henry VI. MCCCCLXI*. London: The Commission of Public Records, 1837.

Nilson, Ben. *Cathedral Shrines of Medieval Europe*. Woodbridge: Boydell Press, 1998.

—. 'The Medieval Experience of a Shrine.' In *Pilgrimage Explored*, edited by Jennie Stopford, 95–122. Woodbridge: Boydell Press, 1999.

Northern Ireland Place–Name Project 'Placenamesni.org.' Accessed 14 July 2018.

http://www.placenamesni.org/resultdetails.php?entry=17513. Accessed 09/09/2018.

Nolan, Rita. *Within the Mullet*. Naas: Leinster Leader, 3rd ed., 2000.

Nugent Louise. 'Pilgrimage and the Augustinians in Medieval Ireland.' In *Households of God: The Regular Canons and Canonesses of St Augustine and of Prémontré in Medieval Ireland*, edited by Martin Browne and Colmán Ó Clabaigh, 215–234. Dublin: Four Courts Press 2019.

—. 'Gathering of Faith: Pilgrimage in Early Medieval Ireland.' In *Proceedings of the Conference of The Archaeology of Gatherings of Sligo IT*, edited by Fiona Beglane, 20–30. Oxford: Archaeopress, 2016.

—. 'St Kevin's Road: Relics of a Pilgrim Landscapes in the Wicklow Mountains.' *In Archaeology, People, and Landscapes: Essays in Honor of Jenna Higgins*, edited by Thomas Finan, 175–216. St. Louis: Institute of European Archaeology Press, 2012.

—. 'A 17th-Century Kilkenny Pilgrim.' *Old Kilkenny Review* 67 (2015): 48–54.

—. 'A Short Note on the Co. Wicklow Labyrinth Stone.' *KAJ*, 2012, 330–34.

—. 'Barrigone Holy Well and the Crimean War: An Unlikely Connection.' *NMAJ* 56 (2016):121–126.

—. 'Exploring the Evidence for Early Medieval Pilgrimage at Kilcolman.' *JKAHS* 13, no. 2 (2013): 23–50.

—. 'Medieval Pilgrims' Tokens and Other Souvenirs in Ireland: A Review of the Archaeological and Historical Evidence.' In *Irish Maritime Heritage. Proceedings of the 3rd Galway International Heritage Conference 2013*, edited by Jim Higgins, 25–46. Galway: Crow's Rock Press, 2013.

—. 'Pilgrimage at Croagh Patrick from Medieval to Modern Times.' In *Recent Explorations and Discoveries in Irish Heritage*, edited by Jim Higgins, 41–55. Galway: Crow's Rock Press, 2017.

—. 'Pilgrimage in Medieval Ireland, AD 600–1600.' Unpublished PhD thesis, School of Archaeology, University College Dublin, 2009.

—. 'The Rian Bó Phádraig. A Reappraisal of an Ancient Pilgrim Road.' Unpublished MA thesis, Department of Celtic Civilisation, University College Cork, 2001.

Nugent, Louise, and Richard Scriven. *Wells, Graves and Statues: Exploring the Heritage and Culture of Pilgrimage in Medieval and Modern Cork City*. Cork: Cork City Council, 2015.

O'Brien, Camin, and David Sweetman. *Archaeological Inventory of County Offaly*. Dublin: The Stationery Office, 1997.

O'Byrne, Emmett. '"A Divided Loyalty": The MacMurroughs, the Irish of Leinster and the Crown of England 1340–1420.' In *Carlow: History & Society. Interdisciplinary Essays of the History of an Irish County*, edited by Thomas McGrath and William Nolan, 272–306. Dublin: Geography Press, 2008.

O'Byrne, Theresa. 'Centre or Periphery? The Role of Dublin in James Yonge's Memorial (1412).' In *Dublin: Renaissance City of Literature*, edited by Kathleen Miller and Crawford Gribben, 16–37. Oxford: Oxford University Press, 2017.

Ó Cadhla, Stiofán. *The Holy Well Tradition. The Pattern of St Declan, Ardmore, County Waterford, 1800–2000*. Dublin: Four Courts Press, 2002.

Ó Carragáin, Tomás. 'A Landscape Converted: Archaeology and Early Church Organisation on Iveragh and Dingle, Ireland.' In *The Cross Goes North: Processes of Conversion in Northern Europe, AD 300–1300*, edited by Michael Carver, 127–52. Woodbridge: Boydell Press, 2003.

—. 'Archaeology of Early Medieval Baptism at St Mullin's, Co Carlow.' *Peritia* 21 (2010): 285–302.

—. *Churches in Early Medieval Ireland: Architecture, Ritual and Memory*. Paul Mellon Centre for Studies in British Art. New Haven and London: Yale University Press, 2010.

—. 'The Architectural Setting of the Cult of Relics in Early Medieval Ireland.' *JRSAI* 133 (2003): 130–76.

—. 'The View from the Shore: Perceiving Island Monasteries in Early Medieval Ireland.' *Hortus Artium Medievalium* 19 (2013): 209–20.

O'Carroll, Ellen. '1996:327. Lemanaghan Togher.' Database of Irish Excavation Reports, 1996. http://excavations.ie accessed 03/02/2017.

Ó Clabaigh, Colmán. 'Anchorites in Late Medieval Ireland.' In *Anchoritic Traditions of Medieval Europe*, edited by Liz Herbert McAvoy, 153–77. Woodbridge: Boydell Press, 2010.

—. 'The Church, 1050–1460.' In *The Cambridge History of Ireland*, edited by Brendan Smith, 355–84. Cambridge: Cambridge University Press, 2018.

—. *The Friars in Ireland 1224–1540*. Dublin: Four Courts Press, 2012.

—. 'The Liber Niger of Christ Church Cathedral, Dublin.' In *The Medieval Manuscripts of Christ Church Cathedral, Dublin*, edited by Raymond Gillespie and Raymond Refaussé. Dublin: Four Courts Press, 2006.

Ó Clabaigh, Colmán, and Michael Stanton. 'Thomas Becket and Ireland.' In *Listen, O Isles, unto Me: Studies in Medieval Word and Image in Honour of Jennifer O'Reilly*, edited by Elizabeth Mullins, and Diarmuid Scully, 87–101. Cork: Cork University Press, 2011.

O'Clery Michael. ed. *Annals of the Kingdom of Ireland from the earliest times to the year 1616 / the Four Masters [Michael O'Clery et al.] ; introduction by Kenneth Nicholls*. Dublin: De Búrca Rare Books, 1990.

Ó Corráin, Donnchadh. *The Irish Church, Its Reform and the English Invasion*. Dublin: Four Courts Press, 2017.

O'Donovan, John, and Eugene Curry. *The Antiquities of County Clare*. Ennis: CLASP Press, 2003.

O'Donovan, John. *Annala Rioghachta Eireann: Annals of the Kingdom of Ireland by the Four Masters, from the Earliest Period to the Year 1616. Edited from MSS in the Library of the Royal Irish Academy and of Trinity College Dublin with a Translation and Copious Notes.* 4 vols. Dublin: Hodges & Smith, 1845.

—. 'The Registry of Clonmacnoise; With Notes and Introductory Remarks.' *JKSEIAS* 1, no. 2 (1857): 444–60.

—. *The Martyrology of Donegal: A Calendar of the Saints of Ireland/Michael O'Clery; Translated from the Original Irish by John O'Donovan; Edited, with the Irish Text, by James Henthorn Todd, and by William Reeves.* Dublin: Printed for the Irish Archaeological and Celtic Society by A. Thom, 1864.

Ó Dufaigh, Seosamh. 'Two Poems on St Patrick's Purgatory.' In *History of the Diocese of Clogher*, Clogher, edited by Henry A. Jefferies, 108-33. Dublin: Four Courts Press, 2005.

Ó Dúshláine, Tadhg. 'Lough Derg in Native Irish Poetry.' *Clogher Record* 13, no. 1 (1988): 76–84.

—. 'Lough Derg in Native Irish Poetry.' *Clogher Record* 3, no. 1 (1988): 76–84.

Ó Floinn, Raghnall. 'Beginnings: Early Medieval Ireland, AD 500–850.' In *Treasures of The National Museum of Ireland*, edited by Raghnall Ó Floinn and Patrick Wallace, 171–212. Dublin: Gill & Macmillan, 2002.

—. 'Clonmacnoise: Art and Patronage in the Early Medieval Period.' In *From the Isles of the North. Early Medieval Art in Ireland and Britain*, edited by Cormac Bourke, 251–260. Belfast: HMSO, 1995.

—. 'Clonmacnoise: Art and Patronage in the Early Medieval Period.' In *Clonmacnoise. Studies. Seminar Papers*, edited by Heather King, 87–100. Dublin: The Heritage Council, 1998.

—. 'Insignia Columbae.' In *Studies in the Cult of Saint Columba*, edited by Cormac Bourke, 136–61. Dublin: Four Courts Press, 1997.

—. *Irish Shrines & Reliquaries of the Middle Ages.* Dublin: Town House and Country House, 1994.

—. 'Late Medieval Ireland, AD 1150–1550.' In *Treasures of The National Museum of Ireland. Irish Antiquities*, edited by Raghnall Ó Floinn and Patrick Wallace, 257–301. Dublin: Gill & Macmillan, 2002.

—. 'The Foundation Relics of Christ Church Cathedral and the Origins of the Diocese of Dublin.' In *Medieval Dublin VII. Proceedings of the Friends of Medieval Dublin Symposium 2005*, edited by Séan Duffy, 89–102. Dublin: Four Courts Press, 2006.

—. 'The Late-Medieval Relics of Holy Trintiy Church, Dublin.' In *Dublin in the Medieval World. Studies in Honour of Howard B. Clarke*, edited by John Bradley, Alan. J Fletcher, and Anngret Simms, 369–98. Dublin: Four Courts Press, 2009.

Ó Floinn, Raghnall, and Heather King. 'Archaeological Investigations at St Ciarán.' In *Clonmacnoise Studies. Seminar Papers*, edited by Heather King, :119–32. Dublin: The Heritage Council, 1994.

Ó Giolláin, Diarmuid. 'Revisting the Holy Well.' *Éire-Ireland* 40, nos. 1 and 2 (2005): 11–41.

—. 'The Pattern.' In *Irish Popular Culture 1650–1850*, edited by James S. Donnelly and Kerby A. Miller, 201–21. Dublin: Irish Academic Press, 1999.

Ó Háinle, Cathal. 'The Pater Noster in Ireland: The Pre Reformation Period.' *Celtica* 21 (1990): 470–88.

O'Hanlon, Rev. John and Rev. Edward O'Leary. *History of the Queen's County.* Vol. 1. Kilkenny: Robert Books Ltd, 1907.

Ó hAodha, Donnchadh, ed. *Bethu Brigte*. Dublin: Dublin Institute for Advanced Studies, 1978.

O'Hara, Alexander, and Faye Taylor. 'Aristocratic and Monastic Conflict in Tenth–Century Italy: The Case of Bobbio and the Miracula Sancti Columbani.' *Viator* 44, no. 3 (2013): 43–60.

Ó hÉaluighthe, D. M.A. 'Saint Gobnet of Ballyvourney.' *JCHAS* 57 (1952): 43–61.

Ó hInnse, Séamus, ed. *Miscellaneous Irish Annals (A.D.1114–1437), Fragment Vol I–III*, Dublin: Dublin Institute for Advanced Studies, 1947.

Ó hÓgáin, Dáithí, ed. *Duanaire Thiobraid Árann: Cnuasach d'fhilíocht Ndaoine ó Oirdheisceart an Chontae*. Baile Átha Cliath/Dublin: An Clóchomhar, 1981.

O'Keeffe, Peter, and Tom Simington. *Irish Stone Bridges. History and Heritage*. Dublin: Irish Academic Press, 1991.

O'Keeffe, Tadhg. *Medieval Ireland: An Archaeology*. Tempus, 2000.

O'Kelly, Michael J. 'Church Island Near Valencia, Co. Kerry'. *PRIA* 59 (1957): 57–136.

—. 'The Belt-Shrine from Moylough, Sligo.' *JRSAI* 95, no.1/2 (1965): 149–88.

O'Laverty, James. *An Historical Account of the Diocese of Down and Connor, Ancient and Modern*. Dublin: James Duffy & Co, 1878.

O'Leary, Patrick. *St. Mullins Illustrated: A Local History and the Life of St. Moling/Compiled from Ancient MSS. with Notes and Traditions by Patrick O'Leary.* Graigue-na-Managh: s.n., 1913.

O'Leary, Patrick, trans. *The Ancient Life of Saint Molyng. Being Translation of an Old Manuscript at Marsh's Library, Dublin. With Notes and Translation by P. O'Leary*. Dublin: James Duffy and Sons, 1887.

O'Loughlin, Thomas. *Celtic Theology. Humanity, World and God in Early Irish Writings*. London/New York: Continuum, 2005.

O'Meara, John. trans. *The History and Topography of Ireland by Giraldus Cambrensis.* Portlaoise: Dolmen Press, 1982.

O Mórdha, P. 'Saint Patrick's Well, Clonfad.' *Clogher Record* 8, no. 3 (1975): 281–84.

O'Neill, Tim. *Merchants and Mariners in Medieval Ireland.* Dublin: Irish Academic Press, 1987.

Ó Riain, Pádraig. *A Dictionary of Irish Saints.* Dublin: Four Courts Press, 2011.

—. *Beatha Bharra: Saint Finbarr of Cork.* Dublin: Irish Texts Society, 1994.

—. 'Boundary Association in Early Irish Society.' *Studia Celtica* 7 (1972): 12–29.

—. *Four Tipperary Saints. The Lives of Colum of Terryglass, Crónán of Roscrea, Mochaomhóg of Leigh and Ruadhán of Lorrha.* Dublin: Four Courts Press, 2014.

—. 'The Calendar and Martrology of Christ Church Cathedral, Dublin.' In *The Medieval Manuscripts of Christ Church Cathedral, Dublin,* edited by Raymond Gillespie and Raymond Refaussé. Dublin: Four Courts Press, 2006.

—. *The Making of a Saint: Finbarr of Cork 600–1200.* Dublin: Irish Texts Society, 1997.

—. *Four Offaly Saints. The Lives of St Ciarán of Clonmacnoise, Ciarán of Seir, Colmán of Lynally and Fíonán of Kinnitty.* Dublin: Four Courts Press, 2018.

Ó Riain-Raedel, Dagmar. 'The Irish Medieval Pilgrimage to Santiago de Compostela.' *History Ireland* 6, 3 (1998): 17–21.

—. 'A German Visitor to Monaincha in 1591.' *Tipp. Hist. Jour.* 22 (1998): 223–33.

—. 'Holy Cross, Co Tipperary: Pilgrimage Site and Boon to Antiquarians,' unpublished article supplied by author.

Ó Ríordáin, Breandán. 'Excavations at High Street and Winetavern Street, Dublin,' *Med. Arch* 15 (1971): 73–85.

O'Sullivan, Aidan, and Donal Boland. 'The Clonmacnoise Bridge: An Early Medieval River Crossing in County Offaly.' *Archaeology Ireland. Heritage Guide No. 11.* Dublin: Wordwell, 2000.

O'Sullivan, Aidan, Conor McDermott, and Matt Seaver. 'Archaeological Excavations at Templeteenaun, Co. Wicklow: A Medieval Chapel on St Kevin's Pilgrim's Road to Glendalough.' *PRIA*, forthcoming.

O'Sullivan, Aidan, Conor McDermott and Graham Warren. 'Stratigraphical Report on Archaeological Excavations at Templeteenaun (Ballinagee Townland), Co. Wicklow. Preliminary Report. School of Archaeology UCD.' Unpublished Excavation Report, 2008.

O'Sullivan, Ann, and Sheehan John. *The Iveragh Peninsula: An Archaeological Survey of South Kerry.* Cork: Cork University Press, 1996.

O'Sullivan, Catherine. *Hospitality in Medieval Ireland 900–1500.* Dublin: Four Courts Press, 2004.

O'Sullivan, Jerry, and Tomás Ó Carragáin. *Inishmurray: Archaeological Survey and Excavations 1997–2000.* Cork: Collins Press, 2008.

O'Donovan, John. *Ordnance Survey Letters Down: Letters Containing Information Relative to the Antiquities of the County of Down Collected during the Progress of the Ordnance Survey in 1834.* Edited by Michael Herity. Dublin: Four Masters Press, 2003.

O'Hanlon, John, ed. *Life of St. Brigid, Virgin: First Abbess of Kildare, Special Patroness of Kildare Diocese, and General Patroness of Ireland.* Dublin: Joseph Dollard, 1877.

Ohler, Norbert. *The Medieval Traveller.* Translated by Caroline Hillier. Woodbridge: Boydell Press, 1989.

O'Keeffe, Grace. 'The Hospital of St John the Baptist in Medieval Dublin: Functions and Maintenance.' In *Medieval Dublin IX. Proceedings of the Friends of Medieval Dublin Symposium 2007,* edited by Séan Duffy, 166–82. Dublin: Four Courts Press, 2009.

O'Keeffe, Tadhg. *Ireland's Round Towers: Buildings, Rituals and Landscapes of the Early Irish Church.* Stroud: Tempus, 2004.

—. *Medieval Irish Buildings, 1100–1600.* Dublin: Four Courts Press, 2015.

—. 'Omey and the Sands of Time.' *Archaeology Ireland* 8, no. 2 (1994): 14–17.

Oldfield, Paul. *Sanctity and Pilgrimage in Medieval Southern Italy, 1000–1200.* Cambridge: Cambridge University Press, 2014.

Orpen, Goddard H. 'Carved Stone near Hollywood, Co. Wicklow.' *JRSAI,* 41 (1911): 183–88.

Orpen, Goddard H. 'The Fitz Geralds, Barons of Offaly'.' *JRSAI* 4, no. 2 (1914): 99–113.

—. 'The Hollywood Stone.' *JRSAI* 19, no. 2 (1929): 176–79.

Orpen, Goddard H. 'The Hollywood Stone and the Labyrinth of Knossos.' *JRSAI* 13, no. 2 (1923): 177–89.

Osheim, Duane. 'Plague Saints.' In *Encyclopedia of Medieval Pilgrimage*, edited Larissa J. Taylor et al., 573. Leiden: Brill, 2010.

Otway-Ruthven, Annette Jocelyn. *A History of Medieval Ireland.* E. Benn, 1980.

Overbey, Karen Eileen. *Sacral Geographies. Saints, Shrines, and Territory in Medieval Ireland.* Turnhout: Brepols Press, 2012.

P. 'Petrification and Pebbles.' *BMLJ* 1 (1825): 488–95.

Paor, Liam de. 'The Early Historic Period: Monks and Traders.' In *Travel and Transport in Ireland,* edited by Kevin Nowlan, 18–31. Dublin: Gill & Macmillan, 1973.

Peers, Glenn. *Sacred Shock: Framing Visual Experience in Byzantium.* Pennsylvania: Pennsylvania State University Press, 2004.

Peraica, M., B. Radic, A. Lucic and M. Pavlovic. 'Toxic Effects of Mycotoxins in Human.' *Bulletin of the World Health Organization.* 77 (1999): 724–66.

Petrie, George. *The Ecclesiastical Architecture of Ireland, an Essay on the Origins and Uses of the Round Towers of Ireland.* Shannon: Irish University Press, 1845.

Plummer, Charles. *Bethada Náem NÉrenn: Lives of Irish Saints/Edited from the Original Mss., with Introduction, Translation, Notes, Glossary, and Indexes by Charles Plummer.* 2 vols. Oxford: Clarendon Press, 1922.

—, ed. 'The Life of Mac Creiche.' In *Miscellanea Hagiographica Hibernica,* 171–286. Subsidia Hagiographica 15. Brussels: Société des Bollandistes, 1925.

—. 'The Miracles of Senan.' *Zeitschrift Für Celtische Philologie.* 10 (1914): 1–35.

—. *Venerabilis Baedae Opera Historica.* 2 vols. Oxford: Clarendon Press, 1896.

—. 'Vie et Miracles de S. Laurent Archevêque de Dublin.' *Analecta Bollandiana* 33 (1919): 121–86.

—. *Vitae Sanctorum Hiberniae* 2 vols. Oxford: Clarendon Press: 1910, reprinted 1968.

Potterton, Michael. *Medieval Trim: History and Archaeology.* Dublin: Four Courts Press, 2005.

—. 'The Archaeology and History of Medieval Trim, County Meath.' PhD thesis, Department of History National University of Ireland Maynooth, 2003 http://mural.maynoothuniversity.ie/5121/. Accessed 30/03/2018.

Power, Rev. Patrick. *Life of St. Declan of Ardmore and Life of St. Mochuda of Lismore. With Introduction, Translation and Notes.* London: Irish Texts Society, 1914.

Powicke F. M, and C. R Heney, eds. *Councils and Synods with Other Documents Relating to the English Church, Vol. II : AD 1205–1313.* Oxford: Clarendon Press, 1964.

Preston, Sarah Marya. 'The Canons Regular of St. Augustine in Medieval Ireland: An Overview.' PhD thesis, Department of History, Trinity College Dublin, Ireland, 1996. http://www.tara.tcd.ie/handle/2262/77241 accessed 10/10/2018.

Price, Liam. 'Glendalough: St. Kevin's Road.' In *FéilSgríbhinn Éoin Mhic Néil,* edited by John Ryan, 244–71. Dublin: Four Courts Press, 1940.

—. 'Rock-Basins or "Bullauns", at Glendalough and Elsewhere.' *JRSAI* 89 (1959): 161–88.

—. *The Place-Names of Co. Wicklow. The Barony of Talbotstown Lower.* Vol. IV. Dublin: Dublin Institute for Advanced Studies, 1983.

Price, Roger, and Michael Ponsford. *St Bartholomew's Hospital, Bristol: The Excavation of a Medieval Hospital 1976–1978. CBA Research Report 110.* York: Council for British Archaeology, 1998.

Prince, John. *Danmonii Orientales Illustres: Or, The Worthies of Devon*. London: Printed for Rees & Curtis, Plymouth, 1810.

Pringle, Denys. *Pilgrimage to Jerusalem and the Holy Land, 1187–1291*. London/New York: Routledge Press, 2012.

Payne Steven, 2015. 'Pilgrims Progress – Posts |Facebook.' https://En–Gb.Facebook.Com/14thcenturypilgrimsprogress/Posts/?Ref=page_internal. Accessed 18 May 2018.

Quaife, P. 'Stone Pilgrims in England and Wales.' *Confratenity of St James Bulletin* 7 (1984): 6–8.

Quinn D.B. 'The Bills and Statutes of the Irish Parliaments of Henry VII and Henry VIII,' edited by D. B. Quinn. *Anal. Hib.* 10, 1941.

Radford, C.A R., and G Donaldson. *Whithorn and the Ecclesiastical Monuments of Wigtownshire. Historic Scotland Guide*. Edinburgh: HMSO, 2002.

Rae, E. 'Irish Sepulchral Monuments of the Later Middle Ages. Part I the Ormond Group.' *JRSAI* 100 (1) (1970): 1–38.

Ralph, K. 'Medieval Antiquarianism: The Butlers and Artistic Patronage in Fifteenth–Century Ireland.' *JASIMS* 7 (2014): 2–27.

Ray, Celeste. *The Origins of Ireland's Holy Wells*. Oxford: Archaeopress, 2014.

Ree, Nona, and John Terry. *Pilgrimage. A Welsh Perspective*. Llandysul: Gomer Press, 2002.

Refaussé, Raymond. 'Introduction.' In *Christ Church Cathedral Dublin: A History*, edited by Kenneth Milne, 1–22. Dublin: Four Courts Press, 2000.

Refaussé, Raymond, and Colm Lennon, eds. *The Registers of Christ Church Cathedral, Dublin*. Dublin: Four Courts Press, 1998.

Richardson, Hilary. 'Visual Arts and Society.' In *A New History of Ireland. Prehistoric and Early Ireland*, edited by Donnchadh Ó Cróinín, 680–713. Oxford: Oxford University Press, 2005.

Richardson, John. *The Great Folly, Superstition, and Idolatry, of Pilgrimages in Ireland; Especially of That to St. Patrick's Purgatory. Together, With an Account of the Loss That the Publick Sustaineth Thereby; Truly and Impartially Represented. By John Richardson, Rector of the Parish of Belturbet, Alias Annah*. Dublin: J. Hyde, 1727.

Riches, Samantha. *St George: A Saint for All*. London: Reaktion Books, 2015.

Ristuccia, Nathan J. *Christianization and Commonwealth in Early Medieval Europe: A Ritual Interpretation*. Oxford: Oxford University Press, 2018.

Robinson, Ven. Archdeacon John L. 'St. Brigid and Glastonbury.' *JRSAI* 83 (1953): 97–99.

Robson, Michael. *St. Francis of Assisi: The Legend and the Life*. London: Continuum, 1999.

Romano, J. F. 'Rome'. In *Encyclopedia of Medieval Pilgrimage*, edited by Larissa Taylor et al. Leiden: Brill, 2010.

Ronan, Myles. 'Religious Life in Old Dublin.' In *Dublin Historical Record* 2, no. 2 (1939): 46–54.

Rosewell, Roger. *The Medieval Monastery*. London: Shire Publications, 2012.

—. 'Medieval Painted and Stained Glass at Worcester Cathedral Priory, Part II: The Priory Cloisters.' *Vidimus Journal* 58 (2010). http://vidimus.org/issues/issue–58/feature/ Accessed 12/06/2017.

Rubin, Miri. *Corpus Christi: The Eucharist in Late Medieval Culture*. Cambridge: Cambridge University Press, 1991.

Ryan, Michael. 'Church Metalwork in the Eighth and Ninth Centuries'. In *The Work of Angels: Masterpieces of Celtic Metalwork 6th–9th Centuries AD*, edited by Susan Youngs, 125–29. London: British Museum Publications in assoc. with the National Museum of Ireland and National Museums Scotland, 1989.

Ryan, Salvador, and Anthony Shanahan. 'How to Communicate Lateran IV in 13th Century Ireland: Lessons from the Liber Exemplorum (c.1275).' *Religions* 9 (3) (2018): 75.

Santiago de Compostela; 100 Ans de Pèlerinage Européen, Europalia 85. Gent: Ausstellungskat, 1985.

Sayer, Jane, and Leslie Watkiss. *Thomas of Marlborough: History of the Abbey of Evesham.* Oxford: Clarendon Press, 2003.

Scally, Georgina. High Island (Ardoileán), Co. Galway: Excavation of an Early Medieval Monastery. Archaeological Monograph Series: 10. Dublin: The Stationery Office, 2014.

Scantlebury, C. 'Tallaght, Co. Dublin: Its Monastery and Its Castle'. *Dublin Historical Record* 16 no.2 (1960): 65–72.

Scott, Brendan. 'The Dissolution of the Religious Houses in the Tudor Dioceseof Meath'. *Archivium Hibernicum* 59 (2005): 260–76.

Sharpe, Richard, ed. *Adomnán's Life of Columba.* Harmondsworth: Penguin, 1995.

Sheehan, John. 'A Peacock's Tale: Excavations at Caherlehillan, Kerry, Ireland.' In *The Archaeology of the Celtic Churches. The Society for Medieval Archaeology Monograph 21*, edited by Nancy Edwards, 191–206. Leeds: Maney, 2009.

—. 'Some Early Historic Cross-Forms and Related Motifs from the Iveragh Peninsula.' *JKAHS* 23 (1990): 57–174.

Shee Twohig, Elizabeth. *Megalithic Art of Western Europe.* Oxford: Clarendon Press, 1981.

Sheingorn, Pamela, trans. *The Book of Sainte Foy.* Philadephia: University of Pennsylvania Press, 1995.

Sherlock, David and H. Woods. *St Augustine's Abbey: Report on Excavations 1960–78. Monograph Series of the Kent Archaeological Society 4.* Kent: Kent Archaeological Society, 1988.

Simington, Robert C. *The Civil Survey AD 1654–1656. Tipperary.* Vol. 1. Dublin: Stationery Office for the Irish Manuscripts Commission, 1934.

Simon, Ben. *Tales, Traditions and Folklore of Ireland's Trees.* Kildare: Crann Publications, 2012.

Slatter, Sharon 'Paying the Rounds at St Patrick's Well, Singland.' *Limerick's Life* (blog), 2017. http://limerickslife.com/paying–the–rounds/. Accessed 12/11/2018.

Smith, Brendan. *Crisis and Survival in Late Medieval Ireland: The English of Louth and Their Neighbours, 1330–1450.* Oxford: Oxford University Press, 2013.

—ed. *The Cambridge History of Ireland: Volume 1, 600–1550.* Cambridge: Cambridge University Press, 2018.

Smith, J. M. H. 'Portable Christianity: Relics in the Medieval West (c .700–1200).' *University of Glasgow Proceedings of the British Academy* 181 (2012): 143–67.

Smyth, Alfred P. *Warlords and Holy Men, Scotland AD 80–1000.* London: Edward Arnold, 1984.

Snoek, Godefridus J. C. *Medieval Piety from Relics to the Eucharist: A Process of Mutual Interaction.* Leiden: Brill, 1995.

Nicholas, Vincent. 'Some Pardoner's Tales: The Earliest English Indulgences.' *TRHS*, 12 (2002): 23–58.

Spears, Arthur. *The Cult of Saint Catherine of Alexandria in Ireland.* Rathmullen: Rathmullan District Local Historical Society, 2006.

Spencer, Brian. 'Medieval Pilgrim Badges. Some General Observations Illustrated Mainly from English Sources.' In *Rotterdam Papers: A Contribution to Medieval Archaeology*, edited by J.G. N. Renaud, 137–47. Rotterdam: Coördinatie Commissie van Advies inzake Archeologisch Onderzoek binnen het ressort Rotterdam, 1968.

—. 'Pilgrim Signs.' In *Late Viking Age and Medieval Waterford: Excavations 1986–1992*, edited by Maurice F. Hurley, Terry Barry, Rose M. Cleary and Orla M. B. Scully, 33–48. Waterford: Waterford Corporation, 1997.

—. 'Pilgrim Souvenirs.' In *Miscellanea 1. Medieval Dublin Excavations 1962–81 (Series B) Vol. 2 Fascicules 1–5*, edited by Patrick Wallace, 33–48. Dublin: Royal Irish Academy, 1988.

—. *Pilgrim Souvenirs and Secular Badges: Medieval Finds from Excavations in London.* London: HMSO, 1998.

St. John Brooks, Eric. '14th Century Monastic Estates in Meath. The Llanthony Cells of Duleek and Colp.' *JRSAI* 83, no. 2 (1953): 140–49.

—. 'The Family of Marisco.' *JRSAI* 1, no. 1 (1931): 22–38.

—. 'The Family of Marisco.' *JRSAI* 2, no. 1 (1932): 50–74.

Stalley, Roger A. *Early Medieval Architecture.* Oxford: Oxford University Press, 1999.

—. 'Sailing to Santiago: Medieval Pilgrimage to Santiago de Compostela and Its Artistic Influences in Ireland.' In *Settlement and Society in Medieval Ireland. Studies Presented to F.X. Martin, o.s.a.*, edited by John Bradley, 397–420. Kilkenny: Boethius Press, 1988.

—. 'The Architecture of the Cathedral and Priory Buildings, 1250–1530.' In *Christ Church Cathedral Dublin: A History*, edited by Kenneth Milne, 95–128. Dublin: Four Courts Press, 2000.

—. *The Cistercian Monasteries of Ireland: An Account of the History, Art and Architecture of the White Monks in Ireland from 1142–1540.* London: Yale University Press, 1987.

—. 'The Construction of the Medieval Cathedral, c. 1030–1250.' In *Christ Church Cathedral Dublin. A History*, edited by Kenneth Milne, 53–74. Dublin: Four Courts Press, 2000.

—. 'The End of the Middle Ages: Gothic Survival in Sixteenth-Century Connacht.' *JRSAI* 133 (2003): 5–23.

Staunton, Michael, ed. *The Lives of Thomas Becket.* Manchester: Manchester University Press, 2001.

Steane, John. *The Archaeology of Medieval England and Wales.* London: Routledge, 2014.

Steward, A., trans. *Felix Fabri (Circa 1480–1483 A.D). The Library of the Palestine Pilgrims' Text Society.* London: London Committee of the Palestine Exploration Fund, 1896.

Stokes, Whitley. 'A Middle-Irish Homily on S. Martin of Tours (Leabhar Breac).' *Revue Celtique* 2 (1875): 381–402.

—, ed. *Félire Óengusso Céli Dé. The Martyrology of Oengus the Culdee.* Dublin: Dublin Institute for Advanced Studies, 1984.

—. *Lives of Saints from the Book of Lismore.* Oxford: Clarendon Press, 1890.

—. *The Birth and Life of St. Moling Edited, from a Manuscript in the Royal Library, Brussels, with a Translation and Glossary, by Whitley Stokes.* London: Privately printed [by Harrison and Sons], 1907.

—. 'The Klosterneuburg Incantation.' *Revue Celtique* 2 (1875): 112–15.

—*The Tripartite Life of Patrick: With Other Documents Relating to That Saint/Edited with Translations and Indexes, by Whitley Stokes.* London: Printed for HMSO, by Eyre and Spottiswoode, 1887.

Stokes, Whitley, and John Strachan. *Thesaurus Palæohibernicus: A Collection of Old-Irish Glosses, Scholia, Prose, and Verse.* Cambridge: Cambridge University Press, 1903.

Stones, Alison, Paula Gerson, Jeanne Krochalis and Annie Shaver-Crandell, eds. *The Pilgrim's Guide to Santiago de Compostela: A Critical Edition.* 2 vols. London: Harvey Miller Publishers, 1998.

Stopford, Jennie. 'Some Approaches to the Archaeology of Christian Pilgrimage.' *World Archaeology* 26, no. 1 (1994): 57–72.

—, ed. *Pilgrimage Explored.* Woodbridge: Boydell & Brewer Ltd, 1999.

Stout, Geraldine. *Newgrange and the Bend of the Boyne.* Cork: Cork University Press, 2002.

Stubbs, William, *Chronica Magistri Rogeri de Houedone.* 4 vols. London: Longman & Co., 1868.

Sullivan, Denis. 'The Cistercian Abbey of Tracton, County Cork.' *JCHAS* 44 (1939): 1–15.

Sumption, Jonathan. *Pilgrimage: An Image of Medieval Religion.* London: Faber & Faber, 1975.

Swan, Leo '1989:021 – 'St Doulagh's, Balgriffin, Dublin.' Database of Irish Excavation Reports. 1989. https://www.excavations.ie. Accessed 10/08/2018.

Swanson, Robert N. *Religion and Devotion in Europe, c. 1215–c. 1515*. Cambridge: Cambridge University Press, 1995.

Sweetman, *Henry*, Savage. ed. *Calendar of Documents Relating to Ireland*, 4 vols. London: Longman for HMSO. 1875–81.

Sweetman, Patrick David. *Irish Castles and Fortified Houses*. Dublin: Country House, 1995.

Sweetman, Patrick David, Olive Alcock and Bernie Moran. *Archaeological Inventory of County Laois*. Dublin: Stationery Office, 1995.

Taylor, Larissa J. et al., eds. *Encyclopedia of Medieval Pilgrimage*. Leiden: Brill, 2010.

Tekippe, Rita. 'Pilgrimage and Procession.' In *Art and Architecture of Late Medieval Pilgrimage in Northern Europe and the British Isles: Texts*, edited by Sarah Blick and Rita Tekippe. Leiden: Brill, 2005.

The Schools' Collection, Volume 0569, page 119. National Folklore Collection UCD https://www.duchas.ie/en/cbes/5162126/5156232/5197390. Accessed 31/03/2019.

Thomas, Charles. *Christianity in Roman Britain to AD 500*. London: Batsford, 1981.

—. *The Early Christian Archaeology of North Britain*. London: Oxford University Press, 1971.

Thomas of Monmouth. *The Life and Miracles of St. William of Norwich*. Edited by Montagu Rhodes James and Augustus Jessop. Cambridge: Cambridge University Press, 1896.

Turpie, Tom. *Kind Neighbours: Scottish Saints and Society in the Later Middle Ages*. Leiden: Brill, 2015.

—. 'Scottish and British? The Scottish Authorities, Richard III and the Cult of St Ninian in Late Medieval Scotland and Northern England.' In *Medieval and Early Modern Representations of Authority in Scotland and the British Isles*, edited by Kate Buchanan and Lucinda H.S. Dean, 124–40. London: Routledge, 2016.

Ulster Society for Medieval Latin Studies. 'The Life of Saint Monenna by Conchubranus: Part I.' *Seanchas Ardmhacha* 9 no. 2 (1979): 250–73.

Ure, John. *Pilgrimages. The Great Adventures of the Middle Ages*. New York: Carroll & Graf, 2006.

Van Hoek, M. 'The Prehistoric Rock Art of the Boheh Stone, Co. Mayo.' *Cathair Na Mart* 13 (1993): 1–15.

Vetromile, Eugene. *Travels in Europe, Egypt, Arabia Petræa, Palestine and Syria*. New York: D. & J. Sadlier & Company, 1871.

Vincent, Nicholas. *The Holy Blood: King Henry III and the Westminster Blood Relic*. Cambridge: Cambridge University Press, 2001.

Waddell, John. 'An Archaeological Survey of Temple Brecan, Aran.' *JGAHS* 33 (73 1972): 5–27.

Wade Labarge, Margaret. *Medieval Travellers: The Rich and the Restless*. London: Hamish Hamilton, 1982.

Wakeman, William. 'Monastic Antiquities of Clones.' *Clogher Record* 3 (1975): 27–340.

Waller, Gary. *The Virgin Mary in Late Medieval and Early Modern English Literature and Popular Culture*. Cambridge: Cambridge University Press, 2011.

Walsh, Christine. *The Cult of St Katherine of Alexandria in Early Medieval Europe*. Burlington, VT: Ashgate Press, 2007.

Walsh, Gerry. 'Croagh Patrick, Glaspatrick/Teevenacroagh.' In *Excavations 1995*, edited by Isabel Bennet, 67–68. Dublin: Wordwell, 1996.

—. 'Preliminary Report on the Archaeological Excavations on the Summit of Croagh Patrick, 1994.' *Cathair Na Mart* 14 (1994): 1–10.

Walsh, Katherine. *Richard FitzRalph in Oxford, Avignon, and Armagh*. Oxford: Clarendon Press, 1981.

Walsh, Maura, and Dáibhí Ó Cróinín, trans. *Cummian, Letter de Controversia Paschali*. Toronto: Pontifical Institute of Medieval Studies, 1988.

Ward, Benedicta. *Miracles and the Medieval Mind: Theory, Record and Event 1000–1215*. Aldershot: Scolar, 1987.

Ward, Jennifer. *Women in Medieval Europe 1200–1500.* 2nd Edition. London: Routledge, 2016.

Ware, James. *The Antiquities and History of Ireland*. Dublin: A Crook, 1705.

—. *The Whole Works of James Ware Concerning Ireland Revised and Improved*. Vol. I. Dublin: Jones, 1739.

Waterman, Dudley. 'An Early Christian Mortuary House at Saul, Co. Down, with Notes on Similar Monuments in Ulster.' *UJA* 23 (1960): 82–88.

—. 'St Mary's Priory, Devenish: Excavations of the East Range, 1972–4.' *UJA* 42 (1979): 34–48.

Watson, Bruce, Trevor Bringham and Tony Dyson. *London Bridge 2000 Years of a River Crossing. MoLAS Monograph 8*. London: Museum of London Archaeological Service, 2001.

Watt, Diana. 'Margery Kempe's Overseas Pilgrimages.' In *A Place to Believe In: Locating Medieval Landscapes*, edited by Clare Lees and Gillian Overing, 170–87. University Park: Penn State University Press, 2006.

Watt, Diane. *The Paston Women: Selected Letters*. Woodbridge: D.S. Brewer, 2004.

Webb, Diana. *Medieval European Pilgrimage, c.700–c.1500*. Basingstoke: Palgrave, 2002.

—. *Pilgrimage in Medieval England*. London: Hambledon, 2000.

—. *Pilgrims and Pilgrimage in the Medieval West*. London: I.B. Tauris, 1999.

Webb, John J. 'The Guilds of Dublin.' *The Irish Monthly* 45, 530 (1917): 507–14.

Weidenbörner, Martin. *Encyclopedia of Food Mycotoxins*. New York: Springer, 2001.

Wessex Archaeology. 'Baliscate, Isle of Mull Archaeological Evaluation and Assessment of Results. Report Reference: 71503.01', 2010. London: Videotext Communications Ltd.

Westbury, Virginia. *Labyrinths. Ancient Paths of Wisdom and Peace*. Singapore: De Capo Press, 2001.

Westropp, Thomas Johnson. *Folklore of Clare. A Folklore Survey of County Clare and County Clare: Folk-Tales and Myths*. Ennis: CLASP Press, 2003.

—. 'Notes on the Antiquities of Ardmore.' *JRSAI* 13 (1903): 353–80.

—. "Slane in Bregia', Co. Meath: Its Friary and Hermitage.' *JRSAI* 31 (1901): 405–30.

White, James F. *Protestant Worship and Church Architecture: Theological and Historical Considerations*. Dallas: Wipf and Stock Publishers, 2003.

White, Newport Benjamin, ed. *Extents of Irish Monastic Possessions, 1540–1541: From Manuscripts in the Public Record Office, London*. London: HMSO, 1943.

Wickham, Chris. *Medieval Rome: Stability and Crisis of a City, 900–1150 (Oxford Studies in Medieval European History)*. Oxford: Oxford University Press, 2015.

Wilde, William. *The Beauties of the Boyne and Its Tributary, the Blackwater*. 2nd Edition. Dublin: McGlashan, 1850.

—. *Lough Corrib: Its Shores and Islands; with Notices of Lough Mask*. Dublin: McGlashan & Gill, 1872.

Wilkinson, J. *Jerusalem Pilgrims Before the Crusades*. Warminster: Aris & Philips Ltd, 1977.

Williams, Bernadette. *The Annals of Friar John Clyn*. Dublin: Four Courts Press, 2007.

Wood, Herbert and Albert Langman ed. *Calendar of the Justiciary Rolls, or, Proceedings in the Court of the Justiciar of Ireland, I to VII Years of Edward II/Prepared under the Direction of the Deputy Keeper of the Public Records by Herbert Wood and Albert E. Langman ; and Revised by Margaret C. Griffith*. Dublin: Stationery Office, 1952.

Wright, George Newenham. *A Guide to the County of Wicklow: Illustrated by Engravings, after the Designs of George Petrie, Esq., and a Large Map of the County, from an Original Survey/By the Rev. G. N. Wright, A.M.* London: Printed for Baldwin, Cradock, and Joy, 1822.

Wycherley, Niamh. *The Cult of Relics in Early Medieval Ireland*. Turnhout: Brepols Press, 2015.

Yeoman, Peter. 'An Archaeology of Pilgrimage.' In *The Oxford Handbook of Later Medieval Archaeology in Britain*, edited by Christopher Gerrard and Alejandra Gutiérrez, 641–57. Oxford: Oxford University Press, 2018.

—. *Pilgrimage in Medieval Scotland.* London: Batsford, 1999.

Yoshikawa, Naoë Kukita. *Margery Kempe's Meditations: The Context of Medieval Devotional Literature, Liturgy and Iconography*. Cardiff: University of Wales Press, 2007.

Zumbuhl, Mark. 'Uí Dúnlainge.' In *Medieval Ireland: An Encyclopedia*, edited by Séan Duffy, 487–88. London: Routledge Press, 2005.

Index

Index of Subjects

Index of Names and Places